EMPIRE IN WOOD

CORNELL STUDIES IN INDUSTRIAL AND LABOR RELATIONS: *VOLUME VII*

Cornell Studies in Industrial and Labor Relations are research monographs developed by faculty and staff of the New York State School of Industrial and Labor Relations.

IN THIS SERIES

PUBLISHED BY

THE NEW YORK STATE SCHOOL OF INDUSTRIAL AND LABOR RELATIONS

A Unit of the State University of New York

at Cornell University

EMPIRE IN WOOD

A History of the Carpenters' Union

BY ROBERT A. CHRISTIE

CORNELL UNIVERSITY

Ithaca, New York

PRINTED IN THE UNITED STATES OF AMERICA BY

W. F. HUMPHREY PRESS INC., GENEVA, NEW YORK

TO *Al Christie and to the memory of his father, Bill: two real, old-time carpenters*

Preface

SEVERAL decades ago the more modern students of American history cried out for a new approach. The political histories of the United States then available, they held, were mere outlines. Before the full history could be unveiled, these outlines had to be filled in with chapters on economic history. Among other chapters calling for their historians in the 1920's were those dealing with the rise of commerce and industry, particularly the trade unions. Charles Beard noted in his *Rise of American Civilization* that the story of these all-important institutions remained as yet unrecorded in 1926. He said with a touch of wonder that the first work on the trade union movement had been published but a few years before.[1]

Professor Beard would be less discontented today. Historical research has since pushed restlessly into fields but little explored in 1926. Land, agricultural, railroad, commercial, and industrial history have all received an ample share of attention since Beard and his contemporaries first pointed the way. Trade union history has, however, lagged behind the field. The fine start made by the Commons group[2] and referred to by Beard was not followed up. By and large the story of historically important individual trade unions has progressed little beyond its 1926 stage of development. And the field of local union history remains almost untouched.

Despite the excellence and careful documentation of the historical work of the Commons group, few answers have yet been made to a whole host of questions in the field of labor history. Why did both the Knights of Labor and the Congress of Industrial

[1]Charles and Mary Beard, *The Rise of American Civilization* (1st ed.), Vol. 1, p. 632.
[2]John Rodgers Commons, *et al.*, *History of Labour in the United States*, 4 Vols.

Organizations experience such terrific but short-lived surges of popularity and then fade gradually into the folds of the American Federation of Labor? Why has the union label been so successful in the United States and how has it been used by local and national leaders? What role has technological change played in the jurisdictional strike, in molding union structure, and in determining the attitudes of workers toward their unions? Did, perchance, philosophers of the labor movement other than Marx and Gompers play a role in the peculiar process whereby the labor movement in the United States was Americanized?

Some but not all of these questions have been answered by the Commons group and its successors.[3] Perhaps Commons and his associates are correct in the answers they have furnished. If so, detailed research in the histories of the various national and local unions will fill in their explanations as histories of the West have done with Turner's thesis. If not, perhaps the same research may reveal a partially or totally new picture of the role of the workers in the history of the United States. At present these questions can only be asked. They cannot be answered because the necessary research has not been done. No other phase of American history comes to mind in which so many important questions have so long been answered only by the work of a single group, engaged in one project, in one period of time.

It is true that since the passage of the Wagner Act in the mid-1930's, the newly developing social science of labor relations has expanded and flourished. Researchers in this field have drawn on older academic disciplines like economics and psychology and created new ones like collective bargaining to place on the records reams of fruitful research. Most of their research, however, has been on the contemporary trade union movement. By and large the workers in this field have based their work on little more knowledge of the past history of the labor movement than was supplied by the original Commons group. The records of most of the hundreds of national unions and thousands of local unions which exist or have existed remain for the most part undisturbed,

[3]In addition to the Commons history, see Selig Perlman, *A Theory of the Labor Movement,* for his answers to the questions which precede this note in the text. The Perlman theory was based on his findings while working on the Commons project.

gathering dust. The labor relations field has thus risen and thrived in what, but for the work of the Commons group, would be a virtual historical vacuum.

The explanation for this neglect is not far to seek. The documents have not been available. Leaders of national trade unions have only rarely opened their archives to the academic historian. This is easy to understand. No one group of men in the recent past and, to some extent, today have been so badly maligned and so little understood. They naturally shy away from the idea of strangers disturbing their files. Further, they have so often in the past been harassed by both government and business that their fears have real substance. Labor leaders and their unions thus now have the same attitude toward historical research that industrial leaders had a few decades back. For similar reasons, research in trade union history is being inhibited now as it was in industrial history a few decades ago.

Still, fruitful work can go on in spite of this handicap. Trade union records other than those controlled by the various unions are available to researchers. When this work was originally undertaken as a doctoral dissertation (1950), aid of union officials was requested. When they declined to open their files, further investigation revealed that a full file of the Carpenters' convention proceedings, journals, and officers' reports were publicly available, beginning with 1881, the year of the union's founding. Further, the proceedings, journals, and officers' reports of the various trade unions with which the Carpenters dealt, of the Knights of Labor, the American Federation of Labor, and the Congress of Industrial Organizations were all also found in public or university libraries. So also were the journals, proceedings, and officers' reports of many of the carpenters' unions which preceded the present one, as well as those of the various employers' associations in the building industry. In addition to these, national, state, and local governmental records and various pamphlets, articles, and secondary works shed much light on the union's past. These together provided the sources upon which this work is based. Other existing records, those held or controlled by the Carpenters' union and never published, were not used. For this reason this work is not a definitive history of the Carpenters' union. Such a history cannot be written until the union yields its files.

Because of the unavailability of these files, the work has certain unavoidable limitations. Many of the local leaders remain vague and shadowy figures, making this more a history of the national office than of the many local and regional parts of the union. There are few details of the day-to-day process of collective bargaining as it developed over the years. Finally, there is little of the work-a-day carpenter in this history of his union. A definitive history of the union would need to treat these aspects fully. Some other phases of the union's history omitted in this work were, however, left out consciously, as a part of the process of constructing an historical narrative. For the absence of these the author bears complete responsibility.

Only one other matter requires explanation, the fact that the work ends in 1941. The historical record was terminated at that time for several reasons. First, as the union centralized its administration over the years, the journals, proceedings, and reports made public contained less and less of the material out of which history may be wrought. By 1941 this material had dwindled to a trickle. Second, it was felt that the union's development had completed an historical cycle by 1941 and that, at this point, a halt could be called and a summation made. Finally, and most important, the type of comtemporary history which would necessarily have to be written about the union's most recent past called for personal interviews with the union's leaders. Under the circumstances already described, this was not possible.

I wish to thank the three members of my doctoral committee, Professors Jean T. McKelvey, Paul W. Gates, and Maurice F. Neufeld, of Cornell University, for their advice and suggestions. I wish especially to acknowledge the important part Professor Neufeld played in the creation of this work. He encouraged my interest in the topic and helped to plan the scope and direction of the research. He read and corrected the completed manuscript as well as the various rough chapter drafts which preceded it. To this thanks must be added for his counsel and advice on a less formal basis, as that of friend. I would also like to thank Dean

Martin P. Catherwood and the Director of Research and Publications, Leonard P. Adams, of the School of Industrial and Labor Relations at Cornell University, for granting the research assistantships without which this work could not have been written. Mrs. Eunice Raimon edited the complete manuscript and offered many suggestions on both style and content, which were incorporated into the work and for which I am greatly indebted. Finally, I thank my wife, Sally Watkins Christie, whose contribution to every aspect of the work at every stage of its development is much greater than she is willing to acknowledge.

R. A. C.

Lafayette College
September 1955

Contents

TABLES

FIGURE

Introduction

WHEN, in the summer of 1953, the executive council of the American Federation of Labor was considering a no-raiding pact with the Congress of Industrial Organizations, its ranking member, William L. Hutcheson, president emeritus of the United Brotherhood of Carpenters and Joiners of America, rose and announced the withdrawal of his union from the AFL. Pressed for a reason, he said that AFL leaders were "more concerned with the affairs of the CIO than...with those of the Federation."[1] He then called the executive council's attention to the problem of conflicting jurisdictional claims among AFL unions which he accused the executive council of neglecting in favor of the no-raiding pact.[2] Advised of Hutcheson's reason for walking out, the *New York Times* wryly commented, "This [concern over the settlement of jurisdictional disputes] came with poor grace from a union that has probably raided more labor unions more often than it has been the victim of such tactics."[3]

In walking out, most informed observers agreed, Hutcheson was bluffing, trying to test the mettle of George Meany, the newly elected AFL president. Meany simply shrugged off the Carpenters' withdrawal and filled their executive council vacancy with another union's representative. When it became apparent that Meany would grant no concessions—jurisdictional or otherwise—to retain the Carpenters, they hastened back into the fold.[4] And the AFL

---

[1] *New York Times*, Aug. 13, 1953, p. 1, col. 1.
[2] *Ibid.*
[3] *Ibid.*, Sept. 10, 1953, p. 24, col. 3.
[4] See the following issues of the *New York Times* for the running account of these events: Aug. 13, p. 1, col. 1; Aug. 14, p. 13, col. 2; Aug. 14, p. 15, col. 7; Aug. 15, p. 11, col. 2; Aug. 15, p. 12, col. 7; Aug. 16, Sec. II, p. 6, col. 1; Aug. 18, p. 32, col. 1; Aug. 19, p. 28, col. 3; Aug. 24, p. 17, col. 4; Aug. 27, p. 1, col. 2; Sept. 9, p. 11, col. 2; Sept. 10, p. 24, col. 3; Sept. 23, p. 27, col. 2.

continued to pass through its seventy-second year with calm assurance.

While the Carpenters were bluffing about remaining outside the house of labor, their jurisdictional sensitivity was not feigned. For well over half a century they have guarded their jurisdiction with such great care and added to it with such frequency that, in 1953, Hutcheson and his son, President Maurice Hutcheson, ruled one of the most heterogeneous union empires ever created. Housed within the confines of this huge and sprawling union are millwrights, furniture workers, pile drivers, and scores of other craftsmen with but this in common: each works with materials that are now, or were once, made of wood.

At one time the carpenter did the tasks performed by each of these craftsmen. Gradually new materials and changing building techniques chipped one, then another of them, from the main body of carpentry. As other trades came to embrace tasks once done by the carpenter, the Carpenters' Union refused to relinquish its jurisdiction over these skills. To have done so would have meant the virtual death of the union. If the present union contained only men who performed tasks done by the carpenter before 1900, it is doubtful if it could muster a hundred thousand members.

Although its leaders nostalgically refer to the United Brotherhood as a craft union, no organization with so richly varied a jurisdiction can be so classified. The carpenter's craft is no more than a point of departure for this jurisdiction. The United Brotherhood of Carpenters and Joiners of America is a multi-industrial union, whose leaders have followed their jurisdiction wherever industrial technology has led it.

The Carpenters could last boast of having a craft union in the 1890's. For, during the first decade of the twentieth century, almost a quarter-century after its founding, changing building techniques forced the United Brotherhood gradually to surrender its craft form. Nor was this the first time a changing building industry caused an American carpenters' organization to revise its structure. In 1724 carpenters were organized into masters' protective organizations. After 1791 this form gave way to the city-wide journeymen's trade union. By the time of the Civil War, the state-wide carpenters' union dominated the craft, and in 1881 the present national union was created. From 1902 to 1912 the United Brotherhood gradually abandoned its craft nature and became a multi-industrial union. Since 1912 it has altered its jurisdiction so many times to absorb new crafts, industries, and subindustries that a list of its jurisdictional claims occupies two pages of the present constitution.

Each of these alterations in union structure met a threat posed by changes in the organization of the industry, in the extent of the labor market, or in the tools of production. Whenever any one of these three factors has changed, carpenters' unions have had to change or cease to exist. This process of administrative response to industrial change provides the major thesis around which this history is organized.

As important as industrial factors are to an understanding of the nature of this union, equally important are the men who have dealt with them. Some of them anticipated these industrial changes and rode to fame because of their foresight. Others as clearly saw them and rode to infamy. Still others saw and fought them, and came to a tragic end. The United Brotherhood has thus had its quota of prophets, practical men, and philosophers. How these men, of widely differing temperaments and outlook, fashioned the history of the United Brotherhood within the limits established by the development of the building industry is the subject matter of this history.

CHAPTER I

The Union, the Industry, and

the Carpenter: Present Day

IN THE year 1947 the United Brotherhood of Carpenters and Joiners of America boasted a membership of 722,000 and a treasury of $9,000,000 in cash and bonds. Few industrial and no craft unions outranked it in size, wealth, influence, or power. That its leaders stood foursquare behind the conservative policies of the American Federation of Labor is understandable. Their predecessors had invented them.

The Apparent Structure of the Union

The 1947 constitution[1] makes provision for a president, a secretary, a treasurer, two vice-presidents, and seven executive board members. The powers of the general president are as extensive as the minds of carpenters assembled in convention could make them. After listing each of his specific powers, the constitution states that "he shall supervise the entire interests of the United Brotherhood." Then, as an afterthought, it provides that "whenever in the judgment of the General President subordinate bodies

[1]The 1947 constitution has been chosen because past-President William Hutcheson gave his only extensive recorded public interview in 1946 to *Fortune* magazine. When the constitution in effect at the time of the interview (the 1947 constitution, passed at the 1946 convention and published in 1947) is read in conjunction with the interview, the two are more revealing than a reading of the constitution alone would be.

...are working against the best interests of the United Brother-hood...[he] shall have the power to order said body to disband under penalty of suspension."[2]

The first vice-president has charge of the label and of the woodworking mills which do or do not use it. He also approves the laws of all bodies subordinate to the national office.[3] The second vice-president is given no specific duties but is essentially a troubleshooter for the general president. Directly under and appointed by the general president are the organizers or general representatives who, in spite of their importance, enjoy neither clearly defined constitutional status nor specific job tenure. The general secretary and general treasurer are clerks rather removed from the main flow of power.

The executive board is composed of seven district members who are elected by both the convention at large and four out of five of the general officers.[4] The general president is chairman of the board and the general secretary, secretary. The executive board has charge of all trade movements and hears appeals on grievances and points of law decided by the general president.[5] Although inferior in power only to the convention, executive board members are subject to the beck and call of the general president who uses them to guide the activities of the various organizers, to direct organizing drives, and to assist the local organizations in the important strikes.

The most important local unit of the United Brotherhood is the district council, which is formed by all of the local unions in a clearly defined economic area, such as a small river valley or a city. Whenever two or more local unions exist, a district council must be formed. The district councils are given jurisdiction over collective bargaining, the framing of work rules, and the admin-

[2]Carpenters and Joiners of America, United Brotherhood of, *Constitution and Laws,* 1947, pp. 10–11.

[3]In 1947 the first vice-president was Maurice Hutcheson, General President William L. Hutcheson's son. In 1952 William Hutcheson stepped down and the executive board appointed Maurice general president.

[4]The second vice-president is not on the executive board.

[5]"Trade movement" is the name given by the United Brotherhood to any demand for changed wages or working conditions.

istration of national discipline. The local unions are simply dues-collecting agencies.

The whole organization meets quadrennially in a convention. Representation at the convention is based on units of five hundred members in each of the local unions. For the first five hundred members, two delegates are permitted, for the second, three. Locals with more than one thousand members are limited to four delegates, and those with less than one hundred members are given one. The district councils are permitted no voting representation at the convention.

The rest of the constitution regulates strikes, benefits, finances, clearance cards, the use of the label, and disciplinary procedure. While it gives extensive powers to the national office, the constitution provides for democratic control in the event that the members should feel democratically inclined. Constitutions, however, do not create democracy; they reflect it. It is necessary to view the United Brotherhood in relation to the building industry to obtain a true picture of the union.

The Building Industry[6]

The building industry is the prototype of those industries considered easiest for trade unions to organize. Competitive, sprawling, sporadic, and, above all, speculative, it is an industry in which the centripetal forces are few and the centrifugal forces many.

Market Structure

The sprawling form of the industry is due to the fact that the finished structure cannot be transported, and materials and labor are also difficult and costly to transport. Table I (p. 4) shows how little intercity and interstate work is done by all building contractors, and how much less by carpentry contractors alone.

This table demonstrates the single most important fact about the building industry: its markets are almost completely local. This fact is as basic and important for the building trades unions

[6]The analysis covers only those aspects of the industry which serve to account for the structure of the United Brotherhood. The "building industry," relative to the unionized carpenter, usually means heavy public or private construction such as museums, factories, and office buildings rather than residential construction. The bulk of this type of construction is confined to the larger urban areas.

Table I.—Location of Work Done by Building and Carpentry Contractors in 1938

Location of Work Done	All Bldg.	Carpentry
In builder's home city	66.1	90.2
In builder's home state (outside home city)	21.4	8.3
Outside of builder's home state	12.5	1.5

Source: U.S. Congress, Joint Temporary National Economic Committee, *Hearings on the Concentration of Economic Power*, 75th Cong., 3rd Sess., Vol. 8, Part 11, p. 5187.

as it is for their industry, for both the unions and management have a localized range of interest; and different traditions, usages, and rules obtain in collective bargaining in each of the various building centers. The effect of this localized market is felt in every realm of trade union activity. Thus, while the cities shown in Table II are within easy commuting distance of each other, the sharp wage differential is obvious.

Table II.—1940 Union Wage Rates for Carpenters in New York City and Boston and Cities Within 50 Miles of Each

City	Hourly Rate	City	Hourly Rate
New York, N. Y.	$1.85	Boston, Mass.	$1.37½
Bridgeport, Conn.	1.25	Milford, Mass.	1.00
Bergen County, N. J.	1.50	Lynn, Mass.	1.25
Essex County, N. J.	1.75	Quincy, Mass.	1.25
Hudson County, N. J.	1.75	Lawrence, Mass.	1.25
Westchester County, N. Y.	1.50	Lowell, Mass.	1.00
Bound Brook, N. J.	1.25	Providence, R. I.	1.17½

Source: "Local Wage Rates," *The Carpenter*, Vol. 60, No. 10, October 1940, pp. 35–53.

Lawrence is but ten miles from Lowell. Yet Lowell carpenters received twenty-five cents an hour less in 1940 than did their fellow union members in Lawrence. This state of affairs reflects the absence of over-all, national control of wage rates. The carpenters accept these differentials as a matter of course and neither desire nor expect any such national control.

Nor does the national union exercise any more control over the other aspects of collective bargaining. In 1914 the executive board of the United Brotherhood asked the convention delegates for power to strike a given intercity employer in cities where he was unionized to force him to recognize the union elsewhere. They also asked for the corollary power to make intercity agreements with these contractors. They promised, however, that such agreements would leave "to [the union in] each locality the *power of home rule as to wages hours and working conditions.*"[7] This request was granted and the present-day constitution gives the board power to "make agreements with employers covering our [the United Brotherhood's] jurisdiction; provided such agreements require employers to conform with the *trade rules of the district* where the work is located.[8]

Beyond this one provision, the constitution says nothing of national control over working conditions. It neither stipulates minimum work standards nor provides rules to guide the locals. Rather, the local unions are given complete power to "make... trade rules for...the members...working in their jurisdiction."[9]

Local autonomy is equally strong in the realm of apprenticeship. For twenty years United Brotherhood conventions toyed with the idea of a national apprenticeship system. Finally, in 1914, a special apprenticeship committee was created. The committee members found that a general apprenticeship plan "cannot apply throughout the [jurisdiction of the] United Brotherhood...owing to ever-varying conditions in the many localities [which] make ...one general plan...impossible."[10] Until 1940 every convention dealing with this problem produced the same negative results. In that year a model apprenticeship plan was finally created. It was, however, only a guide plan providing for local option.[11] It was admitted at the 1946 convention that few locals had picked up the option.[12]

The label, another trade-regulating device, was created by the national union, and the rules regarding its use are detailed in the

[7]Carpenters and Joiners of America, United Brotherhood of, AFL, *Proceedings of the Eighteenth Biennial Convention of Indianapolis, Sept. 28 to Oct. 2, 1914*, pp. 30–31 (italics mine).

[8]UBCJA, *1947 Constitution*, p. 16 (italics mine).

[9]*Ibid.*, p. 22.

[10]UBCJA, *1914 Convention Proceedings*, p. 788.

[11]Carpenters and Joiners of America, United Brotherhood of, AFL, *Proceedings of the Twenty-fourth Convention of Lakeland, Dec. 9 to Dec. 16, 1940*, p. 269.

[12]Carpenters and Joiners of America, United Brotherhood of, AFL, *Proceedings of the Twenty-fifth Convention of Lakeland, April 22 to April 30, 1946*, pp. 354–355.

constitution. But these rules fail to force the various locals and district councils to accept only labeled material. The Pennsylvania State Carpenters' Council asked the 1924 convention delegates to make the lax label laws mandatory. The committee considering the proposal rejected it, holding that it "is impracticable and impossible to legislate local agreements by this [national] convention."[13] In 1936, when the same dispute again arose, William Hutcheson himself stated that he could not and would not force local organizations to accept only labeled wood. The local option on label use stands at this writing.

Although the national office has long been opposed to "grading" carpenters' wages for different types of work, by 1949 at least seven different district councils had established a lower rate of wages for carpenters working on housing than those working on other types of building.[14]

Again, the national office has traditionally favored written agreements. Yet in 1951 so large a district as that in St. Louis announced its first such agreement in thirty years. It reduced its agreement to writing at this juncture not because the national demanded it, but because local leaders felt the Taft-Hartley Act did.[15]

Perhaps the best measure of local autonomy over economic affairs is the position of the business agent. This office, the most important in the union, is the one upon which its whole structure of trade regulation is based.[16] Yet the present national constitution does not regulate this office in any way. In fact the constitution is completely silent on the subject of the business agent.

There will be noted throughout the history of this national union a strange absence of detail about wages, hours, and working conditions. This harks back to the localized market. The national union does not concern itself with these matters. They are not part of its history. If each of its various locals were to cut ties with

[13]Carpenters and Joiners of America, United Brotherhood of, AFL, *Proceedings of the Twenty-first Convention of Indianapolis, Sept. 22 to Sept. 30, 1924*, pp. 361–362.

[14]Miles Colean, *American Housing: A Twentieth Century Fund Survey*, p. 405. These cities were Buffalo, Houston, Jacksonville, Milwaukee, Philadelphia, Richmond, and St. Louis.

[15]*St. Louis Post-Dispatch*, Jan. 9, 1951.

[16]See below, pp. 9, 62–66.

the national office, local collective bargaining would proceed much as it has in the past.[17]

Ownership

There are two general types of owners: the speculative, or temporary owner, who finances construction in order to sell the building at a profit, and the permanent owner. The latter has a long-term interest in the building and will give the contractor relatively more time, since his basic investment is made for purposes to which the building itself is incidental. While delays cost him money, basic capital is not slipping away.

The speculative builder, however, has not a moment to lose. Whether he operates through a contractor or builds himself, his basic goal is to erect the structure in the least possible time. Quality of construction and skill of workmanship are secondary considerations. He operates on a cost-plus basis by adding all that the traffic will bear to construction cost. The less he pays, the greater his profit. He will not deal with a union unless forced to do so. It is this owner who, more than any individual, exaggerates the speculative element in the building industry.

Since this speculator is usually building on the basis of short-term, high-interest loans, he will turn to contractors who are also operating beyond their capital assets in order to avoid the higher prices of the firmly established contractors. Often possessing little general knowledge of the industry, these contractors perform only the organizational function of the contractor by subcontracting until the services of all of the crafts necessary to complete the job are obtained. In their turn, the subcontractors may do the same thing.

It is in degree and not in kind that the pure speculator differs from the regular contractor. While a few large contractors and intercity construction companies possess the vast capital outlay which a foundation-to-roof construction company necessitates, the majority of entrepreneurs subcontract the work in their field. A

---

[17]The national union, of course, has had its function, which, in the light of its history, has been of far greater importance to the members than collective bargaining. For a discussion of this function, see below, Chapter XXI.

minimum of capital is thus risked in this highly speculative industry. In his testimony before the Temporary National Economic Committee, Dr. Willard Thorp presented a list of over sixteen subcontractors engaged to construct one small-scale urban home.[18] This aggregate of subcontractors renders the building industry one of small firms and intense competition. The Temporary National Economic Committee found in 1939 that slightly over half of the firms in the industry employed only three or four workers.[19]

Table III.—Size of Firms in the Building Industry in 1938

No. of Employees	Percentage of Total Employers	Percentage of Total Employees
1	21.77	2.44
2	18.11	4.05
3	13.48	4.54
4	9.39	4.21
5	6.85	3.83
6	4.91	3.30
7	3.90	3.06
8	2.57	2.30
9	2.08	2.09
10–19	9.31	13.95
20–29	2.98	7.94
30–39	1.39	5.25
40–49	.78	3.87
50–59	.51	3.11
60–69	.35	2.53
70–79	.26	2.17
80–89	.18	1.71
90–99	.16	1.65
100–199	.65	9.85
200–299	.17	4.77
300–399	.08	3.16
400–499	.03	1.65
500–599	.03	1.86
600–699	.02	1.27
700–799	.01	1.83
800–899	.01	.67
900–999	.01	.35
1000 and over	.02	3.59

Source: Building Trades Department, AFL, *Report of the Proceedings of the Thirty-third Annual Convention of Cincinnati, Sept. 22 to Sept. 29, 1939*, p. 221.

[18]U.S. *Temporary National Economic Committee Report,* Vol. 8, Part 11, chart facing p. 5174; pp. 5500–5502.

[19]*Ibid.,* p. 5183. When the size of the firms in the building industry is compared to that of firms in all other industries, it is found that in all other industries one-half of all employees work for firms with 250 workers or less. In the building industry, one-half of all workers are employed by firms with 28 or less employees.

The smallest firms are not regularly capitalized business ventures. They are usually no more than rogue carpenters with pretentious company names, lofty ambitions, strong backs, and little capital, trying to worm their way into the contractor class. These jerry-builders threaten the standards of both the union and the established contractor. Since their small jobs take only a few days at most, the union can limit their activities only by the use of full-time, paid representatives familiar with local building activities and empowered unilaterally to strike a job. The all-powerful business agent is thus a natural outgrowth of the competitive organization of the industry as well as of its decentralization.

Because he curtails excessive and cutthroat competition, the business agent is one of the stabilizing influences in the industry. In fact the sum of his activities creates minimum wage, hour, and work quality standards which a recognized contractor or owner rarely disregards and which make for a feeling of kinship between union and management. This feeling is further enhanced by easy access to the entrepreneurial phase of the industry. It is not unusual for two United Brotherhood card holders to sit at opposite sides of the negotiating table. They bargain against a background of well over half a century of trade unionism.

Finances

The bidding system gives this chaotic industry such financial pattern as it possesses. But it is an erratic pattern. Because a job is given to the lowest bidder, a firm's executives do not know in advance which bid will be accepted. Like other costs, the expense of estimating and bidding is pyramided as it moves through the hands of a series of contractors to the customer.

The existence of the bidding system makes the collective bargaining contract an important factor in the industry. If the contractor's bid is to estimate total costs accurately, his labor costs must be relatively stabilized. Once under a contract, the contractor cannot pass wage raises on to the owner, and a contract often runs for two or three years. An unexpected pay raise can wipe out a margin of profit based on anticipated labor costs. The bidding system thus increases the effectiveness of strikes and of the business agents empowered to call them and makes the employer vulnerable to union pressure on still another count.

Temporary Building Site

The builder is also vulnerable to unionization because he creates a highly diversified product on a series of different and temporary sites. Since he rarely knows a year in advance the location, type, or style of structures he will be called upon to erect, he is unable to maintain either an extensive inventory of materials or a permanent force of craftsmen. On one project he may need tons of brick and scores of bricklayers; on the next he may need neither. Under these conditions, the erection of a large structure is a tour de force of organization. Clockwork-like delivery and installation of materials, ranging from huge steel girders to mixed concrete ready for immediate pouring, are demanded in spite of obstacles such as traffic congestion in a large city. The materials and the craftsmen who install them must be carefully marshalled and, like actors in a play, ushered to stage on cue. After the first six weeks of a job, two hundred carpenters may be replaced by hundreds of bricklayers, iron workers, and concrete men. While the builder coordinates these activities, he immobilizes interest-bearing capital, land upon which heavy taxes are paid, and, in the edifice itself, a potential source of revenue. He is penalized for each day's delay in the promised delivery date, thus giving the business agent still further power.

His constantly changing scene of production provides the building trades employer with a difficult problem of personnel recruitment. It is solved for him by the trade unions which recruit and train (by the apprenticeship program) the wide variety of skilled craftsmen needed by the industry; which maintain employment offices (the local union hall) and recruiting agents (the business agents); and which service workers by providing jobs and employers by guaranteeing delivery under any conditions of the desired number of the necessary skills upon call. In return they ask only that employers maintain certain wages, hours, and working rules, without which the unions could not recruit the labor force.

Seasonality

Weather affects the building industry more than most other industries. Unpredictable weather conditions make it difficult for the contractor to plan completion dates with certainty. A contractor with a building in its early stages has most of his employees working out-of-doors. A stormy week will force him to lay off most of his working force. Those laid off may seek work elsewhere, on buildings where the walls and roofs are up and where all work is done indoors, safe from inclement weather. When the skies clear, the contractor may have lost a high percentage of his working force. Again the union comes into play to deliver the necessary craftsmen on a few hours' notice.

Seasonality also affects the carpenter by depriving him of a large percentage of his normal working time. This factor accounts for his higher-than-average hourly wage as well as for his historical sympathy for the eight-hour day and such spread-the-work rules as may be established.

These five factors do more to lend the building industry its distinctive flavor than do any of a host of others which might be cited in a study of the industry itself. Nevertheless, they account only for the existence of strong district councils oriented about the activities of powerful business agents. None accounts for the existence of a national office with extensive, almost absolute, power over the working carpenter. Why have carpenters, working in a strictly localized market, placed so much power in the hands of their national officers?

The Real Structure of the Union

Part of the answer is that the local leaders have not surrendered all of their power. The Hutchesons, father William and son Maurice, have dominated the union on the national level since 1915. In national-local relations, however, there has been much rendering unto the Hutchesons the things which are the Hutchesons' and to local leaders the things which are the local leaders'. The Hutchesons' power has been broadly based on the services which they have rendered to their followers. The Hutchesons are the national agents of the local business agents. The powers possessed by the Hutchesons have been obtained only under economic duress created by jurisdictional encroachments of other crafts. Since jurisdictional threats originate and can be settled only on a national scale, national power is necessary to cope with them.

The Hutchesons have been able to maintain their dominance primarily because of their skill in preserving the carpenters' jurisdiction.

Preserving work for the carpenter is one of the most vital things which the Brotherhood does for the individual dues payer and [William] Hutcheson... [knew] that his own job and power depend[ed] upon the militancy with which he... [fought] any union that claim[ed] jurisdiction over work that carpenters have always done.[20]

When asked how to end jurisdictional strikes, Hutcheson once replied, "There's one way to settle them and only one—give up work carpenters have always done and are entitled to. Is that what carpenters want?" he asked rhetorically.[21] If William Hutcheson had relaxed his jurisdictional vigilance, it is difficult to say which would have disappeared first, Hutcheson or the carpenters' craft.

Power within the union flows in a circle which can best be stepped into during a convention. The general president appoints all members of the powerful convention committees. If rebels should manage to push an antiadministration measure around one of these committees and onto the floor, the general president has the right to silence them with a rap of his gavel. When the convention is over, he appoints the general representatives through whom he influences all district councils. District councils are ruled by a junta of officers whose election is engineered by the business agents, the basis of whose power has already been discussed. The business agents, although elected by local union members, rarely fall from grace. Power to dole out jobs and to call strikes all but guarantees tenure. The business agents, the officers of the district council, and the international representatives pick the convention delegates on the basis of their general tracta-

---

[20]"Boss Carpenter," *Fortune,* April 1946, p. 121.
[21]*Ibid.*

bility.[22] And, in his turn, the general president has all of his powers quadrennially refreshed.

Many a delegate who has acted properly while a convention delegate has later been chosen business agent, if he was not one already. From there he moved up to a district council office; then to an appointment as a general representative; and, finally, into the general offices in Indianapolis as an executive board member or a vice-president. On each level fewer persons share more power. Finally, at the top, the general president is encountered, alone.

This whole organizational structure is based upon the mass of business agents who support everything above them: the district councils, the executive board, and the general officers. Every general officer is a graduate business agent. The position of business agent is a training school for the national officers of the union. The business agents get their power from two sources: from the contractors who are vulnerable to them on all the counts already listed and for whom they provide all the services already listed, and from the carpenters whom they keep employed and whose working conditions they maintain and protect. This hierarchy represents the real structure of power in the Brotherhood because it, and not the constitution, is constructed on economically realistic lines.

If the carpenters want to end this tight national control, they have only to vote all of the business agents—who alone possess direct economic power—out of office. The rest of the machine would then crumble for lack of economic footing. While most of the reasons why the carpenters have not done this relate to the laws of administrative power and of human nature, the nature of the carpenter as a craftsman helps in some measure to explain his failure to alter the United Brotherhood.

The Carpenter

At the 1924 convention of the United Brotherhood, both the committee on the constitution and the body of the convention flatly rejected a resolution requesting that the contractor supply

[22]*Ibid.*, p. 122.

tools for the carpenter. This was done because, in the words of the committee, "every carpenter loves his tools and understands them." This affection strikes closely to the core of the average carpenter's attitude about his calling. He is craft proud. And, as the refusal to accept tools from his employer indicates, he is extremely independent.

Although several factors account for the carpenter's related pride and independence, his strategic position in the construction scheme is the most important. The carpenter is the key craftsman on a construction job. Carpentry alone of the building crafts can require the breadth of knowledge possessed by the architect. The carpenter with complete mastery of his calling stands almost on the same plane as the job engineer.

Unstable conditions of work also account for the independence of the carpenter. Inclement weather, the collapse of a contract because of poor financing, or jurisdictional disputes may pull out from under him overnight what he thought an assured ten-week job. Even if the unforeseen does not occur, in the normal course of events he is dropped from a job with no notice when his part is completed. The carpenter thus hops from job to job and company to company a dozen and more times a year. The company bears no grudge if he quits, and he bears none if laid off. Neither party expects notice. Consequently, if the carpenter knows his employer at all it is because he is an old-timer who has previously worked for the same firm. Usually he does not know him and, in the course of the job, will not come to know him.

Another factor accounting for the carpenter's independence is the casual nature of his trade. There is a streak of the nomad in every carpenter, and itinerancy has, in some measure, characterized the trade since guild carpentry. To this day, many carpenters hobo it around the country from job to job. Subject to immediate dismissal because of material shortages and construction schedules, the carpenter must be a person who adjusts easily to such a day-to-day existence and who does not mind a day or two, or even a week, of inactivity during which to sharpen tools, play cards, or catch up on drinking. The person who accepts such a hand-to-mouth existence is obviously not one who will readily accept responsibility nor desire a fixed schedule, a fixed income, and an assured two-week vacation with pay at the same time each year. There are many carpenters who qualify as superintendents; few will accept the responsibility of being one. The only responsibility most carpenters accept is the craft responsibility that poor workmanship on good material is a sin. To the old-time carpenter this is a creed.

When out of work, the carpenter files his name with the business agent who is, in effect, employment agent for employers and employees alike. Ostensibly, his name is put last on a list of unemployed, and he waits his turn, playing poker or pinochle in the union hall, in the nearest bar, or, and this is unusual for older carpenters, at home by his telephone.

Actually, the business agent awards jobs in order to pay political debts or on the basis of the carpenter's union seniority rather than in terms of his position on the list. A highly skilled old-timer carries much prestige, and few younger members will complain when skipped in his favor. This is shrewd politics on the part of the business agent, for many an old-timer has a sizable following of younger men who will vote with him at election time. The average old-timer, in his day, has carried a score of younger men while they learned the trade.

When the carpenter is informed of a job opening by the business agent, he packs his tools and goes to the construction site. On every job at some time during each day, there is a small knot of carpenters—one familiar with the industry can spot them immediately—standing quietly appraising its merits. "How much carpentry remains to be done?" they ask themselves. "Does the foreman know what he is doing? Does he have control of the men? How much of the valuable inside work is there to be done? How many 'real mechanics' [who will be awarded inside work and will be the last laid off] are there among the carpenters?" When the carpenter has answered these questions to his satisfaction, he approaches the superintendent, who hires him on the spot or not at all. The superintendent cannot estimate even a day ahead whether or not he will need more carpenters. It depends upon too many variables, such as the weather and the delivery of cement.

15

Rarely does the carpenter return if refused. There are too many jobs to cover.

Often when hired he passes the carpenter who was summarily fired. Yet there is little enmity. The other carpenter could not do the work. When the company is efficient, if you cannot deliver you get fired a few hours after starting on the job. Such summary hiring and firing make trained personnel men blanch. Yet these practices are a natural outgrowth of the impermanence and instability of the industry and the result of a half-century and more of custom and usage. In this fashion new carpenters learn the trade. The union never interferes in such summary firing practices; it asks only that union carpenters be hired.

Once hired, he changes into overalls in the carpenters' shack, shoulders his toolbox, and moves up to the building line, as carpenters have done for several centuries. He is given a "buddy" with whom to work, and they work together quietly, rarely even asking each other's name for days after the job starts. He is expected immediately to appraise the nature of the work and to fall in with the pace set by the other carpenters. If he fails, in several hours, a day at the most, the foreman will tap him on the shoulder and tell him to "get your money."

Looking at the working carpenters, the older carpenter can immediately detect which men are highly skilled mechanics and which are not. The latter are "saw and hatchet men," "wood butchers," and "shoemakers." The skilled carpenter works quietly and with an almost grouchy deportment. He is expected to deliver, and if the contractor is efficient and the foreman alert, all concerned know how much he should deliver on a given kind of work. It takes days, even weeks, before an old-time carpenter will unbend sufficiently to talk with those who assist and work with him. Names are rarely used. It is "You," or "Heavy," or "Slim," "get this or that." Those words which are spoken are short and to the point. The efficient carpenter works at top speed as a matter of pride, and, like a well-coordinated athlete, his deftness and economy of motion belie the effort expended. Unless he is doing rough work, his work has to be true, or "plumb," to some figure under an inch.

16

What happens when the carpenter enters the arena of union politics? He is politically naïve. He is inclined to the all-out commitment, the direct and forceful approach for practical rather than theoretical reasons. A man who has to work within an inch or be fired tends to see things as either plumb or on the bias, black or white. Thus, when the Communists infiltered the United Brotherhood, they were dealt with summarily and violently.

Yet, because of their fixed ways and deep-rooted loyalties, the rank-and-file carpenters could never quite convince themselves that established leaders, proved on the practical union front, could misappropriate the union's funds, even when presented with overwhelming evidence. Fixed as they are in their ways, they are devoted to leadership which has been proved by their own uncomplex standards: do they deliver? A leader either delivers or he does not. If he does not quit and is not fired, he is presumed to have delivered, and there is no need to "knock" him. The carpenter dislikes, next to the poor craftsman, the "quitter" and the "knocker." The loyal carpenter has difficulty distinguishing between sincere criticism and treachery. Consequently, in its first sixty years of existence, the United Brotherhood had but two general secretaries, one nationally elected treasurer, and three paid and full-time general presidents. These officers can be criticized for many things. They cannot be criticized for failing to reflect the spirit of the average carpenter.

There appeared in *The Carpenter* of July 1914 a picture of the carpenters who had erected the L. C. Smith Building. They stood on the roof of the completed building, a score or so of walrus-mustachioed old-time carpenters, glowering at the camera. Almost without exception, they had on under their overalls stiff collars, ties, and tie pins. They all wore white shirts, suit coats, and bowlers, derbies, or slouch felt hats. Those without overalls had gold watch chains and fobs stretched across their abundant middles. Their day, perhaps, has passed. The attire certainly has. But it goes a long way toward symbolizing the old-time carpenter's craft pride and character: he came to work attired like his boss. He took pride in neither wearing gloves nor getting his hands very dirty. He worked with his hat on. At the day's end he took off his overalls, folded them atop his tools in the tool shed, washed his scarcely dirty hands, straightened his tie, tipped his bowler a bit more jauntily, and sought out the nearest bar.

Although the carpenter's craft pride and independence have changed but little since the first carpenter sawed the first piece of wood in America, his industry and his union have changed greatly since then. In fact, at one time, because industrial conditions made them unnecessary, the carpenters had no unions. It is in this period that a history of the United Brotherhood of Carpenters and Joiners of America properly begins.

CHAPTER II

The Middleman and the Green

Hand: 1791 to 1881

THREE changes occurred in the building industry between 1791 and 1881 which influenced the development of carpenters' trade unions. One, a change in the basic organization of the industry, called forth the first unions around the dawn of the eighteenth century; another, a widening of the labor market, led to the creation of the first intercity carpenters' unions in the 1860's; and a third, an advance in technology, was responsible for the creation of the present-day national union of carpenters. Prior to the first of these three developments, carpenters were organized under the master-journeyman-apprentice system, through which the trade was regulated. This system will be analyzed briefly in order to explain fully the impact which the first, or organizational, change had upon the carpenter.

The early American carpenter traveled from one isolated frontier settlement to the next, working by contract. He supplied only his skill and a few tools. His customer furnished materials, board, and lodging. If, as merchant, this carpenter bargained well; if, as master, he planned well; and if, as journeyman, he built well, he prospered.[1] He was something more than a carpenter, for he

---

[1] John R. Commons, et al., A History of Labour in the United States, Vol. 1, pp. 66–67.

selected and felled the timber which he later fashioned into beams and boards and then installed. He belonged to no employers' association, since he operated in a relatively noncompetitive market, and to no trade union, since he was both master and journeyman.

With the growth of the first colonial towns, a relatively more complex civilization came into being. The lumberjack, the sawmill hand, and the house builder became three separate persons as the carpenter ceased to choose and fell his lumber and the first "up and down" water-powered sawmills were built.[2] The carpenter settled in the city and opened a shop where, as a combination master carpenter and merchant, he sold directly to the consumer. He looked to the apprentice-journeyman system of the old world for his labor supply.

In the winter the journeyman worked in the master's shop, fashioning the details of the building. During the other seasons he worked outside on the job. He trained the apprentice below him and worked closely with the master who supervised him. Since the master was but little removed in worldly goods from the journeyman, and since the journeyman was not a static wage worker but was biding his time until the opportunity to become a master presented itself, a feeling of common interest prevailed between the two. Consequently no trade unions were formed.

The masters alone formed organizations for the purpose of regulating the trade. The first one was founded in Philadelphia in 1724 and was called the Carpenters' Company. It published a " 'book of prices' for the valuation of carpenters' work...so that workmen should have a fair recompense for their labour." To reduce competition among masters, a rule was passed prohibiting a member from completing work left undone by another member, and a system was inaugurated for the settlement of trade disputes.[3]

Until the end of the eighteenth century, this system operated unimpaired. Then the organization of the industry was completely altered by the rapid growth of the nation. The new unity attained during the formative period (1790–1820) of our present federal

[2]H. C. Mercer, *Ancient Carpenters' Tools in Use in the Eighteenth Century,* p. 281.
[3]Richard K. Betts, *Carpenters' Hall and Its Historic Memories* (Revised ed.), p. 4.

republic accelerated the growth of transportation facilities, commerce, and modern financial and credit systems.[4] Existing cities, as commercial terminals and entry ports, underwent a sharp increase in size. New cities joined the ranks of the old.[5] As offices, factories, warehouses, and docks were expanded to handle the new volume of business, the price of city land underwent a natural speculative increase. Building became more costly, and the small master carpenter could no longer finance the cost of an entire structure. Consequently, speculators with large reserves of idle capital or access to it stepped in as middlemen, between the master and the consumer, and the whole scheme of market and trade regulation pursued by the masters' organizations collapsed for want of direct access to the consumers' market.

The various elements in the industry were completely reshuffled as the middleman shouldered his way into the building picture. The master ceased to be an independent merchant-producer and became instead a small labor contractor. In a labor dispute in Philadelphia in 1791 the masters clearly presented their case to the public as labor contractors whose profits depended on the cost of labor.[6] Without any means of preventing journeymen from becoming contractors, intense competition ensued, and the "bosses cut the . . . [wages] to the bone in order to gain advantage over their competitors."[7]

The journeymen carpenters could either enter the race to become contractors or form trade unions to protect their standard of living. Thus wage-lowering and competitive pressures led to the trade unions formed to counter them.

The first journeymen's trade union of which evidence is available was formed in Philadelphia in 1791.[8] The idea caught and spread. By 1840 carpenters' trade unions had existed in most of the larger cities for four decades. They were present as far west as

[4]Commons, et al., History, Vol. 1, p. 101. From 1791 to 1816 the number of banking institutions in the United States increased from 3 to 246.
[5]Ibid., p. 176. In 1810 there were 11 cities with a population over 8,000, in 1830 there were 26, and in 1840 there were 44.
[6]Ibid., p. 71.
[7]Gabriel Edmonston, "Auld Lang Syne," The Carpenter, Vol. 35, No. 8, August 1915, p. 14.
[8]Commons, History, Vol. 1, p. 69.

Detroit and were active in at least fifteen cities.[9] The unions formed during this period were forced upon the carpenters because they were no longer able to control the market. They were little more than protest organizations. Although a mounting dislike for the do-nothing middleman who induced this competition characterized the period, the carpenters seemed not to understand the middleman's exact role. He was a hazy background figure who, in the normal course of events, rarely emerged to deal with the journeyman. Was he or the contractor responsible for their sad lot? Which should be attacked? In one strike the identity of the adversary was so vague that the strikers directed their settlement offer to both the contractor and the capitalist. "We are," they said, "willing to labour . . . to facilitate the business of the merchant or our employer; the merchant or our employer agreeing [to meet certain demands]." In return the journeymen promised to end the strike.[10]

Neither were the carpenters sure, for trade union purposes, of the exact identity of the contractors. Were these the same masters whose interests were close to those of the journeymen? Or were they capitalists? In some strikes the contractors supported the middlemen. In Boston in 1825 the middlemen addressed the journeymen on behalf of the contractors and signed their address "Gentlemen Engaged in Building." They gave notice that they would support their contractors by blacklisting, by boycotting, and, if necessary, by the lockout.[11] In other cases the contractors moved to support the journeymen. Then the carpenters' strike efforts were automatically directed against the middlemen. By 1825 contractors in New York, Philadelphia, and Brooklyn had supported the journeymen, and in that year the Boston carpenters asked for the same support in their impending strike.[12] At times the contractors

---

[9]*Ibid.*, pp. 365, 380, 386, 488. Carpenters' Organizations were active in Philadelphia, Boston, Washington, Baltimore, New Brunswick, Paterson, Troy, New York City, Poughkeepsie, Albany, Lockport, Buffalo, and Detroit.

[10]J. R. Commons and V. B. Phillips, *A Documentary History of American Industrial Society*, Vol. 6, p. 85, quoting "A Resolution of the Boston Ship Carpenters, May 15, 1832." The demands were long and complex and are not germane to this work.

[11]*Ibid.*, p. 80, "Resolution passed at a meeting of Gentlemen Engaged in Building the present Season" (issued April 21, 1825).

[12]*Ibid.*, p. 78, "Notice to the House Carpenters of the Country" from the Boston Carpenters, April 23, 1825.

were "unscrupulous bosses"[13] and at other times "slaves to the capitalists as we are to them."[14]

Lacking a clear concept of their common enemy, the early trade unionists were unable to found their organizations on a solid foundation from which administrative procedures could be derived and organizational lures set for nonunion carpenters. As a result, prior to 1865 carpenters' trade union movements were more often emotional outbursts against the person of the middleman than carefully planned and guided offensives. On some occasions they threw themselves enthusiastically into local assemblies of mixed trades,[15] on other occasions into politics, and on still others into the cooperative movement. All of these experiments failed, and the various local unions of carpenters ebbed and flowed aimlessly with the tides of depression and prosperity.

Economic developments capable of producing a national union did not materialize until the 1860's. A gradual improvement in transportation which began in the 1850's and continued throughout the 1860's had brought about a major change in the structure of the labor market by 1865.[16] Carpenters were now able to travel cheaply and more rapidly on the new railroad lines to possible jobs in cities heretofore too distant for regular commutation. Job markets were merged and made larger. For the first time carpenters in widely separated cities found themselves competing with each other for jobs.

With carpenters able to journey from city to city, any raise in the wages of a given local attracted a flood of carpenters to that city. Some employers abetted this process by advertising false building booms in various local newspapers. Isolated local unions were thus forced to exchange accurate information on employment and to provide means for union carpenters to travel from town to town without paying a new initiation fee in each town.

Thus did the state-wide union become the next in a long line of

[13]Edmondson, "Auld Lang Syne," *The Carpenter,* Vol. 35, No. 8, August 1915, p. 14.

[14]William Haber, *Industrial Relations in the Building Industry,* p. 273, quoting a labor journal, *The Man,* May 13, 1832, p. 2.

[15]Commons, *History,* Vol. 1, p. 365.

[16]*Ibid.,* Vol. 2, pp. 3–5; Haber, pp. 277–278. In the 1850's 22,104 miles of railroad were constructed and in the 1860's, 16,040.

union experiments. By the end of 1865 there were at least nine in existence.[17] They enjoyed, however, but brief existence and little success, since the political state was not an economic region within which building activities could be controlled effectively. Hence in September 1865, on the invitation of the New York State Carpenters' Union, the state unions held their first convention as the National Carpenters' Union. Almost immediately after its founding this union started to decline, and after 1867 no further evidence of its activities is available.

The apparent reason for the short existence of this union is found in the struggle for power between state and national union officers. The former would surrender no power to the national except that of issuing a national working card. The state unions surrendered this one power because they formed the national for only one reason: to meet the problem of interstate itinerancy.[18] The national working card enabled the itinerant to move from town to town without joining a new union and guaranteed that the card holder would observe local work rules and not undercut the wage rate. Possessed of only one real function, the national officers had little responsibility and less power. The greater part of the National Carpenters' Union's activities were administered on the state level while the national office remained a mere agency through which a working card was issued.

The national officers, however, felt that the state unions were ineffective, and, hoping to strengthen the power of the national office, they bypassed them at every opportunity.[19] This conflict led to disputes about the distribution of power as specific administrative tasks were assigned. The question of whether state or national officers should charter locals, the relationship between national

[17]Carpenters and Joiners' National Union of the United States of America, *Proceedings of the First Annual Convention of New York 1865*, pp. 4–5, 10, 15. The New York State Union was the largest, with 3,370 members. Massachusetts followed with 1,400. Missouri, Michigan, Maryland, New Jersey, Rhode Island, Indiana, and Pennsylvania were also represented at this convention.

[18]*Constitution of the Carpenters & Joiners' National Union of the United States of America,* as adopted in 1865, in *Proceedings,* pp. 22–23.

[19]Carpenters and Joiners' National Union of the United States of America, *Proceedings of the Second Annual Convention of New York 1866,* "Report of President T. W. Harris," pp. 9–10, 46.

representatives on the state level and state officers, the size of the national per capita tax, and a score of other questions brought the struggle to a crisis in early 1866. When the second convention was held in the fall of 1866, all but one of the state unions had dropped out of the national union.

The real reason for the union's failure was the continued vagueness of the carpenters' aims. President T. W. Harris of the National Carpenters' Union told the 1866 convention:

We have no clearly defined purpose; no end at which we are intelligently aiming; no goal which we are trying to reach. Our purposes are general and undefined. Each one is left to project and imagine for himself...our membership are beginning to ask "What does all this mean? Why am I attached to this National Union? What can it do for me?"[20]

Of itself itinerancy, the sole nationalizing force then present in the building industry, was not sufficient to hold carpenters in a national union. As a consequence this union, like so many before it, toyed with politics and cooperation, two of the favorite pastimes of anti-middlemen, reform trade unionists.[21] These diversions hastened the end of their union.

The problem of itinerancy mounted, however, as more railroads were built, and, after 1872, it was joined by a development new to the building industry, an industrial revolution in the machine woodworking industry. As the emergence of the middleman altered the organization of the industry and as the itinerant changed its labor market structure, so did the industrial revolution alter its technology. In fact it completely changed the nature of the carpenter's craft and almost eliminated it as a separate skill.

Although prior to 1872 organizational and market changes had exercised hardship upon the journeyman carpenter, technically he worked much the same as he had a century before, fashioning by hand all of the complicated detail work—doors, windows, newel posts, mantels—outside on the site of the building. In the winter he worked indoors, in the contractor's shop, laying in a stock of such handwork for the building season. This intricate "finishing" work made the greatest demands upon the carpenter as an artisan and hence preserved the identity of his craft and protected it.

[20]*Ibid.*, p. 8.
[21]*Ibid.*, p. 28.

After 1871 a host of woodworking machine inventions rained down upon the unprotected craft. A sander which smoothed wood as fast as a dozen carpenters and a compound carver which turned out six wood duplicates and replaced three-score carpenters were but two of a series of such inventions which lured handicraft work into the factory and effected a major upheaval in the woodworking industry.[22] Table IV speaks for itself.

Table IV.—Hand and Machine Labor Costs in the Woodworking Industry: 1858 to 1896

| | Years | | Labor Cost | |
Item	Hand	Machine	Hand	Machine
50 blinds..........................	1848	1896	$ 87	$ 8.00
12 mantel brackets....................	1889	1896	112	46.00
50 white pine doors..................	1894	1896	113	11.00
1,000 ft. 4½″ yellow pine ceiling........	1859	1895	14	.44
1,000 ft. 3″ oak flooring...............	1858	1895	21	.54
1,000 ft. 4½″ yellow pine flooring.......	1859	1895	12	.36
50 pair yellow pine sashes.............	1858	1895	60	9.00
10 sets stair risers and treads...........	1858	1895	26	2.00

Source: Commissioner of Labor, "Hand and Machine Labor," *Thirteenth Annual Report* (for the year ended Dec. 31, 1898),Vol. 2, pp. 1356–1399. The information in this table was compiled from charts on "Planing mill products" on these pages and is presented in round figures.

The first effect of machine inventions was to give birth to the "green hand"—a woman, an immigrant, or child—who displaced a score of carpenters at half the wages of one. One labor paper held in 1877 that "as improved . . . machinery has advanced . . . hundreds of thousands [of workers] have been . . . thrown in idleness on the pavement. In proof of this it is only necessary to refer to carpentry. . . thousands upon thousands of whose members have been reduced to want."[23]

The windows, doors, and other parts of the building which streamed off the machine, standardized, complete, and ready for installation, allowed for the easy subdivision of the carpenter's

[22]Frederick S. Deibler, *The Amalgamated Wood Workers' International Union of America,* pp. 32–36. In 1850 the woodworking industry turned out a total product worth $58,520.00. In 1900 its products were worth $1,030,906.00 or 7.9 percent of the total value of all American manufactures (*ibid.,* p. 2).

[23]*The Labor Standard* (New York City), Dec. 23, 1877, p. 2, col. 1. Another item of an earlier date in the same paper complained bitterly of a New Jersey factory at which green hands working twelve hours a day turned out one hundred and fifty doors a day for the New York City market (*ibid.,* Oct. 7, 1876, p. 4, col. 2).

work. Carpentry was gradually divided into door hanging, floor laying, stair building, and a score of other special tasks by competing contractors who only paid one-half the wage of a fully trained, all-around carpenter. By the early 1880's Peter J. McGuire,[24] the founder of the Carpenters' Union, complained that "in a few weeks . . . a lad becomes proficient in his part [of the carpenter's craft]."[25] While this lad may have been a "proficient" window setter or shingle installer, he was not a carpenter. He was the outside green hand.

Harassed both in the factory and outside on the building site by the green hand, the carpenter rapidly discovered that still another evil stemmed from the advent of woodworking machinery: piecework. The steady stream of ready-to-install parts which poured off the machines were ideally suited to this mode of payment. And piecework, in turn, was ideally suited to the speed-up. One carpenter complained in 1876 that he had become a floor layer, that he received twenty-five cents for each "square" he laid, and that he was able to lay only three a day.[26]

The pieceworking system effected a basic change in the organization of the industry. Prior to 1872, while the building might have been financed for resale by the speculator, the speculator dealt with one contractor who supplied both labor and material. After the advent of the pieceworker, however:

Speculators. . . [started] putting up shoddy houses on ninety day builders' loans. . . . One of the curses in the carpentry work on these shoddy houses is the system of lumping and subletting or piecework. The lumper. . . takes a whole job at a certain figure; he then sublets it to another, who, in turn, parcels it out to others, who do the work in as rapid. . . a manner as possible—tearing and rushing to get it done. They all have to make a profit, at the expense of [both] the buyer and the laborer.[27]

[24]Peter J. McGuire was of such great importance in both the founding and subsequent development of the union that the whole of the next chapter will deal with him.

[25]U.S. Congress, Senate, Committee on Education and Labor, *Report Upon the Relations Between Labor and Capital and Testimony Taken by the Committee*, 48th Cong., 1st Sess., Vol. 1, p. 352.

[26]*The Labor Standard*, Oct. 7, 1876, p. 4, col. 2.

[27]*John Swinton's Paper* (New York City), Feb. 17, 1884, p. 4, col. 2. John Swinton was a prolabor journalist.

This "speculator" was the hated middleman, who by 1881 was encamped on the carpenter's very doorstep. Under the aegis of the piecework-subcontracting system, he threatened to preside over the disintegration of the carpenter's craft. The most naïve carpenter could no longer question the middleman's identity. He had but to find any green hand butchering wood and there behind him, often literally driving him to greater production, stood the hated middleman. The new speculator and his half-carpenter green hand not only justified a half-century of abstract hatred for the middleman but also anchored it firmly in economic fact. The pieceworker allowed the carpenter to be both philosophical and practical, anti-middleman and job conscious, at the same time. Through the medium of the pieceworker, a half-century of vague antimiddleman sentiment was translated into specific and pragmatic trade union principles.

Consequently, the carpenters were finally able to formulate a logical and consistent trade union philosophy which took into account the working carpenter's grievances and promised to redress them through the medium of a national union. The Brotherhood of Carpenters and Joiners of America was a conscious outgrowth of this philosophy which, for the first twenty years of its existence, colored its every activity.

CHAPTER III

The Philosopher Organizers:

1881 to 1886

THE philosophy of the founders of the union began with a hatred of the pieceworker that was two parts scorn. He was held to be a poor befuddled fool, a "botch." The system, not the man, was at fault. If you wish to hate any class of men, hate the middleman, the monopolist, the speculator, the capitalist. For all these were one man and the pieceworker his pliant tool. The pieceworker was thus only a point of departure for a broad socialist philosophy. All this the founders told the carpenters.

This philosophy was propounded and applied by one man, Peter J. McGuire. For twenty years his personality and philosophy dominated the union. Almost singlehandedly he founded and raised the Brotherhood of Carpenters and Joiners of America to unchallenged pre-eminence among American unions.

McGuire was born of Irish immigrant parents in 1852 on New York's lower East Side. He received little formal schooling before being apprenticed as a joiner in 1867. At night, however, he attended the free lectures and courses at the Cooper Union, then a gathering place for the city's radical and discontented.[1] There he acquired a life-long interest in what scholars then called political economy. Once launched on a study of society, it took him little

[1]Samuel Gompers, *Seventy Years of Life and Labor*, Vol. 1, p. 28.

time to become an advocate of its most violent reorganization. Before he was twenty, he was described by Gompers as an intelligent, big-hearted, but violent and radical advocate of the working-class cause.[2]

During the late 1860's McGuire wandered in and out of virtually every radical group which formed, split, and reformed on the lower East Side. But as a lone native American in obscure groups of radical foreigners, he received little public notice until 1874. Then, in the Tompkins Square rioting of that year, he was catapulted to a notoriety which he rarely lost for the rest of his life. His activity and utterances in the Tompkins Square affair establish the outline of the personality which had such a great influence on the Carpenters' Union.

The depression of 1873 was the worst which had ever struck the country. In New York City, as winter drew on, the unemployed crowded into soup lines and when these were unavailable huddled in doorways and talked darkly of jobs or violence. Although the well-to-do were nervous and the police maintained a virtual cordon around the lower East Side, nothing was done to relieve the poor.

On December 11, 1873, McGuire and a group of radicals called a mass meeting of workers at Cooper Union.[3] Thousands crowded in to hear young McGuire and his friends denounce the city government and demand relief. At the meeting's end a Committee of Public Safety was created to force the city government to alleviate working-class suffering.

Early in January 1874 McGuire headed a subcommittee of the Committee of Public Safety which met with the Board of Aldermen to demand unemployment relief. In a heated discussion, McGuire pleaded with the aldermen, then threatened to throw them out of the window one by one if unemployment relief was not granted. His pleas and threats were both ignored.[4]

The Committee of Public Safety then decided to hold a protest parade from Union Square south to City Hall Plaza, there to hold

[2]*Ibid.*, p. 93. At Cooper Union McGuire befriended Samuel Gompers, with whom he founded the American Federation of Labor (*ibid.*, p. 332), and with whom he remained a close and lifelong friend.

[3]*New York Times,* Dec. 12, 1873, p. 5, col. 1.

[4]*New York Times,* Jan. 12, 1874, p. 4, col. 3.

30

a "monster" meeting. McGuire was placed in charge of arrangements and the parade was scheduled for January 13, 1874.

During the week preceding the parade, the city press was nervous. If only because of its ominous name, the Committee of Public Safety and its leading member, Peter J. McGuire, were constantly denounced by the daily papers. There was talk of a parade ban and of violence if this occurred. On the ninth of January McGuire warned the Chief of Police not to ban the parade. The workers, he said, were determined to get either "bread or blood."[5] Between the tenth and twelfth, tension mounted as McGuire conferred with various public officials. The press was flooded with denunciations of McGuire as a menace to public safety, a demagogue, a loafer, and a "Communist of the most violent type."[6]

McGuire's father, John, a porter at Lord and Taylor's store and a mild man, was appalled at his son's notoriety. He pleaded with him to desist. When Peter refused, his father mounted the steps of their East Side Catholic Church and denounced and disowned him. He accused his son Peter of being an atheist, a Communist, of refusing work, and of living off his father's meager earnings.

The denunciation occurred on the twelfth, as McGuire was on his way to talk with the Mayor about the contemplated parade ban. The papers pounced on John McGuire's words and played them against McGuire for all they were worth. While McGuire was storming at the city officials they confronted him with his father's accusations. When told of his father's act McGuire "burst into tears" and had to be escorted away.[7] The Mayor then banned a demonstration on City Hall Plaza.

Still McGuire held the parade the next day. The thousands of sullen workers with their red flags and sashes and radical slogans frightened the police. As the procession swung into Tompkins Square the mounted police attacked savagely, slashing about them with billy sticks. Hundreds were injured in a pitched battle. All

---

[5] *New York World,* Jan. 9, 1874, p. 5, col. 4.
[6] *New York Times,* Jan. 13, 1874, p. 8, col. 1.
[7] *New York Tribune,* Jan. 13, 1874, p. 5, col. 1; *New York World,* Jan. 13, 1874, p. 1, col. 2; and *New York Times,* Jan. 13, 1874, p. 4, col. 5; p. 8, col. 1.

31

day flying squads of police conducted a reign of terror on the lower East Side. One paper reported that while they were pleased with the actions of the police, "The general sense of justice is outraged by the fact that...Maguire [sic] has not been beaten into insensibility and silence."[8]

The Tompkins Square violence temporarily ended the radical movement on the east coast. Gompers, who had marched with his friend McGuire, was convinced by the rioting of the futility of political radicalism and started his journey to trade unionism. McGuire, however, became more than ever outraged at the capitalist order. "These scurvy knaves know not the volcano ready to burst beneath their feet, and blow them to atoms."[9]

Convinced that the power of the state had blocked the workers' effort to secure justice, McGuire turned avidly to politics. In May 1874 he was one of the leading lights in the formation of the Social Democratic party of North America[10] and was elected to its first executive board. While McGuire had possessed a violent radical spleen, until he formed this party he had no social philosophy. Now for the first time he adopted one which, with some modification, he held until he died. Both the goals and the procedures of the early Brotherhood of Carpenters and Joiners reflected this philosophy.

McGuire's social thought was based on the writing of Ferdinand Lassalle, a German radical. Lassalle held that under the capitalistic system workers could never advance their standard of living. Their wages were held at the level of "bare...existence and propagation" by an "iron" law of supply of, and demand for, labor. To free themselves, however, the workers should not destroy but should capture the capitalist system by forming a workers' political party on the one hand and cooperative societies on the other. Through the political party the workers were to vote themselves control of the government. Once in command, labor was to advance state

[8]*New York World,* Jan. 14, 1874, p. 4, col. 5.
[9]*The Labor Tribune* (New York City), Sept. 9, 1876, p. 1, col. 3.
[10]Commons, *History,* Vol. 2, pp. 230–231. This party became the Workingman's party in 1876 and later, in 1877, the Socialistic Labor party. A few years later, the "ic" was dropped from the name and this party remains in existence at the present time as the Socialist Labor party. For a review of these events, see *ibid.,* pp. 277–290.

credit to each of the various cooperative societies. Through the societies the workers were to purchase all of the industries in the state and to conduct them as producers' cooperatives, eliminating wages and sharing the profits.[11]

McGuire adopted Lassalle's theory of state capitalism and became a tireless itinerant radical agitator. Every speech he made boiled down to a desire "to abolish the present system of wage slavery, by substituting, in its stead, a system of universal cooperative production and distribution."[12]

New England was McGuire's special province, and there was scarcely a hamlet in that region he did not rock with his violent oratory. Windsor Locks and Rockville, Connecticut; New Bedford, Fall River, and Boston, Massachusetts; and well over a hundred other towns heard him split the air with ringing denunciations of capitalism.[13] During the late 1870's he became the leading organizer for the Socialist Labor party. Wherever he went he left behind him talk, discontent, and new sections of the party. One party member described him:

It is worth a long summer day's march to hear McGuire. Sharp, incisive, trenchant, he cleaves asunder, dividing the bones and the marrow. We do not remember having had our spirit so completely refreshed by the free mountain breezes of eloquent statement, well sustained argument and brilliant imagery as...when listening to this man.[14]

When the party supplied the money, McGuire used it; when it did not, he paid expenses himself. Often as not he looked as though he had slept in a box car. Often as not he had. He abused himself without stint. One Boston radical in a letter to the party organ praised his ability but added, "McGuire...is killing himself

---

[11]Ferdinand Lassalle, *Open Letter to the National Labor Association of Germans* (trans. by John Ehmann and Fred Bader). See Commons, *History,* Vol. 2, pp. 205–206, and Selig Perlman, *A Theory of the Labor Movement,* pp. 74–75, for an analysis of the specific background against which Lassalle wrote his *Open Letter.* See also, Selig Perlman, *History of Trade Unionism in the United States,* pp. 74–75, for a discussion of the significance of Lassalle's philosophy in the United States.

[12]*The Socialist* (New York City), April 22, 1876, p. 2, col. 1.

[13]*The Labor Standard,* March 24, 1877, p. 3, cols. 3 and 4; April 7, 1877, p. 3, cols. 3 and 4.

[14]*The National Socialist* (Cincinnati), Aug. 24, 1878, p. 5, col. 4.

working too hard for the cause."[15] He was to pay for this abuse in later years.

Being a good and devout Lassallian, the applied creed meant two things to McGuire: much politics and little trade unionism. On behalf of all Lassallians he wrote in 1877:

[We] think both political action and trade unionism can be used. Not that we mean to have our political action subordinate to the unions! Not that we will compromise our vital principles with their milk-and-water measures! But we shall use them as a means of agitation—to spread our principles among them and have them assist us, if they will.[16]

Consequently, from 1876 to 1878 McGuire spent most of his time urging political action on the trade unions and participating in state and local political campaigns on behalf of the Workingman's party.

During the five years that followed 1876, however, McGuire gradually altered his social philosophy to become a trade unionist. Out of this period in his life came first the idea and then the sub- stance of the Brotherhood of Carpenters and Joiners of America.

McGuire came by his trade unionism in a way thoroughly typical of his undisciplined intellect. He harbored social philosophies as a miser does useless possessions. He was loath to abandon any and equally loath to pass up new ones. He asked of new ideas only that they promise to end the capitalist order. He did not abandon his utopian ideas to become a trade unionist; rather, he shifted their various aspects about to make room for trade unionism.

The first sign of a shift came in 1877. In March of that year, while on one of his many "agitational" tours, McGuire stumbled upon a strike in the Wamsutta knitting mills in New Bedford. When he saw the suffering of the strikers and their fight against the "greedy capitalists," all finer points of ideology were forgotten. He pitched into the fray and in a few days assumed leadership, turning a blind strike into a well-conducted campaign. A strike

[15]*Ibid.*, June 22, 1878, p. 5, col. 2.
[16]*The Labor Standard,* Jan. 6, 1877, p. 3, col. 1. See also *ibid.* and *ibid.,* Jan. 27, 1877, p. 3, cols. 1 and 2, for letters from McGuire emphasizing the role of politics and minimizing that of the trade unions in the revolutionary scheme.

committee was set up, soup kitchens created for the strikers' families, and a nationwide strike support campaign launched. For a month he directed the strike with all the enormous fund of energy at his command.[17]

That the strike ended inconclusively is of no great importance. Of real significance is the fact that during the strike McGuire took his first nibble at the trade union bait. He wrote toward the end of the strike, "Trade unions...have been organized with our [the Socialists'] assistance." He wished it to be known, however, that these were no ordinary trade unions but ones based "upon advanced principles" and formed in conjunction with sections of the Workingman's party.[18]

From this point on, McGuire started a drift to what later became known as "pure and simple" unionism. As 1877 wore into 1878 and 1879, McGuire came more and more to see that "we never can storm the citadel of money power, entrenched as it is behind law-customs, if we have not disciplined our Labor hosts in many a preparatory conflict."[19] While his bitter, almost pathological, hatred for capitalism never relaxed, he became convinced of the futility of direct action. Instead he became convinced that "every concession obtained is forced by organization *and can be maintained only by organization.*"[20]

McGuire moved to St. Louis in the fall of 1878 and immediately became active in both the local Socialistic Labor party and the St. Louis Trades and Labor Alliance. In February 1879 the Alliance sent him to the capital of Missouri to lobby for the creation of a Bureau of Labor Statistics. There he harassed the stunned legislators with all the vigor he had previously directed at the workers. They created a Bureau of Labor Statistics.[21] McGuire saw to it that H. Hilkene, a St. Louis cigar maker, was placed at its head and that he himself became the deputy commissioner.[22]

[17]*Ibid.*, April 21, 1877, p. 3, cols. 4 and 5.
[18]*Ibid.*, April 28, 1877, p. 3, col. 4.
[19]*The Socialist* (Chicago), April 26, 1879, p. 2, col. 4, and p. 3, col. 1.
[20]*Ibid.*, May 3, 1879, p. 2, cols. 2 and 3.
[21]*Ibid.*, May 3, 1879, p. 2, col. 2.
[22]Missouri Bureau of Labor Statistics, *First Annual Report* (for the year ended Dec. 31, 1879), p. 9.

His success in creating a Bureau of Labor Statistics—long a standard demand of American radicals—convinced McGuire of two things. First, he became certain that Socialists should champion practical and ameliorative reform measures for the workers. "Let us do something practically good for them [the workers]: let us gain some tangible result, and it will be no surprise to see them flocking to our support in spite of every prejudice."[23]

This decided upon, he saw trade unions as the best method of luring the men to socialism through the medium of practical reform. Their mission was largely to be one of education:

In the settlement of the labor question, Trades Unions will play a very important part. They are indispensable under our present system. It will be their province to form the intermediary link between the wage system and that of co-operation. As a school of discipline the Unions are invaluable. They bring the heterogeneous masses...together and assimilate them. In their past and present character, they have been a primary school for the study of the industrial problem. And to prepare men for the new state of things will be part of their work. In the future they will be the germ of trade co-operation. To a great extent through them a system of universal co-operation will be conducted and managed.[24]

McGuire thus saw the trade union movement as a "great democratic training school,"[25] through which the workers would gradually usurp the functions of management, learn how to conduct the nation's industries, and prepare themselves for the role of political rulers. "The men," said a labor journal which McGuire supported, "to whom important *future business interests* are to be entrusted, should have been put to the test beforehand and can best be tried in Trades Unions."[26]

Such was the trade union philosophy which emerged from a decade of itinerant agitation. It was to be important for the future of the United Brotherhood and of American trade unionism in

---

[23]*The Socialist* (Chicago), May 3, 1879, p. 2, cols. 1 and 2.

[24]*The National Socialist,* June 15, 1878, p. 2, col. 3.

[25]W. J. Shields, "Where We Stand Today," *The Carpenter,* Vol. 35, No. 4, May 1915, p. 12. Article by William Shields, fifth president of the union, outlining McGuire's idea of the ultimate goal of trade unions.

[26]*The Labor Standard,* Nov. 18, 1876, p. 2, col. 1. (Italics mine.)

general. It is easy to see how out of such a trade union philosophy there could emerge the figure of the business agent so completely entwined in his industry. It is easy to see how such a philosophy could produce peaceful collective bargaining rather than class warfare. In fact, what was later to be called "AFL business union-ism" is McGuire's Lassallian philosophy put into effect but divested of its revolutionary goals.[27]

In amalgamating practical trade unionism and socialism, McGuire lost surprisingly little of his radical fire. Trade unionism merely served "to strip. . .[the labor question] of all minor issues [like wages and hours in order to]. . .come to the main question,"[28] the cooperative commonwealth. "No matter what concession we gain, we should never cease hostilities until every odious remnant of the present industrial system is annihilated."[29]

On his return to St. Louis, McGuire threw himself into trade union work with an intensity which left his associates out of breath and ten steps behind. He turned in early 1880 to his own calling, carpentry, to put his trade union plan into effect. He could not

[27]For a contrary view, see Perlman, *Theory of the Labor Movement,* pp. 193 and 198, and Perlman, *History of Trade Unionism in the United States,* p. 282. Professor Perlman holds that "it was out of this class-consciousness associated with Marx, that there has grown the trade union 'job and wage consciousness' of the American labor movement of today" (Perlman, *Theory,* p. 193). There is, however, little evidence that Gompers and other early AFL leaders were ever Marxists, other than Gomper's word to that effect (Gompers, *Seventy Years of Life and Labor,* Vol. 1, pp. 82–85). McGuire, who was second in influence only to Gompers during the early years of the existence of the AFL, certainly was not a Marxist. Further, McGuire's Lassallian philosophy, with its conscious aim to have organized labor conduct the business and industries of the nation, would seem to explain the development of business unionism more adequately than does Marxism. The most recent scholar to investigate the origins of the AFL has said that a "conservative syndicalism. . .characterized the American Federation of Labor in the first decades after its formation." (Will Herberg, "American Marxist Political Theory," in Donald Drew Egbert and Stow Persons, *Socialism and American Life,* Vol. 1, p. 491). Herberg goes on to describe what he calls conservative syndicalism as not unlike the Lassallian creed held by McGuire (*ibid.,* pp. 491–492). He concludes by noting that "a reinterpretation of old line 'pure and simple' trade unionism from this point of view promises fruitful results" (*ibid.,* p. 492). In any case, more research in the records of the various socialist parties active from 1876 to 1890, in the papers of both Socialist leaders and less well-known leaders of the early AFL and its component unions is required before a definite conclusion as to the origins of the AFL and the aims of its early leaders can be drawn.

[28]*The Socialist* (Chicago), May 3, 1879, p. 2, cols. 1 and 2.

[29]*Ibid.*

have chosen a craft more ripe for his ideas, for by then the middle-man, in the guise of a speculative subcontractor, and the piece-worker had all but torn the trade to shreds. Where better to strike at the hated middleman than through his pieceworker? Where better than on the job to prove to the workers that properly organized and with clearly defined goals they could do away with the middleman? Where better to begin than with the smallest but most noxious variety of this specious growth, the pieceworker?

McGuire raged and fulminated against the green hand, the botch, the wood butcher—the pieceworker. And the St. Louis carpenters flocked by thousands into first one, then two, and finally, four, branches of a local union. By 1881 McGuire had doubled their wage and partially eliminated piecework.

As wages climbed upward, carpenters in other cities eyed the St. Louis labor market as though it were an El Dorado. In the spring of 1881 they descended upon the city in a great deluge and swept aside many of McGuire's hard-won gains. This had also happened in other unionized cities. McGuire wrote in the spring of 1881, "I [have] received letters from all cities asking me... to organize a National Carpenters' Union; I will do so."[30] Thus was the Brotherhood of Carpenters and Joiners of America born.

At a meeting of the St. Louis Carpenters' Union on April 24, 1881, a five-man "Provisional Committee of the Carpenters and Joiners National Union" was formed. McGuire was elected its secretary, and Gustav Luebkert, an old Lassallian comrade of McGuire's, its chairman. A trade journal with McGuire as editor was immediately established. Five days later the hardworking McGuire had the first edition of *The Carpenter* in the mails.

The Provisional Committee selected Chicago, then the center of western radicalism, as the site of the first convention and spread the news broadcast through *The Carpenter*. The Chicago carpenters made necessary arrangements, and the convention opened on August 8. From the outset the struggle over policy turned on the

[30]Letter from McGuire to Philip Van Patten, president of the Socialistic Labor party, April 15, 1881, as quoted in Philip Foner, *History of the Labor Movement in the United States,* p. 499.

question of allotment of administrative powers and was fought between two groups, the "protectives" and the "benevolents."[31]

The protectives, while not completely opposed to benefits, saw the new national primarily as an organization which would enable local bodies better to pursue strikes, to regulate working conditions, and to gain shorter hours and better wages. To accomplish this, they would give the national extensive power over the local unions. The benevolents favored a national union whose only function was to maintain a benefit system. Since in their eyes the national organization was to be a financial clearing house far removed from local union affairs, they wished to give it little power. The dispute thus reduced itself to the problem of how much power the national office was to have over local unions.

It is doubtful if even a man of McGuire's vast energy and talents could have brought the organization into existence in the face of such strong localizing forces were it not for the presence of even stronger nationalizing forces. McGuire constantly preached that specialization, division of labor, the collapse of apprenticeship standards, green hands, and piecework were all due to the advent of machinery. An Ohio machine threatened the Chicago carpenter and the Philadelphia carpenter equally. Moreover, as itinerants the carpenters threatened each other. "There is danger that... high wages will tempt carpenters to come from cheaper cities. Hence every city should be organized [in a national union] and the wages of all advanced to a uniform standard," McGuire told the carpenters.[32] Only real national power, he held, could cope with real national economic forces.

Gabriel Edmonston, head of a Washington, D.C. carpenters union, joined McGuire to form an east-west coalition which successfully pushed the protective point of view. No benefit system was created. Otherwise, the outcome was a compromise constitution which established a weak confederation of local unions. Only three concessions obtained by the protectives were without limitation. A full-time and paid national secretary was created in the

[31]Gabriel Edmonston, "The Genesis of the Brotherhood of Carpenters," *The Carpenter*, Vol. 24, No. 10, October 1904, p. 9.
[32]*The Carpenter*, Vol. 1, No. 1, May 1881, p. 1.

person of Peter J. McGuire; a flat prohibition against piecework was laid down; and a national working-card system was inaugurated to cope with the problem of itinerancy.[33]

Power remained localized and diffused. Although nine national officers were provided, only the general secretary was paid and full-time.[34] An executive board, composed of the nine national officers, was created, but since its members lived at widely separated points it never met. Although a national board of trustees was established to oversee financial affairs, its members were elected by the carpenters residing in the headquarters city. Finally, the convention was given power to move headquarters annually so as to keep it close to the membership.

The financial operation of the national office was also severely restricted. Although the board of trustees was empowered to administer the per capita tax, the tax was set at only five cents per member per month.[35] While the protectives obtained a strike fund into which each local had to put 10 percent of its income, the fund was administered entirely on the local level. National strike aid had first to be sanctioned by a vote of two-thirds of all locals on application of a given local for aid. Then the necessary cash was forwarded by each of the various locals directly to the striking local. It never passed through the national office. The board of trustees possessed only the power to decide how much each local should contribute.

Whether such a loose national organization was forced upon McGuire or whether he desired it, it was a happy arrangement. The independent local carpenters would not have long remained affiliated with a national office which bridled their activities. A tight, detailed, and efficient administration would have sent them scurrying out of the union. Only a loose administration which helped educate pieceworkers to the need for unionism enjoyed a chance of survival.

[33]Edmonston, "The Genesis," *The Carpenter*, Vol. 24, No. 10, October 1904, p. 9.
[34]The other officers were general president, general treasurer, first, second, and third vice-presidents, and a three-man board of trustees.
[35]Carpenters and Joiners of America, United Brotherhood of, AFL, *Proceedings of the Twenty-sixth General Convention of Cincinnati, Sept. 5 to Sept. 12, 1950*, p. 132.

A shadowy and nominal national administration suited McGuire as much as it did the men he led. While he was many things—an organizer, an agitator, an educator, and, after his fashion, a philosopher—he was not an administrator. He did not wish to be burdened with administrative details. Trade unionism in what he called the "present disorganized society" was only a means to an end. It was not to assume a truly important and continuing role until the cooperative commonwealth had been established.

Thus, two months after the Brotherhood was founded, McGuire dropped everything to go to Europe as Socialistic Labor party representative at an International Socialists' convention.[36] When called in 1883 before a Senate committee investigating the state of labor relations, he mentioned his own union only once in fifty pages of testimony.[37] He did speak extensively, however, of unionism as a means to his Socialist ends. His success in organizing a national union caused him to carve out an even more definite niche for the union in his ideological scheme. Not only were unions to educate the workers to the need for socialism and to conduct all industry on behalf of the workers, but they were also to form the political state. After the revolution the representatives in Congress were to be elected on an industrial rather than a geographical basis, through the medium of the various trade unions.[38]

McGuire administered the union along lines dictated by his personality and philosophy. The manner in which he conducted the union can be summed up in three words: organize, agitate, and educate. Said Gabriel Edmonston, "Prior to 1884 the three general terms, 'agitation, education and organization,' had stood to the public in a rather vague way as about the only stated policy of the...union."[39]

[36]Gompers was shocked and surprised at McGuire's move. He wrote, "I urged him not to go for I feared his new organization would wither in his absence." Gompers, *Seventy Years of Life and Labor,* Vol. 1, p. 233. See also, Yurii M. Stekloff, *History of the First International,* pp. 363–365, for a summary of this congress and McGuire's activities in it.

[37]Senate Labor and Education Committee, *Report on the Relations Between Labor and Capital,* Vol. 1, pp. 315–316, and McGuire's full testimony, pp. 315–361, 808–813, 820.

[38]*Ibid.,* pp. 354–355.

[39]Gabriel Edmonston, "When We Declared for Eight Hours," in "History of Labor by Those Who Made It," *American Federationist,* Vol. 8, No. 10, October 1901, p. 406.

41

To McGuire organization was not primarily a battle tactic to be used against the employer, nor even a means of self-help. Rather, it was a way of debating and formulating ideas. When asked by what specific tactic his union would gain its ends, he replied, "Oh, we will find out how to do that eventually. We do not meet night after night without arriving at some plan."[40]

Organization, in turn, was but a precondition to education, and the union one vast classroom. The early leaders of the Brotherhood felt that if the workers could be educated, and then through the worker the public at large, both groups would rapidly come to see the logic and justice of trade union claims. That an "education" might turn either the workers or the public against trade unionism never occurred to them. They were completely taken with the nineteenth-century notion that the facts spoke for themselves and that once uncovered they would speak for trade unionism. In his first official act Edmonston spread broadcast a circular to the carpenters of the United States in which he said:

Education...is an able assistant to help us obtain the objects of our Brotherhood. We must first understand the rights of labor before we can intelligently defend or discuss its claims....We...[must], through numbers, impress the dignity of our just demands on the public. If we are confident we are right, let us convince our fellow workmen, not by force, but by cool argument.[41]

Education was to be spread through agitation, and the two were inseparable. "Unceasing, steady and intelligent agitation is the life blood of the labor movement. Agitation provokes discussion and discussion results in enlightenment and education."[42] Organization, agitation, and education, thus defined, meant little more than pamphleteering and lecturing on cross-country jaunts.

[40]Senate Labor and Education Committee, *Report on the Relations Between Labor and Capital,* Vol. 1, p. 349–350.

[41]Carpenters and Joiners of America, United Brotherhood of, AFL, *Proceedings of the Twentieth General Convention of Indianapolis, Sept. 20 to Sept. 29, 1920,* p. 429. For these reasons, Edmonston stated, the Brotherhood also agreed to work beside scabs. "We think it best as a policy to leave them free and to use no means of getting men into the union except argument and persuasion" (Senate Education and Labor Committee, *Report on the Relations Between Labor and Capital,* Vol. 1, p. 554).

[42]Carpenters and Joiners of America, United Brotherhood of, AFL, *Proceedings of the Sixth Biennial Convention of Chicago, August 4 to August 11, 1890,* p. 11.

For the first five years of the Brotherhood's existence the national office consisted of little more than McGuire's indefatigable, if somewhat chaotic, energies. Wherever McGuire happened to be, there was the national office. Like the old-fashioned businessman, he kept his figures in his head, and those which poured over, on his cuff. The organizing apparatus of the union was simple. If the Brotherhood of Carpenters and Joiners of America announced an extensive organizing campaign in New England, it meant that P. J. McGuire left town for Boston on the next freight. From city to city he agitated and exhorted and, almost by sheer will, kept those locals which were alive, functioning, and brought new ones into being.

In the course of a year McGuire made as many as a dozen organizing jaunts, timing his visits with a strike or some other important event. He was a brilliant and fiery speaker and his visits were considered a great event among carpenters and radical circles in general. He usually spoke for an hour and a half on the "Labor Question" and then, for another ninety minutes, discussed the pros and cons of the issues raised. After a few such visits to a city, he built up a strong personal following which, in later years, was to stand behind him with unquestioning loyalty.

When McGuire was not on the road, he published. The journal of the Brotherhood reflected the philosophy of its founders as much as did the mode of organization of the union. McGuire considered *The Carpenter* his main opportunity to educate the mass of carpenters and kept it full of weighty and learned articles on history, philosophy, and trade unionism. At one point in the 1880's, for the better part of a year a whole page of every issue was occupied by a serialized history of the world. Advertisements offered the carpenters special cut-rate prices of the works of Plato, Ruskin, and other philosophers.

With such general goals and vague uplift tactics, it is but little wonder that the Brotherhood developed no new trade union institutions or organizing techniques. McGuire encouraged the individual carpenter to carry on organizing work and felt the need for no corps of professional organizers. He referred to the men

43

who assisted him as "missionary workers," and the whole tenor of the work was in keeping with the reform goals toward which he was striving. Consequently, no organization which reached into the various regions, states, and cities, and which established a hierarchy of powers, duties, and responsibilities was created during this period. There was but McGuire at the top and beneath him a scattered series of locals.

However pleasant this means of building a union may have been to McGuire, it soon became clear that McGuire was only inching his way toward the millenium. In 1885 the union claimed only 5,789 members.[43] Piecework, the same phenomenon which called the union into being, was staying the union's growth. With their traditional hatred for the middleman and their background in the various reform movements, the founders of the Brotherhood saw the piece-rate system as a means whereby the capitalist system further enslaved the carpenter and destroyed his craft. But the average carpenter had a perfect answer to so-called wage enslavement: become a boss. John Swinton, the philosopher of the late-nineteenth-century labor movement, pointed a finger at the piece-working carpenter and explained why the Brotherhood had failed to grow: "Every mother's son of them expects to become a boss."[44]

Many of the carpenter bosses during the 1880's could point to the piecework system as the means whereby they had risen in the world. In 1884 Morgan Baker, Chicago Local 21, wrote McGuire protesting the ban on piecework. "This section of the general laws ...hinders the organization of the Brotherhood in many localities, and...is opposed by many carpenters. Many of the most successful boss carpenters began for themselves by taking piecework."[45] In each of the first four conventions a strong minority tried to eliminate the piecework prohibition from the constitution. At the 1884 convention members of strong and conservative Local 8 of

[43]U.S. Congress, Joint Industrial Commission, *Report and Hearings on the Relations and Condition of Capital and Labor Employed in Manufacturing and General Business*, 57th Cong., 1st Sess. (authorized by an act of Congress, approved June 18, 1898), Vol. 17, pp. 128–129.

[44]*John Swinton's Paper*, July 1884 (no page cited), as quoted in *The Carpenter*, Vol. 4, No. 8, August 1884, p. 1.

[45]*The Carpenter*, Vol. 4, No. 6, June 1884, p. 3.

Philadelphia led a determined drive to water down the piecework prohibition with a local autonomy clause, but McGuire succeeded in defeating their efforts.[46]

The practical American carpenter cared less about the survival of the craft and more about the survival of the fittest than McGuire was willing to admit. The leaders of the Brotherhood had to devise some kind of lure to attract the practical, conservative American carpenter to their reform organization. But McGuire and his followers refused to water down their reform philosophy. Instead they struck upon a device which both fitted into their reform scheme and gave the carpenter some measure of practical, palpable gain: the eight-hour movement.

[46]Carpenters and Joiners of America, United Brotherhood of, AFL, *Proceedings of the Third Biennial Convention of Cincinnati, August 5 to August 9, 1884*, p. 12; see also *The Carpenter*, August 1884, p. 5.

CHAPTER IV

"Eight Hours for Work . . .":

1886-1890

"DYNAMITE and Blood!"[1] the headlines of the *New York Herald* shrieked on the fifth of May, 1886. Under this headline the details of the Haymarket affair in Chicago and the rioting in Milwaukee,[2] both of which had occurred on the previous day, were recounted in alarming tones. The entire next page of the paper was given over to a description of the rash of strikes then sweeping the country.

The *Herald* described the bloody crescendo to which hundreds of thousands of discontented workers had brought the eight-hour movement. This vast and tumultuous drive, destined to alter the nature of the American labor movement forever, was conceived and launched by five thousand men loosely organized as the Brotherhood of Carpenters and Joiners of America. When the violence subsided, this organization was left fifty-seven thousand strong and completely changed in nature and outlook.

The eight-hour movement affected the Brotherhood in four areas of activity: its relations with the Knights of Labor, with the Federation of Labor, with dual carpenters' unions, and, finally, in its

[1] The *New York Herald,* May 5, 1886, p. 3, col. 1.
[2] The Haymarket affair stemmed from a meeting of eight-hour strikers in Haymarket Square, Chicago. Henry David's *The History of the Haymarket Affair* is the best study of this affair.

own administration and structure. After a description of the Brotherhood's role in this movement, the present chapter will deal with the first three subjects in the order presented, reserving the fourth for the next chapter.

By 1886 the shorter-hours movement had been one of the labor movement's *causes célèbres* for almost a half-century. Like all of labor's nineteenth-century causes, it had been picked up by reformers and integrated into a utopian social philosophy culminating in the inevitable producers' cooperation commonwealth.

Three short-hour theories were in the air in the 1890's: the "share-the-work" doctrine of the trade unions, which held that shorter working hours would create new job opportunities; the "leisure-for-culture" approach, which saw in additional leisure an opportunity for education and hence self- and group-advancement; and the "standard-of-living" philosophy, advocated principally by Ira Steward,[3] that shorter hours would mean increased wants which would, in turn, lead to increased wages as production mounted. McGuire constructed his own eclectic eight-hour philosophy with elements from all three theories and made the drive for shorter hours the chief immediate goal of the Brotherhood. He felt that if but "10,000 men adopt the nine hour rule...it will require 1,100 more men to complete the work now done."[4] The leisure thus afforded all carpenters would create "new wants and aspirations and stimulate a desire for better social conditions."[5] With time to rest and think, carpenters were expected to educate themselves to the point of view that the free enterprise system "adds increase to capital at the expense of the working class."[6]

In McGuire's hands, however, the mild and reasonable eight-hour demand was infused with revolutionary spirit. The workers must "designate one common day to establish the [eight-hour] system, and let them stand by each other to obtain it. This means a general strike, you may say. Well, what of it?"[7] Through an

[3]See Commons, *History,* Vol. 2, pp. 87–92 for details of Steward's important role in the eight-hour movement.
[4]*The Carpenter,* Vol. 2, No. 6, June 1882, p. 4.
[5]*The Carpenter,* Vol. 11, No. 2, February 1891, p. 1.
[6]*The Carpenter,* Vol. 2, No. 7, July 1882, p. 4.
[7]*The Socialist* (Chicago), Aug. 16, 1879, p. 3, col. 3.

eight-hour strike workers would eliminate the three great social evils of the day: rent, interest, and profit. Rent would be replaced by free land and free homes, interest by government banks and government money, and profit by the creation of the cooperative commonwealth.[8]

McGuire and Edmonston chose the Federation of Organized Trades and Labor Unions, an association of national trade unions which the Brotherhood helped form in 1881, as the medium through which to advocate the movement for shorter hours. At the 1884 convention of the Federation, on the instructions of the 1882 convention of the Brotherhood, Edmonston offered, and succeeded in having passed, a resolution calling for an eight-hour movement to begin on May 1, 1886.[9]

The leaders of the Federation of Organized Trades and Labor Unions had turned to the eight-hour movement only as an alternative to the expiration of their little Federation, a development which, in the depression of 1884, seemed all too imminent. They depended on the Knights of Labor, which was then entering its balmy years, to effectuate their bold threat.[10] But the Knights of Labor would have nothing to do with a movement which might very well be taken up by men of the most radical stripe. Its leaders considered the whole eight-hour drive irresponsible, conceived as it was by an organization with nothing to lose. As a result, in a secret circular issued by its leader, Terence V. Powderly, on March 13, 1886, the Knights of Labor denounced the projected eight-hour movement and advised all Knights to hold aloof from it.[11]

There was no turning back at that late date, however. A shot in the dark, fired by an unknown federation of little-known unions in the depression of 1884, struck home at a time of unparalleled working-class upheaval and discontent. By April 1886 it was clear

[8]*The Carpenter,* Vol. 11, No. 2, February 1891, p. 1; *The Carpenter,* Vol. 2, No. 7, July 1882, p. 4.

[9]Federation of Organized Trades and Labor Unions, *Report of the Proceedings of the Fourth Annual Convention of Chicago, Oct. 7 to Oct. 10, 1884,* pp. 8, 14.

[10]Commons, *History,* Vol. 2, p. 378.

[11]Norman J. Ware, *The Labor Movement in the United States, 1860–1896,* pp. 302–303.

that for the first time this discontent had been channeled in a direction which the great mass of workers considered constructive. The leaders of both the infant trade unions and the Knights of Labor were committed to the eight-hour drive whether or not they liked the idea.

During the waning days of April talk of the eight-hour movement mounted with a grim intensity and was given increasingly wide press coverage as May Day approached. Dispatches pouring in from all points indicated that the workers would turn out but would commit no violence if none was done them. Violence was anticipated on all sides, however.

May 1 fell on a Saturday and from Boston to Chicago the workers turned out. The carpenters and the rest of the building trades led the strike in all cities.[12] A description of Milwaukee on May 1 conveys some degree of the tension gripping many of the cities of America which were, for all practical purposes, in the throes of a general strike:

The traditional Sabbath stillness of a Puritan village pervades Milwaukee manufacturing circles. . . . Save for occasional groups of strikers and the rattle of the police patrol wagon on the way to the scene of some disturbance. . . the streets. . . have been deserted.[13]

Then, two days later, after the strike had drawn over three hundred and forty thousand into its orbit,[14] the violence of the Haymarket rioting brought the affair to a dead halt.

In terms of immediate and practical gains, the movement was a failure. Most workers who gained shorter hours had the old working day imposed on them again within a fortnight. It demonstrated, however, that if a specific and palpable gain were held before the workers they could be enticed into trade organizations. And although trade union leaders other than McGuire had done little to effectuate the movement, it "met with an astonishing measure of success considering the imperfect preparations for it and the circumstances under which it was made."[15] The Brotherhood, as

---

[12]The *New York Herald*, May 2, 1886, p. 16, cols. 3–4.
[13]*Ibid.*
[14]*Bradstreet's*, May 15, 1886 (no page cited), as quoted in Commons, *History*, Vol. 2, p. 384.
[15]*John Swinton's Paper*, May 9, 1886, p. 1, col. 6.

initiator of the movement, made the most active gains as local after local reported mass initiations of one hundred, even two hundred, carpenters. Though many of these new members were lost early, enough remained to have increased the membership fivefold by the end of 1886.

The eight-hour strike of 1886 was an accidental straw vote which conclusively demonstrated the workers' sentiment. McGuire was right. Workers would join trade unions, Socialist or not, if the leaders presented them with the hope of concrete gain. Thus was established the first faint contact between radicals like McGuire and the practical American worker. Each had much to teach the other in the next fifteen years. As an older Gabriel Edmonston said in 1901, the eight-hour movement of 1886 "meant a new and very remarkable change in the policy and practice of the labor movement."[16]

The eight-hour movement was a turning point not only for the Brotherhood, but also for the Knights of Labor and the Federation of Trades.[17] The Knights of Labor spun into a precipitous decline. A peak membership of over seven hundred thousand in 1886 had declined by almost two hundred thousand in June 1887.[18] The leaders of the trade unions aided and abetted this decline by pointing out Powderly's opposition to, and their own support of, the eight-hour movement.

The leaders of the Brotherhood were cocky about its new-found strength, and McGuire led an assault of the trade unions upon the Knights of Labor immediately after the eight-hour strike subsided. The assault was not without provocation. Since the founding of the Brotherhood, the carpenters had experienced a certain amount of trouble with the Knights of Labor. In 1884 and 1885, when the Knights of Labor enjoyed its great growth, the trouble became serious. It is necessary to go back to 1883 to trace the dispute to its source.

During 1883 a strong faction in Washington, D.C. Carpenters'

[16]Edmonston, "When We Declared for Eight Hours," p. 406.
[17]Carpenters and Joiners of America, United Brotherhood of, AFL, *Proceedings of the Fifth General Convention of Detroit, Aug. 6 to Aug. 11, 1888,* pp. 11–14.
[18]Selig Perlman, *A History of Trade Unionism,* pp. 94–95.

Local Union One was engaged in a dispute with the national office. The dissenters refused to pay assessments for a new benefits system which had been enacted at the 1882 convention of the Brotherhood.[19] They were opposed by Gabriel Edmonston, the founder of the local. After a year of fighting, the dissenters bolted in December 1883, and, under the leadership of Ira Aylesworth, an opponent of Edmonston, entered the Knights of Labor as a local carpenters' assembly, dual to the Brotherhood.[20] In the course of 1884 the two Washington locals fought a bitter jurisdictional fight both on the job and in the courts. The controversy was unresolved at the time of the 1884 convention of the Brotherhood of Carpenters and Joiners of America.

Such Knights of Labor encroachments were all too common, McGuire told the 1884 convention, but the Brotherhood was too small and weak to prevent them. As the Knights grew, the encroachments increased. Finally, when Knights of Labor carpenters in Troy, New York, refused to work with Brotherhood carpenters, McGuire wrote to E. S. Turner, secretary of the Knights, proposing an exchange of cards. He was refused even the courtesy of a reply. As a result McGuire issued a circular on April 26, 1886, which called for a conference in Philadelphia on May 18, 1886, of all trade union leaders.[21]

The eight-hour movement, with all of its implications, transpired between the convoking and assembling of this conference, which twenty-two trade unionists attended. McGuire was elected secretary and was also appointed head of a committee of five which was to draw up a treaty proposal to present to the leaders of the Knights. The proposal was actually a set of six demands, which amounted to an order for the giant Knights of Labor to do as bid by the tiny trade unions. So extreme were the demands that one of them ordered the Knights not to issue any label which would compete with a label which might be issued by a trade union in the future. McGuire presented this "treaty" to a special session

[19]See above, pp. 38–40, for an account of the protective-benevolent dispute at the 1881 convention.

[20]*The Carpenter,* Vol. 3, No. 10, October 1883, p. 2; *The Carpenter,* Vol. 8, No. 2, February 1888, p. 1.

[21]*The Carpenter,* Vol. 6, No. 5, May 1886, p. 2.

of the Grand Assembly of the Knights of Labor held on May 25, 1886. He persuaded them to appoint a five-man executive board committee to negotiate a treaty with the trade union leaders.

Anti-trade-union forces captured the Knights' executive board before the assembly adjourned, however. Due to the enormous growth of the Knights this special session decided to expand the executive board from five to eleven members. The anti-trade-unionists already had one man on the old executive board. Five of the six new men elected were avowed anti-trade-unionists. One of them was no less a person than Ira Aylesworth, the disaffected Brotherhood carpenter who had bolted Local Union One to join the Knights of Labor.[22] His presence on the executive board hardly augured well for treaty negotiations in which the trade unions were to be represented by the leader of the Carpenters' Union. The negotiations were doomed before they began.

Powderly procrastinated, and no conferences were held prior to the August 1886 convention of the Brotherhood. The leaders of the Carpenters' Union were aware of Aylesworth's presence on the executive board and were spoiling for a fight. The convention passed one resolution forbidding Brotherhood carpenters to join a Knights of Labor Trade Assembly[23] and another advising the carpenters of the United States to buy only "blue label" cigars, thus siding with the Cigarmakers' Union in a dispute they were having with the Knights of Labor.[24] This further exacerbated an already troubled situation.

When McGuire and his treaty committee finally did meet with the executive board of the Knights of Labor on September 28, both sides were too far committed to a policy of warfare to turn back. The negotiations were desultory and broke up with a promise to create a joint committee to investigate mutual grievances. The Knights failed to appoint their part of the committee. When

[22]*John Swinton's Paper*, June 6, 1886, p. 1, col. 1; *The Carpenter*, Vol. 8, No. 4, April 1888, p. 4.

[23]An "assembly" was a geographically determined unit of the Knights of Labor. Smaller cities and towns constituted a "district" assembly. However, a "trade" assembly was based not on geography but on craft and could have either a local or a national jurisdiction. Further mention of the carpenters' trade assembly is made below on pp. 54–55.

[24]*The Carpenter*, Vol. 7, No. 1, January 1887, p. 2.

Powderly failed to refer the matter of a treaty to the Richmond General Assembly, held on October 4, 1886, as he had promised to do, the stage was set for the formation of the American Federation of Labor.

Goaded by the intractability of the Knights of Labor in the matter of a working treaty, McGuire wrote a call to convention of all trade unions. In Columbus, Ohio, on December 8, 1886, the convention met, dissolved the old Federation of Organized Trades and Labor Unions, and formed the present-day American Federation of Labor. McGuire was elected secretary, Edmonston treasurer, and Samuel Gompers president.

As trade union leaders consolidated behind the new federation, differences rather than likenesses between the groups were emphasized. These differences cropped up most violently in Chicago, where the building trades generally and the carpenters specifically had been among the most successful of the shorter-hours strikers in 1886. The Brotherhood carpenters who initiated and directed the movement received the close cooperation of Knights of Labor carpenters during the strike. Due to the success of the strike, the Brotherhood and the Knights of Labor carpenters jointly formed a United Carpenters' Council for the direction and coordination of carpenters' activities in Chicago.[25]

In the early spring of 1887 the United Carpenters' Council directed a successful wage strike of short duration. Later in the spring the employers regrouped their forces and used a bricklayers' strike as a pretext to lock out all building tradesmen. A long and bitter struggle ensued. The national office of the Carpenters came to the aid of its locals in this strike with a $4 weekly strike benefit which had been made possible by the huge membership growth of 1886.

Brotherhood aid was given only to Brotherhood carpenters, however, in spite of the fact that the strike was a jointly administered venture. The Knights of Labor carpenters asked that they, too, receive strike benefits. McGuire refused their request,[26] and the Knights bolted the United Carpenters' Council to form their own

[25]*The Carpenter*, Vol. 59, No. 9, September 1939, p. 15.
[26]UBCJA, *1888 Convention Proceedings*, p. 17.

Progressive Carpenters' Council. A bitter jurisdictional fight with mutual scabbing and recrimination resulted. Resistance to the lockout lost most of its force during the summer of 1887 and the strike ended inconclusively in the early fall of the same year.

Knights of Labor carpenters could hardly fail to see the advantages of the new craft unionism when it was demonstrated so forcefully in terms of dollars and cents. They turned avidly to a form of ersatz trade unionism, the National Trades Assembly. By the time the Grand Assembly of the Knights of Labor met in 1887, there were twenty-two such trade assemblies with some fifty-two thousand members.[27] One of the most ambitious of these was the Progressive Carpenters, or National Assembly of Carpenters, which was conceived by an old enemy of the Brotherhood, Ira Aylesworth, who by this time was firmly entrenched on the executive board of the Knights of Labor.[28] He ardently advocated the creation of a national carpenters' trade assembly. The ability of the Brotherhood of Carpenters and Joiners to pay national strike benefits during the Chicago lockout was a powerful demonstration of craft union effectiveness. It gave great weight to Aylesworth's arguments and finally convinced the other board members of the wisdom of his plan. They gave him free rein.

Using the Chicago Knights of Labor carpenters as a nucleus, Aylesworth busied himself during the last months of 1887 and the first few months of 1888 in forming a dual carpenters' union. Like the other trade assemblies, this union failed because the trade unions had pre-empted the field. The hour was far too advanced for the Knights to change their ways or, more important, to convince the carpenters and other crafts of their honorable intentions. The carpenters' exodus from the Knights which had started after the 1886 eight-hour movement went on unchecked. Between January and June of 1887 at least fourteen Knights of Labor assemblies came into the Brotherhood.[29] After the Progressive Carpenters' Union was launched, the exodus continued. In February 1888 alone six assemblies abandoned the Knights to join

[27]Commons, *History*, Vol. 2, p. 428.
[28]*The Carpenter*, Vol. 8, No. 1, January 1888, p. 4.
[29]*The Carpenter*, Vol. 7, No. 7, July 1887, p. 4.

the Brotherhood.[30] McGuire summed up the failure of the Knights to establish themselves along craft lines: "The Knights of Labor are now taking lessons from the trades unions and are forming themselves on National Trade District lines, which are simply the skeletons of trade unions without either their flesh or blood."[31]

By 1888, although the Knights had been defeated, the long struggle of the previous year had had an effect upon the Brotherhood leaders. The Chicago fight had been but one of a long series of dual union struggles with the Knights. After 1887 the attitude of the Brotherhood's leaders toward dual unionism hardened appreciably. The earlier reform unionism feeling that all unions were members of the labor movement working toward the same goals gradually gave way to the less idealistic feeling that dual unionism was a brand of treason. McGuire summed up this attitude in a pronouncement made in the aftermath of the 1887 jurisdictional disputes. It constitutes one of the earliest definitions of what has since become AFL dogma on the question of dual unionism.

I maintain most firmly that, while we should be ever ready to help all other sister organizations and to practically recognize the common fraternity of interests that exists between all branches of honorable toil, yet, in the management of our own trade affairs, we should never make ourselves subordinate to any other organization, nor should we ever allow a dual form of organization to exist in our trade, for if we do, sooner or later one will be bound to come into conflict with the other. . . . In no case has this been more plainly manifest than in Chicago, where this year certain Knights of Labor Assemblies of carpenters offered to work longer hours for smaller wages while our members were struggling to maintain union rules.[32]

In 1888, having met and defeated the Knights of Labor carpenters, the Brotherhood started a campaign to sweep the field clear of dual unions. The principal targets were the United Order of Carpenters and the Amalgamated Society of Carpenters and Joiners. Both of these unions had been in existence longer than the Brotherhood; it will be necessary to digress briefly to bring their history up to date.

[30] *The Carpenter,* Vol. 8, No. 3, March 1888, p. 1.
[31] *The Carpenter,* Vol. 7, No. 10, October 1887, p. 4.
[32] UBCJA, *1888 Convention Proceedings,* pp. 18–19.

The United Order was an organization of neighborhood lodges confined to the New York City area. It had been organized since 1872 and in 1888 had between three thousand, five hundred and four thousand members.[33] Confined to one city, its members' interests were even more localized than those of the average local carpenters' union. When the Brotherhood was formed the officers of the United Order chose to remain aloof, and they effectively excluded the Brotherhood from the New York City labor market.

The Amalgamated Society was formed in 1860 in England and its first American branch was established in 1868 in New York City. In 1887 it had almost two thousand members, the majority of whom were in New York City locals. The United Order allowed them to remain separately organized in New York because the United Order controlled them in every practical respect.[34]

The founders of the Brotherhood bypassed the Amalgamated Society in 1881 because although the Amalgamated Society claimed national jurisdiction, its leaders were unable to understand the American carpenter and did not adapt their methods to American conditions. In a period when personal leadership was of such importance, its leaders remained distant and alien. This foreignness irked most American carpenters, concerned as they were with the problem of immigration.[35] Until 1887 Brotherhood carpenters looked upon the Amalgamated Society fondly as an older form of trade unionism which, if it had not provided the Brotherhood with a direct pattern, had given it a general sense of direction. The events of 1887, however, had bequeathed the Brotherhood's leaders the altered attitude toward dual unions already described.

With a membership of over twenty-eight thousand in 1887, the Brotherhood was a force for independent carpenters to reckon with, and it first turned its attention to the United Order. Though only a fraction the size of the Brotherhood, the United Order had erected a "wall"[36] about New York City. After the initial successes

[33]*The Carpenter*, Vol. 7, No. 6, June 1887, p. 4.
[34]*The Carpenter*, Vol. 7, No. 7, July 1887, p. 3.
[35]Samuel Higgenbottom, *Our Society's History*, pp. 286–287. This work is a history of the Amalgamated Society of Carpenters and Joiners Union of England.
[36]*The Carpenter*, Vol. 7, No. 7, July 1887, p. 1; D. P. Rowland, "Reminiscences of an Old Scout," *The Carpenter*, Vol. 34, No. 9, September 1914, p. 6.

of 1886, the Brotherhood tried to establish locals in New York but failed since the United Order men refused to work with Brotherhood carpenters. The United Order controlled the United Building Trades Committee and the Board of Walking Delegates and was able to force the Amalgamated Society carpenters to go along with its anti-Brotherhood policy.[37]

Miffed by his failure to organize his home town, McGuire announced in an editorial in the summer of 1887 that he was ready for some "rigid retaliation" if the United Order did not open New York City to his union. When by the end of the summer no New York locals had been formed, McGuire moved. He wrote to J. S. Murchie, the general secretary of the Amalgamated Society, in Manchester, England, on July 18, asking for a mutual card recognition and appealing to his sense of working-class solidarity. The agreement was completed by the fall and was operating by January, 1888. It provided for a mutual exchange of cards and for the services of the business agents of the Amalgamated Society in New York City.[38]

McGuire at last possessed an open sesame to the rich New York market. Armed with it, the Brotherhood carpenters moved in on New York City. They assaulted the United Order from within by using Amalgamated Society cards and from without by encouraging the importation of English carpenters into New York City and by enacting still more recognition treaties with the Associated Carpenters of Great Britain and the General Union of Carpenters and Joiners of England.

English carpenters literally commuted across the Atlantic. They came to New York City in the early spring, worked through the summer, and returned to England in the fall.[39] The "wall" which the United Order erected about New York City was strong enough

[37] *The Carpenter,* Vol. 7, No. 7, July 1887, p. 3. Business agents were referred to as walking delegates at this time. The United Building Trades Council was a federation of all local building trades unions through which the business agents of different trades acted in concert.

[38] *The Carpenter,* Vol. 8, No. 1, January 1888, p. 1; UBCJA, *1888 Convention Proceedings,* p. 19.

[39] *The Carpenter,* Vol. 8, No. 2, February 1888, p. 6.

in its eastern ramparts to give the United Order some degree of protection against continent-hopping carpenters. Now, with the Brotherhood acting as an international labor contractor, those ramparts were breached. The benefits of national affiliation were dramatically demonstrated to the New York carpenters.

Though the United Order forced all members to become citizens in 1888, this did little to counter the Brotherhood's card treaty with the Amalgamated Society. Finally, in March, 1888, the United Order capitulated and agreed to amalgamate. A seven-man committee was elected to negotiate with McGuire.[40] The merger, which was settled at a meeting in Philadelphia on May 13, 1888, was ratified by the Brotherhood's 1888 convention, and the new organization was called the *United* Brotherhood of Carpenters and Joiners of America.

The jurisdictional struggles of 1886 through 1888 strongly influenced the 1888 convention of the United Brotherhood. As a result of the activities of the Progressive Carpenters' Union, the 1886 resolution against dual membership was hardened into law;[41] all existing treaties with carpenters' unions were repealed; and the applications of a half dozen independent carpenter unions, and of scores of carpenter assemblies of the Knights of Labor were approved.[42] The officers of the Brotherhood were then ordered to prepare for another mammoth eight-hour movement on May Day, 1890, with or without the support of the American Federation of Labor.

The delegates of the United Brotherhood introduced the eight-hour motion at the 1888 American Federation of Labor convention and it was passed. A newer and stronger AFL, however, rode tight rein on this movement in order to prevent another Haymarket disaster. It was decided that one union, supported by other AFL unions, would strike for the eight-hour day across the country.[43] In March, 1890, the strongest, largest, and most successful union in

---

[40]*The Carpenter,* Vol. 8, No. 4, April 1888, p. 4.
[41]*The Carpenter,* Vol. 8, No. 8, August 1888, p. 4; UBCJA, *1888 Convention Proceedings,* p. 39.
[42]*The Carpenter,* Vol. 8, No. 8, August 1888, p. 4.
[43]UBCJA, *1890 Convention Proceedings,* p. 19.

the country, the United Brotherhood of Carpenters and Joiners of America, was chosen to inaugurate the movement.

McGuire directed the movement personally, hopping tirelessly from one strike point to the next, working as doggedly for his better tomorrow in victory as he had in defeat. All of this tireless reformer's futile radical agitation of yesteryear was repaid tenfold by the most enormous victory which had ever been won by trade unionism in America. Over 23,000 carpenters in 36 cities gained the eight-hour day, and some 32,000 more in 234 cities gained the nine-hour day.[44]

A changed United Brotherhood assembled in convention in the summer of 1890 as the last sounds of the eight-hour struggle died away. Over 22,000 new members in 258 new locals had been added since 1888.[45] The United Brotherhood had inaugurated the 1886 eight-hour drive and had given it such leadership as it possessed; the Brotherhood had *been* the eight-hour movement of 1890. It had led the trade union struggle against the Knights of Labor, and its leaders, along with Samuel Gompers and Adolph Strasser, had done more to found the AFL than those of any other union. The field had been swept clear of all dangerous rival unions, and the Amalgamated Society was tolerated merely out of sentimentality. McGuire keynoted the 1890 convention with a cry of triumph:

The United Brotherhood [is] in the front rank of labor organizations. It is now the largest and most powerful organization...in the whole civilized world. And its growth is unparalleled, in like time, by any trade union on earth....An immense work has been accomplished. We have spread the gospel of unionism...in every town and hamlet ...and have inspired a spirit of noble and sturdy manhood among the carpenters which...will brook none of the impositions and wrongs of old.[46]

All of these events had occurred under the aegis of the eight-hour movement. From 1886 to 1890 the Brotherhood had been little more than a shorter-hours organization. And although a tribute

[44]*Ibid.,* p. 21.
[45]U.S. Congress, Joint Industrial Commission *Report,* Vol. 17, pp. 128–129.
[46]UBCJA, *1890 Convention Proceedings,* p. 15.

to the personal leadership of McGuire, the overnight growth of the United Brotherhood was equally a testimony to the efficacy of the eight-hour day as a battle standard around which the American carpenter would rally.

Professor Perlman has called the eight-hour theory a philosophical "half-way station between the old 'anti-monopoly' individualism of the past and the self-confident trade unionism of the future."[47] He committed an error of omission, insofar as the Carpenters are concerned, in failing to see that the eight-hour movement was a practical and actual, as well as a philosophical, half-way station between the past and the future. The eight-hour day movement translated past hatred for the middleman into the craft unionism of the future. It may be likened to a cocoon into which utopian unionism disappeared, to emerge four years later as job-conscious unionism.

Prior to 1886 the carpenter had shied away from the Brotherhood, preferring the tangible enticement of the piece-rate system to the indistinct better tomorrow promised by the Brotherhood's leaders. When after 1886 he crowded into the Brotherhood, he literally traded his chance to become a boss for more work and better working conditions. To the working carpenter the eight-hour day meant but two things: a chance to spread the work and to regulate the conditions under which he worked. The material advantages which he could gain from the next trade movement were the sum and substance, the means and end, of his membership in the Brotherhood. Gompers and McGuire, it would appear, learned much more about job-conscious unionism from the workers of America than they ever taught them.

By 1890 American carpenters had buried their own dead past. They then turned to the twenty-year task of articulating the principles and establishing the institutions of the brand of trade unionism which has since been associated with the United Brotherhood. It was to be a vastly different trade unionism than that sought by McGuire. It was to produce a breed of men who differed greatly from McGuire and who opposed him and his broadly socialist trade union goals. These men were the professional organizers.

[47]Perlman, *Theory*, p. 194.

CHAPTER V

The Professional Organizers:

1890-1896

McGUIRE purposely created a weak national administration which reflected his broad educational ends and his organize-agitate-educate means. While his matchless, almost evangelical, skill as an organizer lured thousands of new carpenters into local unions, it did not guarantee their staying there. As a result, during the 1880's and early 1890's local unionists devised for themselves trade union institutions designed to fill the carpenters' day-to-day needs. If these institutions developed along lines hardly foreseen by Mc-Guire, they sprang, at least at the outset, from McGuire's philosophy.

McGuire did not want to destroy capitalism but to have it taken over by the trade unions. He harbored no animus against capital-ists as organizers of productive labor. Rather, he made a fine and perhaps untenable distinction between a capitalist as an organizer of labor and a nonproducing and speculative middleman. As a result, the first Brotherhood carpenters bore little malice toward their immediate employers if they were "genuine" contractors; that is, if they provided materials as well as labor and did not work by the subcontract, hire piece-or-lump workers, or allow work done for them to be lumped. The leaders of the early Brotherhood be-lieved that the legitimate contractor had as much to lose to the pieceworker as did the carpenter. One of the first editions of *The*

61

Carpenter held that "with the workmen...thoroughly organized ...we can soon arrive at a harmonious understanding [to end piecework] with the better class of contractors and boss builders."[1]

Early Brotherhood leaders encouraged the various locals to bargain, conciliate, and even arbitrate, rather than strike the better class of regular contractors. In the spring of 1882 Gabriel Edmonston, through his local, Number One of Washington, D.C., encouraged the bosses to form an employers' organization. In May its formation was announced. Local Union One agreed that its journeymen were to work for none but "genuine" contractors, and the employers agreed to employ only "genuine" carpenters.[2] In New York and Brooklyn, mass meetings were held in 1882 in conjunction with "genuine" contractors. Together, the unionists and their bosses pledged that they would take joint steps to eliminate piecework, which led to intense competition injurious to both contractor and carpenter.[3] Thus the piece-rate system channeled the carpenter's disaffection away from his immediate employer and toward the middleman and established the climate of feeling out of which collective bargaining was later to grow.

High-sounding joint declarations, however, did but little to stop the pieceworker, who was difficult to find, much less eradicate. Working as a subcontractor, he took flash jobs which often were completed in as little as a few days, a week at the most. He moved into a half-completed row of homes or apartments, received material from the speculator, installed the doors, stairs, or windows, packed his tools, and stole silently away. The "genuine" contractors were powerless to combat the pieceworker. Only the union, through the medium of a paid and full-time representative with power to strike immediately any job on which piecework appeared, could combat him. Thus was born the office of business agent.

Carpenter James Lynch, who was probably the first business agent, described in his own words how the post was created:

[1]*The Carpenter,* Vol. 2, No. 3, March 1882, p. 4.
[2]*The Carpenter,* Vol. 2, No. 5, May 1882, p. 8; *The Carpenter,* Vol. 2, No. 6, June 1882, p. 3.
[3]*The Carpenter,* Vol. 2, No. 2, February 1882, p. 2.

A large number of brown-stone fronts were being built by speculators [in New York City]. They would build a block seven hundred feet long and four or five stories high; letting out such work as setting door frames to one class of men at so much each; the putting on of casings to another. This led to special classes of workers known as "door-hangers," etc., according to their special work.

While this practice was strenuously opposed by the union, still it was unable to stop it, as these men were outside of the union and worked all sorts of hours.

In desperation, it was decided to pay a representative to keep after them, so in July, 1883, a walking delegate of the Carpenters of New York City was appointed.

Thus I was taken from the executive office of the Carpenters of New York City and became their *first walking delegate*.[4]

At first the functions of the business agent were not clearly defined and he was called "walking delegate" or "special agent." In some cases he was part of a "committee of walking delegates." As his functions became clearly defined, however, he came to be known as a business agent. By 1890 McGuire reported that a full one hundred cities had business agents.[5] In the following year the business agent was recognized for the first time as an official person by the executive board when it decided that the business agent could be empowered to "collect dues and et cetera."[6] In 1892 McGuire remarked that the use of business agents had become the general custom.

A full-time, paid agent was an expense which few locals could or would carry alone. Hence the district council of local unions also came into being with the business agent. This organization is what the name implies, a council of the representatives of local unions of a given city or other closely knit area, empowered to conduct that portion of local affairs which can best be handled by a body with broader jurisdiction. Quite often the first proud notice that a city, Boston for instance, now had a full-time business

[4]James Lynch, "The First Walking Delegate," in "The History of Labor by Those Who Made It," *American Federationist*, Vol. 8, No. 9, September 1901, p. 347.
[5]*The Carpenter,* Vol. 10, No. 7, July 1890, p. 1.
[6]This was a standing decision of the executive board, made on November 15, 1890.

agent was accompanied by the announcement that the Boston locals had banded together to pay for this luxury.[7]

McGuire announced in 1888 that, while district councils were not yet mandatory, they had sprung up in at least fourteen cities.[8] Following his advice, the 1888 convention made it mandatory for the carpenters of any city with two or more local unions to form a district council.[9] In 1890 there were twenty-six district councils, and they were given power to regulate all strikes.[10] Two years later McGuire reported thirty-two district councils, and they were given all disciplinary power which had previously belonged to the locals.[11] These moves amounted to a mass transfer of administrative, and hence of political, power from the local union to the district council. After 1892 the district council was the real, basic administrative unit of the Brotherhood.

Operating through the district council, the business agent came to fulfill many tasks (other than controlling the pieceworker) which before his advent had gone begging. He effectively negotiated with employers who had previously blackballed any working carpenter presenting union demands. In cooperation with business agents of other crafts, he helped to coordinate and to administer all building trades strike efforts. With his knowledge of the supply of and demand for carpenters, he was able to help the locals regulate the labor market. He became, in effect, a one-man employment bureau with complete knowledge of all new jobs in this casual industry. By maintaining craft standards and eliminating the pieceworker, he aided management as well as the carpenters. He was, in short, a small labor contractor who served employer and employee alike, a middleman. This is a fact of basic importance to both the past and future development of the United Brotherhood. To establish its full significance, it is necessary to retrace several developments up to 1890.

[7]*The Carpenter,* Vol. 7, No. 10, October 1887, p. 1, for notice of the business agent, and district council.

[8]UBCJA, *1888 Convention Proceedings,* p. 19.

[9]*The Carpenter,* Vol. 9, No. 2, February 1889, p. 1.

[10]UBCJA, *1890 Convention Proceedings,* p. 22. See also *The Carpenter,* Vol. 10, No. 8, August 1890, p. 7.

[11]Carpenters and Joiners of America, United Brotherhood of, AFL, *Proceedings of the Seventh General Convention of St. Louis, Aug. 1 to Aug. 8, 1892,* pp. 20, 36.

It will be recalled that the first carpenters' unions arose out of protest against the middleman, and that during the nineteenth century, the carpenter joined with the rest of the labor and reform movement in fostering an antimiddleman or producer-conscious type of trade unionism.[12] The Brotherhood was founded in this tradition, and its first leaders hoped, through the medium of trade unions, to eliminate the middleman as an economic being and then to inaugurate a producers' commonwealth. The carpenter's strong desire to become his own boss, however, struggled with his hatred for the middleman, and he aided and abetted the middleman by taking up piecework. In the eight-hour movement the carpenter, who had previously refused to trade piecework for the vague hope of a producers' commonwealth, traded it for the tangible and immediate gain of shorter hours.

By 1890 it was evident that the system of speculation and subcontracting which has since characterized the industry was there to stay. The carpenters were not as anxious to overthrow this system as they were to control it. Unable to defeat the system, they became a part of it. In order to represent the carpenters' interests, the business agents became middlemen who contracted for labor. Thus did "business" unionism, for the carpenter's craft, at least, have its genesis.

The sum of the business agent's activities clearly established him as a labor contractor. He promised to deliver to the employer a certain number of carpenters possessed of a certain guaranteed degree of skill at a stated time for a stated wage. With the employers or their agents he annually signed a written contract clearly stipulating these promises. In return he received the right to control fully the trade in a given community, to bargain for the wages and working conditions received by the men he supplied, and to replace the old speculator contractor and his pieceworking carpenters as a labor-contractor-middleman.

Here, in the business agent's role as middleman, is the key to the conservatism of the Brotherhood and of building trades unions

[12]See Selig Perlman and Philip Taft, *A History of the Labor Movement in the United States, 1896 to 1932*, pp. 4–5, Volume 4 of Commons, *History*, for a discussion of the general labor movement during the years covered by the text.

in general. The building trades business agent is a more vital part of his industry than are local union officers in any other industry. The industry is literally organized about his figure and functions. Because of his essential role, building trades unions were among the first and most successful in the American labor movement. By the same token, the building trades unions are among the most conservative. For the business agent is not alone an organizer of workers' discontent. He is also a middleman around whom the building industry is constructed. What his left or union hand may choose to do may grievously harm his right or middleman's hand. Thus while the business agent enjoys a position of strength which makes him the envy of many another local union officer, he also bears a burden of industrial responsibility which at times becomes crushing. McGuire's abstract radicalism was a luxury he perhaps could afford. With his strange dual function it was a luxury hardly available to the business agent.

Such a man was not only a middleman, he was also a career man in the trade union field, a professional organizer, a union executive, a member of a union bureaucracy. The union provided his opportunity to rise in the world, to associate with and to ape his boss, and perhaps to climb a bit higher than he. When he obtained his goals, the institutions which had borne him upward became vested interests to be changed as infrequently as possible. He had a stake in the union, the industry, and the community. He decried and deplored every radical manifestation. He was completely dedicated to the present order as long as it provided a niche for his brand of trade unionism.

A glance at the career of any one of these new local leaders bears out their nature as professional bureaucrats. Frank Duffy was the salaried national secretary of the United Brotherhood for over forty years. Before assuming that position in 1901, he held the following offices: representative of Local Union 478 to the New York District Council, thirteen successive times; financial secretary of Local Union 478, four times; business agent, 1896 to 1898; president of the executive council of the New York District Council, six successive times; delegate to the United Brotherhood conventions of 1896, 1898, and 1900; and executive board member, 1900 to 1901.[13] Duffy's career is typical of that of a whole host of young men who rose to power on the local level during the 1890's.

No group could have contrasted more sharply with McGuire than did these men, his followers. They looked different. McGuire was unkempt, with a long drooping mustache and deep-set, burning eyes. He was given to riding freights and to fiery radical oratory, while Harry Lloyd, leader of the Boston District Council, was described as "a good speaker and fair and conservative in all he had to say. He dressed well in dark clothes, wore a heavy gold chain and charm and might have been mistaken for a young lawyer."[14]

They spoke different words. In 1891 McGuire gave his opinion about the ultimate goals of trade unions:

To educate our class, to prepare it for the changes to come, to establish a system of co-operative industry in place of the wage system, to emancipate the workers from subjugation to the capitalists, these are our ultimate objects.

.   .   .

We are approaching a great revolution, which, if based upon organized action, is destined to assume control of the industries and the government of the nation.[15]

A few years later William Huber, a Yonkers, New York, leader, might have been talking about McGuire when he criticized Socialists for being

...visionary, their schemes and isms are only the mouthings of a lot of irresponsible, imaginative fantastical doctrinaries....Our local unions are...being contaminated by even permitting one of their disciples to pollute the floor of their hall and the air of their meeting room with his foul harrange of sedition....I...have taken steps to

[13]Stanley Gipson, "A Carpenter's Voice at the Peace Conference," *The Carpenter*, Vol. 39, No. 5, May 1919, p. 8. See also Robert A. Christie, "A History of the United Brotherhood of Carpenters and Joiners of America," pp. 125–128, the unpublished dissertation upon which this book is based, for a detailed analysis of the careers of all of the more important national officers of the United Brotherhood during the 1890's.

[14]*The Carpenter*, Vol. 9, No. 11, November 1889, p. 4.

[15]*The Carpenter*, Vol. 11, No. 2, February 1891, p. 1.

cleanse the labor firmament of their scurrilous and untruthful literature and proselytizing emissaries.[16]

As the conservative career trade unionists came to fill out the
complement of local leadership after 1890, McGuire became
strangely out of place in his own union. With his violent desire to
reorganize society, he was as incompatible with these men as a
Communist would have been at a 1950 college fraternity convention. For in 1890, as he had been in 1881 and as he was to be till
the day he died, McGuire was an extreme, intelligent, undisciplined, selfless, disorganized radical of the old American school
who could have walked lightly beside Tom Paine or Sam Adams.
When he stood on a platform beside the professional organizers,
nineteenth- and twentieth-century trade unionism met. Like oil
and water, they did not mingle.

Rather, they drew apart, for McGuire would not create, nor
allow others to create, an administrative nexus between the national office and the local bodies. In spite of the phenomenal success of his organizing activity, for the first nine years of its existence
the union had no national administration worthy of the name.
Many experiments were tried.[17] None of them changed the essential fact that the United Brotherhood in 1890 was still being
ruled along lines set down for the little reform organization founded by a group of mad-at-the-world, down-at-the-heel reformers a
decade earlier.

McGuire consciously blocked the growth of an administrative
hierarchy which would have linked the district councils closely
with the national office. In 1884 he suggested that perhaps too many
dollars were being sent to the national office by the locals. His
methods, he said, were simple and required only enough dollars
to carry on the educational campaign.[18] In 1891 he said:

[16]Carpenters and Joiners of America, United Brotherhood of, AFL, *Proceedings
of the Fourteenth Biennial Convention of Niagara Falls, September 17 to September
28, 1906*, pp. 72–73.
[17]For a detailed analysis of the struggle for reform within the United Brotherhood
from 1881 to 1900 see Christie, "History," Chapter V, "The Search for National
Institutions."
[18]*The Carpenter*, Vol. 4, No. 7, July 1884, p. 4.

The tendency of the labor movement is towards simplicity, autonomy and federation. Simplicity of organization, autonomy of function and federation of interests. Workmen have no use for complicated machinery with intricate cogs and wheels in labor organizations. The simpler it is the better [it is] understood.[19]

These words welled out of a strongly held and carefully thought-out conviction about the function and goals of the trade union. McGuire wanted simplicity of organization because he felt that the workers would not become truly active in a union with machinery too complex for them to understand. At best, such a union would attract a group of dues-paying automatons who would allow self-interested trade union politicians to rule for them. When union politicians enter, Socialists exit; they are forced out or they cease being Socialists. And McGuire, as will become clear later, remained a Socialist until he died.

He dreaded, as did so many old Socialists, that trade unionism would become an end in itself; that it would be absorbed by and become an adjunct to capitalism if its machinery became too complex, if it became an accepted institution. He saw trade unions as a funnel through which workers were passed on their journey to socialism. The trade union's main function was to educate, and no elaborate administrative machinery was needed for this task, only "agitators."

As a result, in 1890 the national office had no regional representatives of any kind, no paid and full-time president or executive board, no organizers. There existed no lines of communication between McGuire and the various district councils except that which McGuire provided personally. There did, however, exist strong reasons for erecting such lines. There were the professional organizers. These composed a group of young, ambitious men whose activities were confined to the district council level as long as McGuire would not create regional organizations and expand the national office. They could not become regional vice-presidents or full-time members of the executive board because such posts did not exist. Nor could they become organizers for the same reason. Their ambitions, held unnaturally in check, represented an

[19]*The Carpenter*, Vol. 11, No. 9, September 1891, p. 1.

ominous force which under pressure might burst the bounds of McGuire's paternalistic rule.

And in 1890 the pressure for an expanded national administration was mounting for several reasons. First, the United Order carpenters were trade union members of twenty years' standing in 1890. They had not been organized by McGuire, the United Brotherhood, or its eight-hour movement. They owed little to the national office and could hardly be expected to tolerate long an executive board elected, as it had been since 1884, by the carpenters of one city, Philadelphia. Beside this unrest can be placed the continued technological development of the woodworking industry as a source of pressure for an expanded national office. Woodworking mills were taking an increasingly greater toll of carpenters' work. Mill owners were moving to the countryside to avoid the new and more efficient district council organization of the Brotherhood which was evolving between 1886 and 1890.[20] There advantage could be taken of child, female, and immigrant labor, without fear of interference from the district councils.

The district councils attempted to cope with the threat posed by "unfair, country building material" by binding their employers to use only "union, *city-made* materials."[21] Since country mills lay beyond the jurisdiction of any city district council, however, and since one country mill might market its products in several different district council jurisdictions, only an organizational drive with intercity direction could effectively cope with them. An executive board composed of members from one city was incapable of such direction.

The employers provided a third source of pressure for an expanded national office. After the initial successes of the 1886 eight-hour movement, the builders took a lesson from the union book and in 1887 banded together as the National Builders' Association. They were led by George Prussing of Chicago, Marc Eidlitz of New York, and E. E. Scribner of St. Louis.[22] The new organization

[20]See above, pp. 63–64, for the story of the early development of district councils.
[21]*The Carpenter*, Vol. 8, No. 3, April 1888, p. 5 (italics mine). This was a contract made in the 1880's by the Essex County District Council.
[22]*The Carpenter*, Vol. 7, No. 4, April 1887, p. 4; *The Carpenter*, Vol. 7, No. 6, June 1887, p. 4; *The Carpenter*, Vol. 8, No. 3, March 1888, p. 3.

threw all of its weight behind counteroffensives in the spring of 1887. In Chicago it fought the Carpenters to a draw,[23] and in Toronto defeated them with lockouts.

By the time of the 1890 eight-hour strikes, the builders had tightened their organization and introduced a new arsenal of weapons in their war against the Carpenters. They first used the secondary boycott in the building industry, applying pressure on building material firms to refuse materials to union contractors. The National Builders' Association assisted its affiliated organizations just as the United Brotherhood did its locals by extending them financial aid to resist strikes. This organized opposition took the edge off many of the larger 1890 strikes, and in Wheeling, West Virginia, and Portland, Oregon, two of the larger strikes were defeated outright. In the following spring two huge strikes in Newark, New Jersey, and Pittsburgh, Pennsylvania, into which the national office had poured over $19,000, were defeated by organized employers' resistance.[24] Important strikes were also lost in 1891 in San Francisco, New Orleans, Chattanooga, Seattle, and six other cities across the nation.

It was out of one such Chicago strike that the first mild attack upon McGuire stemmed. The strikers were receiving financial aid from the national office when in May, 1890, they asked for the assistance of a national officer. The Philadelphia executive board dispatched part-time President Rowland to Chicago. Rowland found that the National Builders Association was systematically importing strikebreakers, financing resistance to the strike, and bringing the carpenter leaders into court constantly on conspiracy and picketing charges.

However, Rowland also found that the Chicago leaders had organized the strike well and that the carpenters were standing firm behind them.[25] Unionists picketed railroad stations for a sixty-five mile radius about Chicago, warning itinerant carpenters of the

[23]*Report of the President and Proceedings of the Second Annual Convention of the National Association of Builders of Cincinnati, September 10 to September 14, 1888*, p. 5.

[24]*The Carpenter*, Vol. 11, No. 7, July 1891, p. 1; Vol. 11, No. 8, August 1891, pp. 1 and 2.

[25]UBCJA, *1890 Convention Proceedings*, pp. 13–14.

strike. The Chicago leaders had also initiated a countersuit against the employers for violation of the alien contract labor law by their importation of Canadian carpenters.[26]

Public pressure, however, was mounting against the strikers. Under this pressure, without any consideration of the tactical situation in Chicago, the Philadelphia executive board wired Rowland on April 24 to accept any terms the contractors offered.[27] Rowland felt that such a step would be disastrous in light of local conditions. It would be interpreted as a sellout by the Chicago carpenters and might lose the Brotherhood its Chicago membership. He defied the board members on the ground that he was more conversant with the Chicago situation than they. His decision held, despite the executive board's charge of insubordination, and the strike was later settled by arbitration.[28] Strong employers' resistance met at other points in the eight-hour drive of 1890 demonstrated the inability of a one-city executive board to cope with a national employers' association, and financial aid was withdrawn from strikes in Boston, Philadelphia, Detroit, Louisville, and Portland, in June, 1890.[29]

Pressure for a revised national administration was strong and mounting when the 1890 convention opened. There could have been little doubt in McGuire's mind about the reforms desired by the professional organizers. They wished to have full-time and regionally elected executive board members with power to employ organizers. In 1887 the Massachusetts locals had sent on their own initiative a referendum vote on this question, but McGuire had declared it illegal.[30] Later in that same year the Massachusetts locals tried to form a state organization which McGuire also quashed.[31] At the 1888 convention the local leaders actually succeeded in creating a Board of Seven Vice Presidents, regionally elected, to help the Philadelphia executive board run the organization. However, this board only met once a year, had no

[26]*The Carpenter,* Vol. 10, No. 6, June 1890, p. 1.
[27]UBCJA, *1890 Convention Proceedings,* pp. 13–14.
[28]*Ibid.*
[29]*Ibid.*
[30]*The Carpenter,* Vol. 7, No. 5, May 1887, p. 1.
[31]*The Carpenter,* Vol. 7, No. 6, June 1887, p. 4.

control over finances, and served only to harass the Philadelphia executive board.[32] From 1888 to 1890 the two boards' incessant clashing made a farce of the national administration.[33] At first, McGuire, quite satisfied with the easy-to-handle Philadelphia executive board, stood aloof. Then, having gauged the extent of the professional organizers' strength, he moved to still their protest. At the 1890 convention he shifted his support from the Philadelphia executive board to the new board of vice-presidents and presented the delegates with a new constitution drawn up by himself for their approval.[34]

The new constitution met only one of the demands of the professional organizers and that only part of the way. It created a five-man executive board composed of representatives from each of five districts into which the nation was divided. Its members, however, were not paid and met only four times a year. Further, they were not elected exclusively by members of their districts but by the convention at large. They were given no power to appoint full-time and paid organizers. While a step away from the old one-city executive board, the step was but a short one. The other provisions of the constitution were many, but they changed little that was basic.[35] Administered in McGuire's slipshod fashion, they left the national organization much the same in 1891 as it had been in 1889: a one-man show.

Clinging doggedly to his socialistic aims and educational tactics, McGuire absorbed more and more of the functions of the national office until the man and the office were indistinguishable. The building in which the United Brotherhood had offices, the records, office supplies, and even the general fund of the union were owned in his name. As one of his contemporaries, Frank Duffy, said, "McGuire could have said to the Executive Board, 'Here, gentlemen, get out of this building [the Brotherhood's headquarters], this

[32]UBCJA, *1888 Convention Proceedings,* pp. 33–34, p. 53; and *The Carpenter,* Vol. 8, No. 8, August 1888, p. 4.
[33]See Christie, "History," Chapter V, for details of this dispute.
[34]UBCJA, *1890 Convention Proceedings,* pp. 16, 22, for McGuire's speech introducing the new constitution and *The Carpenter,* Vol. 10, No. 8, August 1890, pp. 4–5, 7, for a resumé of the new constitution.
[35]See Christie, "History," Chapter V, for an analysis of these new provisions.

place belongs to me.' "[36] John Williams, the eleventh general president, summed up the nature of McGuire's rule when he said:

It [the union] was dominated in every vital respect by one forceful personality. All administrative functions were centered in one official.

.   .   .

The serious minded and earnest men who in various sections of the country were leading the Brotherhood [during the 1890's] knew that growth such as they had a right to look for was out of the question until the organization was unshackled and freed from the bonds of a form of paternalism that repressed its spirit and stunted its growth. I know that this was their feeling but they withheld expression thereof because of their loyalty and affection for a great leader and a masterful mind.[37]

Thus in 1892 the Brotherhood faced a strange dilemma. On one hand stood a group of professional trade union career men strongly entrenched behind local institutions of their own creation. On the other stood one of the most fabled figures of nineteenth-century radicalism, as strongly entrenched behind a name and a reputation. While he had built no institutions, he had created the union, through which the local leaders had risen to power. The local leaders were too strongly entrenched behind the real economic power of their business agents to be overthrown on their home grounds. And the personal loyalty which McGuire inspired in the rank and file was too strong for the new leaders to budge him. Either the professional organizers or the philosopher organizer had to give ground if the union was to prosper. Neither gave ground. In 1892 McGuire entered into a ten-year fight with the professional organizers.

The struggle was joined by a combination of the causes already discussed.[38] Increased employer opposition had led to the failure of a whole series of strikes during 1891. Murmurs of discontent

[36]Carpenters and Joiners of America, United Brotherhood of, *Verbatim Proceedings of the Twelfth General Convention of Atlanta, September 23 to September 26, 1902*, p. 108. Two versions of the 1902 convention were published. The one here cited was a verbatim record of a part of the proceedings, the other simply a report of the full proceedings. The former will henceforth be cited as "UBCJA, *1902 Convention Proceedings* (Verbatim)" to distinguish it.

[37]*The Carpenter*, Vol. 35, No. 8, August 1915, p. 18.

[38]See above, pp. 70–71.

were heard as expansion figures fell from a high of 22,275 new members in 1890 to slightly over 3,000 in 1891. When in 1892 the United Brotherhood suffered a loss of 5,500 carpenters, local leaders directed their first faint probe at the base of McGuire's power.

The opposition made a very simple parliamentary move at the 1892 convention which struck at the nerve center of McGuire's one-man rule. They brought to the floor a motion that the executive board members be elected by the assembled delegates of each district rather than by the convention at large.[39] Passage of this motion would have automatically based the power of executive board members on the sum of the powerful city organizations in each of their regions. It would have been but a short time before executive board members, backed by real and articulate regional power, would have chosen from local leaders a corps of professional organizers. The organizers, in turn, would have created a strong following in each of their districts through their ability to dispense national funds. The new locals they created and the strikes won with their assistance would have given them a strong following. Thus the administrative vacuum which existed between the various district councils and the national office would have been filled by several powerful regional organizations, each headed by an executive board member.

That the motion lost by the scant measure of two votes should have been handwriting on the wall for McGuire. With the employers organized nationally and concentrating their forces first on one strike point, then on another, the closest liaison between the various district councils and the national office was necessary. Had McGuire shared his power with the local leaders in 1892, he could easily have translated personal into institutional power.

When, in 1893, the worst depression the nation had ever experienced caught the uneasy Brotherhood a rude blow and lopped off

[39]It will be recalled that the old board of vice-presidents created in 1888 (above, p. 72) had been elected in this fashion and was sufficiently powerful both to bring McGuire over to its side and to undermine, in two short years, the firmly entrenched Philadelphia executive board. When a new executive board was created in 1890, the constitution provided that its members be elected at large rather than by districts.

a full one-half of its membership, murmurs of discontent swelled to a roar of protest. A coalition of local leaders tried to strip McGuire of his power at the 1894 convention. They moved against him personally by introducing a law prohibiting national officers from succeeding themselves in office. It lost.[40] Next, a law making the members of the executive board full-time and salaried organizers was placed before the convention. It lost. Finally, a law making the general president full-time and salaried and seating him on the executive board as a voting chairman was defeated by a vote of fifty-four to twenty-six. With this demonstration that his powers, although no longer unchallenged, were not to be toyed with, McGuire proceeded to consolidate the offices of general secretary and general treasurer in his person.

Although defeated on the floor, discontented members of the union manifested their disapproval in another way. An executive board, three of whose five members were known to be hostile to McGuire, was elected. One member was William Shields, who had been president of the extralegal State Council formed by the Massachusetts carpenters in 1890.[41] Shields led a drive before and during the 1894 convention to initiate a series of district conventions in lieu of the biennial convention, as a means of circumventing McGuire's one-man rule. The other two new members were Albert Cattermull of Chicago and John Williams of New York, whose hostility to McGuire is demonstrated by the fact that they later led a much more deadly and well-organized drive against him. The president elected by this convention was Charles Owens, another trade union careerist from New York City. Since none of these men occupied a full-time office, even operating as a group they could do little to challenge McGuire's methods or power. They immediately prepared their forces for the next convention.

The United Brotherhood rode out the depression still administered according to McGuire's lights. When the 1896 convention met, some four thousand more carpenters had deserted the organization, and membership was back to the 1888 level. The decline in membership crowned a growing conviction among the

[40]UBCJA, *1894 Convention Proceedings*, p. 53.
[41]See above, p. 72.

76

professional organizers that, while McGuire's evangelical brand of trade unionism was fine for organizing a union, it was of but little use in maintaining it. And maintaining the organization was becoming an increasingly difficult task. Employers' opposition remained, and its effectiveness was increased by the depression. The increased incidence of woodworking mills and their greater distance from the well-organized cities also served to underscore the need for a truly national organization with modern administrative apparatus. These mills often marketed their products in dozens of widely separated cities. Uncoordinated district councils could not possibly organize or even locate the mills which supplied their carpenters with building material. Further, a new union, the Amalgamated Wood Workers' Union, had since entered the woodworking industry and was giving certain district councils some measure of jurisdictional difficulty. This, too, required the attention of a national office.[42]

The opposition, which had been too weak to pass its reform measures in 1894, now captured the convention for the first time, and engineered the most furious and effective attack ever directed against McGuire. Powers contained in two whole sections of the constitution were transferred from the hands of the general secretary to those of the general president. The general president received the power to examine and pass on all local regulations, to decide all points of law between both individuals and locals, to suspend all officers on charges pending trial, to control strikes, and to issue all charters. The general president was also given power to appoint all organizers, was put on the executive board as chairman, and was made full-time with a salary of $1,200 a year.[43] President Lloyd said in an article supporting these changes that the new powers would give the general president "active charge of

[42]The whole problem of industrial jurisdiction which first came up in the mid-1890's was new to the Brotherhood. It is of such great importance that part of the next chapter is dedicated to it, and all of Chapter VII. See these chapters for exact details of how these jurisdictional difficulties and McGuire's attitude toward them affected the pattern of opposition to his rule from 1892 to 1898.

[43]"Amendments to the Constitution and Local Rules Submitted by the Ninth General Convention held at Cleveland, Ohio, September 21–29, 1896," *The Carpenter,* Vol. 16, No. 11, November 1896, pp. 2–3.

the entire organization."[44] These measures, McGuire wistfully conceded, stripped him of powers which "he has always had from the time the United Brotherhood first started."[45]

When the votes poured in, the strong grass-roots support which McGuire had built up over the years manifested itself and all the measures stripping him of his powers were defeated. McGuire had vaulted over the heads of the local leadership and found behind them a rank and file unquestioningly loyal to him. He had officiated at the birth of over 90 percent of the locals. He had personal friends in each city and was there by their side in times of trouble. In spite of their on-the-job needs and even their loyalty to local leaders who fulfilled these needs, the carpenters supported McGuire blindly on the referendum. Without a political machine which reached up to the national office, the professional organizers were helpless to capture the secret referendum. They could but watch glumly as McGuire counted the ballots of one more election supporting him, if not his policies.

[44]Henry P. Lloyd, general president, "Important Official Circular," *ibid.,* p. 8.
[45]"Amendments to the Constitution," *ibid.,* p. 2.

CHAPTER VI

The Industrial Revolution:

1896 to 1900

IN THEIR two direct and crude attempts to depose McGuire, the new leaders had learned a painful lesson: not so easily is a king dethroned. Consequently they turned to a skillfully conceived method of wearing away the base of McGuire's power. In the execution of their plan, the new leaders received help from an unexpected quarter: an industrial revolution in the building industry. It had gained momentum in the late 1880's, and during the late 1890's, it broke over the heads of the building trades unionists with a force and fury sufficient to change the whole structure of the industry.

Prior to 1885 new methods of casting iron for lintels, beams, and girders enabled contractors to build to a height of five stories. The Chicago fire of 1871, however, proved the inadequacy of these structures when faced with the menace of fire. Before the skyscrapers could become an important factor in the American building industry, fireproofing was essential. When in 1885 commercial production of rolled or structural steel was rendered possible under the Bessemer process, the industrial revolution got under way. Steel made in this manner, when properly protected, was fireproof. By 1900 structural steel had replaced cast iron in most modern construction.

79

Before buildings could soar to new heights, however, the elevator was necessary. W. B. Baxter, Jr. developed an electrically powered elevator in Baltimore in 1887. Two years later N. P. Otis developed a more successful one in New York City. After Otis founded his company in 1904, the elevator became standard in large buildings, both during and after construction. The elevator combined with new riveting processes to make possible the steel skeleton around which modern skyscrapers are built. The Waldorf Astoria Hotel in New York City was the first building to use both of these new developments in its construction in 1890.

The huge weight of the skyscraper called forth new engineering developments in the field of foundations. After years of experimenting, construction engineers used caissons and compressed air to create bedrock foundations for the Manhattan Life Insurance Company Building and the Mutual Life Insurance Company Building, erected in New York City between 1893 and 1900.

Fifteen years before 1900, E. L. Ransome of San Francisco had invented the twisted bar of steel and had demonstrated that it could be encased in cement to produce reinforced concrete. Gradually during the 1890's this new material replaced the older brick and masonry as filling for the steel skeleton of buildings. By 1905 reinforced concrete had passed the experimental stage.

These and other inventions and processes completely changed the structure of the building industry by the turn of the century. Twenty-five years later, George Otis Smith, director of the United States Geological Survey, could say that to erect a modern building one had but to

take by weight sixty parts of gravel, sand, and crushed stone; fifty-eight parts of tile and brick; twenty-seven parts of building stone; nineteen parts of cement and sixteen parts of steel, with such other ingredients as copper and glass and asbestos and paint...to suit one's taste.[1]

This revolution in building techniques affected the carpenter in four specific ways. First, it changed his most important source of employment from small, local contractors to large, intercity

[1] *New York Times,* Oct. 25, 1925, Sec. IX, p. 12, col. 2. The material for this description of the industrial revolution in the building industry was drawn from Haber, pp. 16–20.

80

construction firms. The small contractor, even when backed by a wealthy speculator, could not undertake the building of a huge skyscraper. The cost of the new equipment alone demanded huge construction companies which had to be highly mobile if they were to keep their expensive capital equipment occupied. Hence large intercity construction companies burgeoned in the 1890's. In 1911 Gompers estimated that "probably a dozen or more great building contractors...do nearly all the construction of modern business buildings throughout the continent of America."[2]

Its second effect was to create an even greater demand for the specialist carpenter. The modern skyscraper had ten, fourteen, even twenty stories of standardized rooms, each with the same floor, door, window, and wall measurements. It became an even simpler task for the contractor to hire a carpenter skilled in only one phase of his task. Consequently a whole spate of specialist carpenters' unions cropped up. By 1904 the general secretary reported the formation of unions among locomotive woodworkers, millwrights, shinglers, dock, wharf, and bridge builders, ceiling woodworkers, and carpenters' helpers.[3]

Third, it created new crafts such as the sheet-metal workers, plumbers, and electricians, many of whom worked on material which replaced wood, and all of whom, while jurisdictional lines were fluid, usurped woodwork related to their job. Complaint against "other trades encroaching upon and stealing our work" was registered at the 1898 convention.[4] By 1904 the delegate from Boston Local 33 complained that "the trade...is being taken, piece by piece, from our control...[by] the Electrical Workers, Wood, Wire and Metal Lathers, Building Laborers, and Sheet Metal Workers."[5]

Fourth, the revolution in building techniques intensified the effect of woodworking mills upon the outside carpenter. The floors

[2]Building Trades Department, AFL, *Proceedings of the Fifth Annual Convention of Atlanta, Nov. 27 to Nov. 30, 1911*, p. 30.

[3]Carpenters and Joiners of America, United Brotherhood of, *Proceedings of the Thirteenth General Convention of Milwaukee, Sept. 19, to Oct. 4, 1904*, p. 68.

[4]Carpenters and Joiners of America, United Brotherhood of, *Proceedings of the Tenth General Convention of New York City, Sept. 19 to Sept. 29, 1898*, p. 65.

[5]UBCJA, *1904 Convention Proceedings*, p. 162.

upon floors of standardized fixtures in a large skyscraper were easily produced by machine. More and more of the carpenter's work disappeared into planing mills. To add further to the carpenter's troubles, a new union, the Machine Wood Workers' International Union, stepped into the picture to claim jurisdiction over these "machine carpenters."

Each problem raised by the revolution in building techniques was a national one. The new construction companies were nationwide in scope. The small specialist carpenters' unions drew members from all parts of the country. The new trades subsisting partly on work traditionally belonging to the carpenter had a national jurisdiction, as did the new union in the woodworking industry. National problems demanded solutions on a national scale. In addition, the last three of these four problems were jurisdictional in nature. The specialist carpenters' unions, the new trades, and the new woodworkers' unions all fattened themselves on portions of the carpenter's jurisdiction. The United Brotherhood, more than ever, had to devise jurisdictional policies on the national level which could be put into effect simultaneously in every district council in the land. This, in turn, called for a union with a strong, centralized administration and centrally directed agents, in all localities, ready to move at a moment's notice. In sum, the revolution in building techniques gave further economic and institutional substance to the administrative reforms for which the professional organizers had long been clamoring.

The jurisdictional problem served to initiate the last and most stormy of the struggles over administration which took place during the McGuire period. On the subject of jurisdictional expansion, McGuire was clearly a "little Englander." In 1900 he told President Huber that the Brotherhood, with eight hundred locals, was becoming too large for its own good and was getting "top heavy."[6] Earlier, in 1894, he lamented the loss of half of the membership but saw it as a good omen inasmuch as the organization was shaking itself down to a hard core of good union men. "We have grown," he said in 1902, "but we have grown at an accelerated

<hr />

[6] Carpenters and Joiners of America, United Brotherhood of, *Proceedings of the Twenty-fourth General Convention of Indianapolis, Sept. 22 to Sept. 30, 1924*, p. 246.

pace, a pace that is dangerous and we must...take means and care to preserve this organization."[7]

McGuire was well aware that for every new member the Machine Woodworkers' Union gained, the Brotherhood would sooner or later lose one. He, however, did not care for the race to obtain dues payers. The important thing was to *unionize* the workers. It did not matter to him whether the worker entered the labor movement through this or that union. The important thing was that he enter the *movement*. McGuire was emotionally obsessed with a concept of united labor and not with the concerns of any given union. "Even though McGuire was the mainstay of his struggling organization, he found time for the...work of the Federation," said Gompers.[8]

True, McGuire had fought the Knights of Labor and the United Order, but he fought them reluctantly and because of structural differences. He felt that each of the two unions was, in its own way, staying the unity of labor. Once unity was achieved through the AFL, however, McGuire saw no further reason for unions to quarrel over membership. It is doubtful if he would have mourned greatly had technological evolution wiped out the Brotherhood, providing that its members were absorbed by other AFL unions.

After 1885 McGuire allowed the leaders of the AFL to organize machine woodworkers.[9] In 1888 he actually asked the carpenters to assist the International Furniture Workers' Union with the formation of locals of factory woodworkers.[10] Finally, the United Brotherhood gave Gompers permission to charter the new International Union of Machine Wood Workers as a full-fledged AFL affiliate.[11] Even Edmonston, who usually sided with McGuire, said of this move, "I can account for this...only by supposing... [McGuire] was hypnotized by the diplomacy of [Secretary] Thomas Kidd of the Woodworkers."[12]

[7]UBCJA, *1902 Convention Proceedings* (Verbatim), p. 143.
[8]Gompers, Vol. 1, p. 332.
[9]U. S. Congress, Joint Industrial Commission, *Report,* Vol. 17, pp. 129–130.
[10]*The Carpenter,* Vol. 8, No. 9, September 1888, p. 1.
[11]"Minutes of the Proceedings of the General Executive Board, Nov. 28, 1890," *The Carpenter,* Vol. 11, No. 1, January 1891, p. 4.
[12]Edmonston, "The Genesis," *The Carpenter,* Vol. 24, No. 10, October 1904, p. 9.

Trouble immediately arose on the local level between the United Brotherhood's professional organizers and the Wood Workers. In New York City, which used more wood trim than any other city and manufactured more than most other cities, the dispute crystallized earliest. Armed with his new AFL charter, Kidd sent organizer Richard Braunschweig to New York City just as United Brotherhood Local 309 was set to sign a contract with Brunswick, Balke, Collender, and Company, one of the largest building fixture manufacturers. Braunschweig intruded with an offer to supply labor for seven cents an hour less than the Brotherhood offered. The firm signed with him, and he recruited non-union labor through an "employment office" in the Bowery. These "carpenters" he then organized as Local Union 172 of the Machine Wood Workers' Union. He had neatly edged Local Union 309 out of the picture.[13]

A violent dispute between the two unions ensued. To discover who first scabbed on whom is impossible. The dispute hung fire through executive board meetings and conventions of both unions until 1894. Kidd appeared before the 1894 convention of the Carpenters and asked that they give all of the machine wood-workers to his union. The delegates complied with his request because, Kidd felt, lacking a label and a system of organizers they were unable to unionize the mills.[14] Jurisdiction over all wood-workers was given to the Machine Wood Workers' Union and all United Brotherhood locals were ordered to help the Machine Wood Workers to organize in the future.[15] McGuire's successors were to rue the day pen ever met paper to consummate this, the "Indianapolis Agreement."

The Machine Wood Workers' Union and the other union then active in the woodworking industry, the International Furniture Workers' Union, decided to take advantage of the United Brotherhood's friendliness to broach the subject of amalgamation. The Furniture Workers and the Wood Workers had had jurisdictional

[13]Letter from G. Wurst, secretary of Local Union 309, New York City, to the editor (*The Carpenter*, Vol. 22, No. 4, April 1902, p. 5.)

[14]American Federation of Labor, *Proceedings of the Twenty-First Annual Convention of Scranton, Pennsylvania, December 5 to December 14, 1901*, p. 252.

[15]UBCJA, *1894 Convention Proceedings*, p. 42.

disputes with each other as well as with the Carpenters. Both possessed, as well, a strong group of old-fashioned German Socialists who were inclined toward industrial unionism and who thought amalgamation a good first step.

In January, 1895, the executive board of the United Brotherhood approved a three-sided amalgamation conference.[16] But McGuire, in keeping with his "little England" policy, flatly rejected the amalgamation offer extended at the conference. The Machine Wood Workers and the Furniture Workers then amalgamated without the Carpenters and formed the Amalgamated Wood Workers' International Union in late 1895.[17]

In spite of the amalgamation, McGuire stood by the Indianapolis agreement. But this was the period (1894 to 1896) during which he was gradually losing his once viselike grip on the organization. To make a national agreement was no guarantee of its fulfillment on the local level. Several of the United Brotherhood locals objected to the agreement and took in renegade Furniture Workers locals which had objected to the amalgamation.

While all this happened, the mill owners took advantage of the lull in union watchfulness to increase their rate of migration from New York and other urban centers into the hinterlands. One of the principal contractors in New York City described the exodus:

Ten years ago. . . [in 1890] the great majority of doors, sashes, blinds, and trim. . .were manufactured within the limits of what today is known as Greater New York. Today. . .not twenty percent of it is manufactured there, and the other eighty percent is shipped, some as far as from Detroit and even west of there.[18]

When "suburban" mills started flooding the New York market with cheap trim, the New York District Council began to complain. Later, the New York carpenters decided to refuse to handle "unfair, out-of-town" trim.[19] In 1896 an "agitation against cheap, unfair, nonunion trim made in outside towns" was started. It

---

[16]"Minutes of the Proceedings of the General Executive Board, January 13, 1895," *The Carpenter,* Vol. 15, No. 3, March 1895, p. 12.
[17]AFL, *1901 Convention Proceedings,* p. 252.
[18]U.S. Congress, Joint Industrial Commission, *Report,* Vol. 14, pp. 108–109.
[19]*The Carpenter,* Vol. 17, No. 10, October 1897, p. 1.

enjoyed some measure of success in Stamford, Connecticut, and in Batavia and Rochester, New York.[20]

When the 1896 convention of the Brotherhood met, feelings ran high on the related subjects of unfair trim and the Amalgamated Wood Workers' Union. They were contributing factors to the 1896 revolution against McGuire already described.[21] McGuire had not only done little to help organize the country mills, but he had also seemingly sided with the Amalgamated Wood Workers. Though pressed to repudiate the Indianapolis agreement, he refused. Such a repudiation would have violated his sense of labor unity and would have added to what he felt was the all-too-rapid growth of the union.

Just as he had sloughed off the attack against his personal powers in 1896, so did he slough off this assault against his jurisdictional policy. The rebels were told that the United Brotherhood would continue to make agreements with other organizations when such agreements tended to promote harmony.

As the struggle against the Amalgamated Wood Workers' Union spread, the clamor against the Indianapolis agreement mounted. In July 1897 the executive board repudiated it, claiming somewhat belatedly that the amalgamation which created the Wood Workers' Union had rendered it void. The board requested that the Wood Workers' Union surrender to the United Brotherhood all mill work which was erected by the carpenter.[22] In a later conference with representatives of the Amalgamated Wood Workers, however, McGuire ignored the board and allowed the Wood Workers to retain jurisdiction over all planing mills, with the exception of those already organized by the United Brotherhood.[23]

The New York District Council immediately protested this agreement, but McGuire replied that the executive board possessed the power to effect such a treaty and that their complaint was poorly taken.[24] Again, in May, the New York District Council pro-

[20]UBCJA, *1898 Convention Proceedings*, p. 32.
[21]See above, pp. 76–78, for a description of the 1896 revolt against McGuire.
[22]"Minutes of the Proceedings of the General Executive Board, July 15, 1897," *The Carpenter,* Vol. 17, No. 8, August 1897, p. 9.
[23]*The Carpenter*, Vol. 17, No. 11, November 1897, p. 7.
[24]"Minutes of the Proceedings of the General Executive Board, Jan. 4, 1898," *The Carpenter,* Vol. 18, No. 2, February 1898, p. 4.

tested that Amalgamated Wood Worker members in Newark accepted a lower wage rate than did United Brotherhood mill-workers. As a result, mills organized by the United Brotherhood could not compete with those organized by the Amalgamated Wood Workers in the open market. The New York District Council leaders asked permission to take in Amalgamated Wood Workers. The executive board replied that the agreement stood, but Kidd would be asked to raise his men's wages in and about New York City.[25]

McGuire courted disaster when he hit the independent, willful, conservative New York unions in their pocketbooks. His jurisdictional policy united the various groups displeased with his rule. Since the fiascos of 1894 and 1896 had taught the opposition the folly of a direct personal assault on McGuire, they turned to a plot which was later described by Executive Board Member John W. Williams:

The Committee on [the] Constitution of the 1898 Convention, with A. C. Cattermull...as chairman and...[myself] as Secretary, undertook its task with seriousness of purpose and a definite appreciation of the primary needs of the Brotherhood. The Committee knew that the time had come to break away from the old order....It knew that if the United Brotherhood was to fulfill its mission and to realize its possibilities, a new course had to be mapped out.

The first and most important step was the conversion of the office of the General President from a mere figurehead into an active and essential factor in the administration...of the organization. The Committee knew the fate of every previous effort to change the Constitution in regard to that office; therefore, it concluded not to recommend another attempt. Instead, it drew upon its practical knowledge of psychology for a plan to gain the result. It was agreed to put forth a number of changes in the Constitution whereby many and varied duties devolving upon the General Secretary were to be transferred to the General President. It was thought that the membership...would not oppose the idea of making the General President the actual, as well as the nominal, head of the organization, so long as it was done without providing...for another salaried office. The Committee also requested

[25]"Minutes of the Proceedings of the General Executive Board, April 5, 1898," *The Carpenter,* Vol. 18, No. 5, May 1898, p. 8.

87

and received authority to prepare [instead of allowing, as had been the custom, McGuire to prepare for it] the official circular submitting the amendments...to a referendum. By this means any scheme that [McGuire] might have contemplated to defeat the plan was frustrated. How well the Committee on [the] Constitution and the Convention gauged the feeling and temper of the members is shown by the fact that out of about fifty...amendments...only two were defeated. Of the wisdom of the course adopted at that time there can be no shadow of a doubt.[26]

In keeping with this strategy, the general president was given the duty of examining and approving all local constitutions and of deciding all grievances. In order better to explain the logic of his decisions to the members of the executive board, the general president was given voice but no vote on the board. Since none of these moves took any money from the close-fisted membership or substantially encroached on McGuire's province, the membership allowed them to stand. The conspirators hoped that when the newly empowered general president demonstrated his value to the organization, he would be given a salary. Until that time he was to make his way as best he could by working for the union at night. The first light taps of a divisive wedge had been struck.

On the subject of jurisdiction, the opposition moved forthrightly behind the leadership of the New York locals. Local Union 476 appealed to the convention against McGuire's 1897 treaty with the Amalgamated Wood Workers' Union. McGuire's convention committee upheld the treaty, but after an angry floor debate the delegates threw the torn-up treaty into his teeth by a decisive sixty-nine to forty vote.[27] Then they revised the jurisdictional clause of the constitution so as to make it amply clear to all machine woodworkers that the Brotherhood was their home base. They also resolved that

...no other carpenters' or woodworkers' organizations of any kind be recognized by the Brotherhood and that no agreement be entered into with other carpenters', woodworkers' or machine-hands' organizations

[26]John Williams, "Our Status—Past and Present," *The Carpenter,* Vol. 35, No. 8, August 1915, p. 18.
[27]Carpenters and Joiners of America, AFL, *Proceedings of the Tenth General Convention of New York City, September 19 to September 29, 1898,* p. 14.

88

by our general officers and further, that all agreements now existing be annulled.[28]

McGuire's policy, if not McGuire, had been repudiated. Cattermull continued to head the executive board, and no less a person than J. W. Williams was elected general president.

With McGuire's peace-and-goodwill policy a shambles, events started to move rapidly. The New York unions held a monster rally to protest unfair trim, to serve notice on the Amalgamated Wood Workers, and to devise campaign strategy. At each of the 1899 meetings of the executive board the problem of organization was discussed. In January the board members decided that "something had to be done to strengthen and build up our organization" and ordered McGuire to prepare an organizing scheme. McGuire refused to suggest a plan, however, and at the April meeting handed the hot potato back to the board members. The board replied by arbitrarily appropriating $5,000 to finance four paid and full-time organizers. Three of the four, A. C. Cattermull, W. J. Shields, and W. J. Williams,[29] were members of the executive board. Bit by bit, the organization was slipping through McGuire's hands, like rope in some gigantic tug of war in which the future was pitted against the past.

McGuire's tired body then came to the aid of the opposition by collapsing. In late 1899 and 1900 there were several notices of his sickness in *The Carpenter,* and just before the 1900 convention the members were advised that his health had failed because of "insomnia and nervous troubles." At this convention it seemed a simple matter to the opposition to consign McGuire and all his pathetic visions of utopia to limbo.

The opposition at the 1900 convention was led by William Huber, who had become general president when Williams resigned in 1899 to take a political appointment with the New York State government. A career trade union official of a decade's standing, he was a big, handsome, confident man, the complete apostle of the new, practical unionism. His presidential address to the 1900 con-

[28]*Ibid.,* p. 63.
[29]W. J. Williams of Atlanta should not be confused with John Williams of Utica, the general president.

vention brimmed with determination and firmness. This man would be no figurehead.

Huber led another frontal attack on the sick McGuire's powers. This time the assault centered about a specific and democratic plan to base the powers of the general officers upon the local membership. Each state was to be designated a "section." Each section was to have a convention in advance of the general convention and was to send instruction-bound delegates, at the rate of one per thousand members, to the general convention. Mileage to and from the national convention was to be paid all delegates by the national office.

The plan was an obvious advance. It based the convention on real units of local power and eliminated rotten borough locals as convention representation units. By paying their fares, it encouraged each section to send its delegates. By binding the delegates with instructions, it prevented administration control of the convention through logrolling deals. Frank Duffy, who was later to become McGuire's successor and Huber's aide-de-camp, headed the committee which reported favorably on this scheme and which led the floor fight for it.

When this reform failed to pass, the Young Turks turned on McGuire and stripped him of his powers, substantially as they had in 1894 and 1896. Again the rank and file rose to McGuire's defense, rejected every measure, and restored McGuire to his full preconvention powers.[30] An immediate howl arose from the local leaders, but a recount sustained the results.

Once again the rank and file had rallied behind McGuire. But now they rallied around a name only. The person was hollow, the marrow all drained out, the fight gone. His old-fashioned, genteel, over-intellectualized, and quaint brand of utopian radicalism was as dead in 1901 as William McKinley, the Populist party, or the Knights of Labor. McGuire proceeded, like a faithful old dog, to die with the loyalties he had lived by.

[30]"A Brief Summary of the General Vote on the Amendments from the Scranton Convention," *The Carpenter*, Vol. 20, No. 1, January 1901, p. 1. The general president, however, retained the powers granted him by the 1898 convention.

CHAPTER VII

The Last Radical:

1898 to 1902

IN 1902 Peter J. McGuire, who as long ago as 1872 had stormed across New York City from Union Square to the crowded ghettos of Spring Street with the crude, hand-painted signs of the First Marxist International, slowly went to bits. The body which he had willfully exposed to a quarter-century of abuse and suffering in the interest of his beloved working class collapsed. The mind, so long the servant of two masters, practical trade unionism and utopian socialism, pulled apart, and led him to commit acts he would otherwise never have contemplated. And, as the century of which he was so much a product expired, he stood defeated, discredited, and bereft of power.

In 1891, at the age of thirty-seven, McGuire stood at the summit of a brilliant career. His achievements were many. He had conceived the idea of a national holiday for workingmen and had induced Congress to declare it Labor Day. He had helped found the Socialist Labor party which, in 1891, was the most powerful radical party in existence. He had helped found the AFL and was its "leading genius...during its early days."[1] He "undoubtedly supplied what ideas the American Federation of Labor had for its

[1] Louis S. Reed, *The Labor Philosophy of Samuel Gompers*, p. 59.

foundation."[2] Even Gompers admitted that besides himself only McGuire provided the early AFL with practical guidance as well as ideas.[3] He had translated the abstract eight-hour day philosophy of the radicals into a practical working plan: he had made the shorter working day a reality for the workers. And, finally, he had single-handedly built the largest and most influential trade union in the land. More than any other man it was he who first amalgamated the philosophy of the foreign radicals with that of American radicals and then translated this philosophy into practical trade union institutions.

Yet, for all his trade union successes, McGuire was not at heart a trade unionist. The coming day he saw dawning was not a trade union, but a Socialist day. He emphasized the first, or trade union, phase of his philosophy only to the temporary exclusion of its other parts. What for McGuire was a temporary means became to the men he led a permanent end. And, as the Socialist fat was melted off McGuire's philosophy, what emerged for them was pure and simple trade unionism.

McGuire's "organize, agitate, educate" trade unionism might have been compatible with his Socialist goals. Pure and simple trade unionism could never be, for its apostles preached both present and future aloofness from socialism. McGuire counseled such aloofness only until sufficient workers were organized. Its apostles preached identity of interest between labor and capital; McGuire held that "employers and employees have antagonistic interests."[4] Its apostles preached that both of the major political parties should be solicited for prounion laws; McGuire thought that "there is very little to expect...at the hands of either the Democratic or Republican Parties for the working people."[5]

Yet although McGuire and the men he led were set out upon different, even antithetical courses, McGuire refused to surrender either his Socialist goals or his trade unionism. Instead he tried to weld these two incompatible metals. "The workingmen even-

[2]Ware, pp. 108, 165–166.
[3]Gompers, Vol. 1, p. 332.
[4]Senate Committee on Education and Labor, *Report*, Vol. 1, p. 350.
[5]"P. J. McGuire's Political Views," *The Carpenter*, Vol. 16, No. 9, September 1896, p. 8.

tually will eliminate all middlemen standing between the worker and the full product of his toil,"[6] McGuire told a group of men in 1894. To whom did he make the statement? To a group of middlemen, business agents, who stood as much as any capitalist between the worker and the full product of his toil, to the 1894 convention of the United Brotherhood of Carpenters and Joiners of America.

These men were simply not interested in the worker's receiving the full product of his toil. They wished only that he get a fair day's pay for a fair day's work and that he allow them to continue to lead him. All the finer points of Socialist theory were lost on them. They despised the Socialists who might gamble away hard-won trade union gains on political action. The Socialists returned the sentiment, and McGuire was caught in the cross fire.

During the mid-1890's socialism experienced a depression-inspired revival, and the Socialists tried to capture the AFL. Instead of opposing socialism completely, McGuire as AFL first vice-president took the position that the time was not yet ripe for trade unions to associate themselves with a Socialist party. "With 8 percent of the wage earners organized...to rush into an independent political party is suicidal and dangerous,"[7] he told the Socialists. "Politically, we [the trade unions] will control this country in forty odd years." And, he added, "The man who is not content to wait will have to."[8]

The Socialists failed in their attempt to capture the AFL, in large measure due to McGuire's opposition.[9] His plea that socialism was just around the corner fell on deaf ears. The trade unionists did not care where it was, and the Socialists rejected McGuire's position as mere rationalization. "Some one will say...[I]was a socialist. Yes, of the trade union kind,"[10] McGuire told the hostile groups, trying vainly to keep a foot on each of two horses which were moving increasingly farther apart.

[6]UBCJA, *1894 Convention Proceedings,* p. 4.

[7]American Federation of Labor, *A Verbatim Report of the Discussion on a Political Program at the Denver Convention of the A.F.L., December 14, 15, 1894,* p. 12.

[8]American Federation of Labor, *Proceedings of the Fifteenth Annual Convention of New York, N. Y., December 9 to December 17, 1895,* p. 99.

[9]For the complete story of the Socialist attempt to capture the AFL, see Commons, *History,* Vol. 2, pp. 509–520.

[10]*A Verbatim Report,* p. 44.

From this point on McGuire was neither socialist fish nor trade union fowl. Although he continued to support the Socialist Labor party, his days as a political radical were behind him. And the professional organizers tried mightily to remove him from power because the Socialist vision he continued to foster prevented him from establishing the kind of union which they felt the industry called for.

Had McGuire completely surrendered either his ideology or his pragmatic trade unionism he might have avoided a tragic fate. But the former was too much a part of his emotional make-up, and the latter the only tangible result of a life's work. He could surrender neither. Rather, he tried to house both within the confines of the same personality. He paid the price of this impossible juggling. Under the burden of hard work and constant opposition, he suffered a collapse so complete as to bring his career to a premature end.

The first signs of his inability to choose between practical trade unionism and socialism became obvious during the mid-1890's. At times McGuire rode high on the crest of a "pure and simple" exhilaration; at times he sunk deep into the doldrums of a socialist despair at ever changing the established order. After opposing an independent labor party at the 1894 AFL convention, he introduced a resolution calling for one at the 1897 convention.[11] In 1898 he reversed his stand again and made a violent speech against such a party.[12] Toward the end of the 1890's his indecisiveness became so serious that in the same articles and speeches he advocated diametrically opposite courses of trade union action. Thus, he wrote in 1897 that "The time is near at hand when the wealth of the world will be...evenly divided among all creators of it, and the great instrument of the equalization of that wealth will be...labor."[13] On the same page of the same issue of *The Carpenter,* he also wrote that the United Brotherhood will "always uphold strict trade union principles and practical trade union

[11]American Federation of Labor, *Proceedings of the Seventeenth Annual Convention of Nashville, December 13 to December 21, 1897,* p. 86.
[12]AFL, *1898 Convention Proceedings,* p. 117.
[13]*The Carpenter,* Vol. 17, No. 5, May 1897, p. 8.

actions free from all isms, fads and experimental abstractions."[14]

McGuire tumbled downhill rapidly after 1894. Abandoned by the Socialists, fought by his own followers, yesteryear's most violent radical had to abandon agitation and become a not-very-efficient clerk. A man who had once held twenty thousand workers spellbound spent all of his time poring over lists of figures or directing stenographers. His violent and explosive sentiments were no longer able to find an outlet. Confined within him, they turned to corrosive juices and ate away at his inner being. He was still a Socialist, to be sure. In 1901 he said, "We should never lose sight of the fact that our efforts after all in reducing the hours of labor and in increasing wages are simply supplemental to the still greater movements of all branches of labor to claim and have the full results of their toil."[15]

But his words no longer carried conviction. Men who had once hung on his every word now walked in sullen, uninterested groups out of the lecture hall to leave him crushed. He was crushed, ironically, by the very reforms he had given his followers as a sop to sustain them on the socialist journey. Now these same men, entrenched firmly behind local trade union institutions, were grown fat and sleek.

The end came when McGuire turned to liquor to ease his troubled mind. He remained away from his duties for days at a time, brooding over his fate in Philadelphia saloons. "Nothing could be more pathetic than the end of his career. Resolute and self possessed, a great hill of strength to the cause of labor, he gradually came, as the result of intemperance, to lose all influence and to exist by the bounty of his friends."[16]

Liquor magnified his existing faults a thousandfold. Never a good administrator, he started blatantly evading official responsibilities. In 1901 he wrote in a letter to Huber, "I . . . can do much more for it [the Brotherhood] if not pestered and annoyed by

[14]*Ibid.*
[15]*The Carpenter,* Vol. 21, No. 1, January 1901, p. 10.
[16]Roland Hill Harvey, *Samuel Gompers: Champion of the Working Class,* pp. 64–65. See also, UBCJA, *1902 Convention Proceedings* (Verbatim), p. 161, 188, 191.

visiting delegations and many...[demands] made on me of the most trifling character."[17]

The manner in which McGuire conducted the national office in 1901 was described by Frank Duffy.

Letters by the hundred were lying around in all directions, begging for a reply, asking the cause of delay, demanding explanations, threatening to bring charges, or to withdraw from the organization altogether. Even these were not answered. They were thrown in a heap on the floor behind the chair of the General Secretary-Treasurer, where they had lain for months, some of them for more than a year, forgotten or ignored.

On the desks, window sills, and other places, were to be found other communications already answered, with properly addressed envelopes, awaiting the signature of the General Secretary-Treasurer. Hundreds of these were three, six and twelve months old. Lawyers' letters threatening to bring suit...and law suits already entered received no attention whatever. Complaints in general were to be found on all sides, while in several instances strikes and lockouts did not receive the slightest consideration or even a passing notice.[18]

The final phase of McGuire's career opened shortly after the 1900 convention closed. Executive Board Members Frank Duffy and W. J. Grimes were sent by the convention to Philadelphia to help McGuire compile a report of the convention proceedings. They moved in on McGuire and found the office a shambles. Attempts to induce him to forsake the local saloons for his work were in vain.

Word of McGuire's condition spread around the country, and in December Chairman Cattermull of the executive board came in from Chicago to put the organization in order. Instead of going directly to McGuire, he went to New York and sought out Duffy. The boys in Chicago, he told Duffy, were in arms about McGuire's neglect of his work. Then he offered Duffy the following proposition: "Pete is not doing his work; he has got to step down and get out and another man go in his place that will. Grimes and

---

[17]Letter from McGuire to Huber, July 23, 1901, in UBCJA, *1902 Convention Proceedings* (Verbatim), pp. 208–209.
[18]UBCJA, *1902 Convention Proceedings*, pp. 33–34.

Walz [two of the five executive board members] will vote together, Miller will vote with me—where do you stand?"[19]

Duffy put him off, and the two journeyed to Yonkers to speak with Huber. The three repaired to a bar to talk. They agreed only that McGuire was finally cornered. Cattermull announced that he wanted McGuire's job. Huber described his answer. "Yes, and that was all."[20] Huber had his own plans and Cattermull played no part in them. He and Cattermull then had a violent scene over the fact that Huber had rented an office for seven dollars a month to conduct the president's affairs.

From this point on, there was a falling out among the conspirators. Duffy sided with his New York neighbor Huber, and his vote tipped the delicate balance within the executive board in Huber's favor. With a majority of the executive board on Huber's side, the succession to the throne was decided. Events now moved rapidly.

At the January 1901 meeting of the executive board, Huber told of the many local complaints about McGuire's "not attending to his duty, failing to answer correspondence, neglecting to pay legal death claims and to send money donated [for organizing purposes] by the Scranton Convention [1900] to different localities as ordered by that body."[21] When Huber wrote to McGuire inquiring about these complaints, McGuire told him to come to Philadelphia and do the job himself. The executive board took McGuire at his word and ordered Huber to appear and assist him. Huber held out for a salary and in contravention to the constitution was granted $100 a month.[22]

Huber arrived in February 1901 and until the next quarterly meeting of the executive board was unable to work with the brooding and recalcitrant McGuire. He reported, "I found the office in deplorable condition, and all efforts on my part to have

<hr/>

[19]UBCJA, *1902 Convention Proceedings* (Verbatim), p. 105, testimony of Duffy. The executive board had five voting members at this time, giving Duffy the balance of power.

[20]*Ibid.*, p. 156, testimony of Huber. The context in which he repeated his explanation of this conversation leaves little doubt that the "yes" was meant ironically.

[21]UBCJA, *1902 Convention Proceedings*, p. 21. Executive Board Member Grimes.

[22]*Ibid.*

Brother McGuire attend to his duties were virtually in vain. I received more complaints, but was powerless to do anything more than call the General Executive Board's attention to the matter."[23]

When the board met again in April, the members took into consideration the administration of the union. Upon auditing the books, they discovered a deficit of $6,300. The board members called McGuire to account. He vehemently denied that there was a shortage but admitted that due to his illness the books might have become muddled. He asked for time. Four days later he appeared at a board meeting and told the members that the books were too confused to adjust immediately. He offered them a personal check to cover the $6,300, however, and promised to have the books in order for the next meeting of the board in July.[24]

When the board met in July, McGuire pleaded that he was at home sick and could not appear. He asked for more time. The board members waited restlessly one, two, three days. On the fourth day Huber was sent to get McGuire. He was not home. He was sick enough, but sick with fear at facing the board. On each of the four days he had set out for the office and each time had ended in a nearby bar gathering courage to meet his antagonists.[25] When, under the threat of legal action, McGuire finally appeared, he was given a date on which to square accounts or be suspended. "I never saw Brother McGuire blanch but twice in my life," said Board Member Grimes, "and that was one of the times."[26]

All of these events transpired in early July 1901. On July 18, when it became clear that McGuire would give them no satisfaction, the board members started perusing the account books. They found that McGuire had

made deposits in the Penn National Bank [in the union's account] for the purpose of deceiving the Board as to the balance on deposit. On 3rd May, 1901, a draft on the Hanover National Bank, New York [McGuire's bank] for $6,300 was deposited by him, but as this draft was obtained from the Continental Title and Trust Company [another of the Brotherhood's banks] in exchange for a cheque of the

---

[23]*Ibid.*
[24]UBCJA, *1902 Convention Proceedings* (Verbatim), pp. 85–90, testimony of Executive Board Member Grimes.
[25]*Ibid.*, pp. 10–11.
[26]*Ibid.*, p. 88.

Brotherhood for the same amount from the Penn National Bank, no additional funds were added to the balance. A deposit of $9,250 of a similar nature was made on July 18, 1901, but in the bank deposit book the figure 1 in the...date was erased for the purpose of making it appear that the deposit was made on July 8, 1901.[27]

McGuire stood accused of writing a total of three false checks each of which was designed to cancel the others out and of altering the books to obscure his deed. Had he become a private assassin for Czar Nicholas, he would not have assumed a role more out of character than that of embezzler of union funds.

Huber and Duffy made the first move. Upon discovering the shortage on July 18, they called in all of McGuire's books. Several days later Duffy was put at the head of an executive board committee to handle all financial affairs. On July 23 the executive board pressed charges against McGuire under the United Brotherhood's constitution and he was temporarily suspended. On July 24 the executive board made Duffy acting general secretary-treasurer, and legal counsel was hired. Huber was advised to complete the prosecution of charges against McGuire under the constitution before taking civil action. Expert accountants were hired who found a shortage totaling $10,074.93.[28] Five days later McGuire suffered a collapse from which he never fully recovered.

The collapse was complete. From this point on, McGuire's actions were erratic and he petulant and, on occasions, childish. He made appointments with the executive board members and repeatedly failed to keep them. He refused to turn valuable papers over to the board, holding them to be his personal property.[29] On some occasions he stormed at the board; on others, he was contrite and humble. A letter he wrote to Huber just before his suspension tells the pitiful story of his condition:

My nervous system was shattered....
Certainly I made mistakes and neglected some details, but that was due to ill health and constant worriment. It was not due to lack of

[27]"Reports of Lybrand, Ross Brothers and Montgomery," Certified Public Accountants, made on Sept. 14, 1901, Oct. 9, 1901, and Aug. 27, 1901, reproduced in *ibid.,* pp. 38–81. The quotation is on p. 62.

[28]*Ibid.,* p. 63, and "Minutes of the Proceedings of the Executive Board," July 18 to July 24, 1901, *The Carpenter,* Vol. 21, No. 9, September 1901, p. 11.

[29]UBCJA, *1902 Convention Proceedings,* (Verbatim), p. 100.

interest in the organization I founded and cherished for so many years. Friend Bill, be kind to me, for I have been sick and need encouragement, not abuse, from those I have stood up for for years.[30]

McGuire, so long a fighter, now fought by reflex, and with such feeble weapons as were still at his command.

In September a struggle ensued for possession of *The Carpenter*. After preparing the September issue, Duffy had to leave Philadelphia. The sick McGuire called the printer to his home and asked him to publish his side of the story. The printer consented and ran off an issue in which many of Duffy's writings were deleted to make way for McGuire's article. McGuire defended himself hotly but vaguely and denounced the new general officers as an overambitious opposition. He was not specific about the shortage of cash.

Duffy returned to the office before all of the copies of the altered *Carpenter* were in the mail. He destroyed the rest, fired the printer, and sent the original issue to all local unions.[31] The whole affair served to heap more coals on an already raging controversy.

The organization was split down the middle. On October 19 the executive board met in search of a solution. The members asked McGuire to appear and to cooperate in drawing up a circular wherein both sides could present their view of the question to the United Brotherhood's court of final appeal, the membership, for a vote. On November 5 such a conference was held and the circular sent out.

In December, on advice of counsel, while the vote was as yet untabulated, Huber decided to open suit against the bonding company for the amount McGuire had allegedly embezzled. He was advised that for the union to proceed with such a suit, McGuire would have to be arrested. McGuire agreed to appear in court without warrant but ignored his promise three successive times. On December 9, 1901, twenty years, four months, and one day after he had founded the Brotherhood of Carpenters and Joiners, Peter J. McGuire was indicted by a grand jury for "making way

[30]Letter from McGuire to Huber, July 23, 1901, *ibid.*, pp. 208–209.
[31]Frank Duffy, "So-called Suppression of the September Carpenter," *The Carpenter*, Vol. 21, No. 12, December 1901, p. 2.

with association property."[32] Before McGuire could be brought to trial, the last ballot came into the office. A full 14,374 members favored McGuire's permanent suspension, but 12,702 others rallied around him. Lacking the two-thirds majority, the suspension was not made permanent.[33]

McGuire appeared at the office on January 2, 1902, and demanded official reinstatement. But since no bonding company would deal with him, he could not provide the $30,000 bond required by the constitution.[34] He stayed out of power. He countered by mailing to all locals a circular on official Brotherhood stationery in which he again maligned Huber and Duffy and defended his record, and which he signed as the official general secretary-treasurer. After this the various locals which supported McGuire also started sending out antiadministration circulars, thus compounding the chaos and breaking down all the lines of discipline. Said Huber:

Our motives were misconstrued and our actions severely criticized. Distorted reports prejudiced some of the members against us. Locals refused to abide by the decisions of the General Officers, withheld their per capita [tax] and even carried on open warfare against [them].[35]

Throughout the first three months of 1902 McGuire intensified his campaign to get reinstated. He had locals write letters of protest to Huber (he himself wrote three), demanding that he be reinstated as a result of the referendum vote. Huber replied that the referendum vote did not dismiss the charges and that in any event McGuire could not be reinstated without a bond.[36]

Finally, on the last day of April, McGuire gave up the fight. He agreed to pay $2,000 "in compromise of the claims of the United

[32]Docket of the Clerk of Quarter Session Court, Phila., Penna., p. 407. Bill of Indictment, No. 177 of the December 1901 Session of the Grand Jury, Letter from Samuel Dash, Assistant District Attorney of Phila., to the author, Feb. 27, 1953; "Report of the General President William D. Huber to the G.E.B.," January 1, 1902, The Carpenter, Vol. 22, No. 2, February 1902, pp. 2–3; UBCJA, 1902 Convention Proceedings, p. 24.
[33]"Report of the Committee on General Vote on Permanent Suspension of G.S.–T.P.J. McGuire," The Carpenter, Vol. 22, No. 1, January 1902, pp. 2–3.
[34]"Report of General President William D. Huber to the General Executive Board, April 1902," The Carpenter, Vol. 22, No. 5, May 1902, p. 2.
[35]UBCJA, 1902 Convention Proceedings, p. 21.
[36]The Carpenter, Vol. 22, No. 5, May 1902, p. 2.

Brotherhood...of $10,074.93 deficit in the account of...Mc-Guire."[37] He then took leave of the labor movement, saying:

I, Peter J. McGuire, formerly General Secretary-Treasurer of the United Brotherhood of Carpenters and Joiners of America, in consideration of one dollar do hereby remise, release, quit-claim and forever discharge the United Brotherhood of Carpenters and Joiners of America for any and all claims I have, or may have or can have....[38]

Whether or not the working carpenter—McGuire's last source of support and one which had yet to fail him—would accept his dollar offer remained to be decided by the 1902 convention.

A bitterly divided group of delegates met in the summer of 1902 to decide the fate of the man who had given each of them his trade union birthright. Said Huber, of the support accorded McGuire:

It was...astonishing...as quite a number of delegates...on the eve of the Convention and even during the earlier part of its sessions were still laboring under the belief that a discrepancy in P. J. McGuire's accounts was an impossibility, that he had been unjustly accused and removed from office by the General Executive Board and the General Officers and maliciously persecuted by them.[39]

Executive Board Member Grimes told the delegates "Now we have arrived here...with a venom so well developed and a spleen so enlarged that if all of us can leave this city...still in one organization...I think we shall have achieved a miracle."[40]

McGuire's trial began on September 23 and lasted for three days. Huber opened proceedings with the remark, "You wanted to have all your dirty linen washed; now wash it."[41] All rules were abandoned, and the seven hundred delegates acted as a huge court of justice, while the critically ill McGuire remained in Philadelphia. Nerves were strained and tempers flared repeatedly, as the various officers mounted the platform to explain their role in the affair.

---

[37]UBCJA, *1902 Convention Proceedings* (Verbatim), p. 126; "General President's Quarterly Report," *The Carpenter*, Vol. 22, No. 9, September 1902, p. 3.

[38]UBCJA, *1902 Convention Proceedings* (Verbatim), p. 126.

[39]William Huber, "Our Twelfth General Convention," *The Carpenter*, Vol. 22, No. 11, November 1902, p. 5.

[40]UBCJA, *1902 Convention Proceedings* (Verbatim), p. 91.

[41]*Ibid.*, p. 35.

All of the petty maneuvering for position came out as the various delegates hurled heated remarks at one another.

On the last day of the debate McGuire stunned the delegates with a surprise appearance. Mental collapse had been followed by physical collapse. Afflicted with rheumatism, dropsy, and gastric catarrh, he could no longer stand erect. Yet, as his words reveal, he labored under an enormous compulsion to explain how he had come to this low estate. He made his final accounting to the union movement:

I have no voice, no care about this little plan and that; I have no part in your little plans and schemes....All I want to say is...keep together; no split, no division, no disorganization....I have always done everything in my power...to bring the men together, the men of our craft, even by humbling myself....I simply want you to judge me by the facts.

. . .

I do not care whether I sink or swim, so long as this organization is maintained.

. . .

I am not lost entirely in this world, but I have enough to wreck me physically; destroy me mentally; but while I live I will fight....

. . .

I throw myself entirely on the mercy...of this convention. After many years of work for the organization I claim no great distinction, but I want fairness.

. . .

For some time I have felt completely broken down and lost in heart to find...so much opposition to me. If some of the men had worked as hard as I did in my own humble way they would be broken down, too, and it was due to sickness, long travels and journeys and in strike movements that I got completely broken down. And I do not want any office in the Brotherhood, even if I am cleared of everything. I want other men to go ahead, and I want this organization to prosper and succeed.[42]

It was not a defense but a plea. When it ended McGuire had spoken the last words he was ever to speak to the workers.

A roll call was held on the motion to accept McGuire's resigna-

[42]*Ibid.*, pp. 142–144, 206.

tion and to close the books forever on this unfortunate page of labor history. By a margin of only 61 votes out of 335 cast, McGuire was expelled from the union.[43]

Thus did a plot laid four years before hatch in 1902. Still one problem remains which can be resolved neither by court record nor convention proceedings: did McGuire actually embezzle the money? It is likely, but not proven, that McGuire used some of the union's funds to defray the cost of his illness. The circumstances under which he did so, however, could constitute a crime, or even a reprehensible act, only to the most caviling of critics. With the knowledge and permission of the various conventions, the Brotherhood's money was banked under McGuire's name until February, 1901, and the union's general fund and McGuire's salary were indistinguishable. In the early days, McGuire often passed up his salary, financed *The Carpenter,* and turned his own earnings over to the union's general fund. The miles he traveled, the abuse he suffered, the speeches he made, and the strikes he led were beyond financial evaluation. Without them there would have been no union to have a general fund, to have a shortage.

To speak of McGuire's owing the union money or the union's owing McGuire money in 1901 was a travesty in every sense but the legal one. Said McGuire when first accused of being an embezzler, "I was actually disgusted with the unexpected demands [to balance the books] made upon me. . . . I have cherished and protected the interests of this organization for twenty years, and saved it thousands of dollars."[44] If McGuire did take the money, he took precious little, for he lived on after 1902 as an absolute pauper. Most of the shortage uncovered by the accountants was undoubtedly due to neglect. But the men who hounded him so mercilessly could not distinguish between neglect and embezzlement. Or perhaps they did not wish to make the distinction.

That McGuire had to be eased out of power somehow, there can be no doubt. That he had to be thrown from power by the means used, there can be much doubt. His successors hauled him to court as a common criminal, discredited him, and exposed the labor

[43]UBCJA, *1902 Convention Proceedings,* pp. 142–147.
[44]UBCJA, *1902 Convention Proceedings* (Verbatim), pp. 208–209.

movement to ridicule for $10,000 they knew he did not possess. They sold their birthright for a mess of pottage.

After 1902 McGuire's crippled and bent form was still to be seen in the old haunts and bars where labor men met. For a time the great names in the labor firmament journeyed faithfully over to Camden to see the old rebel. Then, gradually, he was forgotten and left to die, without so much as a scroll of thanks or a paid doctor's bill.

On the evening of February 15, 1906, he wrote to an old comrade in arms in New England, the scene of some of his earliest trade union triumphs. "I'm very tired of it all, old boy, and, of late, in looking my past in the face, I wonder if the game was worth the poor candle, the more so when I see the ingratitude of those who benefited by our labor."[45]

Later that night he died at home alone with his daughter. His last words, spoken in a delirium, were: "I've got to get to California, the boys in Local 22 need me."[46] He might better have saved his waning breath. The boys in Local 22 did not need him. They had but recently placed one Patrick H. "Pin Head" McCarthy, politician and labor boss extraordinary, in power.

[45]A. Charles Corotis and Charles W. Phillips, *The Life Story of a Forgotten Giant —Peter J. McGuire,* p. 24. This pamphlet is a short sketch (26 pages) of McGuire's life.
[46]*Ibid.*

CHAPTER VIII

"All That's Made of Wood . . .":

1902 to 1912

McGUIRE sincerely believed in the brotherhood of all laboring men. Although, under the pressure of the professional organizers, he sometimes dealt harshly with unions that encroached upon the Brotherhood's jurisdiction, more often he preferred to overlook the encroachment. Never did he concern himself with the potentialities of an expanding jurisdiction. Rarely did the new leaders concern themselves with any other matter.

Headed by Huber, they were alert to every possible sign of encroachment. They struck first at the Amalgamated Wood Workers' Union which had grown to a healthy maturity under McGuire's warm-hearted brotherhood-of-labor policy. For a decade (1902 to 1912) they fought this organization on all fronts. At the end of that period they had wrecked, dismantled, and absorbed it.

Thus began the Carpenters' notorious reputation for jurisdictional aggressiveness. The United Brotherhood's leaders, however, did not attack the Wood Workers' Union in 1902, nor have they since jousted with scores of other unions, without good and sufficient reason. Hence, before describing the conflict this chapter will deal with the general nature of the jurisdictional dispute, which, if it did not originate with the Carpenters, was developed by them to its last refinement.

The Jurisdictional Dispute

The whole problem of jurisdiction provides in a very real sense a watershed for the historical development of the United Brotherhood after 1902. These disputes always influenced and sometimes dictated the structure and determined the policies of the Brotherhood, and they decided the nature of the Carpenters' relations with the other building trades unions and the AFL,[1] with their employers,[2] and with the United States government.[3] As medieval barons surrendered all living comforts to construct their huge, drafty, and dismal castles, so did the leaders of the Brotherhood neglect most fields of trade union activity in order to turn their union into a huge machine for the protection and expansion of the Carpenters' jurisdiction.

As has already been stated, this preoccupation with jurisdiction can be traced to the industrial revolution in the building industry which started in the 1880's,[4] reached full bloom in the period directly preceding the First World War, and shows little present sign of going to seed. Rarely does a year pass without the introduction of some new material for, and some new method of, constructing the nation's offices, warehouses, docks, ships, and homes. With each innovation, a mad scramble for jurisdiction ensues.

The fact that disputes rising out of these jurisdictional innovations were not, either in 1902 or 1952, handled in as orderly a fashion as they might have been can be laid upon the doorstep of the industry. The very disorganization of the building industry, with its plethora of small competitors, hit-and-miss financing, temporary work sites, and seasonality, conspires against the orderly introduction of technological innovations. This disorderliness gave birth to the unions,[5] and the unions, as agencies for job preservation, brought into being the jurisdictional dispute.

For all of its troublesome ramifications, however, the industrial revolution in the building industry found the journeyman a

[1]See below, Chapter IX, "Craft or Industrial Unionism."
[2]See below, Chapter XI, "Label Unionism."
[3]See below, Chapter XV, "The Carpenters and the Government."
[4]See above, pp. 79–82.
[5]See above, pp. 3–11.

handicraftsman and left him one. Had it been sufficiently far-reaching to render the handicraftsman a useless, uneconomic anachronism, from whose labor no entrepreneur could have made a cent, the jurisdictional dispute might never have seen the light of day, and buildings, like airplanes and automobiles, might be made in factories. But it left the highly skilled handicraftsman as essential as it found him. On any job, however large and up-to-date, the basic tools of the carpenter are still the saw and hammer, of the bricklayer the trowel, and of the plumber the wrench. The unions are still the major source for recruiting and training these crafts-men, in spite of the vocational school movement. Thus, another need for the union; thus, another source of jurisdictional jealousy.

The timing of the industrial revolution in the building industry also accounts for jurisdictional troubles. If it had come all at once after the Civil War and had substantially ended within a few decades, the unions born in the 1880's and 1890's might have grown along fairly fixed jurisdictional lines. This, of course, was not the case. The industrial revolution called forth the unions, and the two grew side by side in the late nineteenth and early twentieth centuries. By the time technological change had become a constant in the industry (the years covered by this chapter), unions were fixed institutions upon which both employers and workers had come to depend. In lieu of a unionism constructed on more realistic jurisdictional lines, the craft form remained. It was supplemented only by the jurisdictional dispute and by such modifications of the craft form as these disputes caused.[6]

The Carpenters roared into their jurisdictional fights with an alacrity and an efficiency which made lesser unions shudder at the prospect of a test of strength. Huber and Duffy rapidly discovered that the size of the Brotherhood and the strategic position of the carpenter in the building scheme gave them an advantage which they pressed relentlessly. Before the first five years of the present century passed, the Carpenters had a reputation as the Saracens of the trade union movement. "The boys in Boston," H. M. Taylor, president of Local Union 67 of Roxbury, Massachusetts, wrote in

[6]See below, Chapter IX, "Craft or Industrial Unionism," for an analysis of this modified form, the craft-industrial union.

1905, "believe in going ahead at all times. 'Hold what we have and get all we can' is our motto."[7]

Four years later, in dwelling on jurisdictional troubles, a labor editor wrote, "The old fight of Plumbers v. Steamfitters, Building Laborers v. Cement Workers, and Carpenters v. Everybody else has never been as bitter as now."[8]

An amazed Machinist delegate to the 1915 AFL convention read to his fellow unionists the latest of the Carpenters' claims to jurisdiction in the millwright field. It concluded, "Finally, all work pertaining to machinery...which, with the evolution of time and this craft will come under this jurisdictional claim." Even posterity was invoked as a Brotherhood ally.

Although it would be tedious and profitless to chronicle all of the Carpenters' disputes, a representative cross section of the more important ones provides an inkling of how the Brotherhood was affected by the industrial revolution. Disputes over wood and metal materials were the two most important types. The one with the Amalgamated Wood Workers falls into the first category and will be discussed in this chapter. The disputes over metal products, which occurred chiefly with the Sheet Metal Workers, the Iron Workers, and the Machinists, constitute a separate field of jurisdiction and will be discussed in Chapter XII.

Other less important disputes occurred in the following order. In 1904 the Carpenters engaged the Plasterers; in 1905 the Shipwrights, the Organ and Musical Instrument Workers, and the Laborers; and in 1906 the Hod Carriers. In 1909 they spread their jurisdiction to cover all furniture factories. In 1910, a boom year, disputes were announced with the Metal Lathers, the Marble Workers, the Tile Layers, the Asbestos Workers, the Electrical Workers, and the Elevator Constructors. The Carpenters began to accept members of the Amalgamated Carriage, Wagon, and Auto Workers in 1914, had differences with the Roofers and the Miners as well as with several other unions over cork installation and shingling, and took part in a dispute concerning the manufacture

[7]Letter from H. M. Taylor to the editor in *The Carpenter*, Vol. 25, No. 4, April 1905, p. 27.
[8]*The Labor Compendium* (weekly newspaper published by the National Building Trades Council), July 1909, p. 6, col. 2.

and repair of beer boxes and cases. Part of 1918 was spent battering the United Order of Box Makers and Sawyers into line, and at the 1920 convention disputes were announced with the Coopers and the Maintenance of Way and Railroad Shop Laborers. A few of these disputes were compromised; some, like open cankers, continued to fester and remained unsettled; none was lost.

The Amalgamated Wood Workers' Union

The dispute with the Amalgamated Wood Workers was the first, the most successful, and the most bitter of all the Carpenters' jurisdictional struggles. The background of the dispute and the economic reasons for it have been traced to 1898.[9] The next two years brought forth no new developments. Then, as the professional organizers took command of the United Brotherhood, the attitude of the leaders of both unions started to harden. After several futile attempts at compromise, both unions took their case to the AFL, and in 1902 the AFL executive council officially awarded jurisdiction over all factory woodworkers to the Amalgamated Wood Workers.

Backed by the AFL, the Wood Workers mounted an offensive. Although effective,[10] it was resisted by the Carpenters, both on the job and in the councils of the AFL. Throughout 1902 the Wood Workers, with the moral backing of the AFL, assaulted the United Brotherhood but could not pry the Carpenters out of the mills. Finally, after recriminations and counterrecriminations and a series of heated AFL-sponsored conferences, both sides agreed to put the matter to arbitration.

P. J. Downey, the AFL arbitrator, decided in favor of the Amalgamated Wood Workers' Union. He based his decision on several factors. First, McGuire had allowed the old Machine Wood Workers' Union to come uncontested into the AFL in 1891. Second, in making the 1894 Indianapolis Agreement the Carpenters, or at least McGuire, willingly had conceded jurisdiction over factory woodworkers to the Machine Wood Workers' Union.

[9]See above, pp. 82–87.
[10]Deibler, p. 172, The Wood Workers' voting strength in the AFL rose from 184 in 1902 to 272 in 1903. Each vote represents 100 members.

Third, McGuire had recognized the amalgamation of the Machine Wood Workers' Union and the Furniture Workers' Union which had created the Amalgamated Wood Workers' Union and had not abrogated the Indianapolis Agreement on that account. And, fourth, another agreement had been negotiated with the new union by McGuire in 1897.[11] Nothing points up so clearly as does the Downey award the reasons why the professional organizers wished to rid themselves of McGuire.

The Downey award was a rude shock to the Carpenters. They had accepted arbitration in the faintly lingering spirit of McGuire's brotherhood-of-labor policy. They found that to accept the spirit meant to accept the substance: the loss of their mill jurisdiction. McGuire had left the union in 1902. A year later, with the Downey award, the last trace of his spirit was gone. From 1903 on United Brotherhood officials left the realm of the spirit for those who were spiritually inclined and based their policy on three hard economic facts: first, that technological change took work from the carpenters; second, that unless jurisdiction was maintained over new processes the union and the craft might disappear; and third, that until third parties understood these facts the Brotherhood would not arbitrate questions pertaining to its jurisdiction. "Third Parties" included the AFL.

General Secretary Duffy described the new policy:

When we get down to hard facts the AFL does not approve or disapprove jurisdictional claims at any time. All that they do [sic] is publish them without assuming any responsibility for them. Therefore, if an affiliated organization extends its jurisdictional claims the AFL has no power to prevent it from doing so. . . . We reserve the right to say what our jurisdictional claims shall cover, and we don't propose that they shall be curtailed, altered, or amended through any other agency.[12]

Having made these decisions, the Carpenters pursued a jurisdictional strategy in dealing with the AFL which was to remain fixed for the next half-century. First they denied the right of AFL

[11]"Report of the Committee on the Amalgamated Wood Workers," *The Carpenter*, Vol. 23, No. 3, May 1903, pp. 5, 7–8.

[12]Frank Duffy, "Our So-called Unwarranted Jurisdiction Claims," *The Carpenter*, Vol. 26, No. 3, March 1916, pp. 5–6.

111

leaders to award jurisdictions to a union, holding that its officers could only accept or reject a union's own claim to jurisdiction. Second, they held that AFL officials could never arbitrate but were limited to mediation. This position had the effect of leaving jurisdictional disputes to the arbitration of open battle. Of the Carpenters' effectiveness in this realm the next half-century was to leave little doubt.

The strategy led to struggle, and the struggle called for tactics. Those the Carpenters pursued against the Wood Workers set a pattern for the hundreds of disputes which were to follow. In entering a struggle with another AFL affiliate, the Carpenters possessed one enormous advantage. With the exception of the United Mine Workers, they were the largest union in the Federation. Huge per capita tax payments gave added weight to their voice on the national council of the AFL as well as in its local Central Labor Unions. On either the national or local level they needed but one or two powerful allies to gain a majority vote. Jurisdictional logrolling or, as labor leaders called it, "scratching each other's back," often achieved this.

Another powerful weapon possessed by the Carpenters by virtue of size was their benefits system. This could be used to buy off individual members and whole locals of a poorer and smaller union which could offer fewer or no benefits for the same dues. Hugh Kirk of the Shipwrights' International Union described the Brotherhood's use of this financial weapon in 1908:

The methods employed emulate those of the life insurance companies of our country, namely, they offer to pay greater financial benefits to seceders...than that which they were already guaranteed by the international union of their trade.[13]

The most effective tactic, however, stemmed from the fact that the Carpenters usually erected material over which they were demanding jurisdiction. They installed every piece of building trim turned off woodworking machines. If a firm insisted on stand-

<hr />

[13]American Federation of Labor, *Proceedings of the Twenty-eighth Annual Convention of Denver, November 9 to November 21, 1908*, p. 264.

112

ing by the Amalgamated Wood Workers, the Carpenters boycotted its products. Not wishing to tie up his job, a contractor rapidly changed his supply mills. If he did not he was struck and picketed.

During the remainder of the Carpenters' struggle with the Amalgamated Wood Workers, Huber gradually developed this general strategy and its accompanying tactics with a fine Italian hand. First, to repudiate the Downey award he had to discredit it. He did this by claiming that Downey was ineligible to arbitrate because he had previously been on an AFL grievance committee which heard the dispute. Further, Huber said, he had agreed only to confer, and even though he had accepted Downey as an arbitrator, he was not bound to accept the award. The Carpenters then allowed notices to filter into the newspapers of their headquarters city, Indianapolis, suggesting that "Gompers had written the award."[14]

The Carpenters' rationalizations were lost on both Gompers and the leaders of the Wood Workers. During 1903 and 1904 the AFL declared the Downey award official policy.[15] But, for all of the formal exchanges, the dispute was gradually being resolved on the local level among business agents and in the various building trades councils. The Carpenters were past masters at this type of infighting. In New York the Central Federated Union backed a complaint of the Carpenters that the Wood Workers had organized several of their mills by working nine hours to the Carpenters' eight.[16] The Central Federated Union ordered the Wood Workers to equalize working conditions or get out.

In Baltimore the central body flatly refused to enforce the Downey award, telling Gompers that he was asking local AFL bodies to pull the national federation's chestnuts out of the fire. "Enforce the award on the national level, if you can," they told

[14]American Federation of Labor, *Proceedings of the Twenty-third Annual Convention of Boston, November 9 to November 23, 1903*, p. 243. This source did not specify which newspapers carried the claims.

[15]*Ibid.*, p. 242.

[16]The Central Federated Union was the central body of all New York City AFL locals.

him, "but if you cannot, do not ask local bodies to do so." This state of affairs prevailed in virtually all of the major cities.[17]

At the 1905 AFL convention, a portent of the grim future in store for them was given the Wood Workers' representatives. Their secretary, Thomas Kidd, was dropped from the executive council and Huber took his place as seventh vice-president.

Kidd agreed to confer again in January 1906. At this conference Huber offered amalgamation with an automatic funeral insurance benefit of $200 to all Amalgamated Wood Workers.[18] Kidd refused the offer, claiming that the Carpenters were trying to buy Amalgamated members. The executive board of the Carpenters promptly sent out a notice that all district councils were to admit Amalgamated locals, intact, under terms of this offer.

During 1906 the Brotherhood stepped up the pace of its warfare. In addition to the virtual buying of members, the boycott and even the open shop were used against the hapless Wood Workers. The Carpenters went to the extent of declaring one New York firm, which had been unionized by the Wood Workers for years, unfair.[19] Upon complaint of a Brotherhood local union, an order was handed down by the New York City Central Federated Union which had the effect of prohibiting the Wood Workers from future organizing activities in New York.

The Wood Workers reeled under this assault. The 272 votes their delegates were entitled to at the 1903 AFL convention had fallen to 200 by 1905. When the 1906 convention assembled, these had dwindled to 150.[20]

At the 1906 convention the AFL yielded ever so little to the Carpenters' might. After the combatants had gone through the protocol of mutual denunciation and demand for expulsion, Gompers managed to bring them together for a conference which bore fruit. The Committee on Adjustment triumphantly an-

[17]*The Carpenter,* Vol. 25, No. 9, September 1905, p. 17; *American Federation of Labor, Proceedings of the Twenty-fifth Annual Convention of Pittsburgh, November 13 to November 25, 1905,* pp. 71–72.
[18]UBCJA, *1906 Convention Proceedings,* p. 56.
[19]Deibler, p. 188.
[20]American Federation of Labor, *Proceedings of the Twenty-sixth Annual Convention of Minneapolis, November 12 to November 24, 1906,* p. 46.

nounced that both sides had agreed to amalgamate by November 1908 and would recommend as much to their membership for referendum approval.[21] Huber agreed then and only then to call his charges off the harassed Wood Workers.[22]

A rank-and-file Wood Workers' rejection of the proffered amalgamation was the tocsin which called the Brotherhood to arms again. So fierce did the struggle become that the planing mill owners, caught in the middle, rained petitions for relief down upon the AFL executive council.[23] The Wood Workers began to close their ranks by ousting those members who had supported the amalgamation plan. They then took the offensive in Chicago, one of their strongholds. In early May, 1907, the Chicago Mill Owners' Association announced that after May 12 its members would recognize only Amalgamated Wood Worker cards.

The Chicago members of the Brotherhood literally swarmed down upon both parties to this announcement. Carpenters refused to erect Amalgamated trim. The Brotherhood dealt with the mill owners individually, even going so far as to organize one mill 150 miles away from Chicago at 20 percent less than the Wood Workers' rate.[24] During 1907 2,500 Chicago members of the Amalgamated Wood Workers streamed out of their organization and into the Brotherhood. First one then the next mill owner lowered his standard, until, by the summer of 1908, only a few Wood Workers' locals remained out of the Brotherhood fold. These few were then banished from the ranks of organized labor in Chicago.[25] At the 1908 AFL convention, the Amalgamated Wood Workers had but forty votes.[26]

The leaders of the Carpenters then turned their attention to New York City, where the largest of the wood fixture mills, the Brunswick-Balke-Collender Company, had been organized several years previously by the Wood Workers. William Schardt, chairman

[21]*Ibid.*, pp. 209–210.
[22]*Ibid.*
[23]*Proceedings of the Twenty-seventh Annual Convention of the American Federation of Labor of Norfolk, November 11 to November 23, 1907*, p. 82.
[24]*Ibid.*, p. 270.
[25]Deibler, p. 186.
[26]AFL, *1908 Convention Proceedings*, pp. 47–48.

of the executive board, directed the fight with the assistance of three national organizers. They first declared the company "unfair." To the stunned surprise of the company's executives, their wagon drivers reported bands of carpenters with huge signs, busily pedaling behind them on bicycles, proclaiming to the world at large the company's "unfairness."

The company promptly filed a $50,000 suit against the belligerent bicyclers. The Brotherhood's leaders, by this time wise in the ways of court procedure, held off a final resolution until the company capitulated, broke its agreement with the Wood Workers, and signed up with the Carpenters.[27] The Brotherhood brought the powerful New York Manufacturing Wood Workers' Association to heel by October, 1909, and securely signed to an exclusive agreement by January, 1910.[28] Huber proudly announced that in the first year of the New York offensive three thousand Wood Workers had deserted to the United Brotherhood.[29]

As Huber delivered the Wood Workers one blow after another, their officers and their AFL allies fought a stubborn, though retreating, rearguard action. They gradually surrendered first one point, then another. At the 1909 AFL convention Gompers asked, but refused to force, the Wood Workers to amalgamate with the Carpenters.[30] At the 1910 convention the AFL executive council recommended compulsory amalgamation but was refused by the delegates, among whom sentiment for the all-but-moribund Wood Workers was still strong. Finally, in 1911, the AFL delegates told the Wood Workers to accept either amalgamation or expulsion.[31] The struggle was over; the victory for the Carpenters complete.

President D. D. Mulcahy bowed to the inevitable. He delivered a farewell message on behalf of his organization, now a scant cor-

[27]Carpenters and Joiners of America, United Brotherhood of, AFL, *Proceedings of the Fifteenth Biennial Convention of Salt Lake City of September 21 to October 2, 1908*, pp. 298–299.

[28]"Report of First General Vice-President Arthur A. Quinn," *The Carpenter*, Vol. 30, No. 10, October 1910, pp. 29–31.

[29]UBCJA, *1908 Convention Proceedings*, p. 390.

[30]American Federation of Labor, *Proceedings of the Twenty-ninth Annual Convention of Toronto, November 8 to November 20, 1909*, pp. 290–291.

[31]American Federation of Labor, *Proceedings of the Thirty-first Annual Convention of Atlanta, November 13 to November 25, 1911*, pp. 114–116, 322. The vote margin was 15,374 to 409.

116

poral's guard (four thousand in all) of the immense army of thirty thousand workers he had once led:

They [the Carpenters] have already driven over twenty thousand [wood workers] out of the labor movement. They have got some men, it is true, but in the vast...centers of industries today there is very little effort towards organizing these men and there is less success attained than ever before.[32]

The merger plan was drawn up on January 10, 1912, by Presidents Huber and Mulcahy. The terms provided complete membership in the United Brotherhood of Carpenters and Joiners of America for Wood Worker members, both individually and as locals. The only concession granted them as a national organization was the promise that the next convention of the Brotherhood would appoint a committee composed solely of delegates from factory locals to draw up laws to govern all factory workers.[33]

Thus died a union which, nine years before its death, had been the twelfth largest, and one of the fastest growing, of the AFL unions. It died in spite of a bona fide AFL charter, AFL approval of its label, approval of its stand against the Carpenters by nine consecutive AFL conventions, a favorable arbitration award, and support by the officers and the executive council of the AFL, which was withdrawn only at the eleventh hour.

The expansion of the United Brotherhood's jurisdiction effected a basic change in the structure of the union. The first signs that the leaders were groping their way to some kind of new unionism became evident. They did not call this new unionism industrial unionism, however, but instead referred to their expansion as the complete organization of the craft. " 'One craft; one organization' is our motto," Duffy told the 1904 convention, "and we do not propose to deviate one iota until that end has been accomplished."[34]

Earlier, Duffy had struck somewhat closer to the truth when, speaking in industrial rather than craft terms, he said, "every man employed in the wood-working *industry*...ought to belong to the

[32]*Ibid.*, p. 321.
[33]See below, pp. 195–196, for the results of this committee's deliberation and pp. 197–198 for the subsequent treatment accorded the Wood Workers.
[34]UBCJA, *1904 Convention Proceedings*, pp. 45, 80.

United Brotherhood."[35] In their desire to be in no way associated with the radical ogre of industrial unionism, the Brotherhood's leaders continually referred to any new groups of workers they claimed as "branches of the craft." In subsequent years, the Brotherhood's "branches" were to spread sufficiently far and wide to deprive whole industrial unions of the sunlight necessary to trade union growth.

The leaders of the United Brotherhood had no intention, however, of subordinating the carpenters to the industrial workers. President Mulcahy had accused the Carpenters of wanting to get only those few factory workers they felt compelled to organize and of being willing to wreck a union and strew the unwanted members to the wind to accomplish their goal. And there is much truth in his accusation. When in December, 1903, Huber and Duffy conferred with Kidd and Mulcahy, the two Wood Workers proposed a "federation where we would recognize the cards of each organization." Huber refused, for the same reason McGuire had refused a similar proposal eight years before.[36] In Huber's words, "With the conglomeration of the different trades their organization is composed of it was beyond us to bring about the results they desired." Later he continued, "I have hopes that the *class of mechanics that we claim jurisdiction over* and who belong to... [the Amalgamated Wood Workers' Union] will see the advisability of transferring... to the United Brotherhood."[37]

It is difficult not to construe these statements as meaning, "We want some, but not all, of your men." The "some" wanted were the most highly skilled, who turned out trim once made by the carpenter. As for the lesser skilled, it is likely that the Carpenters felt that they could not effectively house them in the United Brotherhood. One of the better informed contemporary observers, Professor Frederick Deibler, reported after investigating the Wood Workers during the last stages of the dispute that in Chicago and New York City, after defeating the Wood Workers' Union, the Carpenters took in only its most skilled members.[38]

[35]*Ibid.*, p. 45 (italics mine).
[36]See above, p. 85.
[37]UBCJA, *1904 Convention Proceedings*, p. 37 (italics mine).
[38]Deibler, p. 187–188.

Membership figures for the millmen in the Brotherhood during the years of the struggle give further credence to this line of thought. At the outset of the struggle (1904), Frank Duffy reported 60 machine hand locals, with a total membership of 7,917.[39] Three years later, he reported 69, with a total membership of 12,789.[40] This represented a net gain of only 5,272 mill workers, according to official Brotherhood figures. Yet during this same period the Amalgamated Wood Workers reported a loss of 19,000 members.[41] These figures would seem to indicate that over 13,000 workers were lost in the shuffle.[42] There can be little doubt that the Brotherhood took in only those Wood Workers it wanted, allowing the rest to drift.

Thus, between 1902 and 1912, the United Brotherhood cleared the field of its most important rival and spread its jurisdiction over the length and breadth of the woodworking industry, albeit with nose upturned in craft selectivity. Where 68,463 members were reported to the last convention over which McGuire had presided, at the end of 1912 there were 244,388.[43]

Most of the Brotherhood's struggles, at least in their more formal aspects, were fought out in the councils of the AFL. As the Carpenters changed their jurisdictional policy and hence their structure, the AFL was towed in their wake and also changed its jurisdictional policy and structure. A federation greatly different from the one which heard the Carpenters' first disputes in 1902 emerged from the decade of jurisdictional struggles just recounted.

[39]UBCJA, *1904 Convention Proceedings*, p. 65.

[40]Carpenters and Joiners of America, United Brotherhood of, AFL, *Report of General Secretary Frank Duffy for the year ending Dec. 31, 1907*, p. 13.

[41]American Federation of Labor, *Proceedings of the Thirty-second Annual Convention of Rochester, New York, November 11 to November 23, 1912*, p. 65.

[42]The figures given above are only for mill hands organized into millmen's locals and presumably do not include millmen in mixed locals with house carpenters. The Carpenters did not at this time officially publish total figures for all millmen.

[43]Carpenters and Joiners of America, United Brotherhood of, AFL, *Proceedings of the Sixteenth General Convention of Washington, D.C., September 17 to October 1, 1912*, p. 211.

CHAPTER IX

Craft or Industrial Unionism:

1902 to 1912

ONE student of the AFL wrote of the federation as follows:

Of 133 national unions, most of them affiliated with the American Federation of Labor, only 28 may be called craft unions. . . . Only 5 of the national unions claim jurisdiction over all trades in an industry. The remaining 100 are of an intermediate type.[1]

This "intermediate type" is the craft-industrial union, one composed of all or parts of several industries built on tasks once done by the key craft of that union. The United Brotherhood became this kind of union when it had absorbed the first union which had the misfortune to trespass on its jurisdiction. The AFL became a federation of craft-industrial unions when, after ten years of resistance, its leaders were forced to adapt its policy to the Carpenters' tactics. To relate the story of how and why the AFL became a craft-industrial federation it is necessary to return to the 1890's.

Just before the turn of the present century, a foreign observer, Professor Louis Vigouroux, who was studying the United Brotherhood, characterized it as a "double movement," one on the national level of "distinct trades," and one on the various local levels of

[1] T. W. Glocker, "Amalgamation of Related Trades in American Unions," *Trade Unionism and Labor Problems*, John R. Commons, ed. (2nd series), p. 362.

120

"unions interested in the building industry."[2] Professor Vigouroux described the United Brotherhood in this fashion because the emphasis placed by its leaders on building trades council development was sufficiently strong to give its district councils and local unions a definite industrial union cast and to make the Carpenters the leading force in the formation of such councils in all of the middle-size and larger cities of the United States.[3]

The Brotherhood's strange and apparently conflicting emphasis on the craft form on the national level and the industrial form on the city level can be traced to two causes. The first was the localized market structure of the industry, which made the concerns and needs of carpenters in one city separate and distinct from those of carpenters elsewhere.[4] Naturally, under these circumstances the interests of local leaders tended away from the national union.

The second cause was the interrelatedness of building work. Although the skills of carpenters and, for instance, bricklayers are distinct and in no measure interchangeable, each must work closely with the other and with all other crafts on the job. Until the iron and cement workers have done one part of the job, the bricklayers and carpenters cannot do their part. If one building craft strikes, all the other trades are made idle. Consequently, wage demands and strike actions must be coordinated.

For these reasons the new national unions of building trades craftsmen which cropped up in the 1880's and 1890's could not organize without the aid of building trades councils, and the power of the building trades councils in the 1890's grew faster than that of the new national unions. When the industrial revolution overtook the building industry in the same decade, the building trades councils were very nearly autonomous units.[5]

Although almost all of the influences of this revolution led to the growth of national unions in the building trades, strong localizing forces had dug a gully of custom into which most building trades

[2]Louis Vigouroux, *La Concentration Ouvrière en Amerique du Nord*, p. 79.
[3]*Ibid.*, pp. 102–103.
[4]See above, pp. 3–7.
[5]William J. Spencer, "The Building Trades as Organized Prior to the Formation of the Building Trades Department," *American Federationist*, Vol. 23, No. 7, July 1916, p. 559.

council leaders had fallen by the mid-1890's. "Why not meet problems of national scope posed by the industrial revolution by forming a national federation of building trades councils?" many local leaders asked. As a result local building trades leaders started to turn away from their craft nationals and the AFL and toward a national organization of local building trades councils.

Thus was the National Building Trades Council, another child of the industrial revolution in the building trades, born in 1897. It was formed by a group of local building trades councils claiming to represent some fifty thousand workers. Its leaders immediately turned toward industrial unionism, announcing in their first circular that they sought "closer amalgamation of building trades workmen to establish...a national working card [and] an equalization of wages in the different crafts."[6] Its constitution provided only one convention vote for any national union which might join its ranks, while it also granted one vote to each of the many building trades councils.[7]

Because the National Building Trades Council bypassed the craft nationals, and because if successful it could not fail to lead to an industrial union in the building trades, the national leaders of the Carpenters opposed it from the outset. For several reasons, however, their opposition was, at best, lukewarm. First, in 1897 the Brotherhood was still a weak national federation of strong district councils which, on their home grounds, were often more powerful than the national union. Not until a good many years later was the national office of the Brotherhood able effectively to extend its rule to the various cities. As a result many Carpenter locals and district councils affiliated with the National Building Trades Council, and carpenters provided some of its most effective leadership.

Second, the leaders of the Carpenters and of the other building trades unions sympathized with the National Building Trades Council's quest for building trades autonomy. One of the major goals of the men who founded the National Building Trades

[6]National Building Trades Council, "An Appeal to the Building Trades Workmen of America," as quoted in UBCJA, *1898 Convention Proceedings*, p. 61.

[7]"Constitution of the National Building Trades Council," *Weekly Labor Compendium*, Dec. 26, 1897, p. 1.

Council was "to have our differences adjusted by men from our own ranks."[8] Here the founders clearly alluded to the pique which building trades men felt because their affairs were handled by the Central Labor Unions of the AFL.[9] They considered these local bodies not only useless, but also, at times, millstones around their necks. Unions in other industries could wait two weeks or even a month for the deliberations of a Central Labor Union before striking; the building trades unions could not. The very nature of the new industry emerging from an industrial revolution demanded that they strike quickly and silently.[10]

Finally, the Carpenters' opposition to the National Building Trades Council was weak because the council acted as a lever to force Gompers to grant the building trades unions special consideration within the AFL. Although the Carpenters introduced, and the 1897 convention of the AFL passed, a resolution denouncing the National Building Trades Council as a dual union, they also complained to Gompers that the "Federation never attempted to cooperate with the building trades."[11]

Gompers gradually and reluctantly responded to this pressure. He decried to the 1899 and 1900 AFL conventions the independence of the building trades but advised the Central Labor Unions to form distinct, though not separate, building trades "sections."[12] Again, in 1901, he scored the mounting trouble given the AFL by separatist groups of local building trades workers but announced to the AFL convention that in May he had ordered all central bodies to establish subordinate building trades sections.[13]

The formation of the National Building Trades Council presented Gompers with an entirely new problem. Although this organization was as dual as any which ever faced the AFL, its founders were not at variance with AFL philosophy. They were neither advocates of the "one big union" idea of the older Knights

---

[8]UBCJA, *1898 Convention Proceedings,* p. 62.

[9]Central Labor Unions were federations of all AFL local unions in a given city.

[10]F. J. McNulty, "Building Trades Department," *The Carpenter,* Vol. 29, No. 11, November 1909, p. 13.

[11]AFL, *1897 Convention Proceedings,* pp. 62, 104.

[12]American Federation of Labor, *Proceedings of the Nineteenth Annual Convention of Detroit, December 11 to December 20, 1899,* p. 8; AFL, *1900 Convention Proceedings,* p. 9.

[13]AFL, *1901 Convention Proceedings,* p. 18.

of Labor nor close cousins to the radicals who wished to steer the AFL in the direction of socialism. To the contrary, they were among the oldest and most active supporters of the AFL's job-conscious and pragmatic craft unionism. They simply felt that, under the pressure of technological change, the AFL would have to alter its structure.

The industrial revolution in the building trades was wiping out old craft jurisdictions and creating new ones. As a result it was causing disputes among the various craft unions. Both the Carpenters' jurisdictional policy and the separatist movement in the building trades were tactics designed to meet the problem of clashing jurisdictions. The Carpenters were not only standing on their jurisdiction and eliminating all usurpers, supposed and real, but also they were offering the AFL a new policy of "one trade, one union."[14] If applied, this policy would have been an abrupt departure from the policy of chartering distinct crafts independent of the industry. And the National Building Trades Council, in striking out for a closer association of building trades on the local and national level, was also offering a new policy which, applied within the AFL, would have altered its structure. But whatever the nature of the solution, the problem of technologically induced jurisdictional strikes remained the same.

That this problem faced the AFL at all is one of the strange ironies of history. Craft unionism, Gompers' synthesis of the labor problem of the 1880's, had generated by 1900 a host of tiny splinter craft unions. Their existence constituted an antithesis which could be solved only by a new thesis. Mention has already been made of the fact that shortly after the turn of the century the Brotherhood's jurisdiction was being nibbled away by a swarm of small, specialist carpenters' unions.[15] The Carpenters did not suffer alone. Most of the older and larger unions were exposed to the same annoyance because Gompers insisted on chartering any group which could, however vaguely, present itself to the labor world as a trade union.

[14]See above, pp. 117–118.
[15]See above, p. 81.

He did not realize that yesterday's pragmatism could become tomorrow's folly.

A survey of Gompers' chartering activities between 1899 and 1904 shows that he chartered craft unions where often neither craft nor union existed. In 1899 the AFL admitted the Glass Bottle Blowers and the Coal Hoisting Engineers; in 1900 the Chainmakers, Watch Case Engravers, and Wire Weavers; in 1901 the Watch Case Makers, Paving Cutters, and Blast Furnace Workers; and in 1902 the Piano and Organ Workers, the Tube Workers, the Special Order Clothing Workers, the Gold Beaters, the Window Glass Snappers, and the Print Cutters all received charters and entered the AFL. In 1903 the Glass House Workers, Elevator Constructors, and Tip Printers stood up to be counted. In 1904 even the humble Tack Workers struck out on their own. When, in the same year, the smoke finally cleared, it was revealed that a total of seventy-five new international unions had been chartered in the previous six years.[16]

It is obvious that many of these ambitious little trade groups encroached upon established unions just as the specialized carpenters' unions were encroaching upon the Brotherhood. In this policy of blindly splintering the structure of the trade union movement at a time when industry was consolidating is to be found the genesis of the jurisdictional dispute. Crafts splintered and jurisdictions crossed. Finally, in 1900, the AFL convention urged that "narrow conceptions of autonomy be abandoned and that disputes be settled through amalgamation." The convention also warned the executive council that henceforth it would do well to demand a clearer definition of jurisdiction before granting charters.[17]

Throughout 1901 the mounting pressure of jurisdictional disputes made it plain that the next AFL convention would have to formulate an over-all jurisdictional policy both to guide its officers in chartering new unions and to help its member unions in adapting to technological change. The result of the next convention's

[16]American Federation of Labor, *Proceedings of the Thirtieth Annual Convention of St. Louis, November 14 to November 26, 1910*, p. 66.
[17]Lewis Lorwin, *The American Federation of Labor*, p. 68.

deliberations was the Scranton Declaration. Much ado has since been made of this document as the ultimate expression of the AFL's brand of trade unionism. Subsequent AFL leaders canonized it. In point of actual fact, and in terms of the immediate problems facing the AFL at that time, it was one of the most slippery, equivocal, and, therefore, innocuous trade union documents of all time. Its every sentence turns upon itself before its end.

The Declaration starts off by saying that "the future success, permanency, and safety of the American Federation of Labor, as well as the trade unions themselves, depends upon the recognition and application of the principle of [craft] autonomy. . . ." Then this flat-footed craft union stand is rendered meaningless. The sentence ends, "consistent with the varying phases and transitions in the industry." Reduced to essentials, the Declaration left the leaders of the various affiliated unions with two alternatives: strict "organization on trade lines," or "jurisdiction. . .by the paramount organization" in any industry containing closely related crafts.[18]

These were exactly the alternatives which faced the convention when it opened. For what was the position of the Amalgamated Wood Workers in their quarrel with the Carpenters but a demand for organization along what its leaders considered "strict trade lines," or that of the United Brotherhood but what its leaders considered "jurisdiction by the paramount organization in the woodworking industry?" The leaders of the Brotherhood, who were getting more and more short-tempered with the AFL, were not pleased. They saw the Scranton Declaration for what it was, "an ingenious straddle" which "left the matter as it stood before."[19]

This was the background against which the jurisdictional disputes of the Carpenters described in the last chapter got under way. With an industrial building trades union cropping up under the AFL and with the Carpenters relentlessly pressing their "one trade; one union" policy, it remained for the events of the next eleven years to force Gompers to choose between the two interpretations capable of being placed on the ambiguous Scranton Declaration.

The officers of the AFL immediately made it clear which of the

[18]AFL, *1901 Convention Proceedings*, p. 240.
[19]"Delegates' Report," *The Carpenter*, Vol. 22, No. 3, March 1902, p. 12.

two they preferred. Gompers, Secretary Frank Morrison, and Treasurer John B. Lennon all favored sharply defined and, perforce, fairly small craft jurisdictions.[20] In 1902 they admitted fourteen new national unions,[21] some of which represented ridiculously minute crafts. When the 1902 convention met, Gompers announced that the problem of jurisdiction was the most important one then facing union labor, and he noted that every affiliate of the AFL was involved in one or more disputes. Still, he made it plain that he was thinking in terms of paper autonomy rather than practical economics when he said:

It is not an uncommon occurrence for an organization...to so change their...claims to jurisdiction as to cover trades never contemplated by the organization's officers and members; never comprehended by their title; trades of which there is already in existence a national union. And this without a word of advice, counsel, or warning.[22]

He could not have more clearly singled out the Carpenters had he taken Frank Duffy's nose between his fingers and tweaked it. Gompers then asked that the delegates come out flatly against such union raiding.[23]

The Carpenters simmered. Their delegates carried instructions demanding the suspension of the Amalgamated Wood Workers' Union,[24] denying the right of the AFL to decide jurisdictional questions, and threatening to withhold their per capita tax if not given their way.[25] The AFL executive council answered them by strongly supporting their antagonist and rejecting their claims.[26] The majority of the delegates, who shared the Council's sentiments, also refused to grant the Brotherhood any concessions. Instead they ordered the conference which produced the Downey award during the next year. The officers of the AFL refused to recognize that the Carpenters' jurisdictional fights, the AFL's chartering policy, and technological change were all inextricably bound to-

[20]Lorwin, p. 69.
[21]American Federation of Labor, *Proceedings of the Twenty-second Annual Convention of New Orleans, November 13 to November 22, 1902,* p. 41.
[22]*Ibid.,* p. 16.
[23]*Ibid.,* p. 17.
[24]*Ibid.,* p. 52.
[25]UBCJA, *1902 Convention Proceedings,* pp. 195–197.
[26]AFL, *1902 Convention Proceedings,* pp. 140–141.

gether. In chastising the Carpenters they took a moral approach to what was essentially an economic problem.

When during 1902 the Carpenters refused to abide by the Downey award, their relations with the AFL hit an all-time low. They hung on to their affiliation only by the slimmest of threads.[27] *The Carpenter* was weighed down with spirited letters berating Gompers and the AFL. Still Gompers continued blithely chartering small, specialized trade unions. Twenty more were chartered in 1903, several of which trespassed on the Carpenters' jurisdiction.[28]

This extreme application of craft union principles cut the Carpenters to the quick. The dispute with the Amalgamated Wood Workers, in fact the Amalgamated Wood Workers' Union itself, seemed to them the child of this poorly conceived "autonomy" policy, and it demonstrated the dangers inherent in such a course at a time when technological evolution had rendered jurisdictional lines so fluid. An editorial in *The Carpenter* struck back at Gompers through the medium of his own union.

If it is advisable to separate the...mill hands from the United Brotherhood...then it is equally as advisable to separate the filler and binder stripper, the bunch makers, and cigar roller and the packers from the Cigar Makers' International Union; or to separate the Linotype Operator from the International Typographical Union, and the Cracker, Biscuit, Cake and Bread Baker from the Bakers' International Union. Let...each of these branches form a little national body of their own, and the result will be controversies, friction, and complete demoralization.[29]

This editorial struck to the heart of the matter. "Controversy" and "friction" were present; "demoralization," due in very large measure to the internal friction generated by Gompers' "autonomy" policy, had set in.[30] Surveying the turmoil, Gompers found only that "it is not an uninteresting fact...that there were applica-

---

[27]UBCJA, *1902 Convention Proceedings*, pp. 186–187.

[28]American Federation of Labor, *Proceedings of the Twenty-third Annual Convention of Boston, November 9 to November 23, 1903*, p. 40.

[29]Editorial in *The Carpenter*, Vol. 23, No. 11, November 1903, p. 5.

[30]Lorwin, p. 76. He cites this friction as one of three reasons for the AFL's sharp decline in 1904.

tions from one or more international unions for the revocation of the charters of 30 international unions" during 1903.[31]

Although the Carpenters' free-for-all method of settling their jurisdictional troubles hardly redounded to their credit, it is difficult to see how, under the circumstances, they could have done otherwise. They were pressured by the force of economic events on one hand, and on the other by an unyielding AFL policy which not only ignored economic facts, but flew in their face. In the absence of a guiding policy which should have emanated from the AFL in these times of economic transition, the Carpenters were forced to plot their own course.

The AFL maintained its firm stand against the Carpenters throughout 1903. On October 2, the executive council refused official sanction of their new label because it would appear on manufactured goods over which the Amalgamated Wood Workers had jurisdiction.[32] The delegates to the 1903 convention upheld the action of the council by pigeonholing the Carpenters' resolution protesting this action. The Grievance Committee soundly berated the Carpenters for ignoring the Downey decision, and its report ended by ordering the Downey decision to be "sustained and enforced in all localities."[33] This was an open declaration of war.

On the broader question of jurisdiction the leaders of the AFL doggedly maintained their craft autonomy position, vetoing a resolution which would have established a commission to study the "natural causes of the jurisdictional controversies in a clear and concise manner."[34] The executive council plainly took a swipe at the Carpenters by pronouncing that jurisdictional disputes were caused primarily by unscrupulous souls who desired "enlargement of jurisdiction for the sake of the power thus secured."[35] The effect had been mistaken for the cause; the moral approach was still preferred to the economic one.

On the closely related question of separate authority for the

[31] AFL, *1903 Convention Proceedings,* p. 19.
[32] *Ibid.,* p. 179.
[33] *Ibid.,* pp. 136, 243.
[34] *Ibid.,* p. 116.
[35] *Ibid.,* p. 217.

129

building trades unions,[36] the convention created a standing fifteen-man Building Trades Committee to handle all building trades affairs and enlarged the executive council from six to eight vice-presidents so as to include two building trades members. It had been made clear earlier, however, that the full executive council, the butchers, bakers, and candlestick makers, would still determine the final resolution of all building trades matters.[37] The leaders of the AFL were as opposed to giving separate industries special consideration as they were in favor of extreme craft autonomy.

The Committee on the Executive Council's Report enunciated the official position on building trades autonomy when its spokesman said:

We believe that the interests of the building trades can best be served by regarding these trades as part and parcel of the whole movement, not as a separate and distinct entity, having separate, distinct, and peculiar interests. The committee feels that it cannot too strongly deprecate the idea which...underlies the suggestion of a separate authority to deal with building trades questions as such.[38]

The humblest business agent could have told the executive council that while the building trades certainly had many things in common with other unions they just as certainly had other interests that were "separate and distinct" that could be settled only by the building trades unions themselves. The makers of this declaration were sowing the wind. In 1904 they reaped the whirlwind. During that year the AFL continued to encourage the growth of splinter unions by chartering eleven more.[39] At this juncture the two problems of building trades independence and "craft autonomy" dovetailed, and Gompers had a full-blown secessionist movement on his hands.

Chagrined generally by the jurisdictional policy of the executive

[36]The question of separate authority for the building trades was closely related to that of jurisdictional disputes because the building trades wanted separate authority to settle their own jurisdictional quarrels.

[37]AFL, *1903 Convention Proceedings,* pp. 213, 215, 217. At the 1902 AFL convention the first Building Trades Committee was established. It was made permanent and standing at this convention.

[38]*Ibid.,* p. 214.

[39]American Federation of Labor, *Proceedings of the Twenty-fourth Annual Convention of San Francisco, November 14 to November 26, 1904,* p. 40.

council and specifically by the knuckle-rapping administered to them over the Downey award affair, the Carpenters had extended feelers to the National Building Trades Council in 1903.[40] All year long Duffy and Secretary W. J. Steinbiss of the National Building Trades Council carried on a postal flirtation.[41] Finally Steinbiss sent his chief organizer, J. W. Adams, a member of the Brotherhood, to Indianapolis to personally urge the Carpenters to affiliate.[42]

Subsequent events proved that the disaffiliation of the Carpenters was a much more apparent than real threat. While it continued, however, it gave Gompers some difficult moments. More Brotherhood members were on the executive board of the National Building Trades Council in 1903 than members of any other union.[43] On the local level the Carpenters supplied the backbone of the National Building Trades Council's resistance to the AFL central bodies as well as to employers. Furthermore, in wooing the Carpenters Steinbiss had flatly refused membership to the Amalgamated Wood Workers and had given the Carpenters jurisdiction over certain disputed classes of lathing and shingling.[44]

The Brotherhood did not join the National Building Trades Council in 1903 because of the manner in which it weighted the vote against national unions.[45] If Gompers' federation placed too much emphasis on craft autonomy, Steinbiss' placed too much on local autonomy. In the summer of 1903 the Carpenters were faced with two national federations from which to choose, neither of which, given their policies, could possibly meet the Carpenters' needs. Huber took the only course open to him; he formed a third national federation, the Structural Building Trades Alliance.

The Carpenters had been toying with the idea of a third federation for some months before founding it in 1903. In early August

[40]UBCJA, *1904 Convention Proceedings,* p. 140.

[41]For a record of this correspondence see National Building Trades Council, *Proceedings of the Seventh Annual Convention of Sioux City, September 12 to September 17, 1904,* pp. 12–16.

[42]*Ibid.,* p. 16. The United Brotherhood's national officers had done nothing to prevent individual members or local unions from affiliating.

[43]*Ibid.,* p. 15.

[44]*Ibid.,* p. 13.

[45]UBCJA, *1904 Convention Proceedings,* p. 140; see above, p. 122.

Duffy issued a call to conference to six of the largest building trades unions. They met on August 26, made Duffy temporary chairman of the conference group, and decided to call a convention of the "basic building trades." The Structural Building Trades Alliance held its first convention on October 8, 1903, in Indianapolis, the headquarters city of the Carpenters. Nine of the "basic trades" of the building industry were represented.[46] John Kirby, president of the Carpenters Chicago District Council, was chosen first vice-president of the new federation.[47]

The Structural Building Trades Alliance was an interesting and important attempt to resolve the jurisdictional dispute by initiating a new kind of unionism, custom-made for an age of rapid technological evolution. In philosophy and structure it was built to meet the current needs of the Carpenters. It struck first at the AFL policy of issuing charters to splinter crafts born of the industrial revolution. Its secretary, William Spencer, said:

The transformation of the building trade from its old line of construction is another feature that has forced this Alliance to organize. . . .

.　　.　　.

The skilled. . .of every trade [are being effaced] by the substitution of materials, the construction and installation of which can be performed by men of scarcely any training.

.　　.　　.

The natural heirs of building specialties and tributary trades are those men of the *primary* or *basic* traces. . . .Acting in concert, we can . . .claim these specialties that of right belong to us. . . .
It is not the intention. . .of this Alliance to indiscriminately accept to membership the several trades engaged upon building work, since many of the. . .trades simply install. . .one special fixture. . .in the building, and are, therefore, not in any sense strictly building men.[48]

Following this logic the leaders of the Structural Building

[46]Frank Duffy, "Report of Committee Appointed by Gen. Pres. Huber to Attend Conference of Representatives of Structural Building Trades," *The Carpenter*, Vol. 23, No. 11, November 1903, p. 3. This group was composed of the Carpenters, Painters, Plumbers, Bricklayers, Laborers, Iron Workers, Plasterers, Engineers, and Electrical Workers.

[47]UBCJA, *1904 Convention Proceedings*, p. 41.

[48]William J. Spencer, "Structural Building Trades Alliance of America," *The Carpenter*, Vol. 25, No. 3, March 1905, pp. 5–6 (italics mine).

Trades Alliance staked off eight "basic" building fields, designated one trade "paramount" in each field, and awarded jurisdiction over work in the field to the union of that trade.[49] To counter the strong force of localism encouraged by the National Building Trades Council, representation was granted only through the medium of national unions. One of the founders stated flatly that "the men who have inaugurated this movement...want...a National Federation of Building Trades without any Building Trades Councils, all work to be done through the executive heads."[50]

This tolled the death knell of the National Building Trades Council. Its largest national affiliate, the Painters, forsook it for the Structural Building Trades Alliance. The only remaining national unions were a small group of splinter unions which huddled together to escape the icy blasts soon to be sent in their direction by the newly federated basic trades. Over the next five years the Council slipped first into impotency and then into oblivion.

The founders of the Structural Building Trades Alliance were also aware of the problem of separate organization for the building trades which had been plaguing the AFL executive council for four years. Secretary-Treasurer J. C. Skimp of the Painters' Union stated in a letter to Steinbiss that the founders of the Structural Building Trades Alliance "believe the time has come when National Building Tradesmen must do something to protect their interests from the interference of [AFL] central bodies."[51]

The Structural Building Trades Alliance was thus designed to pressure the AFL into taking three steps: stopping the chartering of small splinter unions, supporting the claims of the various "paramount" crafts for amalgamation of all unions within their groups, and organizing the building trades separately within the AFL. When the officers of the AFL made cautious inquiries as to the

---

[49]The eight basic groups and the trades given jurisdiction over them were as follows: wood, the Carpenters; masonry, the Bricklayers; pipe fitting, the Plumbers; decorating, the Painters; plastics, the Plasterers; iron, the Bridge and Structural Iron Workers; motive power, the Hoisting Engineers; common labor, the Hod Carriers (Spencer, "The Building Trades as Organized Prior to the Building Trades Department," p. 562).

[50]NBTC, *1904 Convention Proceedings,* p. 9.

[51]*Ibid.*

purpose of the new federation, Secretary Frank Duffy of the Building Trades Committee gave some inkling of its true purpose in his reply. "[We] hope that . . . the Structural Building Trades Alliance may become part and parcel of the AFL.[52]

The formation of the Structural Building Trades Alliance marked a turning point in AFL policy. In 1905 Gompers admitted only three new unions.[53] This new caution was to become permanent policy. From 1906 to 1910 only seventeen new charters were issued. Palpably fearing the influence of the new federation, in 1906 Gompers also began moving slightly away from his extreme craft autonomy position. He began to emphasize and even to praise the number of amalgamations taking place among related trades.[54] Toward the end of the 1906 convention, on the motion of Chairman Huber of the Building Trades Committee, the convention sanctioned a conference of all building trades officers to be held during the coming year.

The conference was held in Indianapolis in early 1907 and another was held in the spring of the same year in Pittsburgh. Finally, on October 26, a full-dress conference was held between representatives of the Structural Building Trades Alliance and the AFL.[55] The AFL was represented by carpenter Huber and the Structural Building Trades Alliance by carpenter Kirby.[56] The Building Trades Department of the AFL, which eventually grew out of this conference, could not have been more a child of the Carpenters' creation had the United Brotherhood's label been stamped upon its charter.

In his report to the 1907 convention Gompers edged still further away from his extreme autonomy position. "Trade unions are not rigid organizations. . . . In truth . . . [they] are flexible," he said. Then he hailed the jurisdictional dispute as a sign of this flexibility: "The constantly increasing claims to jurisdiction are themselves evidence of the evolutionary character of trade unions,

[52] AFL, *1904 Convention Proceedings*, p. 267.
[53] AFL, *1910 Convention Proceedings*, p. 66. During 1903 and 1904 he had admitted thirty-one new unions (*ibid.*).
[54] AFL, *1906 Convention Proceedings*, p. 14.
[55] Spencer, p. 563.
[56] AFL, *1907 Convention Proceedings*, p. 76.

which endeavor to expand their membership and adapt themselves to the various branches of industry under their jurisdiction."[57]

Toward the end of the convention the Building Trades Committee recommended the creation of a Building Trades Department with separate conventions and with power to charter building trades councils distinct from AFL central bodies. The unanimous passage of this proposal indicates how thoroughly Gompers had succumbed to the pressure applied by the building trades.[58] President Kirby of the Alliance said, "The agitation created and success attained by the S.B.T.A. is the main reason why the building trades were granted complete autonomy over their own affairs without a dissenting vote."[59] Then, speaking of the order issued by Gompers which created the Building Trades Department, Kirby said, "It gives us exactly what we want, nothing less—strict autonomy and the right to charter local bodies."[60]

Having eliminated the problem of autonomy for the building trades, Gompers continued to move closer to the Carpenters on the subject of jurisdiction. In 1909 he had the AFL recognize the Brotherhood's label and began nudging the Wood Workers gently into amalgamation. Finally, at the 1911 convention, the Carpenters were given all they demanded. Chairman James O'Connel of the Committee on Adjustment flatly stated the new policy. "I want to say right in the beginning that our committee is unanimously of the opinion that there is room for but *one organization of one trade* in America, and we are starting right out on that line."[61] The Committee on Adjustment ordered amalgamation for the Amalgamated Wood Workers as an alternative to expulsion.[62]

The action of the 1911 convention of the AFL marks a significant turning point in its history, one of greater significance than the Scranton convention which had simply posed the problem of juris-

[57]*Ibid.*, p. 20.
[58]*Ibid.*, p. 303. See below, pp. 173–180, for the details of the creation of the Building Trades Department and the Carpenter's relations with the Department until 1915.
[59]"Report of James Kirby, President of the S.B.T.A. to the Board of Governors, December 28, 1907," *The Carpenter*, Vol. 28, No. 1, January 1908, p. 12.
[60]*Ibid.*, p. 13.
[61]AFL, *1911 Convention Proceedings*, p. 311 (italics mine).
[62]*Ibid.*, pp. 113–116.

dictional policy in an age of technological change. After a decade of running strife the Atlanta convention of the AFL declared soundly for the principle of organization by the paramount craft in an industry rather than for craft autonomy. No one union had more to do with forcing the AFL into this position than the Brotherhood.

The AFL executive council recognized the importance of the work of the 1911 convention. Its 1912 report stated:

Every effort has been made to carry into effect the spirit as well as the letter of the declaration of the Atlanta Convention of one organization for one trade; that duality and rivalry must cease so far as we have the power to enforce it.[63]

This statement was placed directly above a restatement of the Scranton Declaration and, to put at rest any doubt that it was meant to modify this earlier declaration, the executive council re-defined the term "autonomy." Some people, the council noted, had interpreted the idea of autonomy as being in opposition to that of amalgamation. "No such construction or interpretation can be justly given the term," the report declared. "Every effort has been made by the AFL [and] the Executive Council... to bring about amalgamation."[64] Although the officers of the AFL continued to burn incense before the Scranton Declaration, the Atlanta Declaration guided them in practical matters after 1911.[65]

[63]AFL, *1912 Convention Proceedings,* p. 114.
[64]*Ibid.,* pp. 114–115.
[65]The inauguration of the Building Trades Department and the pronouncement of the Atlanta Declaration together gave the AFL in 1912 a structure vastly different from that which it possessed in 1902. This craft-industrial structure allows for the existence of craft unions where they are feasible. It allows for craft-industrial unions like the United Brotherhood where technological evolution calls for an industry to be organized about its principal trade. And, finally, it allows for separate departments, each with its own structure, to house complete industries where technology calls for industrial unions.

In 1935 this structure failed temporarily to meet the needs of the mass-production workers over issues to be discussed in Chapter XIX. However, in 1955 these issues were resolved by the creation of still another, an industrial, department. The AFL-CIO exists today as the world's largest trade union movement with much the same structure the United Brotherhood helped give the AFL a half century ago.

CHAPTER X

The Struggle for Power:

1902 to 1912

WHILE during the years covered by the past two chapters the new leaders concerned themselves primarily with affairs of jurisdiction, they did not neglect the union's internal political affairs. Although all of the many new leaders agreed substantially upon jurisdictional policy, they did not agree on which persons should administer it. Almost immediately after McGuire had been pushed to one side, they set upon each other. A bitter struggle for power swirled unabated around the higher offices of the union for ten years. This struggle was not so much over policy or structure as over naked personal power; it determined the pecking order. It ended only when a balance of power between the executive board and the other national officers had been struck. At this point the search for national institutions which had started twenty-four years before came to an end, and with it the constitutional history of the United Brotherhood.

The 1902 convention afforded the new leaders the opportunity for which they had waited so long and so impatiently. Like so many schoolboys with the teacher at long last out of the room, they wreaked havoc. The general treasurer's office was made full-time and salaried and separated from that of the general secretary; the general secretary was stripped of all of his policy-making powers and was made a combination clerk, advocate, and major-domo to the general president; the general president was made full-time and salaried at $2,000 per annum, and was given the power to appoint organizers, with or without local sanction, in addition to all of the powers held by McGuire. Provisions were made for the trial of general officers properly accused; two new members were added to the executive board; the per capita tax was raised to twenty-five cents; the general headquarters was moved to Indianapolis; a label was adopted; and new laws were passed regulating officers' reports, finances, and the administration of the journal. Only one of the sixty-five measures passed by the convention failed to pass the referendum: the raised per capita tax.[1]

Shortly after the convention adjourned, the general office was shifted from Philadelphia, the center of nineteenth-century trade unionism, to Indianapolis, the center of early twentieth-century trade unionism. A new and brisk efficiency became apparent in the administration of the organization. Monthly local reports, grievances, strikes, trials, disciplinary cases, and per capita tax payment were all tightly controlled and administered.

The most important issue confronting the organization during the last decade of McGuire's rule, the constitutional position of the executive board, however, still remained. The board was still part-time, unsalaried, and completely independent of the three general officers. Its seven members were still elected at large. And although the general president received some new powers, there was little to choose between McGuire's power in 1900 and Huber's in 1903. The fact that the two men used substantially the same powers in vastly different ways does not alter this basic fact.

Huber immediately started to erect a political machine. The only machine McGuire had possessed was the sentimental attachment of the rank-and-file carpenters. Yet because of what he failed to do McGuire must be given a good measure of responsibility for the machine erected by Huber. He failed to build democratic safeguards around the great power he had amassed. He failed to

---

[1] "Amendments to the Constitution as Adopted at the Atlanta, Ga. Convention, September 15–30, 1902," *The Carpenter*, Vol. 22, No. 11, November 1902, pp. 2–3; "Result of the General Vote on Amendments to the Constitution Submitted at Atlanta," *The Carpenter*, Vol. 23, No. 1, January 1903, chart accompanying p. 16.

create a hierarchy of union executives, starting at the lowest local level and running up through district councils, states, and regions to an executive board responsible at all levels to the membership.[2]

McGuire's reluctance to share power prevented the creation of democratic avenues of approach to the national office and opened a vast gulf between the national office and the local district councils. While the union was small he bridged this gulf personally, but as the union expanded the gap widened, the bridge collapsed, and he lost contact with the district council leaders. When McGuire was finally overthrown, the administrative gap became a power void. No one of McGuire's personal stature stepped forward to fill it, and in the absence of representative administrative machinery the void was filled by the Huber-Duffy machine.

The same men who fought so doggedly in 1900 for a democratic plan of representation did not utter one word of it or a similar plan once in office. Rather they filled the void with swarms of professional organizers and hence with a political machine, for these organizers were hired, fired, paid, and administered completely by Huber. The constitution in no way regulated them. It is with the existence of these organizers that an analysis of the Huber machine must begin.

Organizing in 1902 was a relatively well-paid ($4 per day) and pleasant job for a workaday carpenter. Huber's ability to dole out these jobs, like the ability to dispense any patronage, gave him a substantial power to influence the powerful district councils. Thus obligated to Huber, the organizers took all of the president's powers, implicit and explicit, with them into the field. They also carried with them general office appropriations. As one group of carpenters complained a few years after Huber organized his corps of organizers, the constitution of the Brotherhood did "not provide for the appointment of organizers or for any regulation...[of] the duties or work to be done by them, or for any official regulation as to their appointment or the supervision of their work." They went on to say that in the absence of control, "organizers have been appointed and retained in some localities to the detriment and injury of the United Brotherhood

[2]See above, pp. 68–70, 73–74.

against the expressed will and desire of the members interested, thereby arbitrarily setting aside the rights of local unions."[3]

Furthermore, Huber used the organizers to influence elections and the referendum voting. In one quarterly report, speaking of an imminent vote, he said, "I hope that every officer of the Brotherhood, as well as all of our organizers and business agents will . . . see to it that a favorable vote is rendered from their district."[4] One carpenter complained that "organizers were in the convention for political purposes only . . . [they] had a certain amount of influence in the convention and . . . they used that influence in behalf of certain candidates."[5] In 1910 the organizers at the convention openly admitted that they had caucused as organizers and had manipulated Huber's re-election at the 1906 and 1908 conventions.[6]

At each convention a batch of "fraternal delegates," powers in the various district councils, were present on Huber's invitation. If a local opposition group could engineer the election of nonmachine delegates, they were forced to operate under the stern gaze of the real powers back home. How many working carpenters from San Francisco could, or would, stand up against P. H. McCarthy, Mayor of San Francisco; or from New York City, against Robert Brindell, overlord of the New York building trades?

After 1902 the committees which did all of the real work of the convention were invariably rigged. The presidentially appointed committee members were paid up to $10 a day. This also represented a source of administrative patronage which, if small in number of dollars, was important in terms of control of the convention. Never, after 1900, did the committees fail to report for the administration and against the opposition. One committee, established to hear and judge his report to the

---

[3]UBCJA, *1908 Convention Proceedings,* p. 372. In this case, Huber had sent a group of organizers into Pittsburgh and had taken control of the whole district council out of the hands of the man who had opposed him in the previous election.

[4]*The Carpenter,* Vol. 32, No. 5, May 1912, p. 23.

[5]Carpenters and Joiners of America, United Brotherhood of, AFL, *Proceedings of the Sixteenth General Convention of Des Moines, September 19 to September 30, 1910,* pp. 425–426.

[6]*Ibid.,* p. 426.

convention, at a time when Frank Duffy was being attacked by an especially strong minority, said:

We cannot do otherwise but congratulate the United Brotherhood . . . in having such an able Secretary as Brother Duffy. No man could make any better report. . . . We cannot let the opportunity pass without congratulating our General Secretary for placing such an intelligent and instructive report to our convention. . . . Nothing has been left undone by him . . . to elevate and improve the United Brotherhood. We look upon the report . . . as one of the best . . . ever made in . . . history.[7]

This report speaks volumes on the methods Huber used in choosing the committee personnel.

Delegate George L. Murphy of Tacoma described the convention system erected by Huber as:

Unrepresentative and inadequate because it practically disfranchises a large majority of our Local Unions . . . who find the expense of sending representatives to the convention prohibitive. . . . [This system] throws the control of the conventions, and consequently the policy of the organization, into the hands of a few of the larger unions.[8]

If, perchance, a hostile man or measure did elude the convention, there was still the referendum gauntlet to be run. One referendum vote compilation committee reported that "The present method of election of General Officers seems . . . to be a clumsy and costly one, and if continued will ultimately wreck the organization." The report went on to complain that the referendum system placed a "premium on illegal voting" and that the recording secretary of a local union could disfranchise the whole union by making some minor mistake in filing the returns "either through carelessness or intent."[9]

Nor were such practices uncommon. Referring to the 1912 election, Thomas Ryan of New York, one of the tabulators, said, "You

[7]Carpenters and Joiners of America, United Brotherhood of, AFL, *Proceedings of the Seventeenth General Convention of Washington, D.C., September 17 to September 20, 1912,* p. 604.

[8]Carpenters and Joiners of America, United Brotherhood of, AFL, *Proceedings of the Nineteenth General Convention of Fort Worth, September 16 to September 28, 1916,* pp. 272–273.

[9]"Report of Committee on Compilation of Vote for General Officers," *The Carpenter,* Vol. 31, No. 2, February 1911, p. III, appendix.

could stretch out fifty or one hundred ballots on the table and even to a little curve on the cross all were alike."[10] In the counting of the vote, "ballots were thrown out because they were folded, and some were thrown out because they were not folded."[11] Almost every election from 1904 to 1912 was disputed. The administration won each of them. President William L. Hutcheson subsequently admitted that the election in which he first assumed office (1913) was rigged.[12]

Yet Huber and Duffy had great difficulty in running their machine smoothly. McGuire had been content to maintain a loose organization. Huber tightened it, and the willful locals revolted. While the opposition was never quite able to oust Huber, neither was he ever quite able to control local leaders in their own bailiwicks. The 1902 convention was the first and last from which he exacted a per capita dues boost. Five successive conventions turned him down. Neither did he succeed in raising his salary, in effecting an apprenticeship system, in stopping the use of the initiative to amend the constitution, nor in regulating local benefits and, to some extent, strikes. While he succeeded in consolidating his machine, he did so only after a knockdown, dragout struggle which lasted, off and on, for eight years.

Opposition to Huber first appeared at the 1904 convention. Since, for all its reforms, the 1902 convention did not essentially change the constitution, the executive board was still balanced against the general officers. Under the care of too many cooks the porridge rapidly came to a boil. Between 1902 and 1904 the executive board, led by Chairman Henry Meyer of California, heard that it had been "flimflammed"[13] in the matter of presenting bids for the monthly journal. Upon investigation the members discovered that the printer had informed his competitors that bidding "was a mere formality" and that he would be awarded the con-

[10]*Ibid.*, p. II. Ryan meant that in his opinion the ballots had been marked by one man.

[11]UBCJA, *1912 Convention Proceedings,* p. 638.

[12]"Boss Carpenter," p. 123. William L. Hutcheson was elected second vice-president in 1912.

[13]UBCJA, *1904 Convention Proceedings,* pp. 142–143.

tract.[14] The board then took over the printing of the journal and managed to save $1,000 by instituting a new system of bids.

When the 1904 convention met, the executive board issued an unprecedented report to the convention. It suggested strongly that bribe money might have passed hands in the printing affair and asked that Duffy be forced to keep invoices and a sales book of all future purchases. The report also scored Huber's personal organizers who "rove[d] at will" and who were both expensive and ineffective.

The antiadministration forces tried but failed to capture the committee which considered this report.[15] When the report was finally made on the ninth day of the convention, it completely exonerated the general officers of either negligence or corruption. "This committee," it said, "does not approve of the policy pursued by the...Executive Board in conducting its investigation."[16]

The floor debate on this report occupied most of the next three days. After a good many delegates had gone home, the report received the support of the convention by a 318 to 117 vote.[17] Election of the new executive board was one of the last acts of the convention, and five of the seven incumbents were defeated by the administration slate. Franklin Pimbley, chairman of the committee which had exonerated the officers, led the slate.

Although this revolt was potentially dangerous, in fact it was weak. None of the board members was firmly enough entrenched to constitute a true threat. They fared as well as they did because Huber was still warming to the feel of power. Several of Meyer's moves were portentous, however. He charged Huber with corruption, as Huber had charged McGuire. He made a bid for some of Huber's important administrative tasks. And, most important, he made a mild pass at the organizers, Huber's vital lifeline to the various district councils. These were to become classic tactics in the power game during the ensuing decade.

From 1904 to 1906 Huber had a tractable executive board and

[14]*Ibid.*
[15]*Ibid.*, pp. 143–144.
[16]*Ibid.*, pp. 275–276.
[17]*Ibid.*, p. 282; "Our Thirteenth General Convention," *The Carpenter*, Vol. 24, No. 11, November 1904, p. 2.

143

had no opposition from that quarter. But the carpenters were not yet machine broken, and opposition mounted steadily from 1906 to 1909. In 1906 the opposition came from a coalition, led by August Swartz, of local officers of the Pittsburgh district council. Two years later it came from First Vice-President Tim Guerin, Huber's chief organizer. Both of these men ran for the presidency and were defeated. Neither posed a serious threat because neither had a foothold on the executive board.

Swartz was dismissed by the simple expedient of the executive board's taking over his district council on the grounds of corruption and poor administration of a strike.[18] The board established direct national rule in Pittsburgh, dismissed the existing officers, and shook up and consolidated the locals.[19] Guerin lost an election in which the votes of no less than 204 locals were disqualified for any one of several technical mistakes alleged to have been made in filing the ballots.[20] The executive board rejected an objection over this wholesale disfranchisement,[21] just as earlier it had taken over the Pittsburgh district council.

That the executive board could be a powerful group was not lost on Board Member William G. Schardt, who was eyeing Huber's presidency with interest in early 1909. The 1906 opposition had been grass roots, from the bottom. In 1908 it had come from the top, from Huber's own official family. From 1909 to 1912 Schardt led opposition from the vital middle region: the executive board. The executive board stood midway between the national officers at the top and the local business agents at the bottom. In hostile hands it could easily command on either level or on both. For the next four years the executive board members struck out for control in both directions.

This revolt was no passing thing to be swept aside with a vote counting or a district council reorganization. It was given

[18]J. C. Kephart, "In Justice to the D.C. and to the Members of the Pittsburgh District," *The Carpenter*, Vol. 28, No. 4, April 1908, pp. 36–37.

[19]UBCJA, *1910 Convention Proceedings*, pp. 239–240.

[20]"Report of the Committee on Tabulation of Vote for General Officers," *The Carpenter*, Vol. 29, No. 2, February 1909, pp. 116–118.

[21]"Minutes of the Proceedings of the Second Quarterly Session, 1909, of the General Executive Board," April 19, *The Carpenter*, Vol. 19, No. 6, June 1909, pp. 21–22.

substance from the outset by the presence of William G. Schardt. Schardt was at ease in the high councils, for this was his third two-year term as a board member. He also had powerful connections back home, where he was president of the Chicago Federation of Labor. He manipulated the election of three other local leaders to the 1909–1910 board,[22] thus gaining majority control of the board which, though part-time, had members who were full-time local union officials.

Schardt first reached for a share of Huber's administrative duties at the April 1909 meeting of the board. Henceforth, he ordered, Huber was to clear all purchases of supplies, all appropriations for lawsuits, strikes, and local unions with the executive board. He then flicked lightly at Huber's powerful force of organizers, ordering that they no longer be paid a per diem allowance when in their home town.[23]

Huber was incensed. He called the board "in on the carpet," Board Member Connolly later reported:

It was rather an innovation to me; I was under the impression that we were co-ordinate officers in this organization....We went in...and Duffy and Neale were also present—when the fire works began. We were asked why we "butted in"...and we were given to pretty plainly understand that it was none of our business.[24]

Several days later Schardt asked for the account book with which to audit the stock of office supplies. Duffy begged off on the grounds the book had been mislaid. The stock was not audited.[25] When Duffy produced the long-sought-after book in July 1910, Board Members W. A. Cole and Dan Post checked the stock. As had always been the custom, the other board members rubber-stamped their clearance.

Schardt, however, was suspicious. After the meeting adjourned he lingered in the supply room to thumb through the book. What he saw set wheels turning: erasures, falsifications, and sup-

---

[22]These three were John Walquist of Minneapolis, serving his second term, and Charles Bauscher of New York and Robert E. L. Connolly of Birmingham, both of whom were serving their first term.
[23]"Minutes of the Proceedings of the Second Quarterly Session," p. 22.
[24]UBCJA, *1912 Convention Proceedings*, pp. 531–532.
[25]*Ibid.*, pp. 523–524.

plies sent out with no record of cash received.[26] Here at last was a chink in Huber's armor. Schardt immediately decided to press his advantage. If he kept the book a secret until after the 1910 convention (then but six weeks away), he could run against Huber, reveal this evidence of malfeasance on the eve of the election, and run off with the victory.

Schardt kept quiet, and preparations for the convention were launched. At the convention Schardt and Tom Ryan of Local Union 471, New York City, led a coalition of New York and Chicago rebels against Huber. Both Schardt and Huber were strong men wise in the ways of union machines. In their struggle at the convention they resembled two dualists, thrusting, parrying, and occasionally scoring. Schardt first tried to prevent the seating of fraternal delegates, powers back home in the large district councils and invariably proadministration. He failed. Then he turned to Huber's corps of organizers. He pushed through two laws, one limiting organizers to communities in which two-thirds of the members requested them, and another preventing them from acting as delegates to future conventions.[27] He then turned directly upon Huber and tried to strip him of power to pass on district council and local union bylaws and to prohibit him from effecting local strike settlements. After this failed, the Schardt faction sponsored an amendment making the chairman of the board (Schardt) and the secretary (Connolly) salaried, full-time executives of the union. The amendment gave the chairman of the board the vague power to "devote...[his] entire time to the business and interest of the U.B."[28] Had it passed, the measure would have made Schardt a second general president and Connolly a second general secretary and would have led rapidly to mayhem in Indianapolis.

Schardt had not won the day, but in hobbling Huber's organizers he had scored a telling point. Huber countered with a proposal that the executive board members be made full-time salaried organizers under the direction of the general president. The board

[26]*Ibid.*, pp. 524–525.
[27]UBCJA, *1910 Convention Proceedings,* pp. 432, 425–426.
[28]*Ibid.*, pp. 450–451.

was a pawn in a game of power politics. As Huber had checkmated Schardt's move, so Schardt checkmated his. The measure was defeated. Palpably fearing Schardt's strength in a referendum vote, Huber then tried to have the constitution amended so as to eliminate the referendum vote and to have the convention delegates elect as well as nominate candidates for office. Again Schardt checkmated him.[29]

When Schardt placed himself in nomination against Huber for the presidency, a long and complicated floor fight occurred over the choice of a tabulating committee to tally the election returns. The opposition to the administration captured four of five positions, with Tom Ryan, a free-swinging New York carpenter, in the lead. Bit by bit Huber was surrendering his strong points. The 1910 convention was a major disaster for him. He had lost control of his organizers and of the all-important tabulating committee. Now with the convention at an end he turned to face a hostile executive board in the flush of victory and eager for the kill.

Immediately after the convention disbanded, Schardt held an unprecedented meeting of the executive board at headquarters.[30] Throughout October Schardt, Walquist, Bauscher, and Connolly spent their time scrutinizing every aspect of the administration. Then, late in October at a special evening session of the board, Schardt let fly a thunderbolt. According to Board Member Cole, Schardt "arose in a dramatic manner and said, 'You boys just might as well know there is a great discrepancy in the books.' It struck me like a clap of thunder or a California earthquake. . . . Then I began to realize about the whispers that I heard."[31] The next morning Huber, Duffy, and Neale were called into the board room and told of the shortage, and the services of an expert accountant were engaged.[32]

[29]*Ibid.,* p. 438.
[30]The constitution provided only for quarterly executive board meetings and for none between August and December.
[31]UBCJA, *1912 Convention Proceedings,* p. 566.
[32]"Minutes of the Proceedings of the Fourth Quarterly Session, 1910, of the General Executive Board," October 29, *The Carpenter,* Vol. 31, No. 2, February 1911, p. 22. Lybrand, Ross Brothers and Montgomery, a reliable firm, was engaged for the job. Their manager, Walter A. Staub, was in charge of the subsequent inventory (*ibid.,* p. 37).

From this play of forces a classic pattern of union politics was emerging. The executive board was the chief prize. In 1888 rebels captured the executive board and forced reforms on McGuire. In 1902 a hostile executive board engineered McGuire's downfall. Two years later another executive board tried, but failed, to turn Huber out. At the 1910 convention Schardt tried to make the executive board dual to the national officers. In terms of our federal constitution, this would have been equivalent to the appointment by Congress of a shadow cabinet to help the President administer the government.

In terms of the personal struggle for power, almost every one of these revolts featured at least a hint, and often an accusation, of corruption. McGuire had been pulled from power by such an accusation. Now, in 1910, Schardt repeated these tactics. Said Duffy, "It was politics. . . . Someone [Schardt] was running for General President Huber's position. . . . They wanted to find something wrong at the home office. . . . Then the dirty circulars would go the rounds."[33]

When the executive board left headquarters, Tom Ryan and his tabulating committee roared into the office, spoiling for a fight. The Ryan Committee, on counting the ballots, found false election dates, different types of handwriting signing one man's name, ballots too clean and uncreased to have been handled by individual voters, and a score of other fraudulent techniques.[34] Many examples of fraud in the voting and recording of the vote, as well as in the final tabulation, were revealed.[35] Ryan stated that as the count progressed he was "threatened with violence."[36]

The air was thick with accusations. The general officers were called crooks and the members of the tabulating committee frauds. Huber was accused several times of being drunk,[37] and a good many brawls were but narrowly averted. When the smoke of battle finally cleared on January 24, it was discovered that Huber

[33]UBCJA, *1912 Convention Proceedings*, pp. 471–472.
[34]"Report of the Committee on Compilation of Vote for General Officers, January 24, 1911," p. II.
[35]*Ibid.*, p. V; UBCJA, *1912 Convention Proceedings*, p. 627.
[36]UBCJA, *1912 Convention Proceedings*, pp. 632–633.
[37]*Ibid.*, pp. 632–633, 638, 639.

had won by 131 votes.[38] The chart below shows the number of votes disqualified and the reasons for disqualification. Huber's local supporters had delivered, apparently, just 131 more votes than Ryan and his friends could reasonably disqualify.

Table V. The Disputed Election of 1911: Invalidated Votes

Reason for Invalidation	Number of Votes Invalidated	
	Huber	Schardt
Illegal Markings..	7,153	1,243
No Date on Returns.............................	656	189
Voted Ahead of Time.................................	762	261
Not Properly Attested..............................	536	327
Voted After Date......................................	1,162	607
Held Too Long Before Mailing.......................	2,674	1,574
Total Ballots Invalidated.........................	12,943	4,201

Source: "Report of Committee on Compilation of Vote for General Officers of January 24, 1911," *The Carpenter,* Vol. 31, No. 2, February 1911, pp. LX, LXIII, LXVII, LXXIII, and LXXIV.

While Huber was locked in battle with the tabulating committee, the accountants pored over Duffy's books. On December 31, 1910, they came up with a report which cleared the officers of any possibility of embezzlement.[39] It just as clearly charged Duffy, however, with a degree of maladministration which made McGuire, by comparison, seem an efficiency expert. Schardt had been on firm ground in believing a shortage existed.

The whole affair was aired before the membership in the February 1911 issue of *The Carpenter.* Side by side were printed the accountants' report, the executive board's accusation, a rejoinder by Duffy, an account of the vote for general president, and the majority and minority reports of the tabulating committee. Here matters stood when the new executive board, a pro-Schardt group, met for the second time in the spring of 1911.

The chairman of the new executive board was R. E. L. Connolly, one of the leading lights in the Birmingham district council, and the secretary was Charles Bauscher, business agent of the New York district council. These men could speak with authority, and the board immediately made a palpable bid for power. Its members

[38]*Ibid.,* p. 628.
[39]*Ibid.,* p. 410; "Report of Expert Accountant to General Executive Board," *The Carpenter,* Vol. 31, No. 2, February 1911, pp. 31–37.

rode tight rein on the general officers, closely scrutinizing all administrative details. In the course of its last three meetings in 1911 and the first meeting in 1912, the board sustained Huber in only seventeen out of fifty-two appeals from his disciplinary actions.[40]

After almost two years of retreat, in the summer of 1912 Huber made a bold bid to regain full control. In a letter to Local Union 327 of Cincinnati he announced that organizers, always the key to control of the union, would be eligible as delegates in the forthcoming convention in spite of the ruling passed by the previous convention forbidding their presence. Huber reasoned that this ruling conflicted with other parts of the constitution (although the 1910 convention had instructed him to eliminate all older parts of the constitution which disagreed with any new law) and that the constitution "guarantees to all members certain rights...and no convention of the United Brotherhood has a right to submit to a referendum vote...any law which will take from any member ...rights...guaranteed him by the constitution.[41] This was tantamount to denying members the right to change the law of their organization. In effect, it gave Huber the right of constitutional review.

The struggle over organizers was joined as soon as the convention assembled and "the whole delegation was divided into two camps to fight out the future destiny" of the union.[42] Twenty-five delegates, representing powerful local unions from all parts of the country, protested the seating of organizers. When the majority report of the credentials committee was read, Bauscher contested it with a minority report.[43] In the course of the debate, Duffy, Huber, and P. H. McCarthy spoke for the administration and

[40]"Minutes of the Proceedings of the Second, Third, and Fourth Quarterly Sessions 1911 and First Quarterly Session 1912 of the General Executive Board," as cited in *The Carpenter*, Vol. 31, No. 6, June 1911, pp. 14–26; Vol. 31, No. 8, August 1911, pp. 19–28; Vol. 31, No. 11, November 1911, pp. 20–25; Vol. 32, No. 3, March 1912, pp. 17–25.

[41]UBCJA, *1912 Convention Proceedings*, pp. 21–23.

[42]Frank Duffy, "Our Thirty-Fourth Anniversary—Looking Backward," *The Carpenter*, Vol. 35, No. 1, January 1915, p. 4.

[43]UBCJA, *1912 Convention Proceedings*, p. 20. Huber probably placed Bauscher, a known enemy, on the credentials committee because the contesting forces were so evenly balanced.

150

Bauscher and Ryan for the opposition. Huber took the body of the convention through two roll calls before he went down to defeat. The organizers were not seated.[44]

The convention also took up the report of the tabulating committee and decided, after a long and heated debate, that the "dead past should be forgotten." With this, the whole matter was dropped. The stock scandal, however, was debated hotly and almost caused a brawl. Duffy and Huber, Schardt and the members of the executive board, all spoke and defended their policies. Each group had fought the other to a standstill and no alternative remained but to put the case up to the convention. After all the tactics of popular debate had been exhausted, Walquist raised the basic issue. "The Executive Board [members]," he said, "[are] the representatives of our membership, and the three . . . general officers the same . . . [on] the other side. . . . I am never going to be a tool for the general officers."[45]

Here was the pith of the matter. Since 1881 the union had been divided between two sets of rulers. Ten years of bitter internecine quarreling apparently drove this point home to Huber. This latest revolt convinced him that the fault rested not with himself or with those who revolted but in the union's structure. The delegates to the 1912 convention supported the measures Huber advanced to put an end to the administrative division at the top of the union's structure. They voted to make executive board members full-time and salaried, and they placed them under the supervision of the general president. The general president and general secretary were placed on the board with voice and vote. The former was made chairman and the latter secretary of the board.[46] With the passage of these laws the revolt automatically ended in a victory for the administration forces.

These changes were made by local leaders in their capacity as convention delegates because they had tired of the costly and divisive struggles between the general officers and the executive board which had marred the union's existence since 1884. The delegates

[44]*Ibid.*, p. 56.
[45]*Ibid.*, p. 553.
[46]*The Carpenter*, Vol. 32, No. 11, November 1912, p. 60.

put an end to such struggles by eliminating the executive board as the free, interconvention policy-making arm of the union. By making the general president chairman of the executive board, the delegates placed the whole organization firmly in his grip and demoted each board member to lieutenant in charge of organizing in a given district. Twenty-four years later, Executive Board Member Arthur Martel defined the status the board members have had since 1912. "The Board members of the United Brotherhood have no power whatever...when [not] in session....Between sessions we are subject to the orders and instructions of the General President."[47] That power which the board possessed when in session, Martel might have added, was only paper power.

Thus was a power void created years before by McGuire finally filled in 1912. Henceforth there was to be only one avenue to headquarters: the machine. Deprived of access to the top, subsequent protests were to be pathetic and feeble cries. Since 1912 the United Brotherhood has been troubled by neither grass-roots nor palace revolts. Unity had been purchased at the price of democracy.

Only the last inevitable payment was made in 1912, however. The down payment was made in the 1890's, when business agents were given unbridled power to dispense jobs and to call strikes.[48] Accountable only to a membership more concerned with job control than with the refinements of democracy, the tenure of the business agents was guaranteed as long as they protected and preserved the craft and its working standards. Under these conditions, basic power in the union soon came to rest in the hands of the business agents, who proceeded to entrench themselves behind local union machines.

With the advent of the jurisdictional dispute, the power of these machines was challenged. If they were not settled in favor of the carpenters, many members would have been lost to other unions. Those carpenters who remained would soon have deposed their business agent leaders for failure to protect the craft.

[47]Carpenters and Joiners of America, United Brotherhood of, AFL, *Proceedings of the Twenty-third General Convention of Lakeland, Florida, December 7 to December 15, 1936*, p. 306.

[48]See above, pp. 9, 62–66, for the reasons why the business agents received this power.

But since jurisdictional disputes could be settled only on the national level, local machines had to be consolidated into one national machine. Like local business agents, the national officers had to be empowered to act swiftly and arbitrarily in jurisdictional disputes.

Once McGuire was ousted, the last barrier to consolidation of the various local machines was swept aside. Huber started to merge them into one huge national machine through the medium of a corps of professional organizers, of which each of the members was a graduate business agent. From its national vantage point, this corps directed the various business agents as they went about their appointed task of protecting the carpenter's craft.

Consolidation, however, was rendered a difficult task because of the existence of an independently elected executive board. Such a board was a democratic anachronism resting at the top of an organization which had been rendered basically autocratic by local business agents. Instead of presenting a constitutional safeguard against the abuse of national power, the board served as a readily available approach to that power. Down this avenue marched one group after another of men who challenged not Huber's right to build, but to operate, the national machine. By sealing off this avenue, the 1912 convention put an end to a dispute of thirty years' standing and established the structure of the United Brotherhood as it exists today.

Huber, however, was not to enjoy the pleasure of ruling the newly unified union. Opposition to him personally was so strong that it is likely that he would have lost had he run. By stepping down, he guaranteed the perpetuation of his machine.[49] After a bitter fight, the convention passed a motion to pay him $2,500.

The administration slate then won a complete victory in what a subsequent president of the Brotherhood called yet another rigged election.[50] Bauscher, Connolly, and Walquist were swept off the executive board and a more compliant group took office. James Kirby, an administration man out of Chicago, defeated Schardt for general president, and Duffy defeated Connolly for

[49]UBCJA, *1912 Convention Proceedings,* p. 596.
[50]"Boss Carpenter," p. 123.

general secretary. When Kirby assumed command he became the first general president to rule a truly united organization.

The disputes related in this chapter were between two groups, the executive board and the general officers, to determine which were to be the national agents of the business agents. And as the business agents ruled, so, perforce, would the winners of the struggle have to rule: autocratically. An independently elected executive board represented committee rule in an autocratic situation. It was but a matter of time until the executive board members, like Napoleon's other two proconsuls, were cut down to size.

CHAPTER XI

Label Unionism: 1902 to 1912

IN SPITE of their preoccupation with internal struggles and jurisdictional disputes, the leaders of the Brotherhood pursued the more prosaic and conventional economic activities of the union with dispatch and efficiency during the years covered by the previous three chapters. Membership rose from 122,568 to 218,794 during this decade, and in 1913 the Brotherhood was the largest of the so-called craft unions. Since this growth led the Carpenters into new industrial fields, the union was forced to undergo still further adaptations, both in policy and in structure, to accommodate the workers in these new fields. Policy changes were essential to organize the new millworkers, structural changes to administer their needs as union members.[1] Before describing these changes, it is necessary to return to the early years of the Brotherhood's existence and to trace its relations with the employers up to 1902.

The first effective national intertrade employers' association in the building trades, the National Builders Association, was formed in 1887 as a result of the eight-hour strikes. Although this organization enjoyed some initial successes in the early 1890's,[2] its fortunes started to ebb in the depression of 1893, and its last convention was held in 1899. This decline was due both to the forces of

---

[1] This chapter will deal only with policy changes. The changes in union structure which were made to accommodate the millworkers and which resulted from policy changes will be explained in Chapter XIII.

[2] See above, pp. 70–71.

localism and the endeavor to join diverse trades in "one big [employers'] union." Primarily, however, it declined because its philosophy ran counter to the hard facts of the industry. Its leaders sought the right of the employer to run his own shop without interference from the union, or, in today's terminology, the open shop. In each of the cities where building trades unionism was coming into its own, however, the great majority of contractors found union leaders properly conservative chaps open to reason. Employers repeatedly discovered, as did union leaders, that they stood in a fair way to be of great benefit to each other. Since the National Builders' Association, the only national intertrade employers' association, was antiunion, local employers gradually abandoned both national and intertrade organization for the more limited but more attractive prospect of working with the unions on the local level. Since the unions were set up on a craft basis, so also were the new employers' associations. During the 1890's the employers dropped all pretense of intertrade organization and in all of the major cities dealt with the union of their trade through an employers' organization of the same trade. By the late 1890's none of the major urban centers boasted a citywide building employers' association.

While their employers peacefully slumbered, the union leaders were busily working. Behind the leadership of the Carpenters, they pounded out city-wide, intercraft building trades councils.[3] By the mid-1890's most of the building trades in New York City were in the building trades council,[4] and the same stage of growth had been reached in Chicago, San Francisco, and most other large urban centers. In all of these cities the building trades councils were controlled by a small cabal of business agents.

Thus organized into building trades councils, business agents provided extensive services for the contractors. It took but little time for the organized business agents to look down from their well-fortified position and to see that payments for services rendered could easily be extracted from disorganized and unprotected

---

[3] See above, pp. 120–122.
[4] John R. Commons, "The New York Building Trades," *The Quarterly Journal of Economics,* Vol. 18, No. 5, May 1904, p. 411.

employers. Union racketeering thus came to pass in all of the larger cities during the mid-1890's. In New York City the notorious Sam Parks of the Iron Workers held the building trades in a vise-like grip. In Chicago the colorful Martin B. "Skinny" Madden of the Steam Fitters' Helpers controlled the trades, and in San Francisco the handsome, fluent, and astute Patrick H. "Pin Head" McCarthy was czar of the trades. All were firmly entrenched by the turn of the century.

These men and others like them were, by any definition, beyond the pale of the law. They were not innovators, however. They introduced little that was new to building industry racketeering but simply forced the contractors to pay their share of the expense incidental to mulcting the building public. For over a decade the contractors had made exclusive agreements and price-fixing arrangements with materials dealers, trade union leaders, and with each other. Now these contractors were pressured into paying the piper by trade union leaders as dishonest as themselves but more forceful.

The contractors set up a hue and cry of "racketeering" as these trade union extortionists applied pressure. Then in 1900 or shortly after, the contractors mounted an offensive in many of the larger cities. Slogans of "liberty to work," "individual freedom," and "open shop" were designed to convince the paying public that the contractors were more sinned against than sinners. One business publication, describing the holier than thou position taken by the New York City contractors, pointed out the facts:

What the public hears . . . about arbitration, open shop, liberty to work, ten commandments, and golden rule is all surface talk. Revelations of graft are not isolated cases. Parks was an example, but corruption was deep seated and permeated the trades. The evil is fundamental. The public is beginning to inquire how far the organization of the employers' association was the effect of internal abuses and of illicit disunion among the employers. The Association was necessary not only against the demands of labor but also against the lax code of the building trades. In the course of the connection between labor and the employers each had used and misused the other to such a degree that self respect has vanished. For years the employers in New York City had been inclined to look upon the Manhattan market as a special possession of their own, a local domain. There was a general tendency toward exclusiveness throughout the entire building trades. The idea of "protection" was applied to a certain group of the trades. The employers and labor had different points of view but a similar motive. This protection expressed itself in a gradually developed system of "interference." This weapon of interference whether it worked directly or indirectly, . . . had for its main object the protection of the New York markets. The owners of real estate in New York paid the bill. Labor was a partner and shared in the pie. Parks was at one time a straight fellow but he breathed a poisonous atmosphere in the employers' office. The organization of the employers marks, in a general way, the point at which the loss came in for at least one of the parties. There was no longer enough in it for two. The employers had their protection but the unions made them pay for it. When the employers' association was created it was necessary not only to continue to protect the market but to protect against labor. Labor had lost the respect of the employers as a body. Open market and open shop were not desired but the employers wanted the unions to be less exacting.[5]

Across the country the pattern of increasing unity among building trades employers emerged from 1900 to 1904.[6] In Chicago the employers formed the Building Employers' Conference Committee in 1899, and in 1900 a bitter lockout of a year's duration ensued.[7] In San Francisco the Building Trades Council and the Millmen's Employers' Association locked horns over a United Brotherhood millworker strike in 1901. The Millmen's Employers' Association tried at this point to unite all of the various employers' associations in a city-wide building trades employers' association,[8] but failed.[9] In New York City a jurisdictional strike between the Brotherhood and the Amalgamated Society[10] caused the contrac-

[5]*Real Estate Record and Builders' Guide* (New York City), Vol. 72, Aug. 8, 1903, p. 244, as quoted in Haber, *Industrial Relations in the Building Industry*, pp. 354–355.

[6]*Real Estate Record and Builders' Guide*, Vol. 74, July 9, 1904, p. 58.

[7]Royal Montgomery, *Industrial Relations in the Chicago Building Trades*, pp. 23, 28–32.

[8]Frederick L. Ryan, *Industrial Relations in the San Francisco Building Trades*, pp. 105–106.

[9]See below, p. 160.

[10]The Amalgamated Society of Carpenters and Joiners was the American branch of an English trade union of the same name. At its height it had 9,000 members, and after ten years of intermittent struggle with the Carpenters it was absorbed by the United Brotherhood in 1915.

tors to form the New York Building Trades Employers' Association in 1903.[11] Here too, a long and costly lockout ensued between the new organization and the building trades council.

This fierce and united front convinced the Carpenter leaders that the bosses were intent on destroying building trades unionism. In February 1904 Duffy warned the carpenters to gird their loins for protracted battle.[12] At the biennial convention later in the year, Huber and Duffy dwelt at great length on the new employers' associations and the open shop drive.[13]

The employers remained on the offensive throughout 1904, picking off local Brotherhood unions city by city. In August 1904 the New York contractors locked out the Carpenters.[14] In early 1905, after a compromise settlement in New York, a lockout was ordered in Pittsburgh.[15] The Interstate Association of Builders harassed the Brotherhood in most of the larger New England cities.[16]

The tactics used by the employers revealed their talk of "liberty" to be less than sincere. In Milwaukee the Building Trades Employers Association used the sympathetic lockout. In Louisville the employers had their own business agent with the same arbitrary powers possessed by his union counterpart. In Houston the employers forced materials dealers to withhold supplies from union contractors.[17] Elsewhere they formed company unions, forced the nonunion shop upon industrial contractors, utilized a reference card or "blackball" system, and imported half-skilled labor to replace union carpenters.

Before the employers' offensive was very old, it became clear that its object was not the total destruction of building trades unionism. In San Francisco a building trades employers' asssoci-

[11]Commons, "The New York Building Trades," pp. 415–416.

[12]Frank Duffy, "Circular Letter," The Carpenter, Vol. 24, No. 2, February 1904, p. 3.

[13]UBCJA, 1904 Convention Proceedings, pp. 33, 47–48.

[14]"Quarterly Report of G. P. W. D. Huber of May 1, 1905," The Carpenter, Vol. 25, No. 6, June 1905, p. 18.

[15]Ibid., p. 16.

[16]"What Our Organizers Are Doing," The Carpenter, Vol. 26, No. 3, March 1906, pp. 31–33.

[17]"What Our Organizers Are Doing," The Carpenter, Vol. 25, No. 6, June 1905, pp. 27, 29, 33–34.

ation was never formed because the prime mover for such an association, the Mill Employers' Association, insisted on the open shop.[18] In New York the chairman of the employers' association flatly stated to the union leaders:

If any non-union men are on a building...the Employers Association ...will notify that contractor...that unless he removes those men... at once, we will order our trades withdrawn. We expect to work together hereafter for each other's interests. This is distinctly an arrangement between your association [the Building Trades Council] and ours.[19]

The employers desired not to kill the trade union goose but simply to regulate the production of, and prices for, its golden eggs. As union leaders came to see this, they took a more kindly view of the new employers' associations. By 1906 Duffy reported that the Brotherhood no longer had anything to fear from the employers' quarter.

In San Francisco, because the building trades council under McCarthy had never stooped to graft and because "Pin Head" rode tight rein on jurisdictional strikes, the employers never tried to challenge McCarthy's rule. Exclusive agreements, price fixing, and collusion were the order of the day. In fact, local officers of the Bricklayers, Lathers, and Plasterers were also members of the employers' organization of each of these trades.[20]

In Chicago the lockout of 1900 was settled on the basis of six "cardinal points" propounded by the employers. Neither the closed shop nor the exclusive agreement was banned by these six points. The object of the cardinal points was not to wipe out trade union racketeering but to regulate it and to make certain that the contractors did not become its victims. Thus the cardinal points prohibited the sympathetic strike, the means through which "Skinny" Madden had extracted excessive graft from the contractors, and it regulated union working rules.[21] Monopolistic malpractices con-

[18]Ryan, pp. 105–106.
[19]Commons, "The New York Building Trades," p. 425.
[20]Ryan, pp. 103, 113, 115. Undoubtedly they gained membership because they were small contractors.
[21]Montgomery, pp. 25–26.

tinued for many years to characterize the Chicago building trades in spite of, or perhaps because of, these "cardinal points."

The outcome of the New York City lockouts that occurred from 1903 to 1905 was the New York Arbitration Plan, which specifically called for a closed shop and severely regulated business agents in their relations with Building Trades Employers' Associations but gave them a free hand with nonmember contractors.[22] Although Sam Parks was gone, his spirit lived on. New York City continued to be mired in collusive practices.

Thus, from 1900 to 1906, two equally wiry adversaries met and fought to a draw. Behind a smoke screen of "liberty to work," agreements on future division of the loot were pounded out between two groups of tough old pirate lords. Duffy wrote in 1907:

Why should not our employers organize for the protection of their interests?...They have good reason to protect themselves from... unfair competitors....Fair minded employers...find that the labor union...is a formidable bulwark against unhealthy competition.... Employers' organizations...have come to stay and it behooves the workers to...meet the employers intelligently, fearlessly, and with determination.[23]

Out of this new unity arose a new trade union tactic, label unionism. To trace its rise, it is necessary to return to the year in which the United Brotherhood adopted the label.

One of the first actions of the convention which deposed McGuire was the adoption of a union label.[24] During the next two years its use was desultory and largely confined to New York City. To render the label truly effective, the cooperation of the contractors was required. In San Francisco, after the 1900 mill strike, this cooperation was willingly proffered. In New York City the Carpenters' district council signed a label recognition agreement with the Master Carpenters in 1909, under the terms of which the contractors forced the wood mill employers' association into the agreement. A three-cornered deal provided that both the mills and the contractors conduct union shops and that

[22]Haber, pp. 352–353.
[23]Editorial in *The Carpenter,* Vol. 27, No. 2, February 1907, p. 17.
[24]UBCJA, *1902 Convention Proceedings,* pp. 122–124.

the carpenters work only for members of the contractors' association or the millmen's association.[25] All three parties to the deal profited. The mill owners, guaranteed a monopoly over the purchases of all association contractors, raised prices; the association contractors received a special discount on the mill products they purchased; and the carpenters obtained higher wages by reason of the millmen's higher prices and the association contractors' lower costs of materials.

Of course, the whole arrangement was contingent upon the Carpenters' keeping not only "unfair" trim but also "outside" trim from entering a given city. In many cases they did this. President Huber complained to the 1912 convention that "several times our men have refused to put up...[mill] material although it did bear our label."[26] A few months later the Philadelphia district council complained to the executive board that New York carpenters had refused to handle Philadelphia union mill products even though wages and hours were the same in both cities.[27]

A committee of the Illinois legislature told of the operation of the Chicago exclusive agreement:

Every piece of mill work...manufactured outside of Chicago, save the products manufactured in one plant in Neenah, Wisconsin, and another in Grand Rapids, Michigan, was denominated as "non-union mill work"...and...exclud[ed] from the Chicago market....

. . .

The evidence shows that the operation of the aforesaid arrangement resulted in a practical monopoly in favor of the Chicago manufacturers' millwork to the exclusion of practically all outside materials. Consequently, the Chicago manufacturers have dictated the price for their product, and, as a result, it has risen approximately 200 per cent within the past three years.[28]

To measure exactly the extent of this collusion is difficult. Certainly New York and San Francisco were tied up well before

[25]U.S. Joint Industrial Relations Commission, *Final Report and Testimony*, 64th Cong., 1st Sess., Vol. 2, pp. 1626–1627.

[26]UBCJA, *1912 Convention Proceedings*, p. 113.

[27]"Minutes of the Proceedings of the Second Quarterly Session, 1913, of the G. E. B., April 11," *The Carpenter*, Vol. 33, No. 5, May 1913, p. 28.

[28]Illinois Building Investigation Committee, *Report to the 53rd General Assembly*, pp. 15–16.

World War I, and Chicago before the 1920's. The vice-president of one of the largest lumber companies in the United States, the Paine Lumber Company, expressed the fear in 1910 that unless label unionism was stopped, even though a company "might be successful in organizing a non-union crew it would not be able to market its product except at flag stations and country four corners."[29] The editor of the *New York Lumber Trade Journal* wrote in 1913 that "New York City. . . , conducting the greatest building operations in the world, a center of transportation by both land and sea, is as completely cut off from the benefits of free trade in wood materials as if it were surrounded by a fleet of hostile ships."[30]

Label unionism, as it has just been described, rose simultaneously with the decline of union-management hostility from 1902 to 1908. Since the new tactic was based on a new ally, the employer, it engendered a new opposition, publicly constituted antiunion groups. Deprived of the traditional antiunion weapons like the blacklist and the lockout, the new opposition turned to a new weapon, court proceedings. Time and again after 1906 Brotherhood officers were prosecuted under the terms of the Sherman Act. Some measure both of the severity of the legal assault and of the shift in the Carpenters' tactics may be gleaned from the chart below:

Table VI. United Brotherhood Expenditures for Legal Fees: 1902 to 1914

Dates	Expenditures
1902 to 1904	$ .00
1904 to 1906	8,351.49
1906 to 1908	13,072.65
1908 to 1910	19,203.21
1910 to 1912	35,450.42
1912 to 1914	104,278.83

Source: The above statistics are taken from the following UBCJA *Convention Proceedings* previously cited in full: 1904, p. 111; 1906, p. 191; 1908, p. 190; 1910, p. 223; 1912, p. 374; 1914, p. 272.

The guiding force behind this offensive and the main source of the Carpenters' legal difficulties for over a decade was the Anti-

[29]Letter from Nathan Paine, vice-president of the Paine Lumber Co., to G. W. Dwelle, secretary of the Eastern Door, Sash and Blind Manufacturers' Association, Nov. 28, 1910, as quoted in UBCJA, *1912 Convention Proceedings,* pp. 191–192.

[30]*Anti-Boycott Association Bulletin,* Nov. 10, 1913, unpag.

Boycott Association, an organization founded in 1902 by D. E. Loewe, a Danbury hat manufacturer, and two attorneys, Daniel Davenport and Walter Gordon Merritt.[31] For eight years these men contented themselves with attacking union-inaugurated consumers' boycotts, through the medium of legal suits like the Danbury Hatters and the Bucks Stove and Range cases. By 1910 Merritt and Davenport had rendered this type of boycott ineffective and had almost jailed Gompers in the process. Then the Anti-Boycott Association turned to the producers' boycott and discovered that "The activities of the Carpenters' Union typif[ied] this secondary [or producers'] boycott."[32]

The trouble-shooting lawyers then set their cap specifically for the Carpenters. From 1910 to 1913 injunction servers constantly harrassed various officials of the Brotherhood. At one time, twelve different suits were in progress in New York City alone. In total, almost a hundred suits were entered in the largest court assault directed against a trade union to that time.

The assault was launched in 1910 with the Irving and Casson case. Irving and Casson was both an open shop company and a member of the Anti-Boycott Association, with a woodworking mill in East Cambridge, Massachusetts. Its owners prided themselves on the production of decorative woodwork and in 1910 had the contract for altar work on the Cathedral of St. John the Divine, in New York City. In April 1910 the New York Carpenters' district council struck the church job in protest against the use of the Irving and Casson Company's "unfair" materials. Business agent B. A. French warned the contractor that the Carpenters' district council would "close up...[the rest of the] job tight as a drum" if he tried to replace the men. The Anti-Boycott Association obtained an injunction from a lower federal court. Its terms prevented the Carpenters from striking or threatening to strike because of the nature of the material used on the job.[33]

In 1911 the Anti-Boycott Association's lawyers opened a $200,000 suit in the New York State courts against both the United Broth-

[31]Walter Gordon Merritt, *History of the League for Industrial Rights,* pp. 4–16.
[32]Walter Gordon Merritt, *Destination Unknown,* p. 45.
[33]*Irving v. Joint District Council 180,* Fed. 896, as quoted in *ibid.,* pp. 46–47.

164

erhood and the Master Carpenters' Association of New York City on behalf of another woodworking firm, the Bossert Mills.[34] By these moves Merritt and Davenport were simply maneuvering for position. In February 1911 they struck: a conspiracy case, replete with injunction, was filed on behalf of six manufacturers of wood trim in Wisconsin, Missouri, Iowa, Pennsylvania, and Tennessee,[35] against the Carpenters, the Master Carpenters' Association, and the Mill Owners' Association of New York City.[36] It charged that the three groups conspired to keep "unfair" trim out of New York City and asked that all three be enjoined from doing this in the future. The lawyers asked that limitations be put on the business agent's power to deal with working carpenters and on the local and national offices' power to deal with employers; and that certain clauses concerning the use of the label be stricken from the United Brotherhood's constitution.[37] This was a direct assault on the economic and political structure of the union.

Messrs. Davenport and Merritt rapidly discovered that they had chosen a worthy and resourceful opponent. In March 1911 the executive board went in a body to New York City to study the legal questions raised by these suits and to lay down future strategy. They hired Charles Maitland Beattie to head a battery of legal experts and decreed that the national treasury meet two-thirds of all local court costs.[38] A monster parade was organized in which twenty-five thousand workers streamed down Fifth Avenue to the Cooper Union to hear Gompers denounce the Anti-Boycott Association.

The executive board took over the full expense of all court suits in January 1912.[39] The Carpenters held a huge rally in the Brooklyn Academy of Music on June 21, at which Duffy and

---

[34]*Bossert v. Dhuy 221*, N.Y. 342, as quoted in Frank Duffy, "Another Sweeping Court Decision in Favor of the United Brotherhood of Carpenters and Joiners of America," *The Carpenter*, Vol. 38, No. 1, January 1918, pp. 4–6.

[35]*Paine Lumber Co. v. Neale 224*, U.S. 459, as cited in Merritt, *Destination Unknown*, p. 47.

[36]UBCJA, *1916 Convention Proceedings*, pp. 172–173.

[37]UBCJA, *1920 Convention Proceedings*, pp. 287–288.

[38]"Minutes of Proceedings of the Second Quarterly Session, 1911, of the General Executive Board, April 10," *The Carpenter*, Vol. 31, No. 6, June 1911, p. 18.

[39]"Minutes of the Proceedings of the First Quarterly Session, 1912, of the General Executive Board, January 17," *The Carpenter*, Vol. 32, No. 3, March 1912, p. 20.

several other labor leaders spoke violently against the courts and the Anti-Boycott Association.[40] At their own, and at the AFL's 1912 convention, the Carpenters introduced a resolution calling for the recall of all judges and of their decisions.[41] In February 1914 the national office opened a new law library to guide the officers in future litigation.

By 1914 both the Anti-Boycott Association and the Carpenters had agreed to withhold action on all but the Bossert case, then before the New York State courts, and the Paine suit, then on its way up through the federal system to the Supreme Court. Together these courts would hand down the most authoritative and binding legal decisions in the land. All other cases, perforce, would have to follow their lead.

In pressing their cases, the Anti-Boycott Association lawyers held that the Carpenters' use of their label constituted a conspiracy in restraint of trade and that quite often the terms "unfair" and "out of town" were synonymous when applied to woodwork. The Brotherhood's lawyers contended that if it was lawful for a man to refuse to work with nonunion men, it was equally lawful for him to refuse to work with the fruits of nonunion labor's toil, unfair trim. To press home his point in the Bossert case, Lawyer Beattie brought into court a huge newel post, shaped in the figure of a man, which had been fashioned in a nonunion mill. "Transform," he told the court, "this non-union wooden man into a non-union, flesh and blood man, and the courts will not question the carpenter's right to refuse to work with him. The courts would protect the graven image but not the man!"

The Paine case was the first to be decided. In the spring of 1917 the Supreme Court decided, five to four, with Holmes delivering the majority opinion and McReynolds the dissent, that the Carpenters were innocent of the charge. Holmes held that the Brotherhood simply pursued economic gain, without any malicious motive, and that it did not discriminate in favor of any one firm.[42]

---

[40]"Protest Against Injunction," *The Carpenter,* Vol. 32, No. 7, July 1912, p. 33.

[41]"Report of the Delegates to the Thirty-Second Annual Convention of the American Federation of Labor," *The Carpenter,* Vol. 32, No. 12, December 1912, p. 31.

[42]*Paine Lumber Co.* v. *Neale,* as cited in UBCJA, *1920 Convention Proceedings,* pp. 287–288.

Toward the end of the year the New York State Court of Appeals found for the Carpenters on substantially the same grounds in the Bossert case.[43]

Thus, from 1911 to 1916, the Anti-Boycott Association lost every court case of any note that it pressed against the United Brotherhood. The head of the Anti-Boycott Association went up in the Carpenters' trophy room beside those of the United Order, the Amalgamated Wood Workers, and the Building Trades Department.

The years which transpired between 1902 and 1912 are the ten most important in the union's history. During these years the professional organizers took over and fashioned the union into the type of organization they wished it to be. The last vestiges of McGuire's socialism were purged and his abstract goals and educational tactics replaced by limited goals and practical tactics. The Amalgamated Wood Workers and a host of other unions were trundled out of the jurisdictional area the Carpenters held for their own. The United Brotherhood was made into a craft-industrial union with a jurisdiction covering the whole woodworking industry. Protection of the carpenter's craft in a time of technological change became the most important, virtually the only, task of the national union.

In pursuit of this goal, the policy of "one trade for one union" was foisted upon the AFL. So also was the Building Trades Department. Thus the professional organizers not only changed their own union's structure and policy, but by these moves they also changed those of the AFL. Since this decade the departmental structure has been a basic and important feature of the AFL, its answer to industrial unionism. The policy of "amalgamation of related trades"—another answer to industrial unionism—has also been one of the AFL's basic policies since this decade. As a policy it is nothing more than the application of the Carpenters' "one union for one trade" slogan.

During these same years the United Brotherhood's structure was also changed. The almost constant struggle for power which occu-

[43]Frank Duffy, "Another Sweeping Court Decision," p. 4.

pied the union from 1902 to 1912 was of historical importance not primarily because of the personalities involved but because it emphasized the need for a united national office. When the executive board was placed under the general president's sway, this unity was achieved.

Other administrative reforms fell into a pattern once this most important of all changes was effected. The executive board members were made full-time, salaried employees of the union. Each headed a region. From each of these regions was chosen a group of organizers. They, in turn, kept peace between the national office and each of the various district councils under the control of the business agents. The hierarchy of power, since 1912, reads from bottom to top, as in the following description: Business agents are on the bottom level, each working for a local union. Above them, coordinating activities in a given city, is the district council, with its own corps of business agents and its full-time officers. Above the district councils and coordinating their efforts are the organizers, or general representatives. Their regional commander, who also oversees all of the district councils in his area, is the executive board member from their district, one of seven into which the nation is divided. The second vice-president directs the corps of organizers for his superior, the general president, who has final command of the whole organization.

Wages, hours, and working conditions are almost solely the province of district council officials. When it is necessary, they get assistance from the national office. For the most part, however, the task of the national officers is the protection of the jurisdiction. They do this by putting into effect the policies described in the first two paragraphs of this summary.

The tactics of label unionism, described in the body of this chapter, complete this pattern. The final importance of label unionism rests not as much in the alleged presence of a collusive arrangement between carpenters, contractors, and millmen, as in the fact that it reflected a new type of unionism which had overtaken the Carpenters between 1902 and 1912. That the leaders of the Brotherhood consciously planned label unionism there can be no doubt. In 1904, as their difficulties with management decreased and those with the courts increased, the members of the executive board said, "The old weapon of strike and boycott is. . . robbed of its potency and some new one must be evolved to take its place."[44]

The new weapon was label unionism, and its advent marked a drastic change in the Carpenters' strategy. Gone were evangelical organizing drives in which elements of class warfare were brought into play and direct strike pressure used. In their place arose a unionism of business tactics. Label unionism brought into existence an intricate network of boycotts, sympathetic strikes, and exclusive agreements, and it called the employer into partnership with the union.

On the interunion front, the jurisdictional strike complemented label unionism. By the same strategic maneuvering, whole crafts, industries, and trades were "organized" by the Brotherhood, much as a huge monopoly might force a small local producer into its organization. It is significant that around 1916 President Hutcheson was to insist that henceforth the Brotherhood's organizers should be called "general representatives."

[44]UBCJA, *1904 Convention Proceedings*, p. 141. See also Table VI, p. 163. In the same year (1904) the union recorded its first expenditures for court suits which ten years later were over $100,000.

CHAPTER XII

"Or That Was Ever Made of Wood": 1912 to 1915

CARPENTERS are no respecters of tradition. The United Brotherhood has epitomized the AFL's business unionism only because the Carpenters designed it to meet their own specific needs. When AFL policy has failed to meet these needs, the leaders of the United Brotherhood have felt as free as did John L. Lewis in 1935 to fight it with all the resources at their command. Hence, when it suited their purpose, they swept away the feeble reed of a Scranton Declaration and replaced it with the more realistic Atlanta Declaration. They turned their backs upon pure craft unionism and espoused the doctrine of the "basic crafts" organized about the "principal trade," of which the Building Trades Department was a pale reflection.

After 1912, when neither the basic crafts plan nor the Atlanta Declaration continued to meet their needs, they upended both and went marauding in new fields: the metal crafts. By no stretch of the most belligerent carpenter's imagination could the metal trades be claimed as a part of the woodworking industry. When the Carpenters moved into the metal trades, they pursued a policy of one organization for *two* trades. By the same move, they served notice that they would move into two hundred trades if they felt technological evolution made this necessary. Consequently the

Atlanta Declaration, with its one organization for one trade, was rendered meaningless.

The same forces which caused difficulties with the Wood Workers brought the Carpenters into conflict with the metal trades. Technological change had deprived the carpenter of work by replacing much hand carpentry with woodworking machinery. To retain jurisdiction over this work the United Brotherhood challenged and defeated the Amalgamated Wood Workers' Union. Even as the Carpenters asserted their claim to jurisdiction over the woodworker, wood was being replaced by iron, steel, and sheet metal as the basic material out of which building trim, windows, and roofing was fabricated. A dispute with the International Association of Sheet Metal Workers arose when metal trim replaced wood trim; one with the International Association of Machinists when metal was substituted for wood in the construction of heavy machinery; and another with the International Association of Iron Workers as iron replaced wood in piles, docks, and window frames.[1]

Although these new conflicts signified changes in antagonists and in the nature of the materials disputed and made mockery of the Atlanta Declaration, the Carpenters' basic policy remained the same. They continued to insist on the right to install any object once made of wood. The Atlanta Declaration policy of one organization for one trade had been a convenient means to help the United Brotherhood encompass the woodworking industry, but the Carpenters did not intend to allow this policy to bar them from following technological evolution wherever it might lead. As it led them into the metal trades, they were forced to apply the same basic policy in a new manner.

While occupied with the woodworking industry, the Carpenters paid but scant attention to new metal materials. Then, in 1908, the matter of sheet-metal trim was rudely called to their attention by a New York City building ordinance prohibiting the use of wood in the construction of a building higher than fifty-nine

[1] The first two of these three disputes are discussed in this chapter. The dispute with the Iron Workers is discussed in Chapter XIV (see especially p. 208, n. 26) in terms of the effect of expansion into the metal trades upon national-local relations in the union.

feet.[2] Although there were four hundred carpenters occupied in hanging metal trim, the New York district council had not concerned itself with the new material until this ordinance was passed. To lose all the trim in New York City, however, was another matter. They moved.

In February 1909 the executive board claimed all sheet-metal work for the carpenters. This led to a dispute with the Sheet Metal Workers which, under the New York Arbitration Plan, had to be decided by a third party. On April 23, 1909, arbitrator N. J. Gaynor, a justice of the New York State Supreme Court handed down a decision in favor of the Carpenters to which the Sheet Metal Workers immediately objected.[3]

In preparation for the inevitable conflict, Huber made two shrewd moves. First he induced the New York architects to provide in their specifications for the installation of all metal trim by carpenters. Next he agreed that the manufacture of hollow trim was not included in the Carpenters' jurisdictional claims. This automatically gained for the Carpenters the support of the sheet-metal factory owners who preferred to have a different union controlling installation of their materials from that which unionized their factories.[4] Thus from the outset the Carpenters deprived the Sheet Metal Workers' Union of the power of internal boycott which was such an integral part of their own label unionism.

One of the longest and most intense jurisdictional struggles recorded in labor annals was then launched on its checkered twenty-year career. James Duncan, an AFL vice-president, described the effect which this fight had on a typical job:

The Sheet Metal Worker will begin to install the trim and the Carpenter will sit in a chair reading... [the] morning paper and smoking a cigar; he will be there all forenoon and he will be paid the scale.

[2]D. F. Featherston, "Work the Carpenters Claim," *The Carpenter*, Vol. 29, No. 4, April 1909, p. 28.

[3]In effect, Gaynor said that the difference over new material was only a question of molecular distribution and that although the new trim was not wood, the skill and tools of the carpenter were required to install it (John S. Henry, "Judge Gaynor's Decision," *The Carpenter*, Vol. 29, No. 5, May 1909, p. 34).

[4]Building Trades Department, AFL, *Proceedings of the Fourth Annual Convention of St. Louis, November 28 to December 5, 1910*, pp. 56–57.

At noon time they will change places and the Sheet Metal Worker will sit down and read the paper and... [the contractor] will pay him a day's pay.[5]

The Sheet Metal Workers took the dispute to the Building Trades Department in 1909, almost immediately after it was founded. The Carpenters did not fare well in 1909 in pleading their case before the Building Trades Department representatives, nor did they for the next six years. To explain why, it is necessary to return to 1908, the year of the Department's founding.[6]

The Department held its founding convention in February 1908 in Washington, D.C. and received the first AFL department charter on March 20, 1908.[7] The Department avoided the error made by the National Building Trades Council from the outset by allowing only national unions to be directly represented. To this important extent it was patterned after the Structural Building Trades Alliance. Otherwise, however, its structure was a far cry from the "basic crafts" plan of the Structural Building Trades Alliance. Nineteen trades in all crowded into it, and although carpenter James Kirby was elected president, it rapidly became clear that the smaller unions were determined to beard the United Brotherhood lion in his own den.

The AFL plan of representation by membership was used,[8] but unlike the AFL, roll calls were held on a one-vote, one-delegate basis instead of being weighted by per capita units.[9] This gave a quarter of a million carpenters no more voice in settling a jurisdictional question which vitally affected them than it did to five thousand Marble Polishers who were also organized in a national union represented in the Building Trades Department. Furthermore, voting in the local building trades councils was also on this basis, with no referendum vote provision. Financial support, however, was placed on a weighted per capita basis. In the first year

[5]UBCJA, *1924 Convention Proceedings,* p. 151.
[6]See above, pp. 124–134, for events which led to the creation of the Building Trades Department.
[7]AFL, *1908 Convention Proceedings,* p. 69.
[8]Up to four thousand members, one delegate; eight thousand, two; sixteen thousand, three; and so on.
[9]Building Trades Department, AFL, *Proceedings of the First Annual Convention of Denver, Nov. 24 to Nov. 28, 1908,* p. 18.

of the Department's existence, the Carpenters paid $2,205.00 of a total of $6,799.84 contributed.[10] At the founding convention and in 1909 the representatives of the Brotherhood fought bitterly to have these laws repealed but were defeated by the coordinated efforts of the smaller unions.[11]

In giving their united numbers more voice than they gave to the United Brotherhood delegates, the leaders of the smaller unions guaranteed that the Building Trades Department would not adopt any jurisdictional settlement plan entailing amalgamation of smaller unions with larger ones. The creation of the Building Trades Department solved the problem of autonomy for the building trades within the AFL. It did not solve the related problem of the jurisdictional strike. Thus its effect was to isolate and quarantine building trades jurisdictional squabbles, not to settle them. It was a failure in 1909 because it did not proffer a realistic plan for the settlement of jurisdictional disputes and because it paid even more obeisance than had the AFL to small craft unions. The newspaper of the National Building Trades Council, *The Labor Compendium*, was not far from wrong when it called the Department "a pension bureau for retired building trades officials hanging on the coat tails of the AFL's prestige."[12]

Thus the 1909 Building Trades Department convention, dominated by small unions blown all out of proportion to true size by an unequal vote, did not give a kindly audience to the United Brotherhood's disputes. The delegates had the "principal trade" yardstick offered by the Carpenters in founding the Structural Building Trades Alliance and the treatment Huber had accorded the smaller Amalgamated Wood Workers in mind when they heard the Sheet Metal Workers' plea. They took this heaven-sent opportunity to pare the Carpenters down to size. They reversed the Gaynor award and gave the jurisdiction to the Sheet Metal Workers in what became known as the "Tampa Decision."

[10]*Ibid.*, p. 12.
[11]Frank Duffy, "Report of Delegates to the Second Annual Convention of the Building Trades Department, American Federation of Labor," *The Carpenter*, Vol. 29, No. 11, November 1909, p. 34.
[12]*The Labor Compendium*, March 1908, p. 1, col. 1.

Huber responded in 1910 by extending the constitutional jurisdiction of the Brotherhood to cover hollow metal, and the Carpenters went blithely on their way, taking sheet-metal work pretty much at will and, in the process, casting the unity of local building trades councils to the winds.

After listening to the complaints of a Sheet Metal Workers' representative, the delegates to the 1910 convention of the Building Trades Department rose in wrath and ousted the Carpenters. Never had a face been more grossly spited by the severance of its nose. The Carpenters had contributed one-third of the Department's revenue and had accepted an unfair voting arrangement with a minimum of complaint. The delegates were simply venting their spleen, and they soon paid dearly for their self-indulgence.

For the Carpenters began casting about them mightily and soon pulled the Building Trades Department down about the heads of its officers. They struck every job on which the Sheet Metal Workers held building trades council working cards until the council in question reversed the Department's Tampa award. Within a few months of the Carpenters' ouster, most building trades councils were either divided and quarreling or inoperative, with the situation especially bad in New York City.[13]

Secretary William Spencer of the Building Trades Department complained to Gompers on June 13, 1911 that the Carpenters had "rendered the work of the Department ineffective, causing distress among...locals and a willful and deliberate manifestation to ignore the...Executive Council of the...Department."[14] He finished by asking Gompers to expel the Carpenters from the AFL.

Gompers replied four days later. He had learned from his experience in the Wood Workers' dispute what a fight with the Carpenters could mean. Not only would he not expel the Carpenters but he would order the Building Trades Department to reinstate them. The 1911 AFL convention backed Gompers' stand. The Carpenters remained aloof for awhile, but after Vice-President John Mitchell of the AFL and President James A. Short of the Building Trades Department came and pleaded with

[13]Building Trades Department, *1911 Convention Proceedings,* p. 60.
[14]*Ibid.*

175

Huber, he put the matter to a vote. During 1912 the United Brotherhood reaffiliated.[15]

Huber then went to the AFL executive council with his main complaint, the representation system at the Building Trades Department conventions. The AFL executive council ordered the 1912 convention of the Building Trades Department to reopen this question but recommended no specific action. The delegates closed the question almost as soon as they reopened it and sent it back to the AFL executive council.[16]

With only the sheet-metal trouble pending, Huber turned to the matter of the International Association of Machinists. Its officers were trying unsuccessfully to organize the York Machine Company of York, Pennsylvania. The Machinists had declared the company unfair and through an internal boycott refused to install its machinery. Not so the Carpenters, who promptly installed the disputed machinery, the installation of which, Huber claimed, fell within the United Brotherhood's jurisdiction.[17]

The officials of the Machinists complained about this alleged violation of jurisdiction in a fiery resolution addressed to the 1913 AFL convention. After being toned down somewhat, the resolution was sanctioned. It "requested" the Carpenters to stay away from millwright work. Unsatisfied, the Machinists took the matter to the 1913 Building Trades Department convention. The delegates promptly awarded millwright work to them.[18]

The delegates then turned to the Carpenters' dispute with the Sheet Metal Workers. The Carpenters coyly asked for a conference rather than a flat repeal of the Tampa Decision. The Sheet Metal Workers saw through this change in tactics, however. They knew that if the convention ordered a conference the Carpenters would maintain that the order to confer reopened the question

[15]Building Trades Department, AFL, *Proceedings of the Sixth Annual Convention of Rochester, November 25 to November 29, 1912*, p. 31.

[16]*Ibid.*, pp. 83–84, 126.

[17]The Carpenters claimed the right to install machinery since at an earlier date most machinery was made of wood and had traditionally been installed by carpenters.

[18]Carpenters and Joiners of America, United Brotherhood of, AFL, *Proceedings of the Eighteenth General Convention of Indianapolis, September 21 to October 2, 1914*, pp. 396–397; Building Trades Department, AFL, *Proceedings of the Seventh Annual Convention of Seattle, November 24 to November 29, 1913*, pp. 156–157.

176

of jurisdiction and automatically annulled the Tampa Decision. Even though the convention committee ordered a conference, the floor rejected its recommendation.[19]

Finally the delegates took up the question of representation. Huber had persuaded the AFL executive council to recommend to the Building Trades Department that its representation plan be changed to give any union with seven or more delegates two votes per delegate on a roll call. The Carpenters alone had seven delegates. This recommendation was flatly rejected by the convention.[20]

Thus, from 1910 to 1913 the Building Trades Department had sided with the Machinists; had overturned an arbitration award to deny the Carpenters sheet-metal work; had thrown the Carpenters out of its councils; and had refused to change a representation system heavily and undemocratically weighted against them. The patience of the usually impatient Carpenters with the Building Trades Department was astounding. Now, in 1914, it was exhausted. They started exacting payment.

In February the Carpenters dropped out of the Department and signed an "offensive and defensive alliance" with the Bricklayers' International Union.[21] Through agreements the Bricklayers had with the International Union of Operating Engineers, the International Association of Plasterers, and the Stonecutters' Association of North America, a miniature, informal, and dual Building Trades Department was created.[22] This alliance gave Huber protection from outside the Building Trades Department which he could not get inside its ranks. As one carpenter had earlier told a Building Trades Department convention, "We want a little protection, that is all. . . . In city after city. . .a half dozen

[19]UBCJA, *1914 Convention Proceedings,* p. 394.

[20]*Ibid.,* pp. 390–391.

[21]Building Trades Department, *1914 Convention Proceedings,* pp. 105–106; *Fiftieth Annual Report of the President and Secretary of the Bricklayers, Masons and Plasterers' International Union for the term ending Nov. 30, 1915,* pp. VII–VIII. The Bricklayers' Union was the second largest building trades union and was still outside the AFL.

[22]Building Trades Department, *1914 Convention Proceedings,* p. 48.

trades that would not form one-third part...of the Carpenters ...could put our men on the streets."[23]

Furthermore, by this alliance Huber protected his flanks in case of a protracted struggle with the AFL or the Building Trades Department. Referring to this treaty, President William Bowen of the Bricklayers said that the leaders of the United Brotherhood knew that they were "entrenched because of an alliance with another organization...outside the Department that had alliances with other unions within the Department, and they could very well defy the Department because of...[these] alliances."[24]

Talk of another Structural Building Trades Alliance was revived as the five unions separated themselves from one after another of the building trades councils.[25] It was idle and unrealistic talk, however. The Structural Building Trades Alliance had been based on the existence of clearly delineated jurisdictions within which each of the basic crafts was to be paramount. Under this plan, for example, the Iron Workers were given jurisdiction over all work done on iron materials. In 1914, however, the Carpenters claimed much of the work in the Iron Workers' jurisdiction.[26] Just as the idea underlying the Atlanta Declaration was rendered untenable by technological evolution, so also was that underlying the Structural Building Trades Alliance. The five unions which formed the 1914 alliance had but one thing in common: no one of them had jurisdictional disputes with the other four.

Each of them had jurisdictional troubles outstanding with other unions, however, and they declared open warfare on those unions remaining in the Building Trades Department. In order to supplant the various building trades councils, the alliance unions granted concessions to employers in many cities.[27] Once in control of building in a city, the alliance unions took not only the work

---

[23]Building Trades Department, *1912 Convention Proceedings,* p. 124.

[24]Building Trades Department, AFL, *Proceedings of the Fifteenth Annual Convention of Denver, June 8 to June 11, 1921,* p. 114.

[25]Building Trades Department, *1914 Convention Proceedings,* pp. 105–106.

[26]See below, p. 208, 208 n. 26.

[27]Building Trades Department, *1914 Convention Proceedings,* p. 106. For example, they agreed to sign pledges foregoing the sympathetic strike.

traditionally belonging to them but also the work done by the unions still in the Department.

Once again the Carpenters hung onto their AFL affiliation by a thread. This time, however, Gompers trod more lightly than he had in the Wood Worker dispute. Duffy wrote to Gompers in June of 1914 assuring him that the Carpenters were "not at variance with the A.F. of L. On the contrary, we are as loyal and true as ever, but we are at variance with the Building Trades Department, its rotten methods and system of doing work, and its trickery in getting decisions."[28] When the inevitable demand for the United Brotherhood's expulsion came from the Building Trades Department, Gompers assured Duffy he would block it.[29] In July Gompers ordered the Building Trades Department to reinstate the Carpenters and asked the Carpenters, in effect, their terms for reaffiliation.

The Carpenters told Gompers on August 6 that the following conditions must first be met: one, the Gaynor Award must replace the Tampa Decision; two, voting must be weighted by membership, both in the Department conventions and in the local councils; three, the Machinists must be put out of the Building Trades Department; four, the power of building trades councils' business agents to reverse decisions of Carpenters' business agents must be ended; five, the Department must cease making it compulsory for all local unions to be in the building trades councils; six, a five-man executive council must be created in place of one on which each union automatically named a member; seven, the referendum vote must be used to make official all building trades councils' laws and elections.[30]

At Gompers' behest the 1914 AFL convention complied as much as possible with the Carpenters' demands. Department membership was made voluntary; any organization with seven or more delegates was given two roll-call votes per delegate; and organizations which properly belonged in one department but wished to

---

[28]Letter from Duffy to Gompers, June 8, 1914, quoted in American Federation of Labor, *Proceedings of the Thirty-fourth Annual Convention of Philadelphia, November 9 to November 21, 1914,* p. 139.

[29]*Ibid.,* p. 140.

[30]*Ibid.,* pp. 142–143.

have representation in another department (for example, the Machinists) had thereafter to pay per capita on at least 20 percent of their membership.[31]

These were changes the Carpenters had long sought, and they sent a full slate of delegates to the 1915 convention of the Building Trades Department. A floor fight against seating the Carpenters was led by the Machinists, the Sheet Metal Workers, and the Iron Workers, but to no avail. When the Carpenters took their seats, the other delegates were warned ominously by President William L. Hutcheson, "I don't believe it is necessary for me to say more at this time...but you will perhaps hear from us later on."[32] In order, Hutcheson saw to it that the Tampa Decision was annulled; that the Machinists were ejected from the Department; and "that those gentlemen [who voted against the Carpenters' reaffiliation] were not re-elected."[33] The presidents of the Sheet Metal and Iron Workers Unions were replaced by Hutcheson and his supporters as vice-presidents of the Department.

Although the Building Trades Department was now in line, the Carpenters had not fared as well in the AFL. Gompers was securely on their side, but many union leaders were distressed with what they deemed the Carpenters' highhanded methods. The same AFL convention (1914) which so radically altered the Building Trades Department's constitution for the Carpenters refused to budge an inch on the question of jurisdiction in the metal trades.[34] It heard and ratified the Machinists' claims against the Carpenters and created an on-the-job investigating committee to take a closer look at the sheet-metal controversy.[35]

The better part of January and February 1915 was spent by the committee investigating the manufacture and erection of sheet metal, starting in New York City and going west to Cleveland.

[31]UBCJA, *1916 Convention Proceedings*, p. 198.

[32]Building Trades Department, AFL, *Proceedings of the Ninth Annual Convention of San Francisco, November 23 to November 27, 1915,* p. 36. William L. Hutcheson had assumed office the previous year upon Kirby's death.

[33]See UBCJA, *1916 Convention Proceedings,* p. 223, for the direct quotation and Building Trades Department, *1915 Convention Proceedings,* pp. 114–117 and 95, for the other actions of the convention mentioned in this sentence.

[34]AFL, *1914 Convention Proceedings,* p. 350.

[35]*Ibid.,* p. 417.

In an attempt to strike a middle position, the committee members suggested an exchange of working cards on the installation of trim. Surprisingly enough, Hutcheson supported this plan when it reached the 1915 AFL convention floor, but the delegates, in an even deeper rage against the Carpenters, rejected it.[36] So outraged were they, that when the Machinists' annual complaint reached the floor, the convention recommended that the Carpenters be ordered to vacate the Machinists' jurisdiction under pain of expulsion.[37]

This sense of outrage did not stem alone from the Carpenters' summary handling of the Building Trades Department. It dated back to the 1914 AFL convention when the Carpenters had been ordered to give up all millwright work. The Carpenters' reply had been to draw up a new and more far-reaching set of jurisdictional claims. Four pages of the October 1915 *Carpenter* were covered by these claims, which outlined with painstaking detail and exactitude the areas of millwright work claimed by the Brotherhood.[38]

Further, upon re-entering the Building Trades Department the Carpenters made it plain that they fully intended to continue their alliance with the Bricklayers. Thus, in effect, they continued to hold a big stick over the AFL. When asked to repeal this entente, Duffy replied to Gompers, "We reserve the right to enter into agreements with other trades...and we reserve the right to transact our business in our own way."[39] This, then, was the background against which floor debate on the motion to expel the Carpenters from the AFL was opened at the 1915 AFL convention.

In the long and furious debate over this motion, the Carpenters changed their tactics. Where once they had blustered, fumed, and threatened, they now maintained a baffling silence. These new tactics heralded a basic and far-reaching change in the Carpenters' jurisdictional policy. From 1881 to 1902 they were

[36]American Federation of Labor, *Proceedings of the Thirty-fifth Annual Convention of San Francisco, November 8 to November 22, 1915*, pp. 452–454.
[37]UBCJA, *1916 Convention Proceedings*, p. 212.
[38]"Jurisdictional Claims of the United Brotherhood of Carpenters and Joiners of America," *The Carpenter*, Vol. 35, No. 10, October 1915, pp. 22–26.
[39]UBCJA, *1916 Convention Proceedings*, p. 190.

a craft union. The craft structure was based on the facts that the craft was easy to define and that its members had a mutual interest in preserving craft standards. From 1902 to 1912, technological change made it imperative for the Carpenters to spread across the whole woodworking industry to retain work they had traditionally done. Craft lines became blurred and indistinct, jurisdiction amorphous, and the union's structure craft-industrial.

Although theirs was no longer a pure craft union in 1912 the leaders of the United Brotherhood still had clearly defined jurisdictional goals. They simply demanded for their members the right to continue to make by machine the wood products they once had made by hand. This made their province the whole of the woodworking industry. Thus their jurisdictional policy was reflected in the slogan "one organization for one trade." It was in fulfillment of this policy that the Carpenters created the Structural Building Trades Alliance and fought the Wood Workers and the AFL from 1902 to 1911. When in 1912 the Atlanta Declaration made the United Brotherhood's policy official AFL policy and awarded the Carpenters jurisdiction over the whole woodworking industry, the Carpenters' victory was complete.

Had industrial invention ceased in 1911, the jurisdictional dispute in this field would have withered away as AFL leaders applied the Atlanta Declaration. First one then another of the basic trades would have organized its entire industry about its basic craft, as had the Carpenters. The opposite occurred, however, when technological changes rendered the "one organization, one trade" yardstick of the Atlanta Declaration anachronistic almost as soon as it was propounded. As sheet metal replaced wood trim, the Carpenters found it necessary to compete with the metal trades for jurisdiction. No policy could possibly rationalize the existence of one union in two such diverse trades. The Carpenters offered none.

Rather, they ceased restricting their "one organization to one trade" and demanded jurisdiction over certain classes of metal work. In doing so they left behind them the restrictions of the Atlanta Declarations and adopted a policy of armed and mobile readiness in matters of jurisdiction. They would henceforth be prepared to move into any industry any time one of its crafts started to do work once done by carpenters. With this policy the Carpenters offered no plan such as they had in founding the Structural Building Trades Alliance and in introducing the Atlanta Declaration. A planlessness which left them free, highly mobile, and ready to pounce on any craft intruding on their jurisdiction was the essence of this new, opportunistic policy. President Hutcheson said in 1916:

It would be impossible to clearly define our work in such a manner that the definition would carry us to the goal for which we are... striving, namely a 100 percent organization of carpenters on the North American continent. We find it more convenient and satisfactory to meet these problems [of jurisdiction] as they arise.[40]

To implement this policy the Carpenters made alliances with unions like the Bricklayers which were facing the same jurisdictional encroachments. These alliances were as different from the Structural Building Trades Alliance as the Axis Pact was from the League of Nations. Like the League, the Structural Building Trades Alliance had a plan, the basic crafts idea, and a goal, peaceful settlement of jurisdictional disputes. The new alliance system had neither. Like the Axis Pact, it was based on anticipated and inevitable warfare. The only theory behind the Carpenters' new alliance was the survival of the fittest craft in a constantly evolving industry; it was a theory of jurisdictional laissez faire.

Since the Carpenters had no policy to offer, they offered none. Instead their delegates sat silent while the debate raged about them. They would probably have been turned out of the AFL but for the eloquence of Andrew Furuseth of the Seafarers' Union. Furuseth had no sympathy for the Carpenters. He saw them as "two hundred thousand heads...[with] an immense ravenous stomach to digest every thing they can put into it." He correctly divined that the Carpenters would leave the AFL before they would surrender their claim to work they had traditionally done and that the alliance with the Bricklayers was insurance against this contingency.[41]

[40]*Ibid.*, p. 40.
[41]AFL, *1915 Convention Proceedings,* pp. 412–415, for the full speech.

This was all Furuseth saw, however. He played into the Carpenters' hands. He offered no jurisdictional settlement plan. He did not seize this golden opportunity to confront them with the "one organization for one trade" policy which the Carpenters themselves had foisted on the AFL. Instead he did exactly what the Carpenter delegates wanted him, and the AFL, to do. He ended his speech by shouting, "You Machinists, don't be sissies; when you are attacked, defend yourselves!... If these men haven't got any sense or...decency, teach it to them.... I say to the organizations...being attacked by the Carpenters, 'Strike back.' "[42]

Thus again the Carpenters gained their object, but this time by guile. Their tactics of silence were designed to foist upon the AFL a policy of jurisdictional laissez faire which alone gave them the necessaary latitude to protect their craft in a constantly changing industry. The Machinists' resolution to oust the Carpenters was defeated, and with it any hope of a permanent AFL jurisdictional policy. The Machinists took Furuseth's advice, started immediately trading blows with the Carpenters, and have been doing it with tireless vigor and to little avail ever since.

AFL officials henceforth confined themselves to asking the Carpenters to be reasonable in their claims to jurisdiction. Gompers wrote to the 1916 Carpenters convention:

Of course I realize that it is not an easy matter to try and persuade ...a Convention of men representing your great Brotherhood to recede from a course...already decided. And yet, I feel...that your Convention will rise to the importance of this occasion and...recede from some of the claims of jurisdiction which are not only new to the Brotherhood...but held by many to be unjustified.[43]

To the same convention, President Theodore J. Williams of the Building Trades Department made a speech couched in similarly cautious language.[44]

For the next two years the same policy was pursued. The Carpenters conferred and conferred yet again with the Machinists, the Sheet Metal Workers, the Iron Workers, and a host of other unions

[42]*Ibid.*
[43]UBCJA, *1916 Convention Proceedings,* p. 24.
[44]*Ibid.,* pp. 313–318.

with which they had disputes outstanding. Nothing came of these conferences. The Carpenters continued to do the lion's share of any metal work which they felt fell within their province. By 1917 a policy of unrestricted jurisdictional warfare within the AFL emerged, in which AFL officials acted as referees who intruded only to announce the victors victorious. While unfolding, these battles were called "voluntarism," when settled, "craft amalgamation." Voluntarism is the right of a powerful union to decide the extent of its jurisdiction. Craft amalgamation is the process whereby the stronger of the disputing unions absorbs the weaker. Jurisdictional laissez faire thus described is not so much a policy as the absence of a policy. It is not so much a means of accommodating technological change as a means of institutionalizing the inevitable interunion warfare to which, in the absence of a policy, such change must lead.

While the Carpenters were busy making, then breaking, AFL policy, the process of centralization heralded by the 1912 amendments to their constitution continued unabated. Between 1902 and 1912 Huber had done all of the constitutional spadework which, of necessity, preceded centralizing the union. Centralization after 1912 was pursued in three realms. On the constitutional level, new and supplementary powers were given to the general officers. On the industrial level, a subordinate position in the union was created for recently absorbed industrial workers. And on the political level, all locals were brought under the sway of the national officers by the simple process of cutting the most independent and powerful ones, the New York locals, down to size. These various steps were the last taken by the leaders of the United Brotherhood on the road to complete administrative centralization.

CHAPTER XIII

Hardening into Empire·

1912 to 1915

McGUIRE had led a weak confederation of local unions, and Huber a somewhat stronger federation. Between 1912 and 1917 the Kirby-Hutcheson administrations pounded out a system of control from above which rendered the United Brotherhood a strong and centralized organization. This chapter will deal with measures which were passed up to 1915 to effect administrative centralization and to control the Carpenters' new industrial workers.

Guest speaker Secretary-Treasurer William Dobson of the Bricklayers told the delegates to the 1916 Carpenters' convention:

You have a big organization, an institution that requires a further concentration; there is too much authority here and there, it is too scattered.... [You] need concentration of that authority in order to be able to do business more successfully than in the past.[1]

Dobson's blunt advice was given as part of an intense drive against "localism" launched early in Kirby's administration (1913). Power over the executive board, given him by the 1912 convention, was the trump card. Possessed of this, Kirby could have gained the other derivative and technical powers by fiat had he chosen. Wisely,

[1]UBCJA, *1916 Convention Proceedings*, p. 345.

he played his other cards close to the chest. The chaos of the 1904 to 1912 period had amply demonstrated that if he moved too rapidly he might easily be leading a divided organization.

William Shields, former general president, described the progress of this campaign for increased national powers a few years after its inception:

The present administration has been working...[for] centralization of our forces....Now that we have inculcated into the mind of the worker the absolute necessity of organization, we can with profit turn our attention to the centralizing process, which means less machinery, and the least machinery we operate the greater the saving of our finance and naturally the less friction. The importance of this reform is not as yet fully understood by the membership, but our experimenting will develop results that will prove the wisdom of the departure from the old way to the new.[2]

Kirby retained the creaky Huber machine. He simply kept it better oiled and added a few needed parts. Shortly after he took office, he effected a reorganization of headquarters by dividing administrative tasks among eight separate departments, each of which was headed by a clerk.[3] The first vice-president was placed in charge of the administration of mill locals and the label; the second vice-president of all general representatives.

At the 1914 convention the machine ran so smoothly that all the incumbent officers were re-elected by acclaim. The delegates then gave Kirby several far-reaching powers never possessed by his predecessors. These new laws could and did have important consequences, once applied.[4] The most important legislation passed by the 1914 convention, however, was that which finally disposed of

[2]William J. Shields, "Economy and Management," *The Carpenter*, Vol. 36, No. 10, October 1916, p. 9.

[3]Frank Duffy, "The General Office," *The Carpenter*, Vol. 33, No. 7, July 1913, p. 3. The departments were as follows: Claims, Membership, Stenographic, Income, Expense, Shipping, Stock, and Journal.

[4]See "Amendments to the Constitution Submitted by the Eighteenth General Convention Held at Indianapolis, Indiana, September 21 to October 2, 1914," *The Carpenter*, Vol. 34, No. 11, November 1914, pp. 22–36, for a list of questions submitted for referendum vote, and "Result of the Vote," *The Carpenter*, Vol. 35, No. 3, March 1915, p. 32, for the result of the vote. These laws, why they were passed, and how they were applied are discussed in the next chapter.

the industrial workers absorbed by the United Brotherhood since 1902.

When Huber pushed the United Brotherhood's jurisdiction into the mills, he was not aware of the administrative problems posed by a craft-industrial jurisdiction. The problems of jurisdictional expansion and label unionism were handled with skill, dispatch, and a keen sense of union generalship. These problems, though large in scope, were simple in concept, and Huber and his aides, as craft unionists, were trained to handle them. The economic difficulties posed by the addition of thousands of mills and scores of thousands of millworkers were more subtle and less capable of solution by direct and heavy-handed methods.

All of the problems introduced by the new industrial jurisdiction stemmed from the existence of competitive markets in the woodworking industry. A mill along the upper Mississippi marketed its products in both St. Louis and Chicago; one on the upper Hudson in both New York and Buffalo. Before a mill in either of these regions could be organized and given the use of the label, its wage scale had to be brought into line with that of other mills selling to the same markets. How best to deal with an industry capable of freely transporting and marketing its wood products was a ticklish problem for men like Huber whose trade union philosophy had been developed in an industry with noncompeting markets.

There was only one effective system to meet this problem. First the mill jurisdiction might have been divided into fairly autonomous regions containing all mills whose products competed with each other. The head of a district would know at what rate per hour a mill need be organized to preserve the competitive position of other union mills. All organized mills could then have been awarded the United Brotherhood label. A law might then have been passed preventing the construction carpenters from using any but labeled wood.

Such a system was never enacted for two reasons. First, it would have given the woodworkers more autonomy than the carpenters thought proper; it would have made the woodworkers a virtually independent unit. For such an arrangement would have called

188

for a millman to head the mill jurisdiction and each of its various districts. These officers would then have to be elected by a vote of all millmen. They would need the per capita tax of the mill locals to finance their operations. Successfully pursued such a system would have attracted more mill workers to the union. Some day by sheer weight of numbers they might have wrested control of the union from the carpenters. Second, a law forcing the urban carpenters to install all labeled wood would have wreaked havoc with the system of label unionism which left the district council leaders free to enter into arrangements whereby out-of-town wood mills might also be "unfair" mills. The urban carpenter's high wage rate was based, in part, on this system of label unionism.[5] If, without discrimination, he were to install all labeled wood he might lose the benefits of this carefully planned system.

From the outset those millmen concerned with organizing the industry as a whole were aware of these facts. When the label was first adopted, they requested that it not become a means of "building a wall around New York and other large cities."[6] By this reference to a "wall" they meant the tactics of label unionism already described which excluded wood mill products not made in a given city from that city.

The millmen were not united on this issue, however. Those employed in the larger urban centers around which a wall might be built had much to gain from such a wall. It assured their employers a monopoly of the urban market in which they produced and hence more work for the millmen at higher wages than would be the case without a guaranteed market. The city millmen were thus more concerned with the protection of their specific urban job market through label unionism than with unionizing the industry as a whole. They asked, when the label was first adopted, that it not be issued "to any mill...when such action will...reduce the rate of wages in any city or large town."[7]

[5]See above, pp. 161–162, for an explanation of the mechanics of label unionism.
[6]Carpenters and Joiners of America, United Brotherhood of, AFL, *Proceedings of the Eleventh General Convention of Scranton, September 17 to September 28, 1900,* pp. 44–45.
[7]*Ibid.,* p. 73.

In the making of this demand two facts were implied. First, the urban millmen were more concerned with maintaining their own high wages than with organizing the industry. Second, city mill wages were generally higher than those of other mills. This second fact can be explained only by the existence of label unionism.

Thus the millmen lost their only chance of inducing the leaders of the United Brotherhood to unionize the woodworking industry along realistic economic lines by reason of the support the urban millmen gave the carpenters' policy of label unionism. Both the urban millmen and the carpenters had higher wages to gain from the monopoly tactics of label unionism. Both were willing to sacrifice the opportunity to organize the whole woodworking industry in return for higher wages.

When a label was finally adopted in 1902 it became clear that the mill jurisdiction was to serve the interests of the carpenters and a few urban millmen. No mill districts were created, nor were millmen placed in charge of the mill jurisdiction. In fact, no separate mill jurisdiction was created. Most important, the new laws did not force the urban carpenters to hang only labeled wood. The new constitutional label clause provided only that "it shall be the duty of all district councils to *promote* the use of trim and...[mill]work bearing this label...whenever possible."[8]

These new laws left the urban carpenters free to use the mill jurisdiction in whatever way they deemed best. Lacking any voice in the administration of the label, the woodworkers were powerless to protect their interests. The St. Louis millmen complained to one convention that the district council leaders used the mill jurisdiction as a dumping ground for unemployed carpenters.[9] They also claimed that the outside carpenters refused to allow millmen to do carpentry work by demanding of them a separate and high initiation fee.[10] President Huber admitted that while

[8] Carpenters and Joiners of America, United Brotherhood of, *Constitution and Laws,* 1905, pp. 35–36 (italics mine). See Carpenters and Joiners of America, United Brotherhood of, AFL, *Proceedings of the Twelfth General Convention of Atlanta, September 15 to September 30, 1902,* pp. 122–124, for the balance of the label laws enacted in 1902.

[9] UBCJA, *1904 Convention Proceedings,* pp. 193–194.

[10] *Ibid.*

the outside carpenters helped the millmen in some places, "in other localities the outside carpenters have no use whatever for the man working in the mills; as some say, 'they are a drag on the journeymen carpenters.' "[11] The mill owners, playing up this conflict, warned the millmen in 1910 that if they joined the Brotherhood the outside carpenters would take away their work in the winter.[12] In 1920 the Brotherhood's first vice-president admitted that the outside carpenters had until then done little to assist the millmen.[13]

When the 1910 convention met, Huber boasted that the Brotherhood had over four thousand mills under its jurisdiction. But its leaders still offered no scheme to regulate the woodworking industry. Angry resolutions poured in from millmen at all points of the compass. Most of them complained that the officers had devised no method of equalizing the wage rate of competing mills. One resolution stated:

Our members are not permitted to go from a $3 district into a $4 or $5 district and work for their home wage of $3. Neither should the product of their labor, the millwork, be used to undermine the wage of the better paid worker. It needs no argument to demonstrate that such a system would tend to keep the wages at the level of the lowest paid locality instead of raising them to the level of the locality wherein the manufacturer desires to do business.[14]

To millmen, concerned of necessity with industry-wide standards, chaos seemed to prevail. The craft unionists who led both the national organization and the various district councils were not concerned with the industry as a whole, however, but with the industry as it affected the outside carpenter. They wanted to organize only those millmen who did work previously done by carpenters, and they regulated their means accordingly. In 1904 Huber noted that he had done his best "to organize the mills that

[11]*Ibid.*, pp. 37–38.
[12]Harry Payne, Local 166, Rock Island, Illinois, "Letter to the Editor," *The Carpenter,* Vol. 30, No. 5, May 1910, p. 29.
[13]John Cosgrove, "Our Craft Label," *The Carpenter,* Vol. 40, No. 7, July 1920, p. 16.
[14]UBCJA, *1910 Convention Proceedings,* p. 566.

191

manufacture material for the construction of buildings."[15] In 1906 he said that "strenuous efforts have been put forth to organize the mills *doing work which necessarily comes under the heading of material for the construction of buildings.*"[16]

The Carpenters unionized the mills they did organize from the cities out to the mills supplying the city, rather than from the mills into the markets they supplied. As early as 1901 P. H. McCarthy organized the mills serving San Francisco from the inside out.[17] Throughout 1908 New York was organized in the same fashion. In 1909 it was announced that only four mills serving New York City did not have the Brotherhood label.[18] In 1910 Huber reported progress in mill organization in terms of the large cities. He announced that district councils of San Francisco, St. Louis, New Orleans, Cleveland, Buffalo, and New York City were all picking off the mills which supplied their carpenters with machine-finished building wood.[19]

President D. D. Mulcahy of the old Wood Workers alluded to this system of organizing mills when, in capitulating to the Carpenters in 1911, he said bitterly:

You cannot successfully amalgamate two sets of men [carpenters and woodworkers] whose feelings are so far apart. . . . They [the Carpenters] have got some [mill] men. . . but in the. . . centers of the industry today there is little effort toward organizing these men, and there is less success attained than ever before.[20]

Andrew Furuseth made the same observation in 1915 during the debate on the ouster of the Carpenters already alluded to. He said:

When the wood worker's [union]. . . was absorbed, some of the members stayed with the Carpenters and their condition was somewhat improved because they were in close relation to building; but the men who worked in factories making. . . [wood products] that could be transported everywhere were. . . pretty thoroughly forgotten.[21]

[15]UBCJA, *1904 Convention Proceedings,* p. 37 (italics mine).
[16]UBCJA, *1906 Convention Proceedings,* p. 58 (italics mine).
[17]"San Francisco Strike Won," *The Carpenter,* Vol. 21, No. 2, February 1901, p. 10.
[18]*The Carpenter,* Vol. 29, No. 11, November 1909, p. 14.
[19]UBCJA, *1910 Convention Proceedings,* p. 86.
[20]AFL, *1911 Convention Proceedings,* p. 321.
[21]AFL, *1915 Convention Proceedings,* pp. 412–415.

Two separate incidents demonstrate how the city district councils placed the mills at their service. The Tri-City district council of Rock Island, Illinois, complained throughout 1909 and 1910 that the national office was neglecting their mills. They were able to get no substantial assistance, however. Then, at the 1910 convention, the officers of the Tri-City district council demonstrated that their mills were a part of a distinct economic district bordering the Mississippi whose mills marketed their products in St. Louis and Chicago. With those facts on hand, the officers of the Brotherhood changed the name of the Tri-City district council to "Central Mississippi Valley," changed its jurisdiction accordingly, and contributed two thousand dollars with which to organize the district.[22]

In the course of 1911, after much difficulty, Huber and Kirby succeeded in unionizing the Brunswick-Balke-Collender firm's Oshkosh, Wisconsin, mill. In order to gain a foothold, they accepted the best hourly rate they could get. They were thanked for their efforts at the 1912 convention by a stinging resolution from the Dubuque millmen who said that the Wisconsin mill was able to undersell the Dubuque mills on the Dubuque market. They demanded that Huber abrogate the agreement and turn the new millmen out into the nonunion wilds. Huber was defensive about his role in the making of the agreement but finally agreed to repudiate it.[23]

From the millworkers' point of view, this reverse system of organization had the defect of shaping the industry to fit some of its markets and ignoring the rest. Just as carpenters did not represent the only consumer of mill products, the large cities did not represent the only markets for mill products. With its emphasis on the welfare of the city market, this system could not fail to lead to a steady constriction of the number of mills marketing in a given city.[24] It purposefully subjugated the interests of all mill-

[22]"Proceedings of the Fourth Quarterly Session of the G.E.B.," January 28, *The Carpenter,* Vol. 31, No. 2, February 1911, p. 30.
[23]UBCJA, *1912 Convention Proceedings,* p. 725.
[24]Once the Carpenters controlled the New York market, for instance, they started reducing the number of firms which marketed there until it was all but closed to any but New York firms. This set afoot the events leading to the Paine Case (see

workers to those of a few city millmen and carpenters, and it made the urban areas high wage oases cases in an industrial desert otherwise dominated by a wage-reducing competition.

The millmen were outraged and flooded the 1912 convention with protests. The leaders of the Brotherhood had to face the problem squarely at this convention. Perhaps a quarter of the Brotherhood's membership at this time was in mill and other industrial local unions. Great danger existed of the union dividing into factions, or even splitting into several separate unions, if the complaints of the millmen were not met or countered at this convention.

Huber agreed, in the treaty of amalgamation signed with the Wood Workers' Union in 1912, to establish a committee of millmen to consider the problems of the industry.[25] True to his word, he appointed this committee shortly after the 1912 convention opened. In their report the members of the committee put forth the first sound plan for unionizing the industry to come from the councils of the United Brotherhood. They advised that before any collective bargaining agreement involving the mill jurisdiction be declared binding it be passed upon by a committee of seven millmen, one from each of seven districts into which the mills of the nation were to be divided. This was hardly a definitive answer to the problem of competing mills and unequal wage rates, but it did constitute the only reasonable approach to such an answer: allow the workers in the industry to handle their own problems in their own way. The convention spurned this plan.

The problem was then passed to a special Label Committee. Its members reported that they had "pondered faithfully over the union label question and we are sorry to report to you that as yet your committee is unable to arrive at any plan that is satisfactory, even to your committee." They went on to say that "there is no

---

above, p. 165). The same thing happened in Chicago, in 1918 (Montgomery, p. 104). In San Francisco it happened early in 1901 when the mill owners, having failed to defeat P. H. McCarthy, joined him. After 1901 all millwork used in San Francisco construction had to come from local mills. The wages of the workers went up 25 percent; the price of mill products up to 100 percent, in some cases, and over 50 percent in all cases (Ryan, pp. 95–96).

[25]See above, p. 117.

way of determining, when we see the label on goods coming from other cities, under which conditions it was placed thereon. All that we do know is that the men are organized."[26]

The mill question was no nearer solution at the convention's end than it had been before the convention began. Although the delegates went on to place the first vice-president in charge of the administration of the mills and the label, this served only to place the millmen even more at the disposal of the carpenters, for no provisions were made to have the first vice-president chosen by, or to be in any way responsible to, the millmen.

The millmen's demand for a measure of autonomy was a cloud on the horizon which developed into a thunderhead at the 1914 convention. Local 309 presented a resolution which stated that the "United Brotherhood is fast becoming an industrial organization. . . . This convention. . . [should] instruct. . . our delegates to . . . propagate. . . the principle of industrial form of organization."[27]

The leaders of the Brotherhood then moved to dissipate for all time the threat posed by the millmen. A new type of local, the auxiliary union, was proposed on the initiative of the Committee on the Constitution. However, the Committee's report was vague about the exact nature of the auxiliary union. Under questioning Committee Chairman Dan Featherstone held that the term was not so much vague as elastic. It might easily be confused with *ladies* auxiliaries. But, in point of fact, he said, the Committee had in mind members of other organizations "we have taken over. . . such as the Amalgamated Wood Workers. . . ." This was being done, he said, because "we have sometimes found it difficult to handle certain of their members. . . who. . . were not fully qualified for membership in the Brotherhood. Committee member Pratt was even more frank when he stated:

The object. . .of the committee in specifying auxiliary unions was to give us a chance to handle the men we cannot handle otherwise; to put them off [to] one side under the banner of the United Brother-

[26]UBCJA, *1912 Convention Proceedings,* pp. 801–802.
[27]UBCJA, *1914 Convention Proceedings,* p. 533.

hood, with no voice in the doings of the Local Union[s] or the Brotherhood.

. . .

We would give them a charter from the Brotherhood, but it does not give them the right to voice in our District Councils or anywhere else. But they are under our authority, and must obey the mandates of our General Constitution.[28]

This measure was passed by the convention and, on a favorable referendum vote, incorporated into the constitution.

From 1902 to 1914 the United Brotherhood drifted rapidly away from craft unionism. The work of the 1914 convention halted the drift at the point of craft-industrialism. Although the United Brotherhood claimed jurisdiction over the entire woodworking industry, it was clear by 1914 that the leaders of the Brotherhood did not intend to unionize indiscriminately the whole industry. Rather, they claimed jurisdiction as the paramount trade in the industry in order to police their industry effectively. There is a vast difference between policing and unionizing an industry.

As organizers of the woodworking industry, the interests of the carpenters would have been subordinated to the interests of those who worked on, or with, wood. For to *organize* the competitive woodworking industry the United Brotherhood would need to organize all of its firms and all of their workers. This would have three effects. It would make label unionism—with its principle of selective organization of the industry in terms of its markets— impossible. It would have introduced some very uncarpenterlike "carpenters" into the union—for instance boiler room personnel and shipping clerks—who might attempt to foist industrial unionism upon the carpenters. Finally, both industrial and label unionism aside, there was always the threat that by their very numbers woodworkers might swamp the carpenters in their own union. For all of these reasons, the United Brotherhood in 1914, in spite of its vehement assertion of jurisdiction over the woodworking industry, chose not to be the industry's organizer but its policeman.

As policeman the Brotherhood retained an option to unionize any branch of the industry which, because of technological change,

[28]*Ibid.*, p. 526 for the Featherstone quotation and p. 529 for the Pratt quotation.

might threaten the carpenters' craft. Those workers who were organized were organized selectively. Label unionism, industrial unionism, and the possibility of being swamped by woodworkers were kept firmly in mind when the Carpenters organized woodworkers. Once in the union, those workers who were "difficult to handle" were "put off to one side with no voice in the doings of the Brotherhood." Thus auxiliary membership guaranteed that the United Brotherhood would continue to police the industry for the advantage of carpenters and without any fear of internal upheavals from the industrial workers in the union.[29]

The 1914 laws put the finishing touch on a policy of craft-industrialism which had been evolving since 1902 and which has remained the policy of the United Brotherhood to this time. It is based on a determination to preserve the carpenter's craft at all costs. To do this the leaders of the Brotherhood maintain a loose jurisdiction based on a static principle: all work once done by the carpenter shall continue to be done by him no matter what the nature of the material worked on or the tools and skill used. To implement this policy in the AFL, the Carpenters insisted that the Federation leave the jurisdictional question open and subject to constant change. To implement it within their own union, they made the Brotherhood a carpenter-centered union rather than a carpenters' union. The carpenter's craft is the strategic craft among the many in the union's jurisdiction. By refusing to install products without the Brotherhood's label, the Carpenters have gradually forced into their union all crafts and industrial

[29]Because the union did not publish the information it is impossible to say how many woodworkers were in the United Brotherhood at a given time after 1914, or to say how many of them were accorded auxiliary status. Twenty-one years later there were over 179,000 employed furniture and planing mill workers (Census Bureau, Census of Manufacturers, *Wage Earners in Establishments classified according to number of Wage Earners by Industries*, 1933 and 1935, pp. 10, 18). These two groups comprised at the time only a small fraction of the employees in the woodworking industry, over all of whom the Brotherhood claimed jurisdiction. Yet in the same year the Brotherhood claimed a total membership of only 200,000 (AFL, *1935 Convention Proceedings*, p. IV). Even by this rule-of-thumb measurement it seems clear that the Brotherhood organized few of the woodworkers who fell under its jurisdiction. Further, in the same year (1935) when the AFL turned over to the Brotherhood a whole spate of ready-organized woodworkers, Hutcheson gave them a nonvoting status much like auxiliary membership (see below, Chapter XX, "Label Unionism Challenged").

workers who trespass on their jurisdiction. Once admitted into the union by the selective process just described, these workers are dealt with on terms advantageous to the carpenters. This is craft-industrialism as defined by the United Brotherhood.

The laws determining the exact status of the industrial workers were, like the other constitutional measures enacted in 1912 and 1914, a part of the process of centralization inaugurated by Kirby. That these measures were not effected during Huber's administration indicates that the upheaval of 1902 was essentially an economic revolution. The much quieter upheaval of the 1912 to 1917 period was more of an administrative revolution. During this period the gains made from 1902 to 1912 were consolidated and the administrative machinery of the union adapted to the changes ushered in by these gains.

Before Kirby was able to enjoy the full fruits of his newly broadened powers he died, in late 1915. William Levi Hutcheson of Saginaw, Michigan, then took over the reins of government. He was not to set them aside for almost four decades. This forty-one-year-old, Scotch-Irish giant was born on a farm in Bay County, Michigan. For two or three years he puttered with formal schooling before going to work. "All that is important to a man, to a real man, to a real American" he felt he had learned in his early farm life.[30] Beyond the Carpenters' Union, his self-proclaimed life-long enthusiasms were Methodism, Masonry, and Republicanism. These enthusiasms had neither changed nor abated in 1947.[31]

Hutcheson was apprenticed to a carpenter in 1901, joined the United Brotherhood in 1902, and four years later was business agent of his local. In 1910 he first appeared in the national councils of the Brotherhood at the biennial convention. He protested that the brothers with rheumatism were not getting sufficient consideration and proposed that the Brotherhood sponsor a mineral bath establishment to cure this oversight.[32] His proposal came to naught.

[30]"Boss Carpenter," p. 122.
[31]Ibid., p. 118.
[32]UBCJA, 1910 Convention Proceedings, p. 374.

198

That same year Hutcheson ran for the general executive board and lost. At the 1912 convention he again appeared, and, as a supporter of the administration, was awarded a seat on the Committee on Finances. His second bid for office, made in the election following this convention, was successful. On April 9, 1913, he took office as the first full-time, salaried second vice-president to serve the Brotherhood. A. A. Quinn, head of the New Jersey State Federation of Labor, stood before him as first vice-president. Quinn was a power in North Jersey union politics, however, and did not relish the idea of abandoning his Bergen and Hudson County haunts to his enemies in favor of a $1600 a year job in the Middle West. Hence, on April 22, he begged off because of "eye trouble," and Hutcheson assumed his job. With Kirby's death a year and a half later, Hutcheson had completed his rise from plowboy to union president.

Kirby gave Hutcheson a much more powerful national office than he had received from Huber. It was, however, not nearly powerful enough for Hutcheson's purposes. Kirby had dealt cautiously with the strong district councils. In 1914 he told the delegates that "no organizer...[was] sent into any territory unless assistance was asked."[33] In fact he added: "No organizer is allowed to remain in a district where the membership oppose him, and some times I have removed organizers from localities...owing to the fact that certain elements were aligned against them, and I felt it was not to the best interests of the movement to continue them in that jurisdiction."[34] Where Kirby had tread softly, Hutcheson hurled bolts of thunder. He reserved his first bolt for the powerful, independent, and willful New York City locals.

[33]UBCJA, *1914 Convention Proceedings*, p. 27.
[34]*Ibid.*

CHAPTER XIV

Taming the New York City

Locals

HUTCHESON'S quarrel with the New York City locals was more than a struggle for power. While love of power for its own sake undoubtedly motivated him, the dispute arose inevitably out of certain policies being pursued by the national officers. To understand these policies, it is necessary to examine in another light some points already made.

It will be recalled that the United Brotherhood adopted a new policy of jurisdictional opportunism in 1914 and 1915.[1] In order to implement the policy, Kirby made a treaty with the Bricklayers wherein each union agreed to support the other's jurisdictional claims by mutual striking and boycotting.[2] The 1914 convention delegates thought the treaty a fine tactic and gave the President specific power to enter into national jurisdictional agreements and to make general offensive and defensive alliances.[3]

Under this new policy the various district councils were called upon to support the Bricklayers in matters where their own immediate welfare was not concerned. It was a difficult matter

---

[1] See above, pp. 181–185.
[2] See above, p. 177.
[3] See above, p. 187. Kirby, strictly speaking, did not possess the power to sign the 1914 treaty, but because the treaty was popular, it went uncontested. The 1914 convention then gave the president this power.

to convince the local leaders to strike for anything other than immediate and tangible gain, however, and only a strong president could make and force the various district councils to observe the alliances upon which the new jurisdictional policy was based. Consequently, Kirby brought Secretary William Dobson of the Bricklayers to the 1914 convention to lecture the carpenters on the need to give the general president greater power over the locals so that the United Brotherhood could live up to its treaty obligations. Dobson told the delegates of one instance, in Philadelphia, where the national officers of the two unions, working together under the terms of the treaty, had obtained an especially favorable contract for the carpenters.[4]

The delegates were impressed and cautiously extended power to regulate local affairs to Kirby. He received permission to consolidate as many locals as he deemed advisable; to "take possession of," as well as to examine the books and papers of, any local or district council; to order a strike in any locality in spite of local agreements; and to make local or national agreements with employers where and when he chose.[5] Each of these new laws was necessary to enforce the new treaty system, which in turn was vital to the new jurisdictional policy made necessary by a changing industry.

To make laws was one thing, to force them on the proud, powerful, and parochial district councils was another. The various district councils clearly wanted to gain all the benefits of a national alliance with the Bricklayers, but to surrender no actual freedom of action. They were willing to pass laws giving the general president the power over local affairs necessary to effect such a national alliance. But when they passed these laws, the district council leaders apparently saw only the benefits and not the responsibilities entailed by such an alliance. For when the general president enforced them in order to fulfill the United Brotherhood's treaty obligations, the district council leaders set up an enormous clatter. Secretary William Dobson of the Bricklayers started complain-

[4]UBCJA, *1914 Convention Proceedings*, p. 754.
[5]*Ibid.*, pp. 637, 692; Carpenters and Joiners of America, United Brotherhood of, *Constitution and Laws*, 1917, pp. 9–10.

ing almost as soon as the treaty ink dried about the irresponsible actions of the various district councils. The Carpenters, he held, began strikes capriciously and refused reasonable settlement offers in city after city during the course of 1915.[6] "One organization," he told the Carpenters, "cannot and must not be permitted...to do as it pleases [and to] go out on strike and cause trouble in a city."[7] No one group of carpenters needed taming more than did the New York City locals.

The New York City building trades were a law unto themselves, not only in their relations with other New York City unions but also in their dealings with their respective international organizations, with the AFL, and, after its founding, with the Building Trades Department. Rarely did the delegates to the biennial convention of the United Brotherhood adjourn without first having given special consideration to some complaint, dispute, or demand from the New York brothers.[8]

New York building techniques were a decade or more in advance of those of other cities, and New York building activities involved more capital than those of any other city on the continent. With this early start and larger enterprise, the institutions of building trades unionism came to maturity at a far earlier date in New York City than elsewhere. For example, in the case of the carpenters, the first continuous modern trade unions took root in New York City between 1868 and 1871, over a decade before the United Brotherhood was founded. The business agent, in his modern form, was active in New York City as early as 1883. Most of the Brotherhood's jurisdictional fights first arose in New York City. The New York carpenters were the first to use the union label, and they foisted it on the national organization.

Independent local unions of various building trades were strongly entrenched in New York City years before national unions

[6]UBCJA, *1916 Convention Proceedings,* pp. 339–345. He picked out Alton, Illinois; Los Angeles, California; Detroit, Michigan; New Haven, Connecticut; and Parkersburg, West Virginia, for special attention.

[7]*Ibid.,* p. 344.

[8]For examples, see the following: United Brotherhood of Carpenters and Joiners of America, *1896 Convention Proceedings,* p. 9; United Brotherhood of Carpenters and Joiners of America, *1900 Convention Proceedings,* p. 15; United Brotherhood of Carpenters and Joiners of America, *1906 Convention Proceedings,* pp. 321–326.

were formed. Although the United Brotherhood leaders were among the first to force the New York locals of their trade into the national union, they were not able to do so until nine years after the Brotherhood was founded, and then only after a long and bitter struggle with the New York carpenters. Most other national building trades unions were not even represented in New York City until 1900,[9] and in 1913 this representation remained, at best, nominal.

Between 1900 and 1903, the New York employers organized themselves as the Building Trades Employers Association,[10] and the various building trades unions, through their business agents, formed the Board of Business Agents.[11] Together the two groups regulated New York City building to their own satisfaction and to the exclusion of the various national unions. They settled jurisdictional matters in their own way without consulting national union officers, banned sympathetic striking, and practiced collusion and racketeering on a scale unmatched in any other city.

When Hutcheson first assumed national office in 1913, the various New York City building trades locals were as independent as they would have been without the existence of national unions. The Board of Business Agents refused to accept a building trades council charter from the Building Trades Department (even though, their locals being affiliated with AFL unions, they were obliged to do so) because the Department's laws prohibited agreements such as they had with the Building Trades Employers' Association. At the 1913 convention of the Building Trades Department, the presidents of the various unions evinced growing concern with the reckless autonomy of their New York locals. When they tried to force a charter on the New York locals, however, James Taggart, one of the members of the New York City Board of Business Agents, flatly stated:

[9]"The Story of a Crime," *Painter and Decorator* (official journal of the Brotherhood of Painters, Decorators, and Paperhangers of America), Vol. 24, No. 12, December 1920, p. 523.

[10]See above, pp. 158–159.

[11]The Board of Business Agents consisted of all the business agents of each of the various building trades unions. They met as a group, elected officers, and acted together on strikes, lockouts, and collective bargaining negotiations.

I am convinced that there can be a charter put in New York City by this Department, but what will it amount to? Nothing.

. . .

Within two or three weeks after the Council is instituted in New York City the Secretary [of the Building Trades Department] will ...notify [the] different...organizations that they must live up to the laws. Will they do it? No.[12]

This was the situation when Hutcheson assumed the presidency and turned his attention to New York. His locals in New York City were too many, too strong, and had too many allies, both in the union and management camps, for him to assault directly. Instead, two more devious tactics were used. First he made powerful friends through whom he infiltrated the closed ranks of the New York carpenters. Then, with the assistance of these friends, he outflanked, isolated, and beat the sixteen thousand New York carpenters into line. The most important of these friends was Robert Brindell who, between 1914 and 1920, became czar of the New York building trades.

Brindell was a Canadian who had worked as a dock walloper before migrating to the United States. Drugstore clerking occupied him in Providence, Rhode Island, until 1905, when he moved to New York City. There he took a job as a dock builder's helper[13] and promptly joined the Independent Dock Union which was chartered as AFL Federal Union 12429 in March 1907.[14] Failure to pay dues caused the AFL charter to be revoked in January 1910,[15] and the Independent Dock Union continued as an unaffiliated local. A majority group in the union wished to return to the AFL, however, and during a dispute over the conduct of a strike, they broke away, formed the Municipal Dock Builders Union in

[12]Building Trades Department, *1913 Convention Proceedings,* p. 124.

[13]New York State, Joint Legislative Committee on Housing, *Hearings on New York City Housing,* Annual Session of the Legislature, 1920, Vol. 1, pp. 44–59. This joint legislative committee will be cited henceforth as the Lockwood Committee, after its chairman, Charles Lockwood.

[14]"Report of the Delegates to the Convention of the American Federation of Labor," *Bridgeman* (official journal of the International Association of Bridge and Structural Iron Workers), Vol. 16, No. 1, January 1916, p. 17. A federal union is a local union chartered directly by the national officers of the AFL and belonging to no international union.

[15]*Ibid.*

the spring of 1910, and accepted an AFL charter on July 7. At this time the Municipal Dock Builders Union had one thousand members and the Independent Dock Union three hundred and fifty.[16]

Brindell remained in the Independent Dock Union, gained control of it, and was elected business agent in 1912. In the summer of 1914 he started a flirtation with the officers of the United Brotherhood and the AFL. Why each of these three parties started to deal with the others cannot be categorically determined. The heavy pall of corruption which subsequently surrounded Brindell's name has served to obscure motives during the earlier period when he first won friends and influenced people in the AFL. Possible motives can be strongly suggested, however.

Brindell had everything to gain, hence his motives are easy to divine. The aid of the AFL would help him greatly in uniting the two dock builders locals (one of which had an AFL charter). Brindell would then be in a position to gain ascendance on the docks and to move from that vantage point upward in New York labor circles.

It is difficult to account for the fact that Gompers spent his time personally negotiating with the obscure business agent of a small independent dock workers union if he did not have aims broader than simply inducing the local to affiliate with the AFL. In order to establish the power of the AFL in New York City Gompers wanted to get an AFL Building Trades Department charter in the city, for without the inclusion of the nation's leading city the Building Trades Department would always be something of a farce. It was generally felt around building trades circles in 1915 that the Carpenters had recommended Brindell as a "strong man" well fashioned for the task. It is not at all unlikely that Gompers, on the advice of the Carpenters, decided to back Brindell and to have him force the Board of Business Agents into the Building Trades Department once he had gained some degree of power.

[16]*Ibid.* The Municipal Dock Builders Union was later absorbed into the Iron Workers' Union.

The larger part of the Carpenters' motives was below the surface. If their motive had been only to gain jurisdiction over the dock workers, the Municipal Dock Builders, a federal union, was ripe for the plucking. AFL federal unions were notoriously easy prey for the larger AFL trade unions. Subsequent events indicate that the national officers of the United Brotherhood interested themselves in Brindell rather than in the Municipal Dock Builders in the hope that through him they could gain control of the New York City District Council.

President Kirby, Executive Board Members Tim Guerin and Dan Post, AFL organizer Hugh Frayne, and Gompers closeted themselves in a hotel room with Brindell during the 1914 convention of the New York State Federation of Labor and opened negotiations which rapidly bore fruit.[17] On February 13, 1915, the United Brotherhood went through the formality of "laying claim" to the Independent Dock Union. The AFL executive council responded by an equally formal "investigation" of the claim which consisted wholly of another conference among Gompers, Kirby, and Brindell.[18] Shortly thereafter the Carpenters chartered Brindell's union as Local Union 1456 and claimed the Federal Union of Municipal Dock Builders as well. When the Municipal Dock Builders refused to associate themselves with Brindell even though he had been legitimized by the United Brotherhood, Gompers revoked their federal charter.[19]

Fearing Brindell, the Municipal Dock Builders started casting about for allies in the spring of 1915 and affiliated with the International Association of Bridge, Structural and Ornamental Iron Workers as Local Union 177.[20] Some inkling of their reason for distrusting Brindell was hinted at by President J. E. McClory of the Iron Workers:

[17] *The Carpenters' Trade Journal* (the organ of the New York State Carpenters' Council), Vol. 2, No. 4, September 1914, pp. 24–25.

[18] "Report of the Delegates to the Convention of the American Federation of Labor," *Bridgeman,* Vol. 16, No. 1, January 1916, p. 17.

[19] *Ibid.;* AFL, *1915 Convention Proceedings,* pp. 136–137.

[20] UBCJA, *1920 Convention Proceedings,* p. 314. As a result of a 1909 agreement with the Carpenters, the Iron Workers had jurisdiction over all iron work on the docks *(ibid.).*

206

Large numbers of dock builders were deserting this independent union ...because of conditions in the...Independent Dock Builders Benevolent Union which they refused to countenance...and which we believe would not be countenanced by...the AFL. Those that were responsible for these conditions sought to perpetuate their power...by seeking a local charter from the United Brotherhood.[21]

If President McClory was hinting at graft and corruption in his thinly veiled remarks, at least one person in a position to know felt that Brindell was auspiciously launched on his career of racketeering and extortion by June of 1915.

The one question outstanding in the summer of 1915 was: with which group would the dock building contractors cast their lot? On August 10 they answered this question by signing a favorable three-year contract with Local 177. The sides thus chosen, there was no course but warfare. On August 11, the day after the contract had been announced, the executive board of the Brotherhood sanctioned a strike by the three hundred members of Brindell's union.[22] From the outset, Brindell, Hutcheson, and Gompers preserved the fiction of a wage strike. The members of Local Union 177 were conveniently branded as "dual" and as "scabs." Henry Steers, one of the leading dock builders in the city, admitted for publication, however, that neither wages and hours nor working conditions was at issue. Rather, he inferred that Brindell's ambitions had caused the strike, without mentioning him by name.[23]

With the employers' backing and with over sixteen hundred of the two thousand dock workers in their union, Local 177 stood firm. Its leaders ignored Brindell's sniping tactics and even ignored the award of an AFL investigating committee. By January 1916 the United Brotherhood withdrew financial support and the strike ended with the Iron Workers still in control of the docks. At the 1916 AFL convention Gompers, Hutcheson, and Brindell engineered the Iron Workers' expulsion. The Iron Workers took this

[21]August Holmstrom, "Reply to a Statement of Samuel Gompers Concerning the Charter of Local Union No. 177," *Bridgeman,* Vol. 15, No. 9, September 1915, pp. 622–623.
[22]"Minutes of the Proceedings of the Fourth Quarterly Session, 1915, of the G. E. B.," August 11, *The Carpenter,* Vol. 35, No. 12, December 1915, p. 19.
[23]*New York Times,* Jan. 3, 1916, p. 20, col. 1.

blow, rolled with it, and maintained their position on the docks.[24]

Even suspension had no effect upon the purely economic struggle on the docks. The Iron Workers clung tenaciously to their jurisdiction. However, an important change in the economic pattern occurred during the later summer and early fall of 1917. The entry of the United States into World War I in April 1917 caused an expansion of dock work. Dock building became a matter of great concern to the federal government. McClory's heretofore staunchly loyal dock contractors mysteriously started signing up with the Carpenters. When two of the largest left and hinted at government pressure as the reason, McClory hastened to Washington to plumb the situation. There he found Admiral Frederick R. Harriss of the Bureau of Docks and Yards uninterested in matters of jurisdiction but determined to have the needed docks built.[25] The Carpenters' tactics were first revealed when, toward the end of 1917, Hutcheson threatened to pull twenty-eight thousand men off several government jobs if the Carpenters were not awarded the pile driving then being done by the Iron Workers on a Pelham Bay job.[26]

The war had tipped the scales in the Carpenters' favor by enabling them to bring into play their notorious and effective "absent treatment." Deserted by one dock contractor after another, McClory capitulated on November 13, 1917.[27] Thus ended the first phase of what, for the New York City carpenters, was to be a long and bitter struggle. The second phase of this struggle had gotten underway in January 1916 within the councils of the United

[24]See R. A. Christie, "History," pp. 373–374, for the details of the strike and the Iron Workers' expulsion.

[25]"Report of President J. E. McClory, November 5, 1917," *Bridgeman,* Vol. 17, No. 12, December 1917, pp. 636–637.

[26]*Ibid.,* p. 641. Pile driving, an important part of dock work, was part of the jurisdiction being contested. In fact, an important aspect of this dispute was the fact that it represented another broadening of the Carpenters' jurisdiction into the metal trades. The dispute with the Iron Workers—apart from its implication on the New York scene—was but another phase of the Carpenters' campaign to maintain jurisdiction over all materials that "were ever made of wood." As such it logically complements disputes then (1914–1917) current with the Sheet Metal Workers and the Machinists, the causes and course of which are discussed above in Chapter XII, "Or That Was Ever Made of Wood."

[27]UBCJA, *1920 Convention Proceedings,* p. 334.

Brotherhood. It is necessary to reach beyond this date to the time of Brindell's alliance with Hutcheson to trace this internal phase of the New York struggle.

Brindell was a nobody in 1913. He was not in the AFL. He led only a three-hundred-and-fifty-man group which was the smaller of two dock workers' local unions. Although he sat on the Board of Business Agents, he carried but little weight.[28] Then, in 1914, fortune smiled upon him. The building trades were in the doldrums. Business agents of the Carpenters and other building trades unions were hard put to fulfill the primary obligation upon which their tenure was based, that of obtaining work for the rank and file.[29] Although the war in Europe gave promise of a boom, it was slow in getting under way. The boom, based on foreign trade, naturally enough hit the docks first. As business agent of the Dock Workers, Brindell had more jobs than he could fill when in 1915 the other business agents were having a difficult time keeping a majority of their working force employed.[30] Brindell's power was immediately enhanced by these economic facts. For this and the other reasons already suggested,[31] Brindell was able to add the power and prestige of Hutcheson and Gompers to his forces.

Hutcheson's bestowal of favor upon an outsider, who was not even a carpenter, was not greeted enthusiastically by the ruling hierarchy of the New York district council. They had cooperated enthusiastically enough with Hutcheson and Gompers in legitimizing Brindell in 1914 and 1915 when they were seeking to place their unemployed on the docks, but as Brindell started to gain influence on the Board of Business Agents, they rapidly came to see him in an unfavorable light. The split between the older leaders of the New York district council and the newcomer became open in May as Hutcheson, Brindell, and the Building Trades Employers' Association lined up to bring the New York district council to heel.

[28]Philip Zausner, *Unvarnished*, p. 112.
[29]*Ibid.*
[30]*Ibid.*
[31]See above, pp. 204–206. Brindell's later notoriety as a racketeer has obscured his earlier career. Undoubtedly, however, there are other factors which account for his rise to power from 1913 to 1916. The sources which have aleady been cited fail to provide any more specific details on his career.

As Brindell rose to power, Hutcheson's relations with the New York district council leaders deteriorated. In 1914 the New York carpenters had not received a wage raise in several years. They wanted one and prodded their leaders. Hutcheson, for reasons of his own, did not want the demand pressed and above all did not want a strike in New York. Even though two-thirds of the members present at a district council meeting had voted for a wage demand, the executive board refused to sanction it.[32] Finally, in the spring of 1916, Secretary Elbridge Neal of the New York district council appeared in Indianapolis to wrangle for permission to turn out on May 1, 1916 for a fifty-cents-a-day increase in four of New York's boroughs and a sixty-cents advance in the fifth, Manhattan. After a long session, the board gave reluctant consent. It agreed to give financial aid to any strike which ensued, with the understanding that the district council create its own strike fund and that an organizing drive be gotten under way in preparation for the strike.[33]

Less than three weeks before the turnout was scheduled, on April 10, in line with the new policy of central control, the executive board laid down a rule that no strike was to be undertaken until Hutcheson had had an opportunity to effect a settlement.[34] On April 20 Elbridge Neal was informed that this new ruling applied specifically to New York City.[35] On May 1 seventeen thousand men turned out on schedule. Most of the employers capitulated rapidly, as they usually did in boom times under strike pressure. By the time Hutcheson arrived in New York four days later, fourteen thousand out of seventeen thousand carpenters had obtained their original demands and were back at work.[36]

[32]This dispute is recounted in UBCJA, *1914 Convention Proceedings*, pp. 764–771.

[33]"Minutes of Proceedings of the First Quarterly Session, 1916, of the G. E. B.," January 18, *The Carpenter*, Vol. 36, No. 2, February 1916, p. 28.

[34]"Minutes of Proceedings of the Second Quarterly Session, 1916, of the G. E. B.," April 10, *The Carpenter*, Vol. 36, No. 5, May 1916, p. 22.

[35]Letter from Duffy to E. H. Neal, as quoted in *The Carpenter*, Vol. 36, No. 8, August 1916, p. 56. Brindell, the only important New York leader to remain loyal to Hutcheson in the subsequent struggle, held that Neal "deliberately concealed" this letter from the other officers and the rank and file.

[36]United Brotherhood of Carpenters and Joiners of America, Local Union 376, *Appeal of Local Union 376 of New York City of the United Brotherhood of Carpenters and Joiners of America*, pp. 25, 29; *New York Times*, May 7, 1916, Sec. I, p. 12, col. 3.

Hutcheson's exact moves during his twelve hours in New York City have been disputed. The administration supporters claim that he spent the forenoon of May 5 closeted with the district council officers. At this meeting, Hutcheson's supporters alleged, the district council officers confessed that they could neither protect the United Brotherhood's jurisdiction in New York City nor get further wage raises from the employers' association.[37]

The council leaders saw the matter differently. They said that Hutcheson came to New York City unannounced, spoke only with Brindell and his henchmen, and then met secretly with the employers. Their first inkling of his presence was gleaned, they said, when he strode into the district council office and announced a new settlement and immediate termination of the strike.[38]

There was no difference of opinion on the nature of the settlement. Under its terms the carpenters were to return to work immediately under the old wage rate, the increase obtained by fourteen thousand carpenters having been forsaken by Hutcheson.[39] On July 1 the carpenters in all five boroughs were to get a twenty-five-cents-a-day increase, and on September 1 another twenty-five cents. Under this settlement the Manhattan carpenters lost 10 cents a day which they had gained in the strike, and the carpenters in all five boroughs got their 50-cents raise two months later than they would otherwise have received it.

Hutcheson said that he made this settlement in order to "get rid of the levies of Manhattan locals on Brooklyn brothers who came to Manhattan to get the higher scale."[40] The district council officers felt otherwise. They said that Hutcheson had made a deal with the employers in order to put Brindell in power and through Brindell to bring the powerful New York district council under his uncontested sway.[41]

[37]UBCJA, *1916 Convention Proceedings*, pp. 42–43; "The New York Situation," *The Carpenter*, Vol. 36, No. 6, June 1916, pp. 16–17; "An Open Letter to the Members Regarding the New York Situation," *The Carpenter*, Vol. 36, No. 8, August 1916, p. 56.

[38]*Appeal of Local Union 376*, p. 25.

[39]*Ibid.*, p. 29; "The New York Situation," pp. 16–17.

[40]"Boss Carpenter," *Fortune*, Vol. 41, No. 4, April 1946, p. 123.

[41]United Brotherhood of Carpenters and Joiners of America, New York State Carpenters Council, Circular, as quoted in *Appeal of Local Union 376*, pp. 24–26.

Whatever Hutcheson's motives, he proceeded to enforce his settlement with characteristic vigor. On the afternoon of the night it was to be held, he called a mass meeting of all New York carpenters at the Cooper Union. Although only eight hundred were able to show up on such short notice, Hutcheson acquainted these with his plan. Furious opposition resulted, and he was finally forced to call in the police to quiet the objectors.[42] Forty minutes after opening, the meeting adjourned. Hutcheson hastily caught a train west and left his aides to reap the whirlwind.

It was not long in coming. Almost immediately after Hutcheson's departure the district council held its own protest meeting in Cooper Union and rejected Hutcheson's settlement.[43] A referendum vote on the proposed settlement was held a few days later, and 11,745 carpenters rejected Hutcheson's settlement, while only 119 accepted it.[44] On May 12 the executive board suspended the sixty-three rebel locals and the district council.

The strike continued. Brindell and his followers alone remained loyal to the general president. Neal procured a temporary injunction restraining Hutcheson from exercising his constitutional power of appropriating the property and records of a district council which might be suspended. At a hearing on July 7, 1916, Judge J. A. Mullan, of the Bronx County branch of the New York State Supreme Court, upheld this injunction.[45]

Hutcheson, however, was not without his defenses. He put his economic countermeasures into the hands of General Representative Dan Featherstone, who turned the hiring hall of Brindell's Local Union 1456 into a dual district council headquarters. Letters, the following of which is typical, were sent to all strikers by the employers: "If you want to work call at the International Headquarters, 210 E. 5th Street and get a transfer card to another local in good standing." It was signed by a contractor.[46]

Tactics like these had their effect. On July 23 the *New York*

[42]*Ibid.*
[43]*Ibid.*
[44]*Ibid.*, p. 29.
[45]*Neal* v. *Hutcheson*, 160 N.Y.S. 1007–1010 (1916).
[46]*Appeal of Local Union 376*, p. 26.

212

Times reported that over half of the seceders were unemployed.[47] In August, using a familiar tactic, Brindell denounced the seceders as Socialists and Industrial Workers of the World sympathizers.[48] To label the grizzled old New York business agents radicals took either a virile imagination or a perverse sense of humor. The social cooperation indulged in by these gentlemen began and ended with their activities on the Board of Business Agents.

Here affairs stood when the 1916 Fort Worth convention met in September. It was the wildest convention in the union's history. The New York locals sent a host of delegates who were prepared, if need be, to crash the convention doors in a flying wedge. They were met by a solid phalanx of Fort Worth's finest, who barred the doors. For the duration of the convention they wandered the streets, men dispossessed, buttonholing delegates in bars or hotel rooms to plead their case.

Inside the convention hall all was turmoil. Delegate after delegate rose to protest the expulsion of one-tenth of the union's membership, to demand that the New York representatives at least be heard before they were judged. Time and again Hutcheson's gavel descended in a thunderous crash to cut off all discussion. Its steady rapping accompanied by the words, "You are out of order," drowned all protest.[49] At one time the delegates were on their feet chanting, "Let New York in to hear this trial."[50]

The New York carpenters did not hear their trial. Hutcheson would not have survived the convention had they done so, for he won one vital vote by only thirty-nine ballots. The New York locals had ninety-seven delegates with a good many more votes. On the last day the leader of the opposition, W. S. Bundy of Kansas City, was expelled for demanding a roll-call vote on a motion to have the question of suspension put to a referendum. As the last act of the convention, the suspension was approved.

Shortly after the convention adjourned, Hutcheson is said to have sent a copy of the proceedings to the office of the Building

[47]*New York Times,* July 23, 1916, Sec. I, p. 10, col. 2.
[48]"Open Letter," p. 57 (the Communist party in the United States was not founded until the early 1920's).
[49]UBCJA, *1916 Convention Proceedings,* pp. 395–403.
[50]*Ibid.*

Trades Employers' Association under cover of the following letter. "You will note by the action taken the manner in which this matter was disposed of and inasmuch as the suspended local unions have not complied therewith, I expect immediate action by your Association."[51]

The "immediate action" was probably increased lockout pressure, accompanied by the strong-arm tactics for which Brindell later became infamous. Whatever its nature, it rapidly brought the locals into line. The leaders of the suspended New York district council held conferences with the executive board from November 8 to 10 in New York City and on November 16 capitulated unconditionally.[52]

During 1917 the New York City carpenters were assigned to clear-cut, easy-to-handle, one-thousand-member local unions. Like Napoleon III, who replaced the crooked, narrow, confused streets of Paris with broad, straight boulevards, Hutcheson replaced the many confused New York local unions and made the United Brotherhood as revolution-proof as Napoleon III made Paris.

Hutcheson then came east and appointed each of the local presidents to a new New York district council. A committee at the next convention, appointed to pass on the reconstitution of the district council, ended its report with grim facetiousness: "Slogan to all Districts: DON'T LET IT HAPPEN TO YOU."[53]

As the architect of Hutcheson's victory over the New York rebels, Brindell was well paid for his services. With the Carpenters' district council tucked securely in his back pocket, with Hutcheson backing him firmly, and with dock work booming, Brindell rapidly swept aside all obstacles and by 1918 was czar of the New York building trades. So securely did he tie up the New York district council after he helped quash the revolt that its headquarters was situated on his own property at 12 St. Marks Place.[54]

From the dock workers placed under his jurisdiction by Hutche-

[51]*Appeal of Local Union 376*, p. 31.

[52]"Minutes of a Special Meeting of the G. E. B. Held in New York City," *The Carpenter*, Vol. 36, No. 12, December 1916, pp. 25–31, contains the minutes of these meetings; UBCJA, *1920 Convention Proceedings*, pp. 171–175.

[53]UBCJA, *1920 Convention Proceedings*, p. 550.

[54]Lockwood Committee, *Hearings*, Vol. 1, p. 51.

son, Brindell levied an exaction of fifty cents per man per month. When, in 1918, war building had swelled the ranks of Local Union 1456 to almost five thousand men, this exaction amounted to about $30,000 a year, and made Brindell the highest-paid trade union leader in the country.[55]

Brindell did equally well in his dealings with the dock employers. Hugh Robertson of the Todd, Iron, and Robertson Company reported paying him $50,000 "insurance" to guarantee the peaceful construction of the multimillion-dollar Cunard docks. Frederick Tench of the Tench Construction Company admitted to the payment of one-half of one percent on the construction of five Staten Island piers, a $3,252,673 job.[56]

Brindell was not only a thief, but he was a flamboyant, ostentatious, overreaching thief. The very brazenness of his deeds, if not the deeds themselves, did him in. So effectively did his "strike insurance" tie up New York building that the New York State legislature set up an investigating committee under Senator Charles Lockwood to probe Brindell's affairs. Throughout 1920 this committee investigated Brindell, and in 1921 he was finally brought to trial and jailed. The prosecuting attorney estimated that in the course of his adventuring Brindell had come by close to a million illegal dollars.[57]

Such are the ascertainable facts of the New York affair. One thing alone is certain: as a result of these events, William Levi Hutcheson finally brought the New York district council to heel. Other things are less certain. The events described in this chapter seem to indicate that Brindell was sponsored by Hutcheson for his own purposes. Further, Hutcheson continued to back him in 1919 and 1920, long after it was common knowledge that Brindell was a thief. It seems equally clear that, once their partnership was formed, the two sided with the employers in order to defeat a membership in arms against the partnership. The exact details of Hutcheson's support of Brindell will remain unknown until

[55]*Ibid.*, p. 54.
[56]New York City Estimate and Apportionment Board, Contract Inquiry, *Stenographer's Minutes,* Vol. 1, pp. 122–124.
[57]W. L. Chenery and J. A. Fitch, "The Untermeyer Revelations," *Survey,* Vol. 45, No. 4, January 1921, pp. 491–492.

the appropriate documents are made available. Samuel Untermeyer, the prosecutor who jailed Brindell, felt strongly enough about the Hutcheson-Brindell alliance to wire the Denver convention of the AFL that "the Federation will...be exceptionally fortunate if the Carpenters' Union can rid itself of Brindell, Hutcheson's crony, who has been an evil influence."[58]

Whatever Brindell's subsequent fate, by 1917 a process of centralization which had been evolving since 1898 was substantially at an end. The constitution of the Brotherhood was all any forceful man could ask of a governing document. The industrial workers were tucked securely in their niche. The moral of the New York revolt was not lost on the other locals, and Hutcheson never experienced another regional revolt serious enough to demand the attention of the historian. Outside the union, the AFL had fallen in line with the Carpenters' wishes, and the Atlanta Declaration, as it was being applied, was all the Carpenters could wish. Jurisdictional disputes lingered, but there was not a serious contender in sight for any part of the Carpenters' job domain.

The United Brotherhood of Carpenters and Joiners of America was a trim and centralized fighting machine when World War I overtook the republic. During the war all of the contemporary activities of the union were frozen, as Hutcheson and his carpenters turned to face an entirely new economic experience: collective bargaining under the auspices of the federal government.

[58]"Big Bill Retires," *Time Magazine,* Vol. 58, No. 27, Dec. 31, 1951, p. 12.

CHAPTER XV

The Carpenters and the Government: 1917 to 1920

WHEN the United States government declared war on Germany, peacetime building skidded to a halt. For the first time in their lives, union leaders, workers, and employers were thrown into direct contact with the federal government. The institutions and practices of building trades unionism were set to one side, and the thread of United Brotherhood history which had been slowly unwinding since 1881 was abruptly snapped.

Few of the events of wartime collective bargaining bear much relevance to past United Brotherhood history. Because these developments are interesting and important in themselves, however, and because of the effect they had on the future history of the United Brotherhood, this chapter will present them in some detail. They will be analyzed in terms of the attitude that each of three groups, the government, organized labor as led by Samuel Gompers, and the Carpenters, held toward wartime labor policy.

Functioning in a sellers' market, wartime labor leaders were in a classically advantageous position; the demand for labor far outran the supply. Most of the leaders, however, were understandably torn between patriotism and their sense of trade unionism. Instead of pressing their advantage, they followed Gompers into the war production program with a loyalty equaled by trade unionists in few other nations. Such policy as wartime labor leaders possessed was a mixture of rear-guard actions to hold whatever prewar union advantages they possessed and a highly successful series of organizational forays designed to unionize as many workers as possible and to get the best possible conditions for those already unionized. Most AFL leaders pressed these limited and pragmatic ends carefully, lest they exceed the bounds of loyalty and alienate public opinion.

Hutcheson, however, followed a policy which was greatly at variance with that of the rest of organized labor. Whereas other labor leaders fought a mild and negative rear-guard action, Hutcheson came out positively for an orderly war labor policy based specifically upon prewar union conditions. Prewar union conditions meant many things to many men. To Hutcheson they meant the closed shop. He considered the closed shop the foundation upon which all other "union conditions" of necessity rested. To him a wartime closed shop meant that he be permitted, in cooperation with the various war labor agencies, to train, recruit, and supply all carpenters needed for the war effort and that he have the right to bargain collectively with government and industrial agents to establish the other conditions of work for the labor his union supplied. Hutcheson fought so persistently for the closed shop that he often found himself in open conflict, on occasion to the point of seeming disloyalty, with both the AFL and the government. Neither the government nor the AFL pursued a closed shop, war labor policy. When Hutcheson tried to resolve his differences with the government by striking, a war-aroused public which would not tolerate work stoppages blocked him at every turn.

On the eve of the war, the trade union leaders of the nation met and exorcised pacifism from the body of the labor movement. Labor promised Wilson its full support, and Gompers renewed the pledge on every possible occasion. He neither asked nor received a stipulated labor policy in return for what was, in effect, a no-strike pledge.[1]

The Carpenters, who never burned bridges behind them, were

[1] See Christie, pp. 404–409, for the story of government labor policy during the early months of the war.

skeptical. The United Brotherhood, Duffy reminded Gompers in an editorial in *The Carpenter,* would have no part of a no-strike pledge without specific safeguards to protect the carpenters. "Patriotic manifestos, unsupported by definite administrative plans," said Duffy, "offer no such guarantee."[2] An editorial in the same issue warned the government:

The AFL, with its great army of skilled mechanics, is in a splendid condition today to be of valuable service *if* the Government will have the forethought and vision to avail itself of its assistance in a spirit of cooperation compatible with the democratic ideals for which the labor movement stands.[3]

The government not only ignored the trade unions' offer to recruit labor but it also failed to establish even the semblance of an over-all labor program. Rather, its agents began showering contracts on all sides, paying little or no attention to labor supply or standards. Many nonunion builders received government contracts and, hiding behind the war effort, were able to foster their antiunion programs.[4] By June 1917 Gompers' loyalty program was starting to look suspiciously like a sellout. He was burdened with the complaints of union presidents, chief among them the presidents of the building trades unions since shipbuilding, cantonment, and plant expansion were the first tasks before the government.[5]

In June 1917 Gompers went into conference with Secretary of War Newton D. Baker. Out of this conference emerged the Baker-Gompers agreement, which set a pattern for labor relations during the war.[6] This agreement was simply an isolated and specific pact made to regulate the treatment of craftsmen working on the construction of War Department cantonments. It provided that prevailing wages, hours, and working conditions continue on all cantonment construction contracts. By verbal agreement, however, Baker and Gompers specifically exempted the closed shop from

[2] "A Program for Labor," *The Carpenter,* Vol. 37, No. 5, May 1917, p. 4.
[3] *Ibid.,* p. 18 (italics mine).
[4] Building Trades Department, AFL, *Proceedings of the Eleventh Annual Convention of Buffalo, November 7 to November 10, 1917,* p. 31.
[5] Lorwin, pp. 157–158.
[6] American Federation of Labor, *Proceedings of the Thirty-seventh Annual Convention of Buffalo, November 12 to November 24, 1917,* p. 82.

"prevailing conditions" even in localities where it existed.[7] The agreement also provided for the settlement of labor grievances by a tripartite Cantonment Adjustment Commission.[8] In the eyes of those who signed the Baker-Gompers agreement, it "was a bargain for union scales in exchange for the open shop."[9]

Whether or not Gompers and Baker intended it, this type of agreement immediately caught favor and spread. By the end of 1917 the field of wartime labor relations was so encrusted with tripartite boards that it is futile even to attempt to list them.[10] Practically every division of every bureau of every government department and agency had its own separate little adjustment board. No one agency existed to coordinate the efforts of these boards, and in effect they set competing wage rates for the existing supply of labor.[11]

This rash of tripartite labor boards brought into existence by August 1917 the three major war labor agencies with which the United Brotherhood was to deal: the Cantonment Adjustment Commission, the Arsenal and Navy Yard Wage Commission, and the Labor Adjustment Board of the Emergency Fleet Corporation of the United States Shipping Board. Through these boards labor was given a direct voice in the settlement of all industrial disputes. Their creation silenced to some extent labor criticism of the government's labor program.

Hutcheson, however, was not satisfied. From his viewpoint the Baker-Gompers agreement pattern left much to be desired. He did not object to carpenters working with nonunion men; he simply wanted the United Brotherhood to be given first chance to supply the required carpenters. Hutcheson contended that his union could supply all the qualified carpenters needed by the government

[7]Lorwin, pp. 157–158; War Department, Office of the Secretary, *A Report of the Activities of the War Department in the Field of Industrial Relations during the War,* Sept. 15, 1918, p. 11.

[8]AFL, *1917 Convention Proceedings,* p. 82.

[9]Louis B. Whele, "The Adjustment of Labor Disputes Incident to Production for War in the United States," *Quarterly Journal of Economics,* Vol. 32, No. 4, November 1917, p. 126.

[10]For a partial list, see Willard E. Hotchkiss and Henry R. Seagar, *History of the Shipbuilding Labor Adjustment Board, 1917–1919* (U.S. Department of Labor, Bureau of Labor Statistics, Bulletin No. 287), p. 42.

[11]*Ibid.*

if government representatives would but ask, and he was hurt and embittered by the government's refusal to give the Brotherhood the opportunity to make good its boast. He was also irritated by the fact that the Baker-Gompers agreement did not guarantee the Carpenters the closed shop in the areas in which it had been a hard-fought-for and long-standing tradition. Consequently, Hutcheson refused to recognize the Baker-Gompers agreement or to serve on any of the national tripartite boards set up by, or patterned after, this agreement.

For all of Hutcheson's objections, the war and the war effort continued. Both were backed strongly by a public opinion which would not tolerate nonparticipation because of the little-understood principle of the closed shop. Consequently, although Hutcheson fought the Baker-Gompers agreement and refused as a matter of principle to sign it on a national level, on the local level his carpenters did participate in the war program on a *de facto* basis.

In spite of his distaste for the government's labor program, Hutcheson got along famously with both the Army and the Navy. After a conference with both the Secretary of the Navy and the Secretary of War in the summer of 1917, he was apparently satisfied that in spite of the Baker-Gompers agreement he would be treated fairly by them. He had no important trouble with either of these departments during the war. Military men seemed to understand Hutcheson's abrupt and brusque tactics. It was with the civilian war administrators, the industrialists administering the government's war production, that the Carpenters had their greatest trouble. Specifically, Hutcheson and his lieutenants locked horns most frequently and viciously with the officials of the United States Shipping Board.

Edwin D. Hurley, a self-made shipyard owner, headed this Board and had charge of both the construction and maintenance of the nation's merchant marine. He established the Emergency Fleet Corporation as a government corporation to finance all new ships. The task before the Emergency Fleet Corporation officials in July 1917 was that of creating an industry almost out of thin air. Shipyards had to be constructed where none previously existed. This required the displacement of capital, management, and labor.

Workers had in some instances to be lured thousands of miles to create new shipyards on marshy terrain and isolated riverbanks, bays, and islands. A mass transfer of workers under such circumstances naturally gave rise to confused and turbulent labor relations.

Furthermore, the prospect of juicy profits attracted many speculators unpracticed in either labor relations or shipbuilding.[12] Firms already in shipbuilding made large sums when the government requisitioned their facilities in 1917. Shipyard workers, lured far from their homes, looked askance at these profits when they compared them to their wages and the rising cost of living.[13]

For these reasons shipyard labor, organized and unorganized, was restless when Hurley took over. Together with Gompers and the heads of the AFL Building and Metal Trades Departments, Hurley signed an agreement patterned after the Baker-Gompers agreement in August 1917. Like its guide plan, a waiver of the right to strike was implied but not explicitly stated and no provision for the closed shop or exclusive union recruitment was included. The agreement left the unions free to organize those workers they could and established the tripartite government-labor-public Shipbuilding Labor Adjustment Board.[14] Through this agreement Hurley hoped to quiet worker discontent.

Every union president in the shipbuilding industry signed it but one, William L. Hutcheson. He contended that his signature would imply agreement with the open shop principle conceded in the Baker-Gompers agreement. He firmly maintained:

While we have every desire, intention and thought of assisting the officials of the Government in the crisis we are now passing through, yet at the same time we have no thought or intention of waiving or giving up our rights to maintain for ourselves the [closed shop] conditions we have established.[15]

[12]P. N. Douglas and F. C. Wolfe, "Labor Administration in the Shipbuilding Administration in War Time, Part I," *The Journal of Political Economy*, Vol. 27, No. 3, March 1919, p. 148.

[13]*Ibid.*, p. 149.

[14]Hotchkiss and Seagar, pp. 10–11; P. N. Douglas and F. C. Wolfe, "Labor Administration in the Shipbuilding Administration, Part II," *The Journal of Political Economy*, Vol. 27, No. 5, May 1919, p. 369.

[15]"Report of General President William L. Hutcheson for the Quarter Ending September 30, 1917," *The Carpenter*, Vol. 37, No. 11, November 1917, p. 26.

Still, to keep the door open, Hutcheson had Executive Board Member Tim Guerin sign the agreement.[16] Hutcheson considered, however, that Guerin's signature did not finally bind the United Brotherhood until the executive board passed on it and until he, Hutcheson, added his signature.

The new chairman of the new Shipbuilding Labor Adjustment Board, Everitt Macy of the National Civic Federation, had to move rapidly to counter a deteriorating labor situation. In the absence of a government labor policy, many yard owners refused to bargain collectively.[17] Strikes over wages, hours, and general working conditions were mushrooming. Macy took his board to the West Coast, where the labor situation was most critical. There, during the closing days of 1917, he made a coast-wide compromise settlement which was to set the pattern for the whole industry.

Hutcheson was greatly distressed by the principles involved in the West Coast settlement. As the price of settlement the West Coast labor leaders, following the Baker-Gompers agreement, had traded the closed shop for a 31 percent wage raise.[18] Furthermore, the Macy board decreed a lower wage rate for house carpenters working in shipyards than for ship carpenters. Hutcheson felt that these two moves were interrelated. If the board were to allow the United Brotherhood to recruit labor through the closed shop, he could prove that qualified carpenters worked equally well on ships and buildings without work interruptions. He advised all carpenters working in shipyards to demand the higher scale.[19] On November 20, 1917, he ordered Guerin to withdraw his signature from the agreement creating the Macy board and to cut all ties with that body.[20]

Throughout November and December, Hutcheson sniped at the board. He brought to the board's attention a series of unpleasant working conditions in the shipyards. Carpenters who were recruited by individual contractors through newspaper advertise-

[16]Letter from F. D. Roosevelt, Undersecretary of the Navy, to William Hutcheson, Feb. 21, 1918, as quoted in *The Carpenter,* Vol. 38, No. 5, May 1918, pp. 10–11.

[17]Douglas and Wolfe, "Labor Administration in the Shipbuilding Administration, Part I," p. 149.

[18]*Ibid.,* pp. 156–157.

[19]"Report of General President William L. Hutcheson for the Quarter Ending December 31, 1917," *The Carpenter,* Vol. 38, No. 2, February 1918, pp. 17–18.

[20]*The Carpenter,* Vol. 38, No. 5, May 1918, pp. 10–11.

ments often found no jobs available after traveling many miles. Others were refused jobs because of union membership. Men who were attracted to a distant locality by the promise of high wages often found wages lower than in their home districts. Contractors were left free to hire and fire at will and men fired were left stranded, often without railroad fare. Eight-hour-day and overtime agreements were openly violated. Skilled and unskilled men did each other's work. Housing at isolated shipyards was often poor.[21]

As a result of these abuses, the labor turnover was higher in shipbuilding than in any other industry in the United States. Three men had to be hired in the course of a year to keep each one-man job filled. Between April and October of 1917, 17.1 percent of all possible shipyard working hours had been lost in strikes, and 16.7 percent of all workers and 6.5 percent of all firms had been affected by strikes. The industry had the second-worst strike record of all war industries.[22]

This poor strike record stemmed from the grievances listed above, and they in turn were produced by the lack of a general labor policy on the part of the United States Shipping Board, Hutcheson maintained. Hurley and his aides had failed to devise a clear-cut policy for recruiting, training, and bargaining with a skilled labor force. All of the specific abuses just cited, Hutcheson felt, could be remedied by formulating such a policy.

Hutcheson did not, however, offer criticism without suggesting a solution. It was simple: give the unions involved in shipbuilding the closed shop. For almost a half-century the building trades unions had solved the problems of labor recruitment and training for private contractors in the building industry. The carpenters and the other unions involved in shipbuilding would do the same for the government and its contractors if given the opportunity. Once granted the closed shop, union building trades officials would then meet with the Macy board to devise a mutually acceptable labor policy.

[21]For a review of these grievances, see "Mr. Hurley and Labor," *The Public,* Vol. 21, No. 1038, Feb. 23, 1918, pp. 228–230.
[22]National Industrial Conference Board, *Strikes in American Industry in Wartime, April 6, 1917 to October 6, 1917* (Research Report No. 3), p. 7.

Both Hutcheson's criticisms and his solution were spurned by the United States Shipping Board's labor arm, the Macy board, even as he made them in November and December 1917. In late 1917 and early 1918 the Macy board completed a series of regional wage and working conditions agreements patterned after the West Coast agreement. The agreements signed with union representatives completed the national wage structure for the shipbuilding industry.[23] But that was all they did. The Carpenters' grievances about working conditions were not met, nor was Hutcheson's demand for a closed shop. All of the agreements provided for the mixed shop and for lower wages for workers new to the shipbuilding industry, including carpenters. By February 1918 the board was faced with a classic strike situation. The workers were aroused over working conditions and a wage they thought lower than their skills called for, and union leaders were denied the degree of recognition they sought.

To avert the imminent strike, Hutcheson and the Macy board met in a series of negotiations in the first two weeks of February 1918. During the course of these negotiations the positions of both sides hardened and became clear. The government insisted that Hutcheson sign the agreement creating the Macy board and thus abandon his closed shop demand before he might bargain for improved working conditions. Hutcheson agreed to sign the agreement only if it granted the closed shop to the United Brotherhood. Otherwise he would meet with the board only to negotiate working conditions and wages and without signing the agreement which created it. The board refused.

Hutcheson was aiming high. While he was sincere enough in his demands for the shipyard workers,[24] he had other, more ambitious

---

[23]Hotchkiss and Seagar, pp. 25–40.

[24]These demands were ten in number, and they accurately reflected the grievances of the men and Hutcheson's plan to settle the labor supply problem. They were as follows: the eight-hour day; a half holiday on Saturday in summer; double time for overtime and eight holidays; weekly pay with no pay held back for more than three days; wages paid from time of departure from home city for men traveling to a job; transportation paid and $2.50 daily for traveling expenses; all workers paid up-to-date within twenty-four hours of quitting a job, and United Brotherhood representatives to be allowed in all yards at all times; no strikes or lockouts during the hearing of a grievance; wage raises with guarantees that a minimum wage would not be treated as a maximum wage; all hiring to be done through the United States Employment office, the latter getting its applicants from local United Brotherhood

targets. He was willing to tie up the nation's largest and most vital war industry in order to discredit the Macy board agreement. Behind it was the Baker-Gompers agreement and behind both the issue of the closed shop. If he could discredit the Baker-Gompers pattern in this the most important of all war industries, it was bound to be abandoned as a prototype. Then the government would be without a policy, and in constructing one Hutcheson might make stick his demands for the closed shop.

All of Hutcheson's plans went for naught as the ship carpenters took the situation into their own hands. On February 11 they walked off the job in New York City. Hurley leaped into the breach, blatantly waving the bloody shirt.

While the people of this country are mourning the loss of brave young Americans in the Tuscania horror—while the thousands of American homes are anxiously watching the list of survivors slowly coming in to make certain that another precious life has been snatched from the Atlantic Ocean, a telegram comes—and with it the grim announcement that the carpenters in shipyards are now on strike.

.   .   .

Do you realize that you [Hutcheson] are adding to the fearful danger our soldiers already face...if food and ammunition are not sent over in ships and many ships at once? Do you think the fathers and mothers whose sons are making this sacrifice will sit patiently by and permit this paralyzing of the lifeline between us and the western front to go on?[25]

The "fathers and mothers of America" did not fail to heed Mr. Hurley's cue. Through the public press and their various spokesmen they immediately made themselves the most important factor in the bargaining between Hutcheson and Hurley and effectively prevented any reasonable settlement of the shipyard labor muddle. Billy Sunday mounted the pulpit to denounce Hutcheson as a traitor and the carpenters as slackers. The press pointed him out as a "dangerous man."[26]

---

offices ("Report of General President William L. Hutcheson to the Second Quarterly Meeting of the G.E.B. Covering all Details of Recent Controversy with the U.S. Shipping Board," *The Carpenter*, Vol. 38, No. 5, May 1918, p. 4).

[25]*Ibid.*, p. 7.

[26]Frank Duffy, "The Shipbuilding Controversy," *The Carpenter*, Vol. 38, No. 4, April 1918, p. 4.

Hutcheson, the midwestern Republican, the Mason, the patriot, overnight became a public menace. He did not enjoy at all the position of public ogre which John L. Lewis later assumed with such equanimity in World War II. He squirmed. In a letter to Hurley and to the public he assured everyone that he and his carpenters were a most loyal group of men who were simply trying to redress their grievances.

Neither Hurley nor his ally, the public, would have any of this. On February 15 the walkout spread to Baltimore, and Hurley released another telegram in which he agreed that the carpenters were loyal and that Hutcheson alone kept the United Brotherhood off the Macy board.[27] The next day Hutcheson asked President Wilson to intervene. Wilson replied that if and when Hutcheson got on the Macy board a settlement could be arranged. The whole force of the government was thus arrayed behind Hurley and the public.[28]

Hurley's demand for, and the public's ready offer of, support for his stand points up clearly that, for the duration, labor relations were not to be conducted by the professionals. Whatever the merits of the closed shop in the shipyards, the public would not tolerate a work stoppage to gain it. Public opinion thus established clear limits to wartime collective bargaining. Gompers chose scrupulously to observe these limits. Hutcheson chose to ignore them and found they could not be ignored.

Hutcheson was neatly boxed in by the government on one side, the public on another, his striking carpenters on a third, and his innate sense of patriotism on a fourth. On February 19 he freed himself by inducing the carpenters to return to work with a guarantee of immediate consideration of their grievances.[29] While none of the carpenters' ten demands was fulfilled, neither did the president of their union recognize the authority of the Macy board.

Here matters stood. The United Brotherhood never signed the agreement and the agreement was never changed. In place of a

[27]"Report of General President William L. Hutcheson on the Controversy with the Shipping Board," *The Carpenter*, Vol. 38, No. 5, May 1918, p. 8.
[28]*Ibid.*, p. 9.
[29]*Ibid.*

fixed and legal arrangement. Hutcheson allowed his local leaders to deal with the board on a day-to-day, informal basis.[30]

Hutcheson had been the only one with the temerity to speak out against a war labor policy under which all of the building trades leaders chafed. President Bowen of the Bricklayers recognized Hutcheson's position. He told the delegates to the 1918 Building Trades Department convention, "I want to have it clearly understood that [at] the time he [Hutcheson] was under fire men high in the affairs of organized labor in America ought to have made it clear why he made the stand."[31] Bowen went on to say that while Hutcheson was struggling for the principle of the closed shop which all the trade union leaders wanted and felt entitled to, the other leaders had deserted him, afraid to face public opprobrium.[32] And, after standing alone for a time, Hutcheson too bowed to the force of public opinion, the real architect of wartime labor policy.

The ship carpenters' strike had exposed the inadequacy of the government's whole labor program. It pointed up the fact that no coordinated war labor policy existed and that the tripartite boards, born of the stopgap Baker-Gompers agreement, had not solved the mediation problem and had not even dealt with the labor supply problem. They were, in fact, actively competing for the existing labor supply. A more comprehensive policy was called for. Finally, two months after the carpenters' strike was settled and a full year after war was declared, the government took its first step toward a war labor policy. It established the National War Labor Board.[33]

The establishment of the National War Labor Board was the first recognition by the government that the labor problem was a basic mobilization problem and should henceforth be handled by labor relations experts. It was a concession to the exigencies of the war labor situation and, more important, to the demands of organ-

[30]*Ibid.*, pp. 10–11.
[31]"Report of Delegates to the Twelfth Annual Convention of the Building Trades Department of the AFL," *The Carpenter*, Vol. 38, No. 8, August 1918, p. 44.
[32]*Ibid.*, p. 45.
[33]Richard B. Gregg, "The National War Labor Board," *Harvard Law Review*, Vol. 33, No. 1, November 1919, pp. 39–40; see also U.S. Department of Labor, National War Labor Board, *Report of the Secretary of the National War Labor Board to the Secretary of Labor for the Twelve Months ending May 31, 1919.*

ized labor. Its creation was a step toward the solution of the war labor problem.

Although the charter of the National War Labor Board exhorted vaguely against wartime turnouts, it definitely did not extract a no-strike pledge from labor.[34] No effective penalties against striking workers were provided. The only powers the board possessed were to settle labor controversies by "mediation and conciliation" and to hold hearings to effect this end.[35]

In return for its cooperation, organized labor received almost everything which leaders like Hutcheson had been demanding. The continued existence of the closed shop where it existed and of all other conditions of labor were guaranteed. The customs and practices of localities were set as the basis of any future adjustments in the wages, hours, and conditions of labor. Trade union leaders received the right to organize defense workers, provided only that no coercion were used. Eight hours was declared the basic workday, and the cost of living was declared the yardstick for fair wages. Finally, the Department of Labor was declared the official labor mobilizing agency and was ordered to use the facilities of the trade unions in its recruiting activities.[36] The board was set up as a going concern in late April, and by May 31, 1919, it made 520 awards in 462 separate cases.[37] Considering that it was the first organization of its kind, the board enjoyed an enormous success.

The leaders of the United Brotherhood greeted the War Labor Board with immediate enthusiasm. Only three other unions used the facilities of the board more frequently than the United Brotherhood, and it never experienced any serious difficulty with the board.[38] Throughout the rest of the war either Hutcheson or

[34]Lorwin, pp. 165–166.
[35]Gregg, "The National War Labor Board," p. 41.
[36]*Ibid.*, pp. 42–44, for details of the principles of the War Labor Board. In general, the board acted as a court of last appeal for the wage adjustment boards and a court of first and last appeal for those industries without wage adjustment boards (Lorwin, p. 163).
[37]*Report of the Secretary of the National War Labor Board...*, p. 5.
[38]Department of Labor, Bureau of Labor Statistics, *National War Labor Board; A History of Its Formation and Activities* (Bulletin No. 287), p. 24.

Guerin sat on the board, and the Carpenters cooperated closely with it.

No union played a larger role in the creation of this board than did the United Brotherhood. Hutcheson, from the day war was declared, decried the lack of a war policy, pleaded with the government to utilize the services of unions in recruiting labor, and pleaded for a separate agency designed to handle war labor policy. Hutcheson alone stood steadfast against the stopgap Baker-Gompers agreement and the various agreements and boards it spawned. Hutcheson alone faced public wrath to drive these demands and principles home.

What were the effects of the war on the Carpenters? There can be no doubt that, even in the absence of the best of all possible government labor policies, the United Brotherhood made enormous gains. Membership rose to well over three hundred thousand. These gains were for the most part, however, ephemeral. Most of the workers drifted into trade unionism as a way of keeping up with the cost of living. Under the hot postwar sun of depression and an employers' offensive, this membership melted away. By October 1921 Hutcheson was sending out orders for dues dispensation in an attempt to hold carpenters who, he admitted, had never really been enthusiastic union members.[39]

The employers were not inclined to look kindly upon the government's encouragement of collective bargaining. Many thought the unions pampered and wages too high. The Carpenters, on the other hand, while satisfied enough with war wages, were unwilling to take wage reductions on private building once the plush war contracts ended. When the employers insisted on the 1916 wage levels, a whole spate of postwar strikes cropped up. Carpenters turned out, or were turned out, in New York, Chicago, Boston, Seattle, and other smaller building centers. These disputes marked the start of a new kind of employers' offensive, which was waged with varying degrees of intensity throughout the decade of the 1920's.

The employers' offensive was new because of a new ally, the

[39]"Report of General President William L. Hutcheson for the Quarter Ending December 31, 1921," *The Carpenter,* Vol. 42, No. 2, February 1922, pp. 27–28.

public, and a new tactic, public labor regulation boards. For the first time the war had forced news of elections, murders, and scandals to make way in the newspapers for news of collective bargaining. While the prewar public had been rendered sufficiently aware of the labor problem by events such as Haymarket and the Pullman strike, it had not been aware of labor relations or, more specifically, collective bargaining, the give-and-take between unions and management. Throughout the war the public had had brought to its attention the details of collective bargaining, of wages and arbitration boards, of demanding trade union leaders, of the "rights" of labor and management, and of the threat to public security and welfare that a well-organized strike could pose.

This war-engendered public awareness had the effect of quickening a trend toward public control of labor relations in the building trades which had been mounting since 1906. Opposition to the building trades unions had taken on a quasi-public cast in the early teens because of the loose alliance formed by the employers and the unions from 1900 to 1906. From 1908 to 1917 the Anti-Boycott Association had had the Carpenters constantly before the courts. After the war this opposition took on a completely public character. In Boston, Guerin and Mayor Peters together settled a city-wide building trades strike. In the same year, in New York City, another city-wide carpenters' strike was settled only after a series of special award commissions heard the dispute and after a Justice of the New York State Supreme Court handed down a decision.[40] In 1920 the New York state legislature took the building trades to task.[41] A year later the Dailey Committee of the Illinois state legislature did the same thing in Chicago.[42] In 1921 publicly constituted groups in both Chicago and San Francisco took labor relations completely out of the hands of both the contractors and the trade union leaders and ruled the building trades, ostensibly on behalf of the public, for the balance of the 1920's.[43]

[40]"Report of the General President for the First Quarter, 1919," *The Carpenter*, Vol. 39, No. 4, April 1919, pp. 22–28.

[41]See above, p. 215.

[42]Montgomery, p. 234.

[43]The Chicago group was called the Citizens' Committee to Enforce the Landis Award, and the San Francisco group the Impartial Wage Board of the Industrial Association.

In scores of smaller cities across the country the same pattern emerged during the postwar period, as self-styled public groups created citizens' committees and "impartial" wage boards to control labor relations in the building trades. For better or worse, the war made labor relations in the building trades public property. Under a harsh public scrutiny new groups emerged, new alliances were made by old groups, and new institutions for collective bargaining arose.

CHAPTER XVI

The Triumph of Jurisdictional

Laissez Faire: 1919-1929

UNTIL the war introduced the general public to labor relations, only building tradesmen, and few enough of them, concerned themselves with the problems of the building industry. In the postwar period the public was not only concerned, it was hopping mad over the excesses of this peculiar industry. Jurisdictional strikes and racketeering seemed to the average citizen responsible for the high building costs under which the nation struggled. The public knew little enough about the causes of jurisdictional striking and the financing of the industry, but racketeering anyone could understand.

In the case of the carpenters, the alliance made with the employers during the 1906 to 1908 period[1] had ripened into collusion and then rotted into flagrant racketeering in most large cities. Carpenter Brindell lorded it over the New York building trades. Carpenter William Brims, as leader of the district council, was part of a ruling Chicago junta. Carpenter P. H. McCarthy ruled virtually the entire city of San Francisco through his building trades council political connections. In each of these cities, and they were typical of most, building czars indulged in practices which ranged from mild exclusive agreements to pure extortion.

[1]See above, pp. 161–162.

McCarthy and his employer allies completely tied up the San Francisco building industry with "monopolistic combinations."[2] In Chicago the infamous Article 3, already mentioned, sent the price of material and the cost of building soaring to unimagined heights.[3] Brindell's activities, as described in Chapter XIV, gave the Carpenters a notoriety second only to that of rumrunners in New York City.

William Schardt's Chicago activities were typical of the method used to exact strike insurance from the contractors. Asked to describe how he was forced to pay "strike insurance" on a building being erected by the Liquid Carbonic Company of Chicago, its president, Albert R. Brunker, replied:

A. The business agent of the Carpenters' Union notified us that if we attempted to complete the installation they would strike the whole building, which involved a loss somewhere...around $10,000 or $15,000 a day....We dealt...with a man named Schardt.

       .   .   .

Q. Who was the business agent of the Carpenters' Union?

       .   .   .

A. He demanded $1,800 and we paid him $1,200 to permit the installation of that outfit.
Q. Who paid it to him?
A. The general sales manager....
Q. Where did he pay it to Schardt?
A. ...in the barroom of one of the hotels, [in] one of the booths.
Q. Paid him in currency?
A. He offered him a check and he refused to take it.
Q. Yes. What happened after the money was paid to Schardt, was the work resumed?
A. The work was resumed and completed.[4]

These practices rose and came under attack simultaneously in each of these cities. During 1920 the Illinois and New York state governments established legislative committees. Their public hearings revealed the extent of racketeering on the part of both trade

[2]See above, pp. 162–163.
[3]*Ibid.*
[4]Illinois Building Investigation Committee, *Report to the 53rd General Assembly,* p. 51.

union leaders and contractors.[5] Thus public opinion was aroused against the building trades unions, and a favorable climate for the open shop drive was established.

Brindell was jailed, and the Building Trades Employers' Association assumed control of New York City labor relations before open shop advocates were able to establish a foothold.[6] Elsewhere, however, the open shop made great gains. In San Francisco McCarthy was thrown from power and in early 1922 a "citizens' committee" was formed to oversee labor relations in the building trades. This committee was composed of various businessmen and financiers who forced the open shop under the guise of the "American plan" on the building trades workers of San Francisco.[7] In Chicago the same pattern was repeated. "Nineteen principles" were laid down which, in sum, were similar to the American plan and which fostered the open shop. Another "citizens' committee" was created to administer these principles.[8] In city after city across the country the pattern, with slight regional variations, was the same. The National Association of Manufacturers could boast in 1922 that building was done under open shop conditions in 36 percent of all cities in the United States.[9]

The open shop drive, however, was unique in the building trades. It was not conducted, as it was in other industries, by the employers. In fact, in New York City the Building Trades Employers' Association stepped in as Brindell was forced out, took charge of labor relations, and successfully excluded the open shop.[10] In Chicago and San Francisco the citizens' committee that took command of labor relations was just that, a committee of citizens unassociated with the building industry. Open shop advocates received little voluntary support from established building trades

[5]The New York committee was headed by State Senator Charles Lockwood and the one in Illinois by State Senator Dailey.
[6]Haber, p. 365.
[7]See Ryan, pp. 144–185, for a discussion of the development of the American plan, a system of regulation of labor relations to insure the open shop.
[8]Montgomery, pp. 246–275.
[9]Noel Sargent, "United States Building 1921–1927," *Open Shop Bulletin*, No. 23, Nov. 12, 1928, p. 6.
[10]Haber, p. 365.

employers.[11] Said one of the country's most prominent contractors as the open shop drive gathered momentum, "A closer association between...employers...and organized labor will yield abundant returns.... It is better to deal with union labor than with disorganized labor."[12]

Most contractors based their labor policy on the continued existence of trade unions and benefited greatly from the stabilizing influences provided by the business agents. Their industry had peculiar problems which only experienced building tradesmen could solve. The contractors shuddered at the prospect of placing their affairs in the hands of inexperienced citizens' committees. Said a spokesman for the National Association of Manufacturers, building trades employers "cannot be relied upon to keep [the] building [industry] open shop."[13]

Yet, backed as it was by the general business community and powered by the racketeering revelations, the open shop was a potent postwar threat. The employers moved to meet it through the medium of an "association" movement. The object of this movement was not to edge labor out of the picture but to bring labor relations out of barrooms and dimly lit district council halls and place it in a series of respectable national trade associations where the public could plainly see that all was aboveboard.

The association movement was less sensational, but of more far-reaching importance, than the open shop movement. Between 1918 and 1922 at least eight national associations were formed by the various groups in the industry.[14] The purpose of each was to

[11]See above, Chapter XI, "Label Unionism," where the reasons why contractors generally preferred to deal with the unions are explained.

[12]American Institute of Architects, *Proceedings of the Fifty-second Annual Convention of Nashville, Tennessee, April 30 to May 2, 1919,* p. 144.

[13]*Open Shop Bulletin,* No. 23, p. 6.

[14]In 1918 the National Federation of Construction Industries was founded by the American Institute of Architects; in 1919 the National Board for Jurisdictional Awards was founded by the Building Trades Department; in 1920 the Joint Conference of Architects, Engineers, and Contractors on Estimating was formed; and in 1921 a Joint Conference of the same groups on Standard Construction Contracts. The American Institute of Architects got an American Construction Congress underway in 1920 and in 1921 established a series of local congresses. In 1921 the Associated General Contractors organized the National Conference Board for the Building Industry. In the same year the various economic groups in the industry created the Permanent Committee on Construction. Finally, during 1922, an American Con-

regulate the industry in one way or another. The most important of the lot, for the carpenters, was the National Board for Jurisdictional Awards. It was created in 1919 to cope with the most expensive malpractice of building trades unions, the jurisdictional strike.

By eliminating the jurisdictional strike building tradesmen would demonstrate their good faith to a hostile public. If this, the most basic of all sources of building trades friction, could be eliminated, racketeering and other surface abuses could be coped with easily. The National Board for Jurisdictional Awards was aimed squarely at the public. Said President John Donlin of the Building Trades Department shortly after its founding: "We... are in the public service, the welfare...of the public is paramount."[15] For this reason the Building Trades Department conceived and founded the board.[16]

Every building trades union leader but one, William L. Hutcheson, supported the board enthusiastically. Hutcheson could not, or would not, support the board, because it demanded that all affiliated unions accept jurisdiction over new or disputed materials only with its sanction. This left it free not only to determine the future direction and extent of the Carpenters' jurisdictional expansion but also to shift parts of the Carpenters' jurisdiction to

---

struction Council, which boasted the affiliation of every organized economnic group in the industry, was formed. See "American Construction Council," *The Constructor* (official journal of the Associated General Contractors of America), Vol. 4, No. 5, May 1922, p. 48, for a survey of this congress movement in the building industry.

[15]Building Trades Department, AFL, *Proceedings of the Sixteenth Annual Convention of Cincinnati, June 7 to June 9, 1923*, p. 59.

[16]The structure and scope of the board was briefly as follows. It was composed of eight members, three of whom, through the Building Trades Department, represented labor; and one representative each from the American Institute of Architects, the Associated General Contractors of America, the National Association of Builders' Exchanges, the National Building Trades Employers' Association, and the General Council of Engineers. This board was given the power to assign jurisdiction over all disputed materials to the union the members of the board thought best equipped to handle them. The board met quarterly, heard evidence from all interested unions and employers, and made awards by a majority vote of six of its members. Both unions and employers were bound to abide by board decisions. If a union proved recalcitrant, the Building Trades Department was supposed to discipline it. E. J. Russell, an architect, was chairman. For a more detailed description of the board's creation and structure see E. E. Cummins, "The National Board for Jurisdictional Awards and the Carpenters' Union," *American Economic Review*, Vol. 19, No. 3, September 1929, p. 365.

other unions. Hutcheson ruled an industrial empire which, in 1919, included a whole swarm of trades and subtrades, industries and subindustries. The board was at liberty to take any one of them from the United Brotherhood and give it to another union. The leaders of the United Brotherhood felt in 1920 much as the rulers of Austria-Hungary felt in 1914 about the demands of their minority peoples: allow one group to go, and the whole empire will collapse. What national self-determination meant for Austria-Hungary in postwar Europe, the National Board for Jurisdictional Awards could have meant to the United Brotherhood.

Before the war Hutcheson would not long have troubled himself about the board. He would have destroyed it in a twinkling. The Carpenters' policy of jurisdictional laissez faire demanded that the question of jurisdiction remain open, to be settled only by Carpenters and by the means they chose.[17] But to pursue this policy in 1920 would mean to buck the strong new associational currents released by the open shop movement. The whole industry, from bricklayers to bankers, backed the National Board for Jurisdictional Awards.

Hutcheson faced a dilemma. If he joined the new board he had to abandon a carefully-thought-out jurisdictional policy. If he challenged it he had to fight a united industry and, in the struggle, expose his flank to the open shop movement. He phrased his dilemma thus: "We would be damned if we did and damned if we didn't and the thing was to determine the lesser of two evils."[18] He cautiously joined the board and watched and waited for a sign of its policy.

The board was organized at a Washington, D.C. meeting in February 1920 and handed down nine decisions, three of which affected the Carpenters in minor disputes. At the Carpenters' request, however, the board deferred decision on the all-important question of metal trim. At the April and August board meetings the Carpenters accepted several more minor decisions but again

---

[17]See above, pp. 181–185.
[18]UBCJA, *1920 Convention Proceedings*, p. 450.

asked that the metal trim decision be delayed until after the 1920 convention met.[19]

None of Hutcheson's recorded remarks to the convention revealed the tactics he might use in dealing with the National Board for Jurisdictional Awards. He told the delegates that he would preserve a wait-and-see attitude. The delegates then instructed Hutcheson to put two questions to President John Donlin of the Building Trades Department: how many contractors sponsored the board and what steps were these contractors prepared to take to back the board's decisions?[20] Until these questions were satisfactorily answered, Hutcheson refused to deal with the board.

The questions were a smoke screen. As one of the founders of the board and as its vice-chairman, Hutcheson knew the answer to both. They were merely a stall for more time and were asked in the hope that they would goad the board into making the sheet-metal award in his absence.[21] This hope was more than fulfilled. When the board met in December 1920, Hutcheson refused to sit because his questions had not been answered. The board members heard the metal trim dispute without him and granted jurisdiction to the Sheet Metal Workers' Union. In so doing they laid themselves open to two charges: first, that they had refused a legitimate request for information, and second, that they had heard a case without one of the interested parties being present.

The Carpenters' executive board met after the award was announced and resigned from the National Board for Jurisdictional Awards. Sides were again chosen for another long and bitter fight, with the Carpenters this time pitted against a united industry. "We do not want any rebellions or inter-union fights—we cannot stand for that," said President Donlin to Hutcheson in finger-shaking, schoolmarmish fashion. Replied Hutcheson, "The Brotherhood... is not looking for a fight, but if they have to fight, they will fight all the way."[22]

[19]"Jurisdictional Awards Made," *The Bulletin* (published by the Associated General Contractors), Vol. 11, No. 5, May 1920, p. 32; Building Trades Dept., *1921 Convention Proceedings,* pp. 31–38, gives a list of these proceedings.

[20]"Report of General President William L. Hutcheson for Quarter Ending December 31, 1920," *The Carpenter,* Vol. 41, No. 2, February 1921, p. 30.

[21]Building Trades Dept., *1921 Convention Proceedings,* p. 118.

[22]*Ibid.,* p. 110.

Donlin knocked the chip off by ordering the Carpenters to confer with the board under pain of suspension. The Carpenters refused to confer until the sheet-metal award was voided. Once more they were thrown out of a Building Trades Department whose leaders refused to be convinced of the utter futility of such a move.

On September 7, 1921, Hutcheson issued a circular bidding all carpenters to take sheet-metal work by any possible means.[23] The board countered on February 9, 1922 by issuing a strong resolution singling out the Carpenters as willful saboteurs of the National Board for Jurisdictional Awards. It ordered all contractors to permit only sheet-metal workers to hang metal trim and all architects to order the use of sheet-metal workers on metal trim in their specifications.[24]

Neither side pressed its position vigorously, however, and there were no serious jurisdictional struggles involving the Carpenters during the first six months of 1922. In fact, the Building Trades Department tried to get the Carpenters to negotiate a rapprochement. The Carpenters refused, however, and stated their opposition to "any recognition or observance of the decisions of the National Board for Jurisdictional Awards."[25] Hutcheson's general policy of refusing to support any plan for jurisdictional settlement was clear by the time the delegates to the 1922 Building Trades Department convention assembled. The tactics through which he would implement the policy were made known before they disbanded.

The quickest and easiest way to discredit the board would be to associate it with the open shop movement. Yet, since the board was founded jointly by employers and the Building Trades Department as an alternative to the open shop, such a move seemed impossible. As Hutcheson eyed the member organizations of the board—the Associated General Contractors, the National Association of Builders Exchanges, the National Building Trades Employers Association—he found each impervious to the charge of open shop advocate. When he came to the American Institute of

[23]"Report of General President William L. Hutcheson for the Quarter Ending September 30, 1921," *The Carpenter,* Vol. 41, No. 11, November 1921, pp. 24–25.
[24]Building Trades Dept., *1922 Convention Proceedings,* pp. 87–88.
[25]*Ibid.,* p. 87.

Architects, however, he found the breach he sought in the building industry's prolabor ranks.

For a half-century the architects had held aloof from the rough-and-tumble arena of labor relations in the building industry. They joined the National Board for Jurisdictional Awards because they were concerned with the unsavory reputation which monopolistic practices, racketeering, and jurisdictional disputes had given the industry. Most architects, however, had had little previous experience with labor unions and were not at all sure they supported union principles. In fact, a good many architects were heart and soul behind the open shop movement. At the 1919 convention of the American Institute of Architects one delegate objected to the National Board for Jurisdictional Awards because it "makes us join with the labor unions and forever engages us not to recognize the open shop principle."[26]

The leaders of the American Institute of Architects did not trouble themselves with such fine distinctions. Rather, they viewed the board as a means to take over and clean up labor relations in the building industry. Said E. J. Russell, the architects' representative on the board:

We are going to...educate them [the union leaders] along the very best lines....We are going to get them to consider the question of grading men as to quality and as to wages, and...to consider their time limitations as to the work a man shall do. All of these things will come.

.   .   .

I think this step [the creation of the National Board for Jurisdictional Awards] we have taken is merely the entering wedge.[27]

Goals such as these, the architects felt, were entirely compatible with both trade unionism and the National Board for Jurisdictional Awards. They simply hoped to restrict certain trade union excesses through voluntary and cooperative regulation. At a time when the open shop controversy was raging at fever pitch such a course was folly. To trade unionists the principles at stake were clear and allowed for no middle position. Building tradesmen felt

[26]American Inst. of Architects, *1919 Convention Proceedings*, p. 75.
[27]*Ibid.*, pp. 99–100.

that when workers were graded as to quality and as to wages the closed shop was gone, and with it building trades unionism.[28]

Consequently, if the Carpenters could associate the National Board for Jurisdictional Awards with the open shop drive, they would score a telling point. They would shift from the defensive to the offensive, discredit the board, and disguise their own aim, the destruction of the National Board for Jurisdictional Awards. They succeeded in doing this at the 1922 convention of the Building Trades Department.

The open shop drive and the absence of the Carpenters from the Department were the most serious problems facing the delegates when proceedings opened. Before they closed the Carpenters had succeeded in linking the two together to their own advantage. Suspended from the Department, the Carpenters had no delegates present. AFL President Gompers, however, appeared to speak on their behalf. He revealed that the American Institute of Architects, which was represented on the board, had passed a resolution at its 1922 convention supporting the open shop.[29] Gompers was incensed. He told the delegates, "I cannot ask the Brotherhood of Carpenters to come back and place their case before a body which has declared for the open shop."[30] While the presence of a representative of the architects on the board did not signify that the board had "declared for the open shop," Gompers had found the board's soft underbelly. Although his resolution calling for the Building Trades Department to reject the National Board for Jurisdictional Awards and to take back the Carpenters failed to

[28]Grading labor as to skill and wages would have taken control of labor supply from the business agents, whose power was based on this control. Building trades unions were based on the power of the business agents.

[29]The resolution was designed to implement the following statement made by St. Louis Architect William B. Ittner: "At the time [the Board was formed] there was one community on the open shop basis, that was Los Angeles. Since then, conditions have changed. We have the open shop coming into popularity. That means...that our Board should be instructed to study conditions...and see what changes can be made in order to bring the principle [of the National Board for Jurisdictional Awards] into accord with the sentiment of the Institute." Converted to a resolution, Ittner's plan was backed unanimously by the architects (American Institute of Architects, *Proceedings of the Fifty-fifth Annual Convention of Washington, May 19 to May 21, 1922*, p. 45).

[30]Building Trades Department, *1922 Convention Proceedings*, p. 110.

pass,[31] he had succeeded in linking together the open shop and the board.

Hutcheson's strategy after 1922 was clear. He planned to leave the sheet-metal award an open issue and through it to keep the building trades disunited as the open shop drive mounted. He could then say:

The Board is pro-open shop. It made the sheet-metal award arbitrarily without even hearing the representatives of the Carpenters. It is continuing to back the award in order to foster disunity among building trades unions and to create a breach into which open shop elements can flood. Not only the sheet-metal decision, but the Board which made it, must go.

From 1922 on Hutcheson offered, in effect, to barter building trades unity for the dissolution of the National Board for Jurisdictional Awards. Delegate D. D'Alessandro of the Laborers' Union was fully aware of the alternatives which Hutcheson's strategy left the Building Trades Department. He told the convention, "The Chambers of Commerce are against organized labor. We [of the Building Trades Department] must either fight ourselves [over the National Board for Jurisdictional Awards] or...unite [by taking back the Carpenters] and fight the other side."[32]

When the delegates to the 1922 Building Trades Department convention refused the trade, the Carpenters declared open war. They demanded the right to install all sheet-metal trim. If contractors refused, the carpenters struck. If they could not force the local building trades councils to support them, they formed dual building trades councils to strike with them. Both Los Angeles and Cleveland had two building trades councils. The California State Building Trades Council openly supported the Carpenters and conducted a running battle with the national office of the Building Trades Department. The Department responded by creating a dual carpenters' union. Department Organizer Fred Hock announced, during 1923, the formation of dual locals in Cincinnati, Dayton, Indianapolis, St. Louis, and Pittsburgh.[33] Before the year

[31]*Ibid.*, p. 128.
[32]*Ibid.*, p. 125.
[33]"New Carpenters' Union Forms," *The Constructor,* Vol. 5, No. 12, December 1923, p. 31; UBCJA, *1924 Convention Proceedings,* pp. 203–204.

ended, the dispute, replete with work stoppages, had spread to virtually every important city in the United States.[34]

The open shop advocates took full advantage of the division in labor ranks. In Chicago and San Francisco the building trades entered into a struggle with self-constituted open shop groups which was to last for the balance of the 1920's. All across the country, in Tucson, Los Angeles, Utica, Duluth, and New Orleans, citizens' committees formed by the general business community forced the open shop upon unions and contractors alike.[35] With labor divided and unable to help the contractors resist the open shop and with a public opinion aroused by the revelations of racketeering, one city after another fell to the open shop. By the end of 1923 the National Association of Manufacturers claimed that 39 percent of all communities were building on an open shop basis.[36]

The architects played still further into the Carpenters' hands at their 1923 convention. After holding a long and, on the whole, friendly discussion of the open shop movement, the delegates unanimously resolved that National Board for Jurisdictional Awards decisions should apply only to

members of the Institute [of Architects] in those communities where building operations are carried on under definite agreements between organized labor and organized groups of employers...and...not... where such agreements are not in force.

What the architects were talking about behind the haze of parliamentary jargon was the open shop. When the secretary of the convention rose to second the motion, F. J. Russell, chairman of the National Board for Jurisdictional Awards, said, "The Secretary beat me to it. I should like to have seconded that resolution."[37]

[34]For a description of the extent and location of these disputes see Building Trades Department, AFL, *Proceedings of the Seventeenth Annual Convention of Portland, Oregon, September 26 to September 29, 1923*, pp. 79–83, 106, 122–127.

[35]"Los Angeles an Open Shop Town," *The Constructor*, Vol. 4, No. 1, January 1922, pp. 55, 86; "Open Shop Working Well," *The Constructor*, Vol. 5, No. 6, June 1923, p. 53; "Labor Situation," *The Constructor*, Vol. 5, No. 10, October 1923, p. 46. See also Building Trades Department, *1921 Convention Proceedings*, p. 123, for examples in Boston, Chicago, and Cleveland.

[36]*Open Shop Bulletin*, No. 23, p. 6.

[37]American Institute of Architects, *Proceedings of the Fifty-second Annual Convention of Washington, May 16 to May 18, 1923*, p. 46.

Hutcheson operated behind the scenes at the 1923 Building Trades Department convention. He discussed readmission with the members of the executive council, but they still refused to repudiate the National Board for Jurisdictional Awards. Hutcheson then told them "quite frankly that they [the Carpenters] were not going to recognize the...Board."[38] Either the open shop or the National Board for Jurisdictional Awards and the Carpenters' suspension occupied all of the convention floor discussions. The Carpenters' price for building trades unity was still the death of the board, and the other trades still refused to pay it.

Building trades union warfare continued after the convention. In late 1923 Duffy invoked the support of the AFL, and events started moving in the direction of a Carpenter-dictated settlement. Duffy wrote a letter to the AFL executive council demanding that it quash dual carpenters' unions fostered by the Building Trades Department. The council gave President Donlin ten days to destroy the unions. Donlin refused, saying that "the...Department is to be made the catspaw by the Executive Council in order that the chestnuts of the...Carpenters...might be pulled out of the fire."[39] He then asked the AFL to oust the Carpenters. His request was refused. Donlin had overplayed his hand, and his presidential days were clearly numbered.

Throughout 1924 either the open shop movement or the sheet-metal dispute plagued the building trades. Disputes, usually involving dual unions, spread to Cleveland, Baltimore, New York City, Chicago, and a score of lesser cities.[40] As the jurisdictional disputes spread, so did the open shop, until 40 percent of all cities were claimed by its advocates.[41] When the Building Trades Department convened in November 1924 William Bowen of the Bricklayers said, "You [the delegates] are rushing pellmell into chaos and into dissolution of this body."[42] The Department officials were caught between the National Board for Jurisdictional Awards and

[38]Building Trades Department, *1923 Convention Proceedings*, p. 123.
[39]UBCJA, *1924 Convention Proceedings*, p. 207.
[40]Building Trades Department, AFL, *Proceedings of the Eighteenth Annual Convention of El Paso, Nov. 12 to Nov. 15, 1924*, pp. 71, 75–78.
[41]*Open Shop Bulletin*, No. 23, p. 6.
[42]Building Trades Dept., *1924 Convention Proceedings*, p. 93.

the open shop, and the Carpenters had made it plain that only by destroying the one could the other be met and defeated.

George Hedrick of the Painters replaced John Donlin as president of the Building Trades Department, and William Tracy of the Plumbers replaced William Spencer as secretary, at the 1924 Department convention. Immediately a more conciliatory attitude toward the Carpenters became apparent. Secretary Tracy wrote to the newly elected president of the AFL, William Green, shortly after taking office, that "a better feeling exists between the United Brotherhood of Carpenters and Joiners and its officials and our Department than has existed since. . . [1921]."[43] Green was grateful and hoped that a "clear and definite" agreement could be worked out.[44]

Building Trades Department officials took steps in 1925 to unite some of the divided building trades councils by providing for local option on the seating of the Carpenters' district councils.[45] The following year the Carpenters and the Sheet Metal Workers signed an agreement giving Hutcheson everything he demanded.[46] Green was then able to lure Hutcheson into a conference with the members of the Department during their 1927 convention. They flatly asked Hutcheson his price for reaffiliation. "Kill the National Board for Jurisdictional Awards," he replied. When the convention opened, the executive council of the Building Trades Department had ready a resolution doing as much. Before the body was cold, Hutcheson was back in the Department.[47] Said Delegate John Coefield of the Plumbers:

A number of the officers and members of the Executive Council of the AFL directed their efforts toward destroying that Board [the National

[43]Building Trades Department, AFL, *Proceedings of the Nineteenth Annual Convention of Atlantic City, June 3 to June 7, 1925*, p. 79.

[44]*Ibid.*, p. 80.

[45]*Ibid.*, p. 73.

[46]Carpenters and Joiners of America, United Brotherhood of, *Proceedings of the Twenty-second General Convention of Lakeland, Florida, Sept. 29 to Oct. 9, 1928*, pp. 48–49. Certain details of this agreement did not meet with the approval of the executive board of the Sheet Metal Workers, and it was renegotiated with a special but unimportant provision added. The final agreement was ratified on March 21, 1928 (*ibid.*, pp. 49–50).

[47]*Ibid.*, p. 53; Building Trades Department, AFL, *Proceedings of the Twenty-first Annual Convention of Los Angeles, Sept. 28 to Oct. 1, 1927*, pp. 88–89.

Board for Jurisdictional Awards] because the Carpenters wanted it destroyed. Brother Green pleaded with me to use what little influence I might have with the delegates in that convention to abolish that Board.[48]

The other building trades unionists accepted the board's death as the price of the Carpenters' reaffiliation because the Department was in dire financial straits and sorely needed the United Brotherhood's annual per capita tax of $18,000.[49] In addition, the Carpenters were taken back in order to end disputes in the various local building trades councils, such as those in Cleveland and New York City. This strife rapidly ended once its fomenters, the Carpenters, rejoined the Department.[50] Furthermore, the Carpenters' support was needed in a membership drive planned for the cities of Cleveland, Philadelphia, and Detroit.[51]

That the most important reason for the death of the board was the open shop movement is proven by the action of the 1928 Building Trades Department convention. Answering a request from the employer members of the board to reaffiliate, the delegates praised the idea behind the board but, on motion of Hutcheson, refused to help create another jurisdictional board until "definite assurances can be given to the Building Trades Department that they [the employers represented on the National Board for Jurisdictional Awards] severally agree to employ none but Union Building Trades Mechanics throughout."[52]

As soon as the Carpenters reaffiliated, the open shop movement in the building trades started to lose its vigor. Its high watermark was the 40 percent figure reached in 1924 and maintained in 1925. Then, as the Carpenters made their peace first with the Sheet Metal Workers in 1926 and then with the Building Trades Department in 1927, the percentage of cities building on an open shop basis began to decline. In 1926 the National Association of Manufacturers reported only 31 percent of all cities building under the

[48]*Proceedings of the Fifty-fourth Annual Convention of the AFL of San Francisco, Oct. 1 to Oct. 12, 1934,* p. 532.
[49]Cummins, p. 373.
[50]Building Trades Department, AFL, *Proceedings of the Twenty-second Annual Convention of New Orleans, Oct. 14 to Oct. 16, 1928,* pp. 45–46.
[51]Cummins, p. 374.
[52]Building Trades Dept., *1928 Convention Proceedings,* p. 102.

open shop, and in 1927 only 29 percent. In 1928 the National Association of Manufacturers complained that the open shop gains of the 1921 to 1927 period had been all but wiped out by union activity since June 1927;[53] June 1927 was about ten weeks before the Building Trades Department made its peace with the Carpenters. In his report to the Brotherhood's 1928 convention Hutcheson announced that "while there are still periodical attempts. . .to put into effect the open shop. . .[we] have been able to combat these efforts so that the system has not become anything other than what might be termed 'Local'; only existing in a few localities."[54]

Thus, by 1928, the postwar period in the building industry had come to a close. The various congresses and commissions, like the National Board for Jurisdictional Awards, faded into oblivion. The open shop movement, too, had passed away. None of these innovations had made an impression upon the conservative building trades men or their crazy-quilt industry. Some legendary Rip Van Winkle carpenter, asleep since before World War I, would have been as much at home in 1929 at a Building Trades Department convention as he was in 1916. Jurisdictional laissez faire was back in all its glory, unencumbered either by public conscience, open shop, or jurisdictional award boards.

While these events transpired in the field of external relations, some interesting events were taking place inside the bounds of the United Brotherhood. During the same period this conservative union turned up an active little colony of Communists. For a good many years they bored, like so many sand hogs, within the union, until Hutcheson took drastic and violent steps to end their activities.

[53]*Open Shop Bulletin* No. 23, pp. 6–7.
[54]UBCJA, *1928 Convention Proceedings*, p. 46.

-+ CHAPTER XVII +-

Status Quo: 1920 to 1933

AFTER World War I the United Brotherhood entered a long period in which nothing changed and history stood still. Its constitutional history had stopped in 1912 with the humbling of the executive board and its political history in 1916 when Hutcheson met and defeated the New York brothers. Not one basic constitutional change emanated from the seven general conventions held between 1917 and 1952. Organized opposition to the administration, which presented itself only once during this period, was opposition from outside, rather than from within, the union.

After 1920, a sharp break with the past history of the union is evident. The opposition, ferment, and constant change of policy which had characterized the 1900 to 1916 period ceased. The habits, customs, forms, practices, prejudices, and even persons emerging from this period of conflict became fixed and impervious to change. The internal history of the United Brotherhood has been marking time since 1920.

There were no more organizing drives, for as a *Carpenter* editorial said shortly after Hutcheson assumed office, "Brilliant 'drives' in which much ground is won only to be wrested back at a later date...have never characterized the fight the labor movement is making."[1] At the beginning of the decade, in 1920, and near its end, in 1928, Hutcheson told the convention delegates that the

[1]Editorial, "The March of Progress," *The Carpenter*, Vol. 36, No. 8, August 1916, p. 33.

organizing staff confined itself to settling jurisdictional disputes and solving trouble with the employers. It did little or no organizing.[2] In fact Hutcheson objected to the very name "organizer" and told the 1928 convention delegates that it was a misnomer. Staff members were his personal representatives, he said, and a better name for them was "representatives."[3]

Since they were not actively sought, few new members joined the union during the 1920's. In the closed shop cities there was a natural turnover as old members died and new carpenters joined the trade. In certain communities the locals lapsed; in others new ones sprang up. But these changes canceled each other out and the union's membership, like its history, marked time. In 1920 there were 331,500 members, and in 1929 322,000.[4]

Partly because few new members entered the union and partly because of tight control from the top, no new blood entered the leadership. Between 1920 and 1929 the seven district members of the executive board came up for election three times. Four new individuals joined the board, yet only one of them gained office by running against an incumbent. The rest were appointed by Hutcheson upon the death or resignation of the incumbents. In the only other change among the general officers, First Vice-President John Cosgrove resigned, Second Vice-President G. H. Lakey moved into his position, and James Gauld was appointed as the new second vice-president.

Most of these new officers rose to prominence by starting out as business agents, working up through the ruling hierarchy of one or another of the district councils, being appointed general representative, then rising to a general officership. Duffy, who entered the national office in 1900, Neale, who became treasurer in 1902, and Hutcheson maintained themselves firmly in office. They changed only by getting a little older and a little grayer.

Like the carpenters they led, these men were fixed in their ways.

[2] UBCJA, *1920 Convention Proceedings*, p. 22, and *1928 Convention Proceedings*, p. 304.
[3] UBCJA, *1928 Convention Proceedings*, p. 304.
[4] *Proceedings of the Fortieth Annual Convention of the AFL of Montreal, June 7 to June 19, 1920*, p. 37; *Proceedings of the Fiftieth Annual Convention of the AFL of Boston, Oct. 6 to Oct. 17, 1930*, p. 38.

New ideas about society at large, the regulation of the trade, or the conduct of the union were strictly forbidden. As the general executive board members said in an official circular, they would "not countenance any action on the part of our members in departing from the well tried methods...that have been successful in years gone by."[5]

Even the journal of the union reflected the dearth of new ideas. One student of labor relations said of *The Carpenter* that it "exudes a quaint Victorian aroma," which "recaptures the folksy flavor of a bygone day."[6] Columns once filled with long, learned articles by the radicals of a past age thundering against the "capitalist order" were replaced by notes on court suits, details of jurisdictional strikes, and long, dull pages of "useful information." Such philosophy as did emanate from the leaders came in the form of an endless stream of inspirational poetry which Frank Duffy sprinkled across the pages of *The Carpenter*. The following is typical:

Do you wish to acquire all the money you need?
    Then save just a little today.
Don't think you will suddenly fall into luck,
    It seldom happens that way.
Your chance for a fortune will always be slim
    Until you've a sum to invest;
So make up your mind that right now is the time,
    Begin now to feather your nest.[7]

Although the leaders of the union propounded no social philosophy, they did possess one which gradually emerged in their practice rather than their comments. They were staunch defenders of the status quo, conservative much in the same manner as the small midwestern businessmen of the 1920's. One delegate was ousted from the 1920 convention because his remarks were "largely an attack upon the existing social order."[8] When the officers of the AFL appeared before the executive board to solicit United Brotherhood funds for, and an endorsement of, the AFL-backed National Non-Partisan Political Campaign, in 1920, the executive

---

[5]UBCJA, *1940 Convention Proceedings*, p. 184.
[6]Herbert Harris, *American Labor*, pp. 167–168.
[7]*The Carpenter*, Vol. 42, No. 1, January 1922, p. 11 (title page).
[8]UBCJA, *1920 Convention Proceedings*, p. 184.

board refused both.[9] Hutcheson declared a resolution to approve the action of the AFL in supporting the La Follette Progressive party, which came before the 1924 convention, out of order.[10] Yet in the same election campaign he gave active support to Coolidge.[11]

When a resolution came before the 1924 convention asking for tighter job control to prevent the bosses from speeding up and firing at will, Hutcheson's committee rejected it, saying, "Every brother should be his own keeper in this matter. The subject is a broad one, having for its foundation the changing of some of the fundamental principles on which society exists, and which cannot be so changed."[12]

Hutcheson and his lieutenants carefully divested the union of all social overtones and made it a straightforward, cold business proposition. "When we become members...we are investors in the biggest paying proposition that we could have chosen for our investments," reads an article in the 1928 edition of *The Carpenter*. Continuing in the jargon of the stock market the writer said, "We looked over the available information, sized up our chances, became satisfied of the solvency of the organization,...talked it over with friend wife perhaps, and decided in our minds, that here was a good investment."[13]

With such a philosophy it is little wonder that the leaders put as much energy into the purchase of a Florida fruit farm and the packaging, shipping, and selling of "United Brotherhood of Carpenters and Joiners' Citrus Fruit" during the early 1920's as they did into organizing. When the following two notices were printed in *The Carpenter* but six months apart, however, there was some cause for wonder. The first notice stated, "1,665 local Chambers of Commerce following the example of the United States Chamber of Commerce,...are pledged to the principle of the 'open shop.'" The second stated, "On invitation of the Chamber of Commerce of

---

[9]"Proceedings of the Second Quarterly Session of the General Executive Board, April 6," *The Carpenter*, Vol. 40, No. 6, June 1920, p. 28.

[10]UBCJA, *1924 Convention Proceedings*, p. 299.

[11]Lorwin, p. 225, n. 34.

[12]UBCJA, *1924 Convention Proceedings*, p. 329.

[13]Heber White, "Membership—An Investment," *The Carpenter*, Vol. 48, No. 8, August 1928, p. 24.

Indianapolis the [Executive] Board, believing it to be in the best interests of the organization, decided to affiliate."[14]

Only one aspect of the United Brotherhood changed after 1920. That was Hutcheson's power, which grew in an almost geometrical progression. Between 1920 and 1924 Hutcheson passed on 621 membership appeals from his authority, 54 of which continued up to the executive board on further appeal. Not one was reversed.[15] Neither was he reversed on any appeals between 1924 and 1928. His own words best describe how he ruled his followers. "We are what we consider a democratic organization...and when we want... [our members] to do something we first advise them of the fact and then if they don't do it, we are liable to say, 'Well, you are going to do it.'"[16]

As the union thus marked time, Hutcheson drew a thick veil of secrecy about all of its activities. The long, informative, and in large part verbatim convention proceedings of the 1902 to 1912 period were replaced, after 1913, by shorter, less informative ones with few direct quotations. The published proceedings of the two conventions between 1924 and 1928 together occupy scarcely two-thirds the shelf space of those of 1912. During the 1920's the union ceased publishing in its public documents its new constitutional amendments and the reports of its referendum vote tabulating committees. Finally even the annual reports of membership were barred from the public eye. The union pushed through the roaring twenties and into the hungry thirties in the still, hushed, and unchanging quiet of an autocratic rule.

But if little changed in its musty Victorian interior, many changes were taking place outside the union during the 1920's. The Communist party, full of proletarian vigor, was born. Its members were immediately attracted to the United Brotherhood. This union, the second largest in the country, led by conservative Republicans, and therefore according to Communist doctrine hardly a trade union at all, seemed to them a prime target for conversion

[14]John P. Frey, "The Open Shop," *The Carpenter*, Vol. 47, No. 5, May 1927, p. 25; "Quarterly Proceedings of the Executive Board, September 29, 1926," *The Carpenter*, Vol. 46, No. 11, November 1926, p. 45.
[15]UBCJA, *1924 Convention Proceedings*, p. 43.
[16]AFL, *1934 Convention Proceedings*, p. 526.

to Marxist ways. Consequently, during the 1920's they launched a carefully planned assault upon the United Brotherhood.

Rather than attack the strong and well-entrenched Brotherhood directly, they chose to infilter its ranks and then to try to capture its leadership. To do this, the Communist party covertly sponsored the Trade Union Education League, under the leadership of William Z. Foster.[17] As the League's attempt to penetrate the building trades unions got under way in 1922 and 1923, its leaders published a small sheet, the *Progressive Building Trades Worker*, and opened headquarters in Philadelphia, New York, Chicago, and Detroit,[18] from which the drive to capture the United Brotherhood was directed. They worked to implement a long-winded, eighteen-point platform which included a series of internal reforms in the Brotherhood, ostensibly designed to make it a more democratic organization,[19] a plan for the amalgamation of all building trades unions into one big union, a labor party, affiliation of the United Brotherhood with the Red International, and recognition by the United States government of Soviet Russia.

The Trade Union Education League was able to establish a strong foothold in the United Brotherhood because of Hutcheson's recklessly autocratic methods. So taut was his rule that a strong opposition was cast into the hands of a minority of planted Communist borers. This opposition was strong, however, only in the sense that it was united and vociferous. It had no roots in the building industry, captured no business agents, had few high-ranking local and no national officers, and had no semblance of organizational background in the union. Consequently, it differed sharply from the 1909 to 1912 revolt which was led by Ryan and Schardt. This new opposition might be described as a flying wedge

[17]David Saposs, *Left Wing Unionism*, pp. 48–50.

[18]*Appeal of Local Union 376 to the Membership of the United Brotherhood of Carpenters and Joiners of America to the Twenty-second General Convention from the Decision of General President William L. Hutcheson and the General Executive Board*, p. 67. This was published by the Trade Union Education League, a Communist front organization. It has been checked carefully with other existing sources, and while the conclusions its authors draw from the facts are usually unwarranted, the facts seem to be reliable.

[19]*Ibid.*, pp. 75–76. This platform is too long to be reproduced here. For example, it asked for local election of organizers, election instead of appointment of the general convention Rules Committee, and biennial conventions.

which penetrated first one part of the organization then another and was each time thrown back hard, until in 1925 it was shattered completely.

The breach into which the Communist opposition flooded was opened by the "Home Affair" of 1920. Hutcheson had always been strongly taken with the idea of a home for aged carpenters.[20] He raised the question of an old age home before the 1920 convention. Opposition was strong, however, and the officers were given permission only to look into the advisability of establishing a home.[21]

Throughout 1921 and 1922 various officers of the union were wined and dined by Florida land speculators. In March 1923 the executive board sent out a long circular, heavily weighted in favor of creating a home in Florida. It ended by asking the carpenters to vote for or against the purchase of a home. In June the executive board announced the favorable passage of the measure and, in December, the purchase of a home site near Lakeland, Florida.[22] The price of the land alone came to almost a half-million dollars.[23] When the rank and file discovered the cost figures, pandemonium broke loose. Even a Hutcheson supporter admitted that "there was [not] a city or local union...that did not criticize this man [Hutcheson] from one end of the land to the other."[24]

Protests against the purchase of the land deluged the national offices. The carpenters of Everett, Washington, found through their own inquiries that the votes of at least thirty locals had been falsified and that the home measure had lost by at least 196 votes. C. J. Mulcahy of Providence, Rhode Island, then took charge of the opposition. He initiated a vote to abandon the project, behind which he marshalled two hundred and eighty locals representing some seventy thousand members. The board, constitutionally bound to put the matter to a vote under these circumstances, refused because, among other reasons, Mulcahy's petition was

[20]See above, p. 198.
[21]UBCJA, *1924 Convention Proceedings*, p. 188.
[22]*Ibid.*, pp. 189–194.
[23]*Ibid.*, p. 115. The eventual cost of the completed home was $4,000,000 ("Boss Carpenter," *Fortune*, April 1946, p. 276).
[24]UBCJA, *1936 Convention Proceedings*, p. 268.

typed and not handwritten and because it did not have the union's seal affixed.[25]

As earlier events indicated it would be, the 1924 convention was a holocaust. The opposition was led by Mulcahy and Morris Rosen, a Trade Union Education League plant in Local Union 376 of New York City. With the support of various opposition locals scattered throughout the country, these two men introduced one resolution after another designed to undercut Hutcheson's power. The resolutions were the same ones introduced by every opposition group which had ever reared its collective head at a Carpenters' convention and need not be repeated again. They were aimed primarily at cutting the executive board and the organizers away from the general officers and at lessening the direct powers of the general president, in and out of the convention. Not one passed.

Throughout the convention Hutcheson stalled Mulcahy's repeated attempts to bring a protest against the purchase of the home to the floor. For well over a year Mulcahy had been stalking Hutcheson. According to the left-wing opposition, Hutcheson paid him back dearly during the convention. The following events are alleged by the opposition to have befallen Mulcahy on the night of September 22, 1924, during the convention:

Mulcahy went over to a restaurant and after leaving...a man stepped out of the shadows, kicked him and pushed him down; then went away.

.   .   .

[Later] a covered automobile passed him as he was walking and stopped a short distance ahead of him. A man got out, stood on the curb, and kept his head concealed in the car. He stood this way until Mulcahy came along ahead of him, when he stepped back and swung out with his left hand hitting Mulcahy on the right eye and knocking him down. The car then drove away [with] the assailant...inside.[26]

Whether or not he was assaulted, Mulcahy was present and in fine voice during the last session of the convention, when the home

[25]"Quarterly Proceedings of the General Executive Board, 1924, March 20," *The Carpenter*, Vol. 44, No. 5, May 1924, p. 39.

[26]Progressive Building Trades Worker, *What's Wrong with the Carpenters' Union?*, p. 36. The remarks made about the pamphlet *Appeal* (above, n. 18) also apply to this source.

matter was finally taken up. He asked that the executive board conduct a second vote on the establishment of a home.

Hutcheson: "The motion...is not debatable...."

. . .

Delegate Mulcahy: "Do I understand then that the appeal of Local Union No. 632 will not be heard before this convention?"

Hutcheson: "It is laid on the table indefinitely."

Delegate Mulcahy: "I appeal from your decision."

Delegate Mulcahy refused to obey repeated requests...[to] come to order.

Hutcheson: "Delegate Mulcahy will be recorded in the proceedings as no longer a delegate in this convention.[27]

Although bitterly defeated in the convention, the opposition managed to run a slate in the election. Willis K. Brown, of Local Union 103, and Rosen split the opposition by both running for Hutcheson's office. James Walsh of New York contested the incumbent John Cosgrove for first vice-president, and Mulcahy ran against Tim Guerin for the first district executive board post. John Halkett, Brindell's successor as czar of the New York Building Trades Council, was elected chairman of the Tabulating Committee,[28] and the United Brotherhood went through the throes of still another contested election.

Hutcheson won the election by a walkaway, but an enormous cross-country hue and cry was set up over the counting of the vote.[29] The most important protests came in from Pittsburgh, Brown's local in Peoria, and St. Paul. With these protests Hutcheson started the big and the final purge.[30] From 1925 to 1928 he established a procedure of first allowing dissenters to speak their little bit, then taking one of two courses: either sending them trundling out of the union or demanding contrite and self-abasing

[27]UBCJA, *1924 Convention Proceedings,* p. 361.
[28]*Ibid.,* p. 257.
[29]Hutcheson received 77,985 votes and Brown 34,436. Rosen received 9,014. (Rand School of Social Science, *American Labor Year Book, 1925,* p. 67).
[30]See "Quarterly Proceedings of the Executive Board, 1925," March 30, *The Carpenter,* Vol. 45, No. 5, May 1925, p. 31, for a list of the various counts of vote fraud with which Hutcheson was charged.

apologies which permitted them to remain in the union only on tenure of good behavior. Hutcheson was the final arbiter of what did and did not constitute good behavior.

He turned first to those who protested the election. Only the Pittsburgh people were to be feared, for the opposition had captured the local union machine and the district council had lodged the protest which came from that quarter. President E. W. Williams of the Pittsburgh district council was given a hearing in March 1925, at the general headquarters. The executive board listened to his story, rejected his charges, and then bundled him on his way. An innocuous little note in the executive board proceedings subsequently stated that "consolidation" of the Pittsburgh locals was proceeding on schedule.[31]

Hutcheson then turned to the other, more isolated dissenters. Herbert Elmore, W. K. Brown's representative at the ballot count, had sent in a violent protest corroborating that of the Pittsburgh people. The executive board felt that Elmore required some investigation. Duffy crooked his finger, and Elmore came scurrying to Indianapolis. In the presence of the United Brotherhood's attorney, James Carson, Elmore contritely and categorically swore that every word in his notarized statement was false.[32]

The St. Paul dissenter, L. F. Kringel, had been more bold in his accusation. He had said that Duffy had arbitrarily thrown out the ballots of no less than nine hundred local unions. Since he had been more bold, he had to be more contrite to regain official favor. Said he, "I am more than willing to admit that it [the protest] was an error of mine for which I owe you an apology, and am glad to do so, hoping that you may be able to overlook the error on my part." He was then forced to accept a public reprimand from his local and to promise never again to commit a like crime.[33]

As Hutcheson conducted his mopping-up operation, the Communists set up an enormous protest. They published circulars, pamphlets, cartoons, and a weekly paper in which Hutcheson was

[31]"Quarterly Proceedings of the Executive Board, 1927," June 20, *The Carpenter*, Vol. 47, No. 8, August 1927, p. 46.

[32]"Quarterly Proceedings of the General Executive Board, 1925," June 17, *The Carpenter*, Vol. 45, No. 8, August 1925, p. 32.

[33]UBCJA, *1928 Convention Proceedings*, p. 214.

either ridiculed or savagely denounced. Hutcheson next moved to silence the left wing, roaring that "there are only two 'isms' that should enter into our organization—that is unionism and Americanism, and all other 'isms' or advocates...should be kicked out and kicked out quickly."[34] He struck out at them by forming a series of junketeering executive board committees and subcommittees which struck at any Communists or any opposition associated with the Communists. The following excerpts from the transcripts of several of the hearings are typical:

Q. "Did you ever attend any meetings at Folkets Hus on Hirsh Boulevard?"

A. "Yes, lots of times."

Q. "The pictures of Lenin and Trotzky hang very prominently on the walls there, do they not?"

A. "Yes."[35]

In another case:

First Vice President Cosgrove: Do you believe in Industrial Unionism?"

Morris Rosen: "I believe in amalgamation."

Cosgrove repeats the above question several times and Rosen gives the same answer. Cosgrove then gets angry and says: "That means yes."

W. T. Allen: "Are you a Communist?"

Rosen: "I refuse to answer that question. I believe it is unconstitutional to ask it."[36]

First to be swept aside was F. W. Burgess, of Local Union 8, Philadelphia. "Scurrilous literature," the executive board found on January 5, 1925,[37] had been sent out by this man who had conducted Brown's campaign for the presidency. Duffy, Cosgrove, and Neale led Arthur Martel and J. W. Williams, both executive

[34]UBCJA, *1924 Convention Proceedings,* p. 4.
[35]*What's Wrong,* p. 18 (transcript of the trial of Nick Olsen of Local Union 181, Chicago, on Nov. 25, 1924 issued by the Progressive Building Trades Worker, publisher of this pamphlet).
[36]*Appeal,* p. 70.
[37]"Quarterly Proceedings of the General Executive Board, 1925," January 5, *The Carpenter,* Vol. 45, No. 3, March 1925, p. 30.

board members, to Philadelphia to right the wrong. Burgess was heard and expelled at the end of the month.[38] With his departure the opposition in Philadelphia was dead.

Hutcheson turned to Detroit on January 9, 1925, and ordered William "Bud" Reynolds expelled. The crime was membership in the Trade Union Education League; of related interest: Detroit had gone to Rosen by forty-one votes in the election.[39] In spite of the fact that Hutcheson had General Representatives Sam Boterill and William Alger campaigning in that city, Reynolds had managed to capture the vice-presidency of the district council, the presidency of his own Local Union 2140, and strong rank-and-file support.

Duffy informed the members of Local Union 2140 by mail, on January 10, that they were to expel Reynolds. When they refused, Lawyer Carson obtained an injunction against Reynolds' participation in union affairs. Reynolds defied it, however, and there ensued some ugly episodes involving violence, avowals by Hutcheson's supporters that "no goddammed radical[s]...are going to run this town," and, finally, police action.[40]

Duffy led an investigating subcommittee out to Detroit. The committee recommended lifting Local Union 2140's charter if the members did not drop Reynolds and having Hutcheson take over the district council.[41] The exact details of what followed are not available. Whatever happened, Local Union 2140 caused no further trouble, and Reynolds disappeared from the scene.

Finally, Hutcheson leveled his sights on New York and blasted Brother Rosen from the United Brotherhood in early 1926. It was the last of the purges, the last of the United Brotherhood's *opéra bouffe* left wing, and the end of opposition, comic or real, in the United Brotherhood. Rosen, who led the Trade Union Education League drive on the Brotherhood, led New York Local 376. He entered it in early 1923 and within the year led a "progressive" slate which wrested control of the union from "the old gang that

[38]*Ibid.*, p. 35.
[39]*What's Wrong*, p. 42.
[40]*Ibid.*, pp. 42–45.
[41]"Quarterly Proceedings of the General Executive Board, 1925," March 28, *The Carpenter*, Vol. 45, No. 5, May 1925, p. 30.

was loyal to Hutcheson."[42] When Rosen looked into the affairs of the old treasurer, Meyer Rudinsky, he found, through accountants, that at least $1,100 was missing and had clearly been embezzled. After his local expelled him Rudinsky went to Hutcheson, who immediately demonstrated an avid interest in the books of the local. He sent Guerin to take possession of the books. Rosen refused to turn them over to Guerin, fearing that they would disappear and with them the evidence. He stood on a clause in the constitution which allowed the general officers to examine a local union's books but only within the local's jurisdiction. Rosen interpreted this to mean in the local's office, and Guerin got no books.

Duffy polished his gavel, packed his luggage, and was off to another trial. In June 1926 the committee which he headed found Rosen and all the members of Local Union 376 guilty as charged and reported that Rosen had refused to surrender the books to conceal the fact that the local's funds had been given to the Trade Union Education League. Local Union 376 was suspended, and several of Rosen's followers in other New York locals were ousted. In this fell swoop Rosen, the man who had run against Hutcheson for president, and Walsh, the man who had contested Cosgrove for first vice-president, were scooped out of the organization. Those Local Union 376 carpenters who were reinstated were barred from any office within the gift of the union for five years.[43]

As far as Hutcheson's vigilant investigating committees, business agents, and general representatives could peer, all was calm and properly conservative in the United Brotherhood in 1927. True, the Trade Union Education League people were setting up an enormous clatter, distributing pamphlets and caricaturing Hutcheson in ridiculous cartoons, but they, and not Hutcheson, were on the outside. Those who had in the past veered a bit too far to the left were all carefully stamped and placed to one side in the organization, under the terms of contracts like the following.

[42]UBCJA, *1928 Convention Proceedings*, p. 242.
[43]See UBCJA, *1928 Convention Proceedings*, pp. 240–245 for Rosen's side of the story, and pp. 245–255 for Duffy's remarks in rebuttal.

I, the undersigned, do hereby promise and agree that I will in no way affiliate with or give support, assistance or comfort to the Trade Union Education League, or any similar or kindred organization.

In subscribing to the above, I do so of my own free will and accord, and agree that should I violate said agreement or pledge, it is understood that my membership in the United Brotherhood of Carpenters and Joiners of America will be forfeited without complaint by me.[44]

Yet something rankled inside of Hutcheson, and he allowed Rosen and several others of the opposition to appear at the 1928 convention, where he stalked them as the Romans did the early Christians, for the pure enjoyment of the spectacle. Duffy and Hutcheson, working as a team, maneuvered Rosen, who was under suspension subject to convention appeal, to the platform to state his case. A delegate objected strenuously, but Hutcheson insisted. "Please come to the platform," he told Rosen, "and stand here beside the flag, the one you don't think so much of."[45] When Rosen requested a fair chance to speak, Hutcheson told him ominously, "I will take care of [you]. . .afterwards. Go as far as you like."[46]

Rosen must have been, after his fashion, a very brave man. He was also a very foolish one. He launched into a long, factual denunciation of Hutcheson on trade union grounds.

Duffy, in rebuttal, centered his attack on Rosen's undoubted Communist affiliation. After mounting his appeal to a near frenzy, Duffy leveled an accusing finger at Rosen and told the hushed delegates, "There are two of us here on the platform today—Morris Rosen and myself. The organization is not big enough for both of us. Either he goes out or I go out, and I'm not going out." In the ensuing uproar Rosen escaped violence only by the narrowest of margins.

President Hutcheson: "Please get out of this building and off the Brotherhood's property as quickly as possible."

A delegate: ". . .I would. . .request. . .that we grant him a safe conduct until he has left the city of Lakeland."

[44]*Appeal,* p. 59.
[45]UBCJA, *1928 Convention Proceedings,* p. 240.
[46]*Ibid.,* p. 240.

President Hutcheson: "That will be done. I am going to ask every member of the Brotherhood in this room to do this—just show that you are real men and do not lay your hands on the likes of him until he gets out of our sight."[47]

Then the delegates indulged themselves in a mass public purge. The proceedings require no comment.

Delegate Flynn: "That is only one, Mr. Chairman."

President Hutcheson: "Let us deal with the rest of them tomorrow morning."

Delegate Flynn: "Are the names of the destructionists available, those who are seated in the hall? If they are, let's deal with them the same as we have with Rosen."

President Hutcheson: "It is in order, and the secretary will give the names of the members you refer to."

Secretary Duffy: "Robert Golden, 1164."

President Hutcheson: "Please rise. You are accused of being a Communist."

A delegate: "I move...that Robert Golden be expelled from the Brotherhood."

The motion was seconded and carried unanimously.

President Hucheson: "You will please follow your pal out of the building."

When Golden attempted to resist...President Hutcheson said: "Get out...and do not make it necessary to put you out."

Secretary Duffy: "Nathan Rosen, 1164...."

President Hutcheson: "He is not present, but we can take the same action."

Secretary Duffy: "Thomas Schneider,...2090."

President Hutcheson: "He is present as a delegate. What is your pleasure?"

A delegate: "I move that Thomas Schneider...be expelled from the Brotherhood."[48]

[47]*Ibid.*, p. 255.
[48]*Ibid.*, p. 255.

By this time it was late in the afternoon, and the delegates had spent their energy. The purge was called off for dinner, and a special committee was given the rest of the alleged Communists to handle as it saw fit.[49] The committee heard from eleven men in all, three of whom were ousted as Communists. Eight of them supplied affidavits of noncommunism. Of these, two were given a "clean bill of health" and six were put on probation because a "disturbing element has been...active lately in Chicago."[50]

When he placed these men on probation Hutcheson cast his net wide, perhaps no wider than he had planned but wide enough to catch several not very Red brothers. Unlike Rosen, they did not bring up the issue of whether or not it was constitutional to ask their political affiliations. Unlike Rosen, they asserted vehemently their noncommunism. These men had but one thing in common with Rosen: they too had opposed Hutcheson. One of their number, pleading against being put on probation, said, "We have been trying to...put new blood in the organization.... Without opposition you would be stagnant and dead."[51]

Several of the Chicago brothers pleaded with the convention to lift the Red onus off them. Said Delegate William Burgbacher:

I am a young man thirty-five years of age...and to think I have come to this, my first convention, and be[en] accused of being a Communist by someone unknown to me.

.   .   .   .

It is a terrible feeling to have that black mark against me....I will have that in my system the rest of my days. It is a thing that has worried me and spoiled my whole pleasure. I say that if the person who gave my name in does not stand up and say so, there isn't a drop of red blood in him.[52]

Pete Trimmer next spoke his piece. He pleaded his service as a marine in France, his wounds, his decorations, his family lineage, and even that his name in Dutch meant carpenter. Then he simply pleaded.

[49]*Ibid.*, p. 256.
[50]*Ibid.*, p. 332.
[51]*Ibid.*, p. 335.
[52]*Ibid.*, pp. 332–333.

264

This is a crisis in my life... [and] you are here witnessing a procedure that will probably wreck a man's life.

. . .

I may have said a thing [against the leadership] which now escapes my notice, but as I stand here before God and you men...I am a good citizen of the United States and an A-1 member of the United Brotherhood of Carpenters and Joiners of America, and you will wreck my home if you place me on probation. Allow me to be a free man.[53]

Both pleas fell on deaf ears.

Delegate Louis Long, who had contested William Brims, the boss of the Chicago carpenters, for re-election, spoke for all the men put on probation when he said: "My opposition...has been [only] to those fellows, turncoats, that held office [in the Chicago District Council]....I am not affiliated with...the Communists or with those other fellows that have anything against the organization."[54]

Hutcheson, who had gone to such great lengths to document the communism of Communist Rosen, offered no evidence of the guilt of Long and his fellow accused. Since the burden of proof rested on the accuser, in the absence of such evidence the men concerned were clearly not proven Communists. Long was correct when he said he and his five friends were placed under a pall because they were dissenters. In reply to Long's contention that his activities constituted only loyal opposition, Hutcheson's New York lieutenant, Halkett, replied, "That is fine up to a certain point...but ...when the majority has spoken, we must desist from opposition to this organization."[55] Opposition was what Hutcheson sought to destroy, whether it was Red, white, blue, or a combination of the three. The five dissenters had to recant and accept probationary membership, whatever its embarrassment and implication, as an alternate to loss of their livelihood.

The Carpenters' brush with the Communists was at an end. The delegates then brought the convention to a rousing finale by rising

[53]*Ibid.,* p. 333.

[54]*Ibid.,* p. 335. By "turncoats," Long probably referred to Brims, the head of the Chicago district council, who had but recently (1926) been indicted and found guilty of collusion with the employers to raise building prices (*U.S.* v. *Brims,* U.S. Supreme Court, Vol. 272, p. 549 [1926]).

[55]UBCJA, *1928 Convention Proceedings,* p. 335.

to sing "Home Sweet Home," "God Be With You," and the "Star Spangled Banner."[56]

The personalities involved in this latest opposition movement are of no great importance. Hutcheson was simply playing a game with the Red brothers, a game in which the dice were heavily loaded in his favor. When the time came, he rolled his seven, swept in the stakes, and sent the Red brothers packing with little other than their memories, mimeograph machines, and some faded cartoons to solace them. More important than the opposition itself is its historical significance.

It differed radically from the prewar opposition led by William Schardt and Thomas Ryan described in Chapter X. The dissenters of the 1920's did not gain so much as a foothold in the national office. The five national officers and the seven-man executive board presented an arms-linked and united front against the radicals. With the independent executive board gone, the radicals were without an approach to the national office. With the latter's victory over the New York locals as a precedent, they had even less chance of capturing and retaining control of any influential district councils. United Brotherhood quarrels ceased being those of business agent against business agent after 1916 and became those of business agents united from local to national office against political radicals.

The other significant aspect of the story told in this chapter is Hutcheson's method of dealing with political radicals. The United Brotherhood was among the first important unions to be assaulted by the Communists and the very first to develop a technique for repulsing the assault. The techniques described in this chapter Hutcheson used again and again from 1925 to 1950 to nip in the bud any attempts to capture his union. They were to become familiar to another generation: the touring subcommittees, the Communists' avowal that certain questions were unconstitutional, the purging of guilt by public confession, and the guilt by association charge of the noncommunist opposition.

Whether or not these were the best of all possible techniques, they served to keep the union out of Communist hands, in the

[56]*Ibid.*, p. 341.

hands of trade unionists, and, more specifically, in the hands of one group of trade unionists: William L. Hutcheson and his associates. Since 1924 no one has ever contested the incumbent president in a United Brotherhood election.

With the Communists gone and the storm abated, Hutcheson once again lapsed into his routine. When in 1929 the depression overtook the organization, Hutcheson and his lieutenants accepted it philosophically. The salaries of the general officers, which between 1924 and 1928 consumed $128,986.38 of the Carpenters' money, consumed that much and $35,353.62 more between 1928 and 1932.[57] The membership figures, which had marked time during the 1920's, began to backtrack after 1929, at first slowly, then rapidly.[58] There was no evidence of concern, even over this development. Official union documents and pronouncements were completely silent on the subjects of possible union growth and actual union shrinkage. No organizing plans to reclaim the loss of membership came from the high or low councils of the union. Within the confines of the United Brotherhood all was as peaceful as an isolated meadow in the summer sun. The machine droned on, lazily, contentedly, and efficiently, like meadow bees. Nothing changed.

Then suddenly, three bolts crashed upon the United Brotherhood, shattering the silence surrounding Hutcheson: Franklin Delano Roosevelt, John L. Lewis, and the Congress of Industrial Organizations. Roosevelt personally created a board for jurisdictional awards in the building industry with the force of federal law behind it, thus assaulting and ultimately rendering untenable the United Brotherhood's policy of jurisdictional laissez faire. By creating the CIO, Lewis pulled a whole industry out from under Hutcheson and seriously threatened the United Brotherhood

---

[57]*Ibid.*, p. 83; UBCJA, *1936 Convention Proceedings*, p. 177. In the latter period the total general officers' salary figures were $164,340.

[58]In 1929 they stood as they had in 1927 at 322,000 members. In 1930 this figure dropped to 303,200, and by 1933 it was down to 205,800 (American Federation of Labor, *Proceedings of the Fifty-fifth Annual Convention of Atlantic City, October 7 to October 19, 1935*, p. 32).

policy of label unionism. Although each of the next three chapters will deal with one phase of this three-pronged drive against the United Brotherhood, they are essentially one unit. Chapter XVIII will deal with the challenge to jurisdictional laissez faire, Chapter XIX will deal with the Carpenters' relations with the CIO, and Chapter XX will deal with the assault on label unionism.

Jurisdictional Laissez Faire

Challenged: 1933 to 1941

WHEN the Carpenters succeeded in destroying the National Board for Jurisdictional Awards, they met and countered the greatest threat that had ever been presented to their policy of jurisdictional laissez faire. As they did so, however, they might well have heeded the warning that Franklin D. Roosevelt, who was then president of the American Construction Council, issued to the building industry generally: "Unless we control ourselves, the government is undoubtedly going to step in in some form in the coming years."[1] By destroying the National Board for Jurisdictional Awards, Hutcheson unwittingly set the stage for government regulation of the building trades unions. But in 1927, at the height of a wild decade, government control of industry seemed the last possible contingency, and Hutcheson kicked the board to shambles with impunity.

The Carpenters re-entered the Building Trades Department in 1927, and a year later the Department again entertained complaints about the United Brotherhood's jurisdictional aggressiveness. Over the Carpenters' violent objections the 1928 Building Trades De-

[1]Franklin D. Roosevelt, "For Self-Government," *The Constructor,* Vol. 4, No. 6, June 1922, p. 15. The American Construction Council was a congress of labor leaders, contractors, architects, engineers, and even bankers interested in the building industry. Roosevelt was its first president.

partment convention approved a plan to create another board for jurisdictional awards. In 1929 Hutcheson again walked out of the Department. His ostensible reason was the Department's failure to reduce its per capita tax from three-quarters of a cent to one-half a cent per member.[2] Actually Hutcheson left because he wished a completely free hand in jurisdictional matters.[3]

Once out of the Department the Carpenters revived an old tactic. Together with the Bricklayers and the Electrical Workers,[4] they formed a triple alliance. Each of the alliance unions staked off the jurisdictional domain its leaders thought technological evolution entitled it to and which it could not have claimed in the Department. The Carpenters abrogated all previous agreements with the Iron Workers and moved against them and the Elevator Constructors in several cities. The Bricklayers staked out claims against the Plasterers and the Cement Workers.[5] Said Plasterer N. L. Colleran:

In Pittsburgh they [the triple alliance]...sent...a full representation ...to appear before the builders, and enumerated all the branches they intended to claim. They named all the branches and subtitles of those branches, making it appear...that they had more affiliated [trades] than they had.

Brother [Frank] Feeney said they were pirating. That word isn't strong enough....[The members of] that Alliance...formed [it not] to defend themselves...[but] to take work away from someone else.[6]

[2]Building Trades Department, AFL, *Proceedings of the Twenty-fourth Annual Convention of Boston, October 1 to October 3, 1929*, p. 103.

[3]Lorwin, p. 382. See also *1928 Building Trades Department Convention Proceedings*, p. 102, for the motion introducing this jurisdictional plan; pp. 102–103, for Hutcheson's remarks; and pp. 104–110, for debate and passage of the motion. Other than forcing the Carpenters to quit the Department, this jurisdictional plan played no important role and need not be outlined or discussed.

[4]The Bricklayers were the second largest and the Electrical Workers the third largest of the building trades unions. Both, like the United Brotherhood, were Building Trades Department expatriates. The Bricklayers left the Department in 1927 because they were dissatisfied with a Department ruling in a local building trades council dispute, and the Electrical Workers left in 1931 in protest against the same Board of Jurisdictional Awards which caused the Carpenters to bolt in 1929 (Building Trades Department, AFL, *Proceedings of the Twenty-ninth Annual Convention of Atlantic City, Oct. 2 to Oct. 4, 1935*, p. 58; and Building Trades Department, AFL, *Proceedings of the Twenty-fifth Annual Convention of Vancouver, Sept. 30 to Oct. 2, 1931*, p. 64).

[5]Building Trades Dept., *1931 Convention Proceedings*, pp. 98–99, 101.

[6]*Ibid.*

270

The two sides were fighting hammer and tongs in a tradition almost sacred to the building trades when Franklin Roosevelt entered the White House. During World War I Roosevelt had been afforded a close view of one of Hutcheson's worse temper tantrums. In the shipyard strike of 1918 he learned of the independence of the building trades men.[7] During the early 1920's, as head of the American Construction Council, Roosevelt was given an even more intimate view of the workings of the building industry. Although in 1922 he had called for voluntary control of the industry by its leaders as an alternative to government control, during the middle and late 1920's he saw the industry relax back into its old competitive planlessness. When he became president, he was well aware of the building industry's need for unity and cooperation.

Had he not been, events would soon have awakened him to the need. Building had been among the first of the basic industries to slip into a decline in 1928, even before the crash of 1929. It had stayed persistently in the doldrums during the 1930's and, with 67 percent of its workers unemployed when Roosevelt took office,[8] was a thoroughly sick industry. Roosevelt and his advisors felt that the rest of the economy could not possibly be revived until the building industry was made well again. Building was designated as one of the ten basic industries upon whose revival an upsurge in the rest of the economy was contingent when Roosevelt turned to the problem of industrial recovery.[9]

Roosevelt induced Congress to pass the National Industrial Recovery Act, based on the principle of industrial self-regulation and operating under government supervision through a system of fair competition codes. These codes regulated prices, wages, hours, and production in each of the various industries and were drawn up by trade associations in each of the nation's industries. Although the National Industrial Recovery Act also gave workers the right

[7]Roosevelt, as assistant secretary of the Navy, dealt extensively with Hutcheson during the shipyard strike described above, pp. 223 n. 16, 225–228.

[8]National Recovery Administration, Division of Review, Southgate Haynie, *Evidence Study, No. 7, of the Construction Industry,* June, 1935, p. 81.

[9]Hugh S. Johnson, *The Blue Eagle, from Egg to Earth,* p. 235.

to bargain collectively through their unions,[10] since most workers were unorganized in 1933 labor had little voice in the drawing up of the various codes of fair competition.

However, a higher percentage of building trades workers were unionized, and building trades unions were more firmly entrenched than unions in other industries. Building industry leaders, consequently, were faced with strong union opposition as they drew up a code of fair competition. From the outset the building trades unions demanded that the master code provide a thirty-hour, five-day week and 1929 wage levels and that they be consulted on all subsidiary codes. It shortly became clear, however, that Building Trades Department officials were to be permitted only to criticize and comment on the code and were not to help prepare it. Creation of the code was entrusted to the Construction League, an organization of contractors, architects, engineers, and building materials dealers.

The code provided for wages well below 1929 levels and for a forty-eight-hour week and an eight-hour day. Building Trades Department officials immediately protested the code. They asked that a new one be drawn up and that labor be given a voice in its creation. They were paid no heed, however, and the code drawn up by the Construction League was accepted temporarily, on August 11, 1933, by the National Recovery Administration.[11]

For the next three months Building Trades Department officials fought doggedly to prevent the Construction League's code from being made permanent, to obtain their minimum wages and hours, and to gain a larger voice for labor in the administration of the code. They pleaded their case before public hearings of the National Recovery Administration, the Planning and Research Division of the National Recovery Administration, in conferences with General Counsel Donald Richberg, Deputy Administrator Malcolm Pirnie, and Administrator General Hugh Johnson of the NRA, with Secretary of Labor Frances Perkins, Senator Robert Wagner, and finally they went directly to Roosevelt in a long

[10]*Ibid., passim,* for background of the act's passage and operation.
[11]See Building Trades Department, AFL, *Proceedings of the Twenty-eighth Annual Convention of San Francisco, September 26 to September 28, 1934,* pp. 60–64, for the story of how the construction code was drawn up.

meeting on January 16, 1934. Roosevelt ordered the Construction League's code to be scrapped, placed Major George Berry, a labor member of the National Recovery Administration, personally in charge of the new code, and ordered him to consult with the building trades unions in drawing it up.[12]

The tenacity of the Building Trades Department officials brought results. In the final code Department officials gained a compromise forty-hour week and a forty-cents minimum wage. Most important of all, a twenty-one man National Construction, Planning, and Adjustment Board was created to administer the code. On it sat ten union men, ten management men, and a public chairman. This board was given responsibility for all "planning and direction" in the building industry as long as building was regulated by the National Recovery Administration.[13]

Since the Carpenters were not in the Department Hutcheson took little part in the fight over the code.[14] Unions in the Department had as much to lose from a code hostile to labor as did the United Brotherhood, and Hutcheson let them fight his fight. He watched developments warily, however. At first nothing in the National Recovery Administration seemed to threaten his interests. Everything seemed in order. Then, the government and the Building Trades Department combined to hit Hutcheson with the most extreme plan for the settlement of jurisdictional disputes ever written. Drawn up on Roosevelt's personal request, it had long sharp teeth which Hutcheson saw sinking deep into the United Brotherhood's jurisdiction and tearing off generous portions.

When Roosevelt received the final code of fair competition for the building industry he noticed a glaring omission: no means of settling jurisdictional disputes had been provided. In his letter to General Hugh Johnson putting the code into effect, President Roosevelt ordered the National Construction, Planning, and Adjustment Board, as its first act, to create a jurisdictional awards board.[15] When the board met in Chicago on August 16, 1934, it announced the creation of a new plan for the settlement of juris-

---

[12]Solomon Barkin, *Negotiating the Construction Code*, pp. 9–26.
[13]*Ibid.*, p. 26. The final code was adopted on Jan. 31, 1934.
[14]AFL, *1934 Convention Proceedings*, p. 531.
[15]Building Trades Department, *1934 Convention Proceedings*, p. 85.

dictional disputes. The plan was to be administered by a permanent three-man National Jurisdictional Awards Board. These men were not to be connected with the building industry. The board received power to enter a dispute or potential dispute on its own initiative, to approve all future union treaties and jurisdictional agreements, to decide which union should have jurisdiction over all existing materials and work, and to allocate jurisdiction over new materials. The three board members were to be paid and full-time government employees of the National Recovery Administration. Beneath the National Jurisdictional Awards Board was a two-man Committee of Temporary Adjudication, composed of the chairman of the National Construction, Planning, and Adjustment Board and the president of the Building Trades Department, which was empowered to meet and settle all disputes as they arose. If necessary, an arbitrator was to be appointed. The committee's decisions were binding but were subject to change by the final award of the National Jurisdictional Awards Board.[16]

Shortly after the plan was announced President Roosevelt issued an Executive Order making the board federal law. He then ordered the Building Industry Code of Fair Competition amended to read:

No member of the [building] industry shall directly or indirectly cause or permit an employee...or other person responsible to him to cause an interruption of work by a jurisdictional dispute. No member of the industry shall by act, direction or otherwise cause, foster or encourage a jurisdictional dispute.[17]

Any violation of this order was assumed to be "*prima facie* unfair competition"[18] and a violation of federal law.

By placing the National Jurisdictional Awards Board's day-to-day administrative functions partially in the hands of the president of the Building Trades Department,[19] the plan gave the few small unions left in the Department power and prestige vastly out of proportion to their size, and the weak and bungling Building

---

[16]*Ibid.*, pp. 101–103. All of the details in this and the two previous paragraphs are from this source.

[17]*Ibid.*, p. 103.

[18]*Ibid.*

[19]As a member of the Committee of Temporary Adjudication he temporarily decided all jurisdictional disputes.

Trades Department was made a force with which to cope. The Carpenters, who had been proceeding at will outside the Department, kicking over a building trades council now and again, perked up their ears and fixed their attention firmly on the newly powerful Department. And then, although a big man, Bill Hutcheson proceeded to move back into the Department with the speed of light. In fact he bulled his way back in with such force that the building trades wing of the house of labor was to collapse under the impact.[20]

Hutcheson and his two allies, the Bricklayers and the Electrical Workers, then proceeded to build one new department and the members of the original Building Trades Department another. The labor world was treated to the comic spectacle of two Building Trades Departments, each of whose member unions were in good standing with the AFL, attacking the other on every possible occasion. The remainder of this section will tell the story of this split and of the struggle between the two Departments.

Roosevelt had ordered the new jurisdictional board created in January 1934. Shortly before the final plan for the board was approved by the National Construction, Planning, and Adjustment Board, Hutcheson gave in to Green's "persevering and patient" pleas and returned to the Department.[21] Almost immediately he and his two allies started jockeying for power. According to President M. J. McDonough of the Department, they began a "campaign of barter and intimidation...to bring about the...disruption of the Department."[22]

Hutcheson's attitude bristled with belligerency. Shortly after deciding to reaffiliate he sent a circular advising all carpenters that the triple alliance between the Carpenters, the Bricklayers, and the Electrical Workers would continue, the Building Trades Department notwithstanding; that the various district councils were under no obligation to affiliate with local building trades councils if they felt it would be to their disadvantage to do so, and that

---

[20]There can be no doubt that the creation of the new jurisdictional board was the cause of Hutcheson's attempt to get back into a Department which did not want him (see remarks of Delegate W. J. McSorley of the Lathers, AFL, *1934 Convention Proceedings*, p. 498).

[21]*Ibid.*, pp. 523–525.

[22]Building Trades Department, *1935 Convention Proceedings*, p. 58.

275

membership in the Department did not change "in any way our jurisdictional claims. . . ."[23]

When the 1934 Building Trades Department convention met it was apparent that the triple alliance was preparing to take over the Department. The smaller unions, which had worked so hard to defend building trades union standards before the National Recovery Administration, were to lose power just as they were about to enjoy the fruits of their labor. Consequently, the Davids turned on the three Goliaths and barred them from membership. President Green's long and impassioned plea to reconsider their action fell on deaf ears. The delegates refused even to allow Hutcheson to speak.[24]

Despite McDonough's dogged resistance, the 1934 AFL convention ordered the Department to readmit the triple alliance within forty-five days or watch the executive council set up a new department. McDonough ignored the ultimatum, and on November 26, 1934, the founding convention of Building Trades Department Number Two was held. The triple alliance was able to lure the International Union of Operating Engineers, the Hod Carriers, Building, and Common Laborers' International Union, the International Association of Marble Polishers, and the International Brotherhood of Teamsters and Chauffeurs out of the original Department.[25] J. W. Williams was borrowed from the executive board of the United Brotherhood to act as president of the new organization.[26] Two Building Trades Departments, identical twins except in size, stood glowering at each other.

One of Williams' first acts was to take Building Trades Department Number One to court to strip it of its treasury and papers. William Green, who testified on behalf of Department Number Two,

[23]AFL, *1935 Convention Proceedings,* pp. 117–118.
[24]Building Trades Department, *1934 Convention Proceedings,* pp. 104–107.
[25]AFL, *1935 Convention Proceedings,* p. 122. These four unions took 84,443 of the 288,662 members out of the original Department and into Department Number Two. Department Number Two had 443,733 members as compared to 204,229 in Department Number One (figures are from Building Trades Department, *1934 Convention Proceedings,* pp. 93–94, and AFL, *1934 Convention Proceedings,* p. 35).
[26]"Five Rounds," *Time Magazine,* Vol. 26, No. 18, Oct. 28, 1935, p. 12, said "Carpenter Williams is the stooge of Carpenter Hutcheson."

placed himself in a paradoxical situation by appearing as a witness in the mandatory injunction suit filed against affiliated organizations of the American Federation of Labor, when only two years ago he advocated the passage of the [Norris-LaGuardia] Anti-Injunction Act, which is now a law.[27]

The injunction was not granted, and the court held that Department Number One was the only legal one.[28] Once again the usual rash of jurisdictional strikes spread across the country as the two groups struggled for primacy.[29]

The day when the Carpenters could start jurisdictional fights with impunity was long past, however. While the government did not immediately interfere in the quarrel between the two Departments,[30] its power to do so hung heavy over the building trades. Consequently, a battle which might have lasted a decade, had it started in the 1920's, ended within the year.

Green lured representatives of the two Departments into one room at the 1935 AFL convention. Before the convention adjourned Referee George H. Harrison of the Railroad Clerks proudly announced that an agreement had been reached. Under its terms a six-man committee of three members from each of the two Departments was established to prepare for a special convention in March, 1936. Six separate meetings of the committee were held before the special convention met in March.

At this convention both sides moved cautiously. So suspicious were they on the one hand but so great was the need for one Department on the other that the dilemma was solved only by dividing the one Department neatly between the two factions. Even before the two Departments were officially glued together, the Carpenters and their two allies caucused and decided to elect one of their number as president.[31] Consequently, the "Williams" faction got the presidency and four of the eight seats on the execu-

---

[27]Building Trades Department, *1935 Convention Proceedings*, p. 64.

[28]AFL, *1935 Convention Proceedings*, pp. 123–124.

[29]*Ibid.*, pp. 107–127, and Building Trades Department, *1935 Convention Proceedings*, pp. 54–69, for full details of the dispute as interpreted by both sides.

[30]The government did not interfere, presumably, because neither the National Construction, Planning, and Adjustment Board nor the National Jurisdictional Awards Board had yet organized and established administrative procedures.

[31]UBCJA, *1936 Convention Proceedings*, p. 4.

tive council; the "McDonough" faction, the secretary-treasurership
and the other four seats. Representation was to remain the same as
before the split, with the Carpenters alone getting dual voting
privileges.[32]

How J. W. Williams became president may best be told in his
own words:

It was brother Hutcheson who put me in there, and I appreciate the fact
that he had confidence enough in me to put me in such an important
position as that, at the crucial time it occurred.

. . .

The greatest handicap I had to overcome was the fact that I was a
...protege of Brother Hutcheson.[33]

Each faction came out of the reunion convention as surly and
suspicious and with forces as evenly balanced as when it entered.
They had not compromised; they had only heard a referee state
the rules, shaken hands, then repaired to their corners. It still
remained for one of the two to capture the Department.

There could be little doubt as the 1937 convention rolled around
that one of the two groups would end the uneasy truce. There was
less doubt which of the two would win. As the convention met:

The nineteen international building trades unions were, as usual, claw-
ing at each others' throats. Out of what has become the annual cat-fight
it presently emerged that William L. (Big Hutch) Hutcheson, perennial
president of the big and rich Brotherhood of Carpenters... [was] more
definitely than ever—the boss of the Department.[34]

As a result of a series of hotel-room caucuses Hutcheson kicked
the 1936 settlement to shambles. In a move that "verged on the
insulting" to the smaller craft unions, he made one of his allies
president and another secretary-treasurer.[35] He then lifted for his
side five of the eight vice-presidencies, modestly reserving the

[32]See the Building Trades Department, AFL, *Proceedings of the Thirtieth Annual
Convention of Tampa, Sept. 11 to Sept. 13, 1936, pp. 64–96,* for further details on the
reorganization of the Department.
[33]UBCJA, *1936 Convention Proceedings,* pp. 4–5.
[34]"Seven Unions Against Twelve Unions," *Architectural Forum,* Vol. 67, No. 11,
November 1937, p. 439.
[35]*Ibid.,* p. 440.

eighth for himself.[36] Never again, during the period covered by this study, did he lose control of the Department.

During the struggle just recounted several sharp departures from past practice were made by the building trades unions. The Luce publication *Architectural Forum* felt that out of the 1934 to 1937 period there emerged several "factors [which] in their role will be relatively long-term manifestations." These new factors were Building Trades Department "unity" and the "smooth settlement of jurisdictional strikes."[37] It would be an exaggeration to say that in 1937 Hutcheson's iron rule of the Department represented all that the word "unity" implies or that, henceforth, there was a "smooth settlement" of jurisdictional disputes. However, the Department, largely because of a change in the Carpenters' policy, was moving slowly in the direction of both.

Unity, for the Building Trades Department, meant one thing: that the Carpenters stay in the Department. An analysis of the Carpenters' relations with the Department before and after Roosevelt formed the National Jurisdictional Awards Board demonstrates the change in their tactics. In 1934 the Department had been in existence twenty-six years. During this time the Carpenters either quit or were suspended on four different occasions and were outside the Department for a total of fifteen years.[38] In the nineteen years between 1934 and 1953 the Carpenters never once left the Department.

Before 1934 the Carpenters treated the Building Trades Department cavalierly and were constantly ready, almost eager, to leave its confines. In 1921 they were ousted when, had their delegates not abstained from voting, they could have prevented their expulsion.[39] In 1929 they quit because the per capita tax was too high when it might have been changed with a flick of Hutcheson's cigar.[40] These tactics represented a conscious attempt to foist jurisdictional

[36]Building Trades Department, AFL, *Proceedings of the Thirty-first Annual Convention of Denver, Sept. 29 to Oct. 1, 1937,* pp. 172–175. Joseph McInerney, of the Marble Polishers Union, was elected president and Herbert Rivers, of the Hod Carriers Union, secretary-treasurer.

[37]"Seven Unions Against Twelve Unions," (continued) p. 58.

[38]Building Trades Dept., *1935 Convention Proceedings,* pp. 57–58.

[39]See above, p. 240.

[40]See above, p. 270.

laissez faire upon the building trades. Jurisdictional laissez faire prevented the other unions from settling down, depriving them of the necessary time to pull the cloak of tradition about their jurisdiction, and placed the Carpenters in a position to maintain a constant harassing action through the medium of an alliance system. It kept the jurisdiction of every other union full center in the bead of the Carpenters' gunsight.

In 1933 it appeared that, with the assistance of the Bricklayers and Electrical Workers, Hutcheson was about to pull the trigger on the smaller unions. Then Franklin Roosevelt entered the picture. From that day on the building trades were to know no peace from the government. They were harassed and hounded, accused and analyzed by an antagonist who, no matter how hard Hutcheson tried, simply could not be brought under the jurisdiction of the United Brotherhood's constitution. A full list of the government agencies with which the building trades had dealings would all but exhaust the alphabet. Among others there were the United States Housing Authority, the Works Progress Administration, the Public Works Administration, the Civilian Conservation Corps, and the Tennessee Valley Administration. Hutcheson had to make certain that these agencies were directed by the "right" people and pursued the "right" policies in the industry and in their labor relations. This could be done only through the medium of the Building Trades Department.[41] The avid interest of the New Deal in construction completely revived an all-but-moribund Building Trades Department and gave it prestige beyond its founders' wildest dreams.

In the light of this new prestige the Carpenters could not stay out of the Department, which is but another way of saying that jurisdictional laissez faire was gradually to come to an end. Exactly this happened. Although the Carpenters retained their alliance

[41]For instance, in the Building Trades Department, AFL, *Proceedings of the Thirty-third Annual Convention of Cincinnati, Sept. 27 to Sept. 29, 1939*, the actual proceedings and reports, minus welcoming speeches, took up 118 pages (pp. 82–200). Of these pages, the following were concerned with the relations of the building trades with the government: 86–88, 91–101, 119–120, 124–129, 131–132, 140–143, 156–157, 163–165. In addition, four out of ten resolutions introduced concerned dealings with the government (p. 236, Index) and three out of nine speakers were government employees (p. 229, Index).

intact when they created Building Trades Department Number Two, it seems to have been gradually placed to one side, forgotten, and allowed to die. No further talk is recorded of this alliance after 1936. There is no evidence that another was made.

If, with this new-found unity, jurisdictional disputes did not come to an immediate end, jurisdictional laissez faire did. These two phenomena must be distinguished. Jurisdictional disputes are a fact, not a policy. Their existence is deplored by everyone, even the Carpenters, experienced and proficient though they are at fighting them. Jurisdictional laissez faire, however, was a policy which, granted technological evolution, was followed by the Carpenters and hence by the Department. It signified that jurisdictional disputes would be settled not by compromise, precedent, or any quasi-judicial procedure but by simply fighting it out, bare knuckled.

Roosevelt's forceful creation of the National Jurisdictional Awards Boards in 1934, however, served notice on the building trades unionists to come in out of the jungle, clean and spruce themselves up, and learn civilized economic manners. Like Jack London's Buck, they were never completely able to ignore the call of the wild, and jurisdictional disputes continued after 1934. If the building trades did not eliminate the jurisdictional dispute, however, union leaders, in general, were at least aware of the need to do so. Hutcheson, specifically, could no longer base his policy on the continued existence of the jurisdictional dispute.

Statistics substantiate these two related facts. From 1908 to 1934 the Carpenters spent exactly one year, 1921, affiliated with a jurisdictional awards board. From 1934 to 1953 they did not spend one year outside such a board.

When, in 1936, the two departments were glued together, the one thing upon which all the delegates agreed was the need for a jurisdictional awards board. They set up an elaborate plan for the settlement of disputes through the Department, a plan which prohibited work stoppages in the course of jurisdictional disputes and which provided for a permanent paid referee who was to make awards on behalf of the Department.⁴² This plan was changed several times. It did not end the jurisdictional strike, but, most important, it was not scrapped and the Carpenters continued to remain a party to it. To no one, even the Carpenters, was the jurisdictional strike any more than a necessary evil after 1934. It was certainly no longer an integral part of their policy.

Jurisdictional laissez faire, then, as a policy of the Carpenters and as a characteristic of the Building Trades Department, was over by 1941 in the sense that each of the nineteen unions in the building trades admitted the overriding need to end the jurisdictional strike. Their leaders felt:

The settlement of these jurisdictional disputes by the organizations within the Department will more than anything else eliminate the possibility of adverse legislation being enacted by the Congress against the building and construction trades unions.⁴³

Building trades men in general, however, and carpenters in particular, are conservative men who change old habits slowly and with great reluctance. While all of them admitted that jurisdictional disputes must end and none of them any longer based their policy on their continued existence, they still failed to eliminate them. They paid the anticipated price: a government law against the jurisdictional strike.

When the Republican Congress for which Hutcheson had so long fought was elected in 1946, one of its first acts was to replace the Wagner Act with the Taft-Hartley Act. Two of the most important provisions in the act were Section 8 (b)(4)(D), which prohibited, by government use of injunctions, the jurisdictional strike, and Section 10 (k), which gave the National Labor Relations Board power to hear jurisdictional disputes and to make awards.⁴⁴ Counsel for the National Labor Relations Board, Robert Denham, made it immediately plain that if the Building Trades Department did not take steps to end jurisdictional striking, he would.⁴⁵

⁴²See Building Trades Dept., *1936 Convention Proceedings,* pp. 73–88, for a copy of the plan and the debate which preceded its adoption.
⁴³Building Trades Department, AFL, *Proceedings of the Thirty-fourth Annual Convention of New Orleans, Nov. 13 to Nov. 15, 1940,* p. 225.
⁴⁴Charles Gregory, *Labor and the Law,* p. 428.
⁴⁵Bureau of National Affairs, *The Taft-Hartley Act—After One Year,* p. 101.

As a result the officers of the Building Trades Department in conjunction with the National Labor Relations Board created in 1948 the National Joint Board for the Settlement of Jurisdictional Disputes.[46] Although the federal government had nothing to do with the administration of the Joint Board, its power to enjoin jurisdictional strikes had brought it into being and kept it alive and powerful.[47] And although William Hutcheson disliked the board and, in fact, tried to destroy it as he had all previous jurisdictional award boards, he failed.[48] With the power of the government behind them the other building trades unions were sufficiently powerful to ignore Hutcheson's views.[49] Government control was the last full fruit of the United Brotherhood's policy of jurisdictional laissez faire. Hutcheson had finally met an enemy he could not defeat. He observed gloomily to the 1950 convention of the United Brotherhood that "unless we get together with the other trades and crafts and reach a mutually agreeable understanding, [jurisdictional] disputes would revert to [National Labor Relations Board] Panel Hearings and we would have to take whatever was given us."[50]

Not the least of the reasons why the building trades demonstrated a new unity in the 1930's was the fact that in the middle thirties there existed an "enemy in the labor movement...far more dangerous to...this labor movement than even the employers' associations."[51] Teamster Dan Tobin spoke about four words which few AFL men uttered, and none uttered lightly, in 1936: Committee of Industrial Organizations. This federation, like the New Deal which did so much to foster it, calls vividly to mind

[46]For a review of the Board's structure and its scope, see Building Trades Department, AFL, *Proceedings of the Forty-first Convention of Cincinnati, Nov. 10 to Nov. 12, 1948*, pp. 127–130.

[47]"Building Arbitration Machinery Starts May 1," *Business Week*, No. 972, April 17, 1948, pp. 115–116; "Formula for Peace in the Building Trades," *U.S. News and World Report*, Vol. 24, No. 8, Feb. 20, 1948, p. 48.

[48]*New York Times*, Jan. 31, 1949, p. 6, col. 5.

[49]*Ibid.*

[50]Carpenters and Joiners of America, United Brotherhood of, AFL, *Proceedings of the Twenty-sixth General Convention of Cincinnati, Sept. 5 to Sept. 12, 1950*, p. 103.

[51]Building Trades Dept., *1936 Convention Proceedings*, p. 80.

the already strangely dated depression decade. The decade was the grandparent, and the New Deal the parent, of the CIO. And the CIO, once born, launched the second and most dangerous attack upon the United Brotherhood, the attack upon its craft-industrial structure.

→ CHAPTER XIX ←

Craft-Industrialism Challenged:

1933 to 1941

One board from a Northwest log may go into the making of a cradle while another board may become part of a casket, but cradle or casket, the board is prepared and handled by men affiliated with the United Brotherhood....From the man who swings the axe..., to the man who wields the sandpaper on the finished product, the wood is handled by men affiliated with the United Brotherhood. In every process from logging to cabinet making, only Brotherhood men are employed.[1]

THIS statement hailed the fact that the United Brotherhood was vertically integrated in its industries to a degree few other unions could boast in the mid-1930's. It also indicated that the United Brotherhood was making no claims to craft unionism in the 1930's. Rather, its leaders recognized it as "a craft union, taking in all the branches of the industry."

The policy of the United Brotherhood was still craft-industrialism, as it had been since 1911. By the time John L. Lewis was preparing his bolt, this policy had made the United Brotherhood a union which had followed the technological evolution of its principal craft so scrupulously that it now had several complete industries nestled snugly within its jurisdiction. This is the prime fact to be kept in mind, for unless it is understood completely the

[1]"Carpenters Include All Woodworkers," *The Carpenter*, Vol. 57, No. 12, December 1937, p. 24.

events surrounding the creation of the Committee of Industrial Organizations make little historical sense. For Lewis did not leave the AFL. Hutcheson pushed him out.

The dispute which divided the AFL in 1935 was not primarily one between the advocates of craft unionism and those of industrial unionism. Rather, it was between the advocates of craft-industrial unionism, led by Hutcheson, and those of industrial unionism, led by Lewis. President Green made this amply clear while testifying before the Senate Committee on Education and Labor shortly after the CIO was created. He went to great pains to explain that his federation contained many craft-industrial unions. He then gave an example. "While the basic membership of the International Association of Machinists...comprises...skilled craftsmen ...[it] also includes within its membership unions composed of a single craft, single trade as well as wholly industrial unions...."[2]

During the now famous 1935 debate which erupted in blows between Hutcheson and Lewis, Delegate John P. Frey, an old AFL hand, declared that he, for one, was confused by the dispute. Why, he said, "We [the AFL] have had for fifty-five years so-called industrial unions...; and we have had so-called craft unions, many of which are more industrial than those so-called."[3]

This evidence makes it clear that not craft unionism and the Scranton Declaration but craft-industrial unionism and the Atlanta Declaration were threatened by Lewis. At one point in the 1935 debate Lewis berated the policy of "the last quarter of a century."[4] His lieutenant, Van Bittner, said to Hutcheson's group, "You are just twenty-four years behind the times."[5] Both referred to the year 1911, the year of the Atlanta Declaration.

In the course of the struggle with the CIO Hutcheson dropped all craft pretense and openly admitted that it was an industry, and not one of its crafts, for which he was fighting. The executive board of the United Brotherhood declared:

[2]U.S. Congress, Senate, Committee on Education and Labor, *Hearings on S. 1000, S. 1264, S. 1392, S. 1550, S. 2133, Bills to Amend the National Labor Relations Act,* 76th Cong., 1st, 2nd, and 3rd Sess., Vol. 1, Part 4, p. 663.
[3]AFL, *1935 Convention Proceedings,* p. 554.
[4]*Ibid.,* p. 535.
[5]*Ibid.,* p. 636.

The AFL gave the United Brotherhood of Carpenters and Joiners of America jurisdiction over the *wood-working industry* of North America, [and] that jurisdiction must be observed and protected at all hazards and all costs and under no circumstances or conditions can the AFL grant charters to other groups in the *wood-working industry*.[6]

Hutcheson did not oppose organization along industrial lines because he was craft minded. On the contrary, he had collected such a wide variety of industries under the Carpenters' jurisdictional claim that, had he chosen, he could very well have organized the whole of several industries. However, the United Brotherhood's policy of policing an industry, rather than organizing it, prevented this.[7] Had Hutcheson organized completely all the industries under his jurisdiction his union would have ceased being a carpenter's, or even a carpenter-centered union, as skilled carpenters were overwhelmed by unskilled millmen and lumberjacks.

Hutcheson would undoubtedly have been a much happier man had the unskilled and semiskilled workers within his jurisdiction remained quiescent. For reasons to be discussed shortly, they did not do so. Lewis shrewdly saw that the unskilled of the mass-production industries could not possibly be organized on a craft, or even a craft-industrial basis. They could only be organized on a straight industrial basis. Hutcheson, for all his protestations to the contrary, had little to fear from the organization of the great mass-production industries like steel and automobiles.[8] Rather, he feared the principle involved. He knew that the principle of industrial unionism was narrower than that of craft-industrialism and was afraid that if the principle of industrial organization were accepted by the AFL, the United Brotherhood stood in a fair way to lose both the woodworking and the lumber industries to new, ambitious industrial unions. Ironically, Hutcheson opposed Lewis not because he was narrower in his assertion of jurisdiction but because he was broader.

[6]"Regular Meeting of the Executive Board, 1939," June 5, *The Carpenter*, Vol. 59, No. 7, July 1939, p. 19 (italics mine).

[7]See above, pp. 195–198.

[8]In fact, in 1934 Hutcheson gave Lewis permission to organize these workers along industrial lines with no mention of the maintenance carpenters involved (AFL, *1934 Convention Proceedings*, p. 593).

287

Neither Hutcheson nor Lewis, nor, in fact, anyone in the AFL, however, brought the problem of organizing the unorganized to the fore. Rather, it welled out of the mass protest of millions of underpaid and insecure workers, brought by five years of depression and grinding poverty to the point of blind despair. Roosevelt gave them hope, in many respects as blind as their despair, and through Section 7(a)[9] of the National Industrial Recovery Act seemed to point a finger to trade unionism as a specific way out of their plight. Although Section 7(a) proved a slender reed on which to lean, the unorganized workers accepted its promise avidly and literally stormed the unions. From 1933 to 1935 they pounded upon the AFL's door, demanding admission. Scores of thousands were admitted into federal unions,[10] where they were put into escrow while the officials of the AFL decided their ultimate fate. Millions more stood outside in the unorganized cold while the great debate raged.

Nothing in the history of the AFL had prepared its leaders to cope with such a vast social upheaval. The eight-hour movement of 1886 to 1890 had been a whimper, the burgeoning of unionism from 1900 to 1904 a meek cry, compared to this overwhelming clamor of social protest which dinned in the ears of AFL officials while they debated. Whether they liked it or not, they were forced to deal with the hot molten metal of social revolution and to mold it into an orderly trade union institution. And the quarter-century of history of which Lewis spoke, and which has been here summed up as craft-industrialism, blocked them at every turn.

Some index of the vastness of this upsurge can be gleaned from the lumber industry, with which the United Brotherhood was specifically concerned. Between 1933 and 1935 thousands of lumber

[9]Section 7(a) guaranteed workers the right to organize and bargain collectively through representatives of their own choosing. It was but poorly enforced, however, and while it gave much encouragement to unions, it passed out of being when the National Industrial Recovery Act was invalidated by the Supreme Court in 1935.

[10]A federal union is a local union organized and chartered directly by the national officers of the AFL and belonging to no international union. Such unions are formed when the work done by their members falls under the jurisdiction of no existing AFL union. After enough such federal locals are formed in a given industry, the AFL either gives them to an existing international trade union or forms a new international out of the federal unions in one industry.

workers stormed into one hundred and thirty federal unions. In 1932 there had not been a baker's dozen of lumber workers' federal unions. Although these workers were to be had for the asking, the AFL had done little to secure them. Their organization, for the most part, was completely spontaneous. The AFL put a few organizers in the lumber camps and printed, from time to time, a mild little pamphlet called the "Lumber Letter."[11] For their edification, this letter told the half-starved lumberjacks how much soft wood was produced in the Southeast between 1920 and 1930 and how Shingle Weavers' Union Number So-and-So was infusing the spirit of trade unionism into this or that little hamlet in Idaho or Alabama. Like the men who printed it, this pamphlet failed completely to understand the nature, gauge the temper, or meet the needs of the lumberjacks. Still they flooded into the federal unions. They had no other place to go.

Throughout the 1920's, though these workers had been placed under the United Brotherhood's jurisdiction, Hutcheson had not raised a finger to organize them. Nor did he in 1933 and 1934 when they were frantically pounding on the door of the house of labor. He took them into the United Brotherhood, in 1935, only when their organized numbers were too many, and their din too deafening, to ignore. Even then he took them not because it might benefit them but because:

In the course of the years methods of work in the lumber industry have greatly changed. The logs taken into the lumber mill come out in the shape of flooring and finished products ready for assembly in building. Much of the work formerly done by the carpenter on the construction site is now done in the mill.[12]

They were taken because it was necessary to do so in order to "police" the industry.

The restive lumber workers' demand for unionization was the rule rather than the exception. In most of the basic, mass-production industries the clamor for unionism mounted after 1933. When the leaders of the AFL met in convention in the fall of 1933 they decided to organize the workers in mass-production industries only

[11]*The Lumber Letter,* Nos. 3 through 8, October 1934 to May 1935, *passim.*
[12]AFL, *1935 Convention Proceedings,* p. 127.

when given permission by the international unions whose jurisdiction was concerned. Then the mass-production workers were to be held in federal unions until they could be divided among the AFL unions claiming jurisdiction in a given industry. However, in what was almost an admission that this constituted no definitive answer to the problem, a conference of all union presidents was called to give further consideration to the problem during 1934.[13]

This conference met in January, 1934, and decided to place the main emphasis on an organizing campaign and to allow the question of jurisdiction to mark time. When the 1934 convention met, Lewis, who had assumed leadership of a group of industrial unionists, felt that the formula established at the January conference "has not worked out as well as some of the delegates...believe it should."[14] He then induced the delegates to approve a resolution which came out flatly for industrial organization, saying that they "realized that in many of the [mass-production] industries...a new condition exists requiring organization on a different basis to be most effective."[15] The executive council was then directed to unleash a vast organizing campaign among these industries. When the resolution passed, with mild assurances to Hutcheson that his jurisdiction would not be violated,[16] Lewis seemed to have won his every point.

Lewis was courting a vast disappointment, however, for in 1935 Green sent a swarm of mellow old business agents into the restive mass-production industries. The campaign in the lumbering industry was typical. After Green pushed the one hundred and thirty federal lumber and sawmill unions into the United Brotherhood, Hutcheson sent Pacific Coast Executive Board Member Abe Muir, a former business agent, into towering forests afire with discontent. Muir was accustomed to dealing with city contractors, many of whom were themselves union men and most of whom welcomed the union. He walked into the North woods where employers were full well prepared to use machine guns, tear gas, and howling, professionally led mobs to exclude the union. The mild Scot tried to

[13]AFL, *1934 Convention Proceedings, pp. 587–588.*
[14]*Ibid.,* p. 588.
[15]*Ibid.,* p. 587.
[16]*Ibid.,* p. 593.

lead loggers who were "real he-men, with hair on their chests. They
...chew[ed] snuff...and...[drank] their hooch and...[made] no
pretense at being tin angels."[17] These men were rough-and-tumble
direct actionists, with a "Wobbly"[18] background and possessed of a
democratic tradition reminiscent of earlier frontiersmen. They
strongly resented Muir's leadership, for he neither understood
them nor the problems of their industry.[19] Muir's advent caused
difficulty and disputes which were, on the whole, an "outright loss
to the cause of unionism" in the Northwest woods. While some
gains were registered, these were few, and far less than might have
been made had Green given the lumberjacks only money and
guidance and otherwise allowed them to erect their own union.[20]

Nor did the situation vary in other basic industries. Lewis said:

Instead of leadership the AFL gave them [the mass-production workers]
a number of chicken-livered business agents who knew nothing except
collecting dues, issuing some charters and keeping peace and harmony.
Their business agents feared any kind of upsurge as something 'radical,'
or, of course, dangerous.[21]

Lewis felt he had been hoodwinked. Few enough industrial
locals had been established by this halfhearted drive, he told the
delegates, and they were "now dying like grass withering before the
autumn sun."[22] "They seduced me with fair words," he said of the
AFL leaders at the 1935 convention. "Now...having been seduced
I am ready to rend my seducers limb from limb."[23]

He had his chance at the same convention. He tried a direct
resolution for industrial unionism. It failed. Each of his allies then
put forth resolutions thinly disguised but seeking the same end.
But however adroitly he moved, the lumbering form of Big Bill
Hutcheson slowly arose and blocked his path. Lewis threw the
words of Shakespeare, biblical quotations, and a barrage of statis-

---

[17]Stanley F. Horn, *This Fascinating Lumber Business*, pp. 75–76.
[18]That is, they had an Industrial Workers of the World background.
[19]Vernon Jensen, *Lumber and Labor*, p. 290.
[20]*Ibid*. The story of Muir's experience with the lumber workers is continued below,
pp. 293–299.
[21]Saul Alinsky, *John L. Lewis*, p. 77.
[22]AFL, *1935, Convention Proceedings*, p. 535.
[23]*Ibid.*, p. 538.

tics at the implacable Hutcheson. Finally, when all else failed, he threw a bone-jarring right fist to the big carpenter's jaw.

Hutcheson had just silenced another of Lewis's supporters with a "point of order." As the delegates looked to President Green for the usual ruling in Hutcheson's favor, Lewis leaped to his feet and roared at Hutcheson, "This thing of raising points of order all the time...is rather small potatoes." Hutcheson shot back, "I was raised on small potatoes. That's why I'm so small."[24] Lewis lumbered over to Hutcheson and told him at close range that his opposition was "pretty small stuff."[25] Hutcheson angrily replied, "We could have made you small and kept you off the Executive Council, you crazy bastard."[26]

At this point Lewis caught Hutcheson flush on the jaw and took a weaker right in return. Then, both men wildly clutching each other, they crashed through a table and down to the floor. With the delegates in an uproar, President Green pounded his gavel futilely as the leaders of the two largest and most powerful unions in the land rolled about on the floor, pummeling each other.

The blow that landed on Hutcheson's jaw was delivered on cue and with the careful precision of a choreographer sending his prima ballerina on stage. Lewis told his biographer:

Bill Hutcheson represented symbolically the kind of leadership in the American Federation of Labor that the workers of this country detested. It was Bill Hutcheson...who successfully blocked every single move that was made in the direction of industrial unionism. All I will say is that I never walked an aisle so slowly and grimly as I did that day in the 1935 Convention.[27]

At the end of that aisle stood Bill Hutcheson. Several well-chosen expletives were exchanged, a sharp scuffle ensued, and a new phase of labor history was inaugurated. John Frey said with a touch of nostalgia that this convention marked "a definite turning point [and] that from now on our Federation of Labor will never again

---

[24]*Ibid.*, p. 727.
[25]"Boss Carpenter," p. 278. This quotation and the one which follows are from a previously cited article based on a personal interview with Hutcheson, and the words are probably his version of the words spoken.
[26]*Ibid.*
[27]Alinsky, p. 78.

be just what it was."[28] He could not have been more right. Twenty-four days later eleven industrial unionists met in Lewis's Washington office, and the Committee for Industrial Organization was born.

Hutcheson's struggle with the CIO was limited to one industry, but what it lacked in breadth it made up in bitterness. It was fought with the lumber workers, and it was among the most violent of all the AFL-CIO disputes. Its roots stretch beyond the 1935 AFL convention to March 1935, when the lumber workers were turned over to the United Brotherhood, months before the CIO had come into being. At the time they entered the United Brotherhood the lumbermen were organized as the Northwest Council of Sawmill and Timber Workers, an industrial federation of federal lumbermen's unions. This council was given no autonomy but was placed directly under the national office, and it was in the charge of General Representative Abe Muir.

Strike fever was mounting among the big trees when Hutcheson sent Abe Muir to assume command of his new charges. From the very outset, Muir wished to avoid a strike.[29] The lumber workers felt otherwise, however, and when they met in convention on March 23, although they accepted Muir's leadership they also laid a series of demands on the operators' doorstep.[30] May 6 was set as the trigger date.

Although some lumberjacks traded axes for picket signs in late April, Muir was able to keep his surly charges on the job, even after the May 6 deadline, in one of the largest lumber centers, Longview, Washington, while he negotiated. By the morning of May 7 a third of the lumbermen were out, another third remained voluntarily on the job, and the final third worked only on Muir's specific orders.[31] On May 9 the terms of Muir's agreement which, it was widely known, he wished to have considered a model settlement were

[28]AFL, *1935 Convention Proceedings*, p. 552.
[29]Jensen, p. 167. For a detailed story of the struggle and the history of the International Woodworkers' Association, which grew out of it, see Jensen, *passim*.
[30]These demands were as follows: the union as sole bargaining agent; six-hour day and thirty-hour work week; overtime and holiday pay; seniority; vacations with pay; pay raise from between forty and fifty cents an hour to seventy-five cents (*ibid.*, p. 165).
[31]*Ibid.*, pp. 167–168.

revealed. He had fulfilled but a fraction of his followers' demands.[32]

The voting lumber men threw the agreement back into Muir's teeth by a thumping nine-to-one majority, and the strike continued. By May 12 approximately 90 percent of all operations in the Douglas fir region were down.[33] On May 14 Muir negotiated his "model settlement" with the three mills of the McCormick Lumber Company in St. Helens, Oregon, and Port Gamble and Port Ludlow, Washington. The workers in the Washington mills accepted the settlement, but those at St. Helens refused even to vote on it and tried unsuccessfully to persuade the workers in the other two mills to reject it.[34]

With his settlement twice rejected, control was slipping through Muir's hands. To check the trend, he peremptorily ousted Norman Lange, whom Muir felt led the insurgents, from his position as vice-president of the Northwest council. When the council next convened he forced it to approve Lange's ouster under threat of losing all United Brotherhood strike assistance. After two days of debate the delegates backed Muir's actions, and the conservatives were in control of the council. The convention lowered the original strike demands to conform to the terms of Muir's model settlement.[35]

Lumberjacks are not carpenters, however, and although Muir controlled the regional organization, the insurgents still controlled many locals. The strike continued. Muir now moved again to force his settlement on the all-important Longview mills. On May 28 he went into a conference with state labor officials and the operators. Their main concern was how best to stop the strike. It was decided to use no more secret ballots among the workers and to have Muir force a settlement on the men. Muir warned the more bellicose rank-and-file leaders that the United Brotherhood would abandon them if they again rejected his settlement. On the evening of May

---

[32]The agreement included a base wage of fifty cents an hour, time-and-a-half pay for overtime, and union recognition but no "sole bargaining rights" (*ibid.*, p. 169).

[33]*Ibid.*, p. 170.

[34]*Ibid.*

[35]*Ibid.*, p. 171.

28 about one-third of the Longview workers attended a meeting and accepted the Muir settlement.[36]

Then Muir moved to wrest control from the rank-and-file insurgents throughout the Northwest jurisdiction. He issued an order for reorganization of all local strike committees. The workers in one local replied by soundly thrashing two of his emissaries.[37] On June 1 Muir announced that the strike was over[38] and that the workers were to return on the best conditions available, under pain of expulsion. The workers ignored him, and on June 6 four hundred insurgent delegates met at Aberdeen, Washington, renewed the original strike demands, and formed the Northwest Joint Strike Committee, which was dual to the Northwest council now controlled by Muir. This committee was never disbanded, although Muir repeatedly denounced it. The strike continued.

Muir went on a charter-pulling campaign in July to force the men back to work. At Longview, which had been captured by insurgents who reimposed the strike, he proceeded to divide the one local into two new plant locals.[39] The mills opened with one-fifth of their former working force, with the former president of an earlier company union at the head of one of the new United Brotherhood locals,[40] and with the National Guard in armed readiness to enforce Muir's rule, if necessary.[41]

At Everett, Washington, where the workers had rejected his settlement 1,500 to 3,[42] Muir pulled the local charter and replaced it with six plant charters. Here violence cropped up. Riot clubs and tear gas were used by state police to prevent the insurgents from keeping the mill closed. An angry crowd of twenty-five hundred stormed the labor temple to prevent Muir's new locals from meeting. Only the guns of the State Police prevented further bloodshed.[43]

At Aberdeen, Washington, Muir separated the more radical

---

[36]*Ibid.*, p. 173.
[37]*Ibid.*, p. 174.
[38]*New York Times,* June 2, 1935, sec. I, p. 33, col. 5.
[39]Jensen, p. 180.
[40]Selden C. Menefee, "How the Lumber Strike Was Broken," *The Nation,* Vol. 141, No. 3661, Sept. 4, 1935, p. 276.
[41]Jensen, p. 180.
[42]"How the Lumber Strike Was Broken," p. 276.
[43]Jensen, p. 182.

loggers from the sawmill workers by issuing two charters where there had previously been only one. Only a smattering of the mill's 4,100 workers moved into his new locals, however. The National Guard in Aberdeen was fair, and the situation was handled better than elsewhere. The workers at first stood behind the original local.[44] The operators would deal with their employees only through Muir, however, and in late July the strike ended. With only one-third of the men voting, they decided to join Muir's local.[45]

Across the length and breadth of the Northwest the situation was the same. Tear gas, riot clubs, and fixed bayonets marched the workers gradually away from their announced objectives. Here the troops aided the operators against both union forces; there Muir received help against the insurgents. By mid-August, tired of opposition from every possible quarter, the lumber workers returned to work. A troubled silence then descended over the big trees.

In order to consolidate his shaky regime, Muir called a conference of all lumber workers in October 1935. Here, using a tactic reminiscent of the refusal of every United Brotherhood ruler since McGuire to set up regional groups, he announced his intention of killing the Northwest council and ruling directly through district councils. He then set up a series of deliberately small regional and craft district councils.[46]

Muir broke the strike, then reshuffled the locals, as Hutcheson had done in New York in 1916. He had the lumber workers neatly lined up, and he prepared to march them into the vast reaches of the United Brotherhood organization. But the lumber workers would not march anywhere they themselves did not choose to go. When Muir destroyed the Northwest Council of Timber and Sawmill Workers, the lumber workers, at a Portland convention, countered by changing their dual Northwest Joint Strike Committee into the Federated Woodworkers' Union. Although it possessed no United Brotherhood charter and was to all intents and

[44]*Ibid.*, p. 183.
[45]*Ibid.*, pp. 183–184.
[46]*Ibid.*, p. 204. The plywood workers, shingle weavers, and boom men were set off into craft district councils. Besides these, eight geographic district councils, equivalent to the regular Carpenters' district councils, were set up.

purposes a dual organization, its founders chose to stay in the United Brotherhood while they awaited further developments.

The struggle now moved to the national councils of the Brotherhood. The Carpenters had not held a convention for eight years. In 1936, however, the ominous rumblings of revolt from the western forests made a convention imperative. Sixteen delegates, representing seventy-two thousand lumber workers organized into a dual union, appeared before the convention. They sent their demands before them. Highly incensed, Duffy read them off: two representatives on the executive board, full voice and vote on all matters affecting the lumber industry, three-fifths of their twenty-five cents per month per capita tax returnable to them.[47]

Duffy, incredulous and angry at the audacity of these ragtag-and-bobtail industrial workers, mounted the rostrum in his favorite role of trouble shooter. The leaders of the United Brotherhood, he said, had noted the presence of these workers for years. Although they possessed jurisdiction over them, they had not wanted them. When the product of their mills came into competition with the outside carpenter, however, the United Brotherhood took them in. "We spent the carpenters' money in order to organize them, so that we could control the trade," Duffy said.[48] He then went on to tell of the financial sacrifices made by the United Brotherhood on behalf of the lumber workers. He made it clear, however, that these workers "wanted a cheap organization and they got it." Unable to pay the full per capita tax, they were nonbeneficial members. "They are only in this convention on probation." They were present only because the executive board had been kind, had stretched a point, and they were there only as "fraternal delegates, so that [they]...may become acquainted with us and our method of doing business."[49] The lumber workers' delegates were seated without vote, but they were allowed to address the convention. They next met with a subcommittee of the executive

[47]UBCJA, *1936 Convention Proceedings*, p. 28.

[48]*Ibid.*, pp. 21–25. The words quoted are found on p. 25.

[49]*Ibid.*, pp. 22–23. The per capita tax was seventy-five cents a month. The lumber workers, who earned about forty-five cents an hour at this time, paid only twenty-five cents a month.

board but were granted only minor concessions.[50] They left the convention as discontented as they had entered it.

At the convention's end the sixteen lumber workers immediately journeyed north to closet themselves with John L. Lewis in Washington. Lewis still hoped to induce the AFL to recognize his Committee for Industrial Organization, however. He refused to aid the lumber workers on the ground that he was interested only in organizing the unorganized.[51] The weary and homeless lumber workers then made the long trek back to the West Coast. There they told the second semiannual convention of the Federated Woodworkers of their treatment. Having no place to go, the delegates retained their affiliation with the United Brotherhood.

When they returned to the Northwest, the tide was running strongly in favor of the CIO. Lewis's organize-the-unorganized campaign was enjoying a phenomenal success. By June 1937, when the Federated Woodworkers convened for the third time, Lewis was openly raiding the AFL. He sent two of his chief lieutenants, John Brophy and Harry Bridges, to address the delegates. Hutcheson was invited but refused to appear. Brophy and Bridges advised the delegates of their "second class" membership in the United Brotherhood and invited them to join the CIO. When the convention voted to hold a referendum vote of the membership, the United Brotherhood lost by a three-to-one margin.[52] On July 20, 1937, the first convention of the International Woodworkers of America met with Lewis's blessing.

By one stroke of a pen, one hundred thousand workers were swept out of the United Brotherhood. The shift has been characterized as overwhelming: the United Brotherhood possessed a nucleus of strength in only three lumber centers.[53] In August 1937 Hutcheson gathered his battered and torn corporal's guard about him, formed the Oregon-Washington Council of Lumber and

---

[50]*Ibid.*, pp. 313–314. The concessions included a subcommittee of the executive board to investigate the industry; the use of the Brotherhood label; certain lumber firms to be placed on the unfair list; and a possible organizing campaign with lumber workers doing the organizing work.

[51]Jensen, p. 206.

[52]*Ibid.*, p. 210.

[53]*Ibid.*, pp. 212–213.

298

Sawmill Workers, and turned to face the first dual union to dare trespass on the carpenters' jurisdiction in a quarter of a century.

A bitter knockdown-and-dragout struggle ensued.[54] At its height, from 1937 to 1940, this struggle was the most extensive and bitter of all the many AFL-CIO disputes. While it raged it included mob, vigilante, and goon-squad actions, mass picketing and counter-picketing, boycotting and counterboycotting. Some employers tried to avoid the boycott by dramatic moonlight bootlegging of logs past union picket lines. Even a pitched, water-borne battle was fought on one occasion between CIO and AFL boats patrolling the rivers which bore disputed logs to the mills.[55]

For almost three years this struggle, from which neither side emerged completely victorious, held the Northwest lumber communities in its grip. The dispute raged at boiling point from 1937 to 1939, then gradually simmered down to a campaign of harassment and denunciation. By 1940, although much bitterness still existed, under the pressure of employer resistance the two unions were cooperating on a limited scale.[56] In that year the United Brotherhood claimed thirty-five thousand lumber workers, most of whom worked in the sawmills.[57] The International Woodworkers of America claimed one hundred thousand members including virtually all the forest workers. And thus a dispute, the immediate causes of which went back to 1935 and the historical causes back to 1911, ended in an uneasy truce which, at this writing, is yet to be resolved.

The depression schism in the labor movement has two separate implications for this history. For the AFL it proved what historians have long known: the AFL was a slow starter but a steady, skilled,

---

[54]It is unnecessary to tell the details of still another of the United Brotherhood's many jurisdictional disputes. Although the faces, settings, and slogans were different, the tactics varied but little from those used by the United Brotherhood in previous struggles. The story has been well told by both sides, see *Senate Education and Labor Committee Hearings,* (76th Cong.) Vol. 1, Part V, pp. 874–899, 933–989; Vol. 2, Part 7, pp. 1220–1247, 1319–1327; Vol. II, Part 8, pp. 1480–1483, 1515–1539; Vol. 3, Part 18, pp. 3432–3433. Certain tactics used by the Carpenters will be described and analyzed from one specific aspect in the next chapter.

[55]*Ibid.,* Vol. 1, Part V, pp. 938–941.

[56]Jensen, p. 255.

[57]UBCJA, *1940 Convention Proceedings,* p. 42.

and enduring runner. Possessed of a tested and flexible policy in craft-industrialism, its affiliated unions spread out and took in workers of every stripe from all industries, until, in the period following World War II, it truly represented a cross section of American labor. When the history of the AFL in the 1930's and 1940's is written, it will undoubtedly show that John L. Lewis and his CIO were to the AFL what Luther's Ninety-Five Theses and the Reformation were to the Catholic Church. It will also show that Hutcheson's jaw played substantially the same role in the later drama as the door of the Wittenberg Cathedral played in the earlier one.

The CIO reformation did not call forth any great changes in the United Brotherhood. True, the format of *The Carpenter* was modernized during the middle 1930's, and a few of the older general officers died off between 1930 and 1940. But Duffy still edited the journal and his inspirational poetry still decorated its pages. The new general officers were carbon copies of the old.

Outside the Victorian interior of the United Brotherhood, however, changes were occurring on all sides. The tactics of label unionism were being applied in an atmosphere markedly different from, and more hostile than, any since the turn of the century. This atmosphere produced both the New Deal and the CIO. The New Deal created the National Labor Relations Board, and the CIO gave it a significance ominous for the Brotherhood.

→ CHAPTER XX ←

Label Unionism Challenged

WHEN the lumber workers migrated from the United Brotherhood, Hutcheson lashed out at them with all the boycott tactics at his command. The Northwest was thrown into a turmoil. Lumber operations in many communities slowed down and then ceased as the United Brotherhood, with only a smattering of lumber workers under its standard, grappled with the International Woodworkers of America. The Woodworkers' Union could not open the mills. The Carpenters laughed at their plight.

"Why cannot I have employment when workers in my division of operation have...affiliate[d] with the International Woodworkers of America...?" a *Carpenter* article pictured the average lumber worker as asking. The answer:

Products are made to be sold! That's why.

. . .

It is the assistance that a Local Union derives from affiliation with a national that can enforce *boycott* that justifies the national or international's existence.

. . .

[The] woodworkers...should have considered the case in the foregoing light before they voted to affiliate with an international that was helpless to give assistance in the one field that is essential to the existence of any labor union.

. . .

The A. F. of L. controls the building trades unions and...similarly the A. F. of L. controls the Teamsters' Union...which likewise must handle

301

the product. If these two outside armies of workers refuse to handle a product produced under the Committee for Industrial Organizations banner, the employer involved must necessarily close his plant, since he would be unable to dispose of his product.

. . .

Why don't they [the leaders of the International Woodworkers of America] admit that a union is strong or weak depending on its power to *boycott* efficiently?[1]

This statement speaks volumes on the Carpenters' trade union philosophy as it had developed in the middle thirties. Theirs was a boycott-centered union. Long ago Hutcheson had ceased calling his field agents organizers. This was honest; they did not organize. They herded workers into their union through boycott and other secondary pressures. This was label unionism in its last refinement: a unionism which hugged every curve and contour of its industry and used its marketing structure to boycott employees and employers into line.

Hutcheson's first reaction, almost a reflex, after the International Woodworkers of America was formed was to spread broadcast a circular which ended with the words, "Let your watchword be 'No CIO lumber or millwork in your district!' and let them know you mean it."[2] A list of fifty-three mills organized by the Woodworkers was then given to all retail lumber dealers with appropriate words of warning. Many order cancellations resulted. In some cases, losses to the operators of International Woodworkers of America mills ran into the millions.[3]

The Carpenters made no bones about their use of the boycott in the Woodworker dispute. They used it solely and simply to force the workers into the United Brotherhood. Governor Martin of Oregon frankly characterized the Carpenters' use of the boycott in his state as an attempt to "starve the employees back into the [Carpenters'] union."[4] A *Carpenter* editorial spoke openly of the

[1] Lester C. Voris, "Boycott Power Lost by Deserters," *The Carpenter,* Vol. 57, No. 12, December 1937, p. 12 (italics mine).
[2] "Special Circular from the General Executive Board," (undated), *The Carpenter,* Vol. 58, No. 3, March 1938, p. 36.
[3] Walter Galenson, *Rival Unionism in the United States*, p. 47.
[4] *Senate Education and Labor Committee Hearings* (76th Cong.), Vol. 2, Part 8, p. 1525.

fact that the boycotted Portland mills were "Formerly a stronghold of IWA dual activity...[and] suffered greatly due to their unfair listing while under IWA control." The article continued, "Upon re-affiliation of the Portland workers [with the Carpenters], this unfair listing was removed, and orders once again began to pour into the Portland mills."[5]

Wherever the Woodworkers had a majority, a similar pattern emerged.[6] When the men left the United Brotherhood and joined the Woodworkers, the Carpenters put in a new charter, threw up a picket line, and slammed on the boycott. Usually the mill closed. Often there was violence, and the troops were called in. Always the Carpenters sat back, hands folded, waiting for their war of attrition to tell. And tell it did. Throughout 1938 and 1939 the tide turned slowly in favor of the AFL. By 1940 the Carpenters had about one-third as many lumbermen as did the Woodworkers. Only three years before, the lumbermen had deserted the United Brotherhood almost to a man.

The Carpenters had made gains but they were fighting uphill. For the Carpenters to fight uphill, however, was something new. Prior to 1935 the odds would have been high, the battle short, and the victory assured. But after 1935 the lumberjacks had behind them a new and powerful ally, the National Labor Relations Board. Not that the Board members consciously sided with either of the antagonists, they simply gave the lumberjacks the right to vote. They usually voted for the International Woodworkers of America and called down upon themselves the harassing tactics just described. Hence when the Carpenters boycotted, they boycotted against not only other unions and other workers but against the results of National Labor Relations Board elections, against "industrial democracy," against a federal agency, against federal law.

[5]"Portland Now 100 Percent A. F. of L.," *The Carpenter*, Vol. 58, No. 5, May 1938, p. 19.

[6]This occurred in Linnton, Oregon, in Gray's Harbor and Tacoma, Washington, and in scores of other towns and cities. See *Senate Education and Labor Committee Hearings* (76th Cong.), Vol. 1, Part 5, pp. 954, 960–961; Vol. 2, Part 8, pp. 1524–1526, for the struggle in the above towns, and Vol. 1, Part 5, pp. 933–989, for a review of the whole Washington-Oregon struggle as seen by various lumbermill officials.

One owner was dazed and bewildered at the boycott which the United Brotherhood clamped upon his products. He said, "Our customers...were bombarded with letters and wires from various locals of the Carpenters and Joiners (AFL) throughout the country to the effect that our products were boycotted, all of this because we were observing faithfully the National Labor Relations Act."[7]

At the Inman-Poulson mill in Portland the Carpenters picketed, boycotted, and closed the plant in which the International Wood-workers of America dominated. They refused to recognize a National Labor Relations Board payroll certification of the Wood-workers and refused to enter an employee-representation election under National Labor Relations Board auspices, holding that majority elections did not solve a national problem of jurisdiction.[8] Board Member Edwin Smith was shocked and held this to be the first case in which a union refused to abide by a Board certification.[9] Even President Roosevelt chimed in with the observation that the tie-up in the Northwest was an "impossible situation."[10]

The board, the Carpenters replied, might hold elections merrily. If the United Brotherhood lost them, the big trees would rot in the ground. The Carpenters conceded that the board had "jurisdiction over employee-employer relations...in a given operation." But there its power ceased. "It had no jurisdiction compelling outside unions to handle the finished product." It could not "guarantee to the employer dealing with the majority of his employees that every product of his machine would be immune to any boycott."[11]

Edwin Smith roared back, "The Carpenters' Brotherhood, asserting merely a paper sovereignty, has proceeded to make it impossible both for the employers concerned and their workers to earn a livelihood."[12]

The Wagner Act was all right, retorted the Carpenters, but

[7]*Ibid.*, Vol. 1, Part 5, p. 954.

[8]"State Governor vs. NLRB," *Labor Relations Reporter* (pub. by the Bureau of National Affairs), Vol. 1, No. 15, Dec. 13, 1937, p. 5.

[9]*Ibid.*

[10]"Labor and the State of the Union," *Labor Relations Reporter,* Vol. 1, No. 19, Jan. 10, 1938, p. 2.

[11]"Boycott Power Lost by Deserters," p. 12.

[12]*Senate Education and Labor Committee Hearings* (76th Cong.), Vol. 1, Part 5, p. 978.

"someone should tell the Board that its tactics smell to high heaven."[13]

Smith answered that the Carpenters boycotted "not only to prevent the workers...from exercising their...right [to a free choice of unions] under the [National Labor Relations] Act but, in fact, to prevent them from working at all."[14]

Thus did the National Labor Relations Board, a new antagonist, shoulder to the fore. This was a development entirely unforeseen by the creators of the Wagner Act. It was also inevitable. For the board members followed a course which could not fail to bring them into conflict with the Carpenters. They asked workers within the United Brotherhood's jurisdiction to vote on whether or not they wished to remain there. The leaders of the United Brotherhood felt that "the Board has given an insurgent group the rights of belligerents"[15]; that its electoral machinery gave workers the right and the means to overthrow union government established by generations of union workers and based on decades of experience in collective bargaining. The Carpenters referred to the National Labor Relations Board elections as "an illusory, impossible promise of [a] so-called 'rank and file' vote."[16]

In the presence of these votes the United Brotherhood's long-established and hard-fought-for jurisdiction was put up for sale. Not only the lumberjacks but any group of workers—the planing-mill hands, furniture workers, millwrights, sheet-metal workers—could vote themselves out of the United Brotherhood and, backed by a federal law, establish a dual union. The Carpenters had fought bitterly to prevent even the friendly AFL from passing on their jurisdiction. Now they were forced by law to watch a group of industrial workers, "radicals," decide the extent of their effective jurisdiction. Without the CIO the Wagner Act was a nice little law which might, from time to time, enable the Carpenters to "police" their jurisdiction. Granted the CIO, the new law was a lance

[13]Editorial, "Labor Board Presses On," *The Carpenter*, Vol. 58, No. 10, October 1938, p. 24.
[14]Edwin S. Smith, "Dangers to Labor from Within and Without," in *Labor Relations Reference Manual*, Vol. 1-A, p. 939.
[15]Editorial, "Shall Government Control Unionism?" *The Carpenter*, Vol. 58, No. 9, September 1938, p. 38.
[16]"Boycott Power Lost," p. 12.

pointed at the union's vitals. There was but one thing to do: change the law.

Throughout 1938 the Carpenters took broader and broader swipes at the board. Finally, under pressure from Hutcheson and other union leaders who felt the same about the board, William Green opened a campaign to amend the Wagner Act. Since the amendments were not passed, the matter need not be pursued further.[17] In the course of the Senate hearings on the amendments, however, the Carpenters' quarrel with the International Woodworkers of America and with the National Labor Relations Board played a dominant role. Evidence relative to the Carpenters' dispute with the board occupied at least 166 pages of the record.[18] Director George Kidwell of the California Department of Industrial Relations charged that the United Brotherhood's quarrel with the National Labor Relations Board in the California lumber district "became the spearhead of the national fight for wrecking the Wagner Act. Move after move was made for the sole reason of discrediting the board and in open defiance of the law of the United States."[19] Senator R. E. Holman of Oregon repeatedly brought the Carpenters' West Coast dispute to the attention of the Senate Education and Labor Committee as a prime example of how the National Labor Relations Board fomented labor war.

It became increasingly clear in 1939 that the Carpenters were aiming to discredit the board by boycott action and then, through behind-the-scenes pressure, to tear the Wagner Act apart. The government accepted the challenge and singled out the Carpenters for the greatest assault ever launched by the federal government against a union. "All the power. . ., resources and. . .knowledge of the Government were arrayed against us," said Hutcheson in 1940.

[17]Editorial, "National Labor Relations Board," *The Carpenter*, Vol. 58, No. 12, December 1938, pp. 22–23. See American Federation of Labor, *Proceedings of the Fifty-eighth Annual Convention of Houston, Oct. 3 to Oct. 13, 1938*, pp. 139–140, for the amendments, and Harry Millis and Emelie Brown, pp. 347–354, for the AFL attempt to pass them.

[18]*Senate Education and Labor Committee Hearings* (76th Cong.). The exact pages are Vol. 1, Part 5, pp. 874–899, 933–989; Vol. 2, Part 7, pp. 1220–1247, 1319–1327; Part 8, pp. 1480–1483, 1497–1501, 1515–1539; Vol. 3, Part 18, pp. 3432–3433.

[19]*Senate Education and Labor Committee Hearings* (76th Cong.). Vol. 1, Part 5, p. 877.

Before describing this assault, it is necessary to trace the events which led to it. The building industry was as important to the New Deal's recovery program in 1939 as it had been in 1933. Yet, for all of Roosevelt's doctoring, the industry had responded very little. It continued to lag behind the rest of the economy and, in 1939, was still depressed. *Fortune* likened it to

a display of fireworks that had been rained on. For years it has threatened to explode in a pyrotechnic spectacle. For five years the New Deal has applied fire to its fuses. And for five years it has sputtered feebly, at intervals...and gone out.[20]

Doctoring was still thought necessary, but in 1939 the method of treatment changed radically.

In 1934 Roosevelt joined with industry leaders to limit business competition through the National Industrial Recovery Act. It failed. Now, in 1939, he turned against industry leaders and by investigations, grand jury indictments, and prosecution under the Sherman Act tried to stimulate business competition. At his request Congress formed the Temporary National Economic Committee in 1939 to investigate the concentration of economic power in American industry and the decline of competition. This group investigated for months and published, from December 1, 1938, to April 26, 1940, twenty-four volumes of hearings and forty-three monographs on the American economy. While it sat it probed with relentless fingers into every facet of American economic life.

One of the Committee's first subjects for study was the construction industry.[21] It found the industry encrusted with bottlenecks, collusive practices, and restraints of trade. Thurman Arnold, head of the Anti-Trust Division of the Justice Department, who played a leading role in the Committee hearings, was convinced that only by attacking the dozing industry "on a Nation-wide scale, and simultaneously, [could] all the various combinations which are creating the log jams in the building industry [be destroyed]."[22]

[20]"The Trouble with Building is...," *Fortune,* Vol. 17, No. 6, June 1938, p. 100, cont. on p. 103.
[21]*Temporary National Economic Committee Report,* Vol. 11, *passim.*
[22]Department of Justice, "Report of Assistant Attorney General Thurman Arnold, in charge of the Anti-Trust Division," in the *Annual Report of the Attorney General of the United States for the Fiscal Year ended June 30, 1939,* p. 40.

Working with the largest appropriation ever received by the Anti-Trust Division, Arnold struck. In a press release of November 20, 1939, he announced a huge drive against the building industry. The ultimate goal of the drive was to encourage competition by eliminating five malpractices: feather bedding, graft and extortion, union refusal to work on new materials, price fixing, and jurisdictional strikes.[23] Arnold held all of these practices to be in restraint of trade. In late 1939 and 1940 eleven grand juries rained indictments on the heads of persons in the building industry.[24] Although the attack was directed against the entire industry, the Carpenters bore the brunt. Their local and national officials were placed under indictment by the hundreds. Big Hutch turned to face the greatest crisis in the history of his union. Thus did the drive which had started out generally against the industry, and which had ended specifically and particularly against the Carpenters, get under way.

The immediate objects of this drive are apparent. Roosevelt had entered his anti-big-business phase, and he gave trustbuster Arnold free rein. The drive had another goal, however, unmentioned but implicit in the indictments and of overriding importance to this study: the implementation of trade union democracy and the destruction of label unionism.

The issue of trade union democracy was raised by the Carpenters' boycott activities against the International Woodworkers of America and the National Labor Relations Board. During the hearings of the Senate Education and Labor Committee on amendments to the Wagner Act, Robert Maxwell, attorney for a group of Northwest mill operators, asserted that, democracy notwithstanding, the Carpenters' boycott activities were in restraint of interstate trade. Senator Frederick Stiewer of Oregon saw a closer relationship between the restraint of trade and the trade union democracy issues. In a letter to Attorney General Robert Jackson, he said that

[23]Department of Justice, "Application of the Anti-Trust Laws to Labor," (public statement release of the Division of Enforcement of the Anti-Trust Laws of the Justice Department, Nov. 20, 1939), passim.

[24]Corwin Edwards, "The New Anti-Trust Procedure as Illustrated in the Construction Industry," Public Policy, Vol. 2, No. 1, p. 326.

a minority of lumber workers in the United Brotherhood had told the majority:

The rights guaranteed to you by the law of the United States will be withdrawn and defeated through our influence [that is, by use of the boycott]. We deny your right to self-organization. We say, on the contrary, that you enjoy legal rights only if you select us as your bargaining agency. In other words, you may work if you get a license from us. If you attempt to act on your own judgment and to exercise your legal right of self-organization we will resort to an illegal boycott and make it impossible for your employer to sell his products. You will yield to us or starve.[25]

Little could be done about this, the Senator continued, under the present law.

It is reasonably clear that the Department of Labor and the National Labor Relations Board are without jurisdiction and are without power to bring this boycott to an end. Secondary boycott is not defined as an unfair labor practice and apparently the act contemplates no means of dealing with it. I know of no power adequate in this situation except the power conferred by the anti-trust law. If this be true, it is a fact of special concern to you because Section 4 of such law provides...that it shall be the duty of the District Attorneys of the United States, under the direction of the Attorney General, to institute proceedings in equity to prevent and restrain such violations.[26]

This letter was sent in early 1938, a few months before its recipient turned Arnold loose on the Carpenters' union.

The Justice Department's court assault was a means of asserting the Wagner Act's "industrial democracy" over the boycott tactics of label unionism. By attacking the United Brotherhood on grounds of restraint of trade, the government replied in kind, although obliquely through the Sherman Act, to the attack the Carpenters had launched on the National Labor Relations Board.

The issue of trade union democracy goes even deeper than the National Labor Relations Board, however. There were people in the government who actively hoped that the board's elections would give the workers an opportunity to speak out against their

---

[25]"The Problem of Inter-Union Boycotts," *Labor Relations Reporter,* Vol. 1, No. 20, Jan. 17, 1938, p. 9.
[26]*Ibid.*

leadership, if they chose, and thus to put the leaders on their toes and further democratize the various national unions.[27] Thurman Arnold was one of these. Even as he prepared his assault on the Carpenters, he wrote:

Why...is it today so difficult to enforce the Wagner Act without bitterness and conflict?

The answer...lies in the failure of government to confine organized labor to legitimate labor objectives. The right of collective bargaining is being enforced in favor of labor organizations which are using the right for illegitimate purposes, against the interests of consumers, against the interests of efficiency, and against the interests of labor itself. Industrialists found themselves forced to deal with unions many of which are nothing more than corrupt political machines that use the right of collective bargaining against the interests of the rank and file of laborers. Many unions are interested in restricting output, in building trade barriers between states, and even in discriminating against working men themselves for the advantage of a few. Many of these unions are undemocratic in organization and their leaders maintain themselves in power by coercion. Such types of organizations inevitably lead to corruption on a large scale.[28]

Then, to make sure he was not misunderstood, he immediately launched into a two-page description of the United Brotherhood as the prime example of this kind of union.[29]

Arnold associated the lack of democracy in the United Brotherhood with label unionism and label unionism, in turn, with restraint of trade. He hoped the Sherman Act might be used to lop off the worst excesses of both trade union autocracy and label unionism. Charles H. Tuttle, the Carpenters' general counsel, said that Arnold had set himself up

as an arbiter and referee over all labor disputes, frictions and contentions that may arise, and if in the opinion of that bureau [the Anti-

[27]Harry Millis, who headed the National Labor Relations Board in 1940 said: "Old and responsible union officers sometimes complained that they were forced as a result [of the Wagner Act] to give excessive attention to keeping members satisfied....But the net effect must have been to promote democracy and rank-and-file participation in their unions. The major loss was to the weak or inefficient union, or the "racketeering union," since, given a free choice, in general the votes go to the organizations that serve their members best" (Millis and Brown, p. 171).

[28]Thurman Arnold, *Bottlenecks of Business*, pp. 241–242.

[29]*Ibid.*, pp. 242–244.

Trust Division of the Justice Department] the strike or labor activity is unjustified...then to proceed against it by indictment.

Tuttle maintained that Arnold sought to induce the courts to give the government the power to distinguish between justified and unjustified trade union activities.[30]

Tuttle was right. By cooperation between two federal administrative agencies, the Justice Department and the National Labor Relations Board, and the federal courts, the Wagner Act was, in effect, to be amended so as to project it into the internal affairs of trade unions. Thus:

The National Labor Relations Board is authorized...to prohibit 'unfair' practices by employers, but it does not have the power to control such practices on the part of labor. But if only the employers are to be restrained, and not labor, what happens to the theory that the government is impartial...between labor and capital? The answer which Mr. Arnold has given is that labor, too, must observe fair play, and the weapon which he proposes to use is the familiar weapon of the Sherman Act.[31]

Through a fast National Labor Relations Board-to-Justice Department-to-Supreme Court shuffle, the administration planned to write unfair practices by labor into the Wagner Act as early as 1939. Thus did the Roosevelt administration anticipate generous portions of the Taft-Hartley Act by almost a decade.

The executive council of the AFL set up labor's clarion call against the court assault, saying that it would "resist with all the power at its command the present reactionary efforts of the Department of Justice to control organized labor." Joseph A. Padway, counsel for the AFL, held the attack to be "the most reactionary, vicious, outrageous attempt in the last dozen years on the part of any department of the Government to bring labor unions under the provision of the Anti-trust laws. Labor stands aghast and horrified at this bold attempt."[32]

For his part, Hutcheson shrewdly gauged the extent and im-

[30]UBCJA, *1940 Convention Proceedings,* pp. 214–215.

[31]H. S. Commager, "Labor Unions and the Sherman Anti-Trust Act," *Scholastic: The American High School Weekly,"* Vol. 36, No. 2, Feb. 12, 1940, p. 13 (cont.).

[32]"Sherman Act and Labor Unions," in *Labor Relations Reference Manual,* Vol. 5, p. 1148.

portance of the assault. From the outset he said that whatever part of the United Brotherhood's structure seemed to be under attack, the government was actually aiming at the policy of label unionism or, as he phrased it, at the right of the United Brotherhood "to use the label and carry on affairs... in the manner they have been carried on for over 40 years."[33] The government's court assault attacked the whole structure of unionism built up by Huber, Kirby, and Hutcheson since McGuire's demise. Thus, with the stakes established and both cases stated, it remained for the federal courts to determine wherein justice dwelled.

In all, the United Brotherhood received seven grand jury indictments for restraint of trade under the Sherman Act. In keeping with the government's dual aim, all of the indictments had one of two objects. One group of indictments was directed against the use of the boycott only because it restrained trade by "building a wall" about a city. The object of these indictments was to implement laissez faire in the industry. Indictments placed against the United Brotherhood in Pittsburgh, New Orleans, Chicago, and San Francisco fell into this category.[34]

The Pittsburgh indictment was typical. It covered the officers of the Pittsburgh district council; fifteen lumber supply companies; their trade organization, the Lumber Institute; and the Master Builders' Association formed by the contractors. The indictment charged that the Pittsburgh district council refused to work on lumber materials made outside Pittsburgh even though the United Brotherhood had organized these firms. It also found that the United Brotherhood made agreements with firms outside Pittsburgh under the terms of which they were prevented from marketing their products in any city where the mill rate was higher than that paid in their mill. The indictment held that these Pittsburgh mills would have been unable to compete in an open market with larger and more efficient out-of-town firms. Consequently the dealers, the contractors, and the Carpenters had entered into a three-cornered collusive agreement whereby material manufactured outside Pittsburgh was excluded from the city. The Car-

[33]UBCJA, *1940 Convention Proceedings*, p. 47.
[34]*Ibid.*, pp. 48–50; and UBCJA, *1946 Convention Proceedings*, p. 185.

penters were alleged to have enforced the agreement by refusing to work on such material.[35]

The second group of indictments was also directed against boycotts. These were pointed at boycotts against a union certified in a National Labor Relations Board election, however, and were designed to back up the board and implement industrial democracy. These three indictments were filed in New Orleans, Chicago, and St. Louis.[36]

The Chicago indictment is typical of this second group. It charged that in 1938 the Carpenters agreed to enter a National Labor Relations Board election at the plant of the Harbor Plywood Corporation in Hoaquiam, Washington, which, at the time, marketed many of its products in Chicago. The International Woodworkers of America won the election, and the Carpenters immediately placed the Harbor Company on their boycott list. Two months after the election Chicago carpenters struck a job on which materials made by the Harbor Company were being installed. The indictment returned against the Carpenters' district council of Chicago and one of the millmen's locals found that they restrained interstate trade to the end of destroying an International Woodworkers of America local.[37]

The indictments were but seven of eighty-one returned in late 1939 against various persons and organizations in the building trades.[38] Out of the welter of cases on his hands Arnold decided to stand or fall on one, the St. Louis indictment against the Carpenters. It was handed down in September 1939 and, when tried in the St. Louis Federal District Court in early 1940, was won by the Carpenters. The Department of Justice took the case directly up to the Supreme Court in April and it was heard in December 1940. Said lawyer Charles Noyes, "Unless this decision is reversed, the comprehensive program of the Justice Department for proceeding

[35]"Pittsburgh Pa. Indictment," *The Carpenter,* Vol. 60, No. 4, April 1940, pp. 23–32, contains a verbatim copy of the indictment.
[36]UBCJA, *1940 Convention Proceedings,* pp. 48–51.
[37]*Ibid.,* pp. 48–49. See "Chicago, Ill. Indictment," *The Carpenter,* Vol. 60, No. 4, April 1940, pp. 18–22, for a verbatim copy of the indictment.
[38]Charles E. Noyes, "Restraints of Trade in the Building Industry," *Editorial Research Reports,* Vol. 1, April 23, 1940, p. 311.

against all types of building trades restraints will be severely handicapped, if not completely stopped."[39]

He was correct. Whatever the Justice Department's specific and immediate aims, the assault raised legal issues of basic and far-reaching importance to labor. The problem facing the Supreme Court was whether or not the activities of labor organizations came under the Sherman Act. If they did, the Department of Justice could proceed with the rest of its cases, assured of a high percentage of victories. If they did not, the rest of the cases would have to be abandoned. More important, if labor did come under the Sherman Act, the government would have the right to regulate the practices of labor unions as well as those of the employers. This right would have then been gained through the medium of the common law, a judicial mill which on occasion can grind out legislation in an exceedingly quiet fashion. Thus would Roosevelt have amended the Wagner Act without resorting to the politically spotlighted legislative arm of the federal government. The Wagner Act is the rock upon which the latest labor citadel, the CIO, was built. To change it to restrict trade union activities might well have cost the Democratic party dearly.

The specific background of the St. Louis case, which became known as the Hutcheson case, was as follows. Both the United Brotherhood and the International Association of Machinists claimed jurisdiction over certain classes of millwright work. When the Anheuser-Busch Beer Company decided to erect a new tank plant in St. Louis it awarded the millwright work to the Machinists. In a National Labor Relations Board election the employees, too, decided that they wished to install the disputed machinery under the aegis of the Machinists. The Carpenters responded by striking Anheuser-Busch's carpenters, by throwing up a picket line, and placing a secondary consumers' boycott on the company's products.[40]

Counsel Tuttle held that this was a "common, ordinary, garden-variety kind of strike" and that the picketing and boycotting fell well within the scope of legitimate trade union self-help activities.

[39]*Ibid.*
[40]UBCJA, *1940 Convention Proceedings*, pp. 216–217.

Department of Justice lawyers contended that the United Brotherhood's activities were in restraint of trade under the law of precedent as decided in the 1921 Duplex case. This case had placed trade union activities much like those used by the United Brotherhood against the Anheuser-Busch Company under the scope of the Sherman Anti-Trust Act as amended in 1914 by the Clayton Act.[41] The final issue came to be: had either common-law decisions made or statutory laws enacted since the Duplex decision placed such "self-help" trade union activities outside the scope of the Sherman Act as amended by the Clayton Act?

In February 1941 the Supreme Court found that such trade union activities were no longer under the scope of the Sherman Act.[42] This momentous decision reversed two decades of legal precedent and "virtually took organized labor entirely out from under the Sherman Act."[43] This decision stands at the time of this writing as the definitive decision on labor and the Sherman Act.

The scope of the victory which the Carpenters had won for organized labor was breathtaking. Hutcheson did not exaggerate when he said:

This was a signal victory. It was and has been the first case and fore-runner of all decisions affecting labor, on the right to Picket, the right to Boycott, the right to circulate statements, the right to assume and maintain jurisdiction, the right to persuade other trades to quit with us, the right to call strikes on other jobs and the right to enforce our laws as made by the membership of the United Brotherhood.[44]

By upholding the broader "self-help" trade union practices, the Supreme Court indirectly held to be legal the whole structure of label unionism as practiced by the United Brotherhood. By uphold-

[41]See Gregory, chapters 7, 8, and 10 for the legal background of the Sherman Act, the Clayton Act, and the Duplex case.

[42]United States v. Hutcheson, 312 U.S. 219 (1941). Justice Frankfurter, who wrote the majority decision, decided that a federal law of 1932, the Norris-LaGuardia Anti-Injunction Act, had amended the Clayton Act of 1914 so as to take labor activities such as the court was concerned with in the Hutcheson case, out from under the Sherman Act. He held that the Norris-LaGuardia Act had rendered legally obsolete the reasoning pursued by the Supreme Court in the 1921 Duplex case. The Frankfurter opinion has been thoroughly analyzed and criticized by Gregory, pp. 271–272.

[43]Gregory, p. 277.

[44]UBCJA, *1946 Convention Proceedings,* pp. 181–182.

ing the United Brotherhood's right to "assume and maintain jurisdiction," the Court caused the United Brotherhood's jurisdiction to take precedence over the electoral machinery of the Wagner Act whenever the two came into conflict. As a consequence of the Hutcheson decision, "the Court acknowledged that rival union factions are free to fight out the new interunion dispute... with the channels of interstate commerce as their battleground quite regardless of their effect on consumers markets."[45] Still another head, that of New Dealer Thurman Arnold, went up in the United Brotherhood's trophy room.

There is a vast historical irony in the fact that one of the most liberal governments the United States ever had, embarking on an antimonopoly drive which had roots sunk deep in the tradition of American radicalism, should have chosen the Carpenters as its target. For the United Brotherhood was founded by a man schooled in the antimonopoly tradition. McGuire had participated in every political fad, from the Greenback party to the Populist movement, which had ever taken an antimonopoly position. No American radical loathed the great monopolies more profoundly. And, but thirty-three years after his death, the one political administration most nearly committed to McGuire's general political goals chose his union for its first antimonopoly target.

Nothing points up as much as this attack upon the Carpenters how deep-rooted was the difference between McGuire and the men who deposed him. Their policies—jurisdictional laissez faire, trade union alliances, craft-industrialism—all led to label unionism. And label unionism led to the very monopoly tactics against which McGuire, as a traditional American radical, had fought. History

[45]Gregory, p. 285. In Gregory's opinion this court victory left the United Brotherhood free to enter into the three-cornered collusive agreements with materials dealers and contractors to keep materials made outside a given city from entering that city (*ibid.*, pp. 278–279). This victory, however, like that over the National Board for Jurisdictional Awards during the 1920's, was pyrrhic. The boycott tactics of label unionism continued and, in the minds of Senator Robert Taft and Representative Fred Hartley, became oppressive. Consequently the Taft-Hartley Act, Sec. 8 (b) (4) (C) and (D), specifically prohibited the use of the secondary boycott to contest a National Labor Relations Board election or to press a jurisdictional dispute (*ibid.*, pp. 427–428.)

completed a circle when an administration which McGuire, if alive, would have given his complete support attacked the union to which he had dedicated his life. It is historically fitting that the target of the antimonopoly drive, William L. Hutcheson, entered the United Brotherhood the same year it cast out Peter J. McGuire.

CHAPTER XXI

The Worth of the National Union

to the Carpenter

WHAT has been the worth of the United Brotherhood to American carpenters? For most unions this question is answered by measuring tangibles like wages, hours, and working conditions and intangibles like industrial democracy. Because of the localized market structure of the building industry, however, these benefits, both tangible and intangible, are dealt with on the local level.[1] Consequently the worth of the carpenters' national union must be judged by a different and more basic standard of measurement from that of wages, hours, and working conditions, or even of industrial democracy.[2]

What, then, is that standard? The present union was founded only when technological changes in the building industry threatened to take from the carpenter work he had traditionally performed, thus depriving him of his livelihood. From that day to this the

[1]To be sure, locals call in the national from time to time for advice and aid in bargaining. But this is rare and confined for the most part to the larger city organizations. Most important, it is not required by the constitution. The almost complete freedom with which the locals deal with their employers is indicated by the fact that the all-important office of business agent is in no way regulated by the national constitution. See above pp. 3–6 for an explanation of the union's localized bargaining structure in terms of the building industry.

[2]It must be recalled that strong and continuing local unions existed almost one hundred years before they united to form the present national union. The national union is the creation of its local unions.

primary task of the Carpenters' union has been to retain for the carpenter the work done by him in 1881. Nor is this difficult to understand: a union can hardly perform its conventional task of improving working conditions unless there is work for its members to do. The ability of the union to retain for the carpenter jurisdiction over work traditionally done by him is the basic standard by which the worth of the United Brotherhood to its members must be judged. A brief review of the history of the United Brotherhood will reveal the degree of success which the present union has enjoyed in this realm.

Until 1881 neither the reorganization of the building industry nor the broadening of its labor market sufficiently threatened the carpenter's livelihood to call forth a successful national union. The former produced the middleman and local unions but failed to lead a permanent national union. The latter gave rise to the itinerant carpenter and, as a direct consequence, the National Carpenters' Union of 1865, which was but short-lived.

Only when the ills born of the middleman and the itinerant were joined by those born of technological change was the present national union launched. New woodworking inventions, which displaced the all-round carpenter with both the "inside" and "outside" green hand, threatened to deprive the carpenter of huge portions of his work. Thus the present-day union was born to preserve work for the carpenter.

The first two decades of the union's existence were characterized by a struggle for pre-eminence within the union between the advocates of two forms of unionism, nonideological and ideological. While the advocates of the latter (at first led by McGuire and, toward the end, consisting almost only of McGuire) lost the struggle, their contribution to the cause of unionism was substantial. It was McGuire's hope for a reorganized society which powered the new union during its first years. It was McGuire's radical zeal and tireless organizing energies which provided a cocoon in which a more practical brand of unionism could develop. And, finally, it was McGuire's tireless mind that conceived the eight-hour drive, which was of such prime importance to both the United Brotherhood and the American labor movement.

Through the medium of this drive, events were set in motion which destroyed the Knights of Labor, pushed the American Federation of Labor to the fore, and established the United Brotherhood as the largest trade union in America. This movement provided the long-sought-after meeting ground on which the ideological radicals and practical workers could come together, compromise, and form workable national unions.

But for the United Brotherhood the compromise was evanescent. As the new union flourished, its local leaders were forced to fashion trade union institutions—the business agent and the district council—in order to dominate an unstable and speculative industry. The leaders produced by these institutions were as conservative and practical as the men they led—too practical to travel long down the same road with the ideological trade unionists. One by one the latter were either dropped by the way or converted, until only McGuire remained.

Perhaps McGuire might have lived out his life as an ideological front for a practical union had not new and more radical technological changes overtaken the United Brotherhood in the 1890's. Once again the carpenter was threatened, this time by a changing industry which had no place for the nineteenth-century journeyman carpenter. Other crafts and still more mechanical inventions called for a stronger national union, one dedicated primarily to preserving work for the carpenter. McGuire could not make the rapid and positive adjustment which the emerging new industry demanded. As a result he was ignominiously hustled out of the trade union movement. The twenty-year-long struggle between ideological and practical trade unionists was put to rest as the latter swept the field at the 1902 convention.

Since that date the history of the union has been dominated by the leitmotif of work preservation. Not an administrative technique, a structural development, nor a conscious policy has been developed since then which cannot be traced back to it.

Huber's first task as United Brotherhood president was to regain the jurisdiction over the woodworkers which McGuire had allowed to lapse. His second was to construct a jurisdictional policy designed to preserve the carpenter's work in an age of technological change. He achieved both goals through one set of tactics.

When the AFL refused to recognize the carpenters' claim to jurisdiction over the machine woodworkers, Huber opened war on the Amalgamated Wood Workers' Union. Then he created the Structural Building Trades Alliance, a federation dual to the AFL. The jurisdictional warfare was a stick behind Gompers and the Structural Building Trades Alliance a carrot before him. He took the carrot. In 1908 Gompers created the Building Trades Department partially in the image of the Structural Building Trades Alliance. Then, in 1911, he gave the United Brotherhood jurisdiction over the Amalgamated Wood Workers' Union and over all North American woodworkers. Thus, in one short decade, Huber both garnered jurisdiction over the woodworkers and forced organized labor to recognize his "all that's made of wood" policy. Broadened to apply to all AFL unions, the policy was called "one organization for one trade."

To Huber, then, must go the credit for devising a jurisdictional policy sufficiently broad to preserve for the carpenter access to work he had traditionally done, work which in the absence of such a policy might have gone to other and newer trades or to industrial workers unassociated with the carpenters' national union. This policy lies at the core of an understanding of the relationship between the national union and the working carpenter. It was devised to attain the simple goal of work preservation which the working carpenter set for his union.

In pursuing this policy Huber changed the United Brotherhood from a confederation to a federation. If as a federation the powers of the national office were limited, so also was the technological threat with which the national officers had to cope. For only the woodworking unions threatened the Carpenters' jurisdiction. But in the few years which followed Huber's retirement the threat broadened as still further technological change brought the United Brotherhood into conflict with several of the metal crafts. To meet this new threat more changes were made in the structure, administration, and policy of the union—changes which served to convert the United Brotherhood into a centralized union.

After 1912 the carpenters lost an increasing amount of work to the metal trades, and Huber's "all that's made of wood" policy was no longer broad enough to protect the craft. Consequently his successors Kirby and Hutcheson broadened it by adding "or ever was made of wood" and prepared to do battle with the carpenters' new foes.

This new departure made the old idea of "one organization for one trade" meaningless and left the Carpenters without a logical argument to present to the AFL in demanding jurisdiction over metalwork. Once again technological change sent the Carpenters outside the AFL in search of support for their jurisdictional policy. This time they erected an alliance system centered on a mutual aid pact with the then independent Bricklayers. Such a system, however, demanded tight national control over the various locals. When the Brotherhood promised the Bricklayers that the Ypsilanti locals would strike in support of the Bricklayers, the Ypsilanti locals had to strike or the whole treaty system would have been voided.

For this reason the general president received power in 1914 to make and break local agreements. Possessed of this power, he was able to enforce the new alliance system. Those local unions who ignored the alliance in their local agreements could henceforth be forced to mend their ways. Thus, from 1914 to 1924, the Carpenters maintained their alliance with the Bricklayers to which all locals were forced to conform in their various agreements. From 1931 to 1934 another such alliance was entered into with the Bricklayers and Electricians which imposed the same restrictions on locals.

The purpose of these restrictions was not to dominate local bargaining but to give the United Brotherhood aid in its various jurisdictional struggles through the medium of the alliance system. But for whatever reason the restrictions were made, they increased the control of the national office over the locals. Thus the United Brotherhood adopted a more centralized administrative structure primarily to protect the jurisdiction, which, as has been noted, is but a means of preserving work for the carpenter.

This serves to explain the apparent paradox of the joint existence of a powerful national office together with almost completely localized collective bargaining. The powers of the national office can be understood only if their use is understood. In matters of jurisdiction the power of the national office over locals is complete, because the need for such power has been proven time and again by events. In matters of collective bargaining the power of the national office is nominal, because events have proven such power not only unnecessary but impracticable.

Whenever local autonomy in matters of collective bargaining stands in the way of the effective exercise of national power in the jurisdictional realm, the latter takes precedence. This principle was demonstrated for the first time in the dispute between William Hutcheson and the New York City locals. The specific issues in this dispute did not directly involve either the alliance system or the jurisdiction. But they did concern the then recently passed laws empowering the president to regulate local agreements. These laws were passed at the behest of the Bricklayers, primarily to enforce the alliance system, which in turn was erected solely to protect the jurisdiction. The whole dispute with the New York locals was no more than the successful attempt of a powerful man to give substance to these laws. With Hutcheson's victory over the New York locals, the United Brotherhood achieved a degree of centralization but little altered at this writing.

Thus far only the main outlines of this centralized organization have been traced in terms of work preservation. The details can easily be fitted in on the same terms. Label unionism was created as a means of organizing factories which took work from the carpenters and of guaranteeing that only United Brotherhood mill products would be installed. Auxiliary membership was created to assure that the industrial workers would not dominate the organization. Jurisdictional laissez faire was adopted as the policy most likely to leave the Brotherhood free to retain work it had traditionally done. All of these policies were established by 1920 in the interest of work preservation.

323

The United Brotherhood's history since 1920 can be understood only in terms of a series of assaults on an administrative structure dedicated to jurisdictional preservation. The first assault, on jurisdictional laissez faire, came from a united building industry in the 1920's, took the form of the National Board for Jurisdictional Awards, and was defeated by the United Brotherhood. The second assault came from the federal government in 1934. It took the form of the National Jurisdictional Awards Board which died, along with the National Industrial Recovery Act, before it could function. Its threat, however, put the Carpenters permanently in the Building Trades Department, associated them permanently with some sort of a jurisdictional controls board, and ended their alliance system.

The assault by the Communists during the 1920's was essentially an attempt to steer the carpenters away from work preservation and back to ideological unionism. But since the carpenters had long since made the choice between these alternate forms of unionism, the Communists were given short shrift.

The court assaults, directed in the first instance (1917) by the Anti-Boycott Association and in the second by the Department of Justice (1941), were aimed at the policy of label unionism. Had either been successful, the Carpenters' ability to organize their woodworking mills would have been seriously impaired. In turn, their structure as a craft-industrial union would have been threatened. At the heart of the issue, the union's main function, preservation of the carpenter's work, would have been placed in extreme jeopardy.

Finally there was the assault on the United Brotherhood's craft-industrial structure. It was led by the CIO and was the most serious of all the assaults on the United Brotherhood. Had Lewis and his woodworker followers been successful, the United Brotherhood would have been pushed, step by step, back to where McGuire had left it. CIO industrial unions would have gradually divested the United Brotherhood of its various jurisdictions like so many vultures stripping a carrion until only the bare bones, the carpenter's craft remained. The lumberjacks did go. Had their departure been easier and their union more successful, they would have been followed by furniture workers, woodworkers, and sawmill workers. When the exodus of specialized workers was over, the few remaining carpenters would have been at the mercy of any marauder. And these abound in the building trades.

With the union dead, the half-century struggle to preserve the carpenter's work would have ceased. The few remaining "pure" carpenters might have formed a tight little union like that of the Stonemasons. The rest would have been divided among the other building trades. It was this grim vision that haunted Hutcheson when he rose to challenge John L. Lewis in 1935 and set afoot the run of events which led to the AFL-CIO struggle.

In this fashion the United Brotherhood has preserved over the years a pool of work for the carpenter. But this has not been done without cost. The first part of this chapter has totaled the gain. The following pages will total the cost and attempt to strike a balance.

Before the 1870's the carpenter worked much the same as he had a hundred years earlier. Starting in that decade technological change renovated the craft. Some carpentry and the hand tools, like the adz, necessary to perform it simply disappeared. Some came to be done by machine operators. Much of the remainder was taken over by other crafts as new materials replaced wood.

The United Brotherhood has preserved work for the carpenter by maintaining jurisdiction over these new materials, machines, and processes. It could not completely preserve the carpenter's skill, however. In the process of maintaining jurisdiction over iron windows, steel piles, and sheet-metal trim, as well as over all woodwork, the average carpenter has lost much of the delicate handicraft skill he once had.[3] No one man can achieve peak efficiency in such diverse tasks as building cement stairs, "finishing" altar work, and erecting concrete forms. It is in recognition of this fact that the United Brotherhood's constitution refers to the various "divi-

[3]This is not to say that the "old-time," all-round carpenter is extinct. There are simply relatively fewer such carpenters than there were in 1870. Craft pride and the completely skilled carpenter still remain and are important to an understanding of the union. Further, if the contractors did require such skilled carpenters, the United Brotherhood would undoubtedly be able to fill the need as rapidly as it arose.

sions and subdivisions of the craft," and to carpenters as "wood-working machine" operators, "bench hands," "stair builders," "millwrights," "dock carpenters," and a host of other names, as well as simply "carpenters."[4] The sum of the jobs the carpenter performs in several years may call for all of these varied skills. For this reason some carpenters gradually acquire them. Most, however, are content to emphasize one skill—stair building or form work, for example—and to find most of their work in that line.[5]

The effect of specialization is found in the Department of Labor's official job descriptions. Here, under the heading "carpenter," are found no less than twenty-three separate occupations, all related to, but distinct from, the main craft.[6] Many of these specialists, though United Brotherhood members, are not all-round carpenters. In fact, most of their special skills are so easily learned that confusion exists as to where a handyman ends and a carpenter begins. For this reason

any estimate of the number of carpenters is subject to considerable uncertainty. This is a trade where census figures are probably excessive, because of reporting of handymen and other partially trained workers . . . as journeymen carpenters. The number who may reasonably be called carpenters is probably over 500,000 . . . , not all of whom are capable of doing the most exacting types of work.[7]

Thus has the United Brotherhood preserved work for the carpenter while the industry has divided his skill.

Where preservation has given, division has taken away. The United Brotherhood's local leaders have been forced to barter unconsciously but nonetheless effectively the highest of all possible wages for preservation of the carpenter's work. The chart opposite shows the results of their barter.[8] On the whole it re-

[4] UBCJA, *1951 Constitution*, p. 5.

[5] Department of Labor, Bureau of Labor Statistics, *Employment Outlook in the Building Trades* (Bulletin No. 967), p. 44.

[6] Department of Labor, U.S. Employment Service, *Job Descriptions for the Construction Industry*," pp. 133–197.

[7] *Employment Outlook in the Building Trades* (Bulletin No. 967), p. 48.

[8] The lines on this chart indicate the national average of carpenters' wages and those of five other skilled building trades crafts. These averages were weighted by the number of craftsmen receiving each of the various local craft union rates which, added together, constitute the national average. It should be noted that these lines represent annual arithmetic averages. Data upon which a frequency distribution or

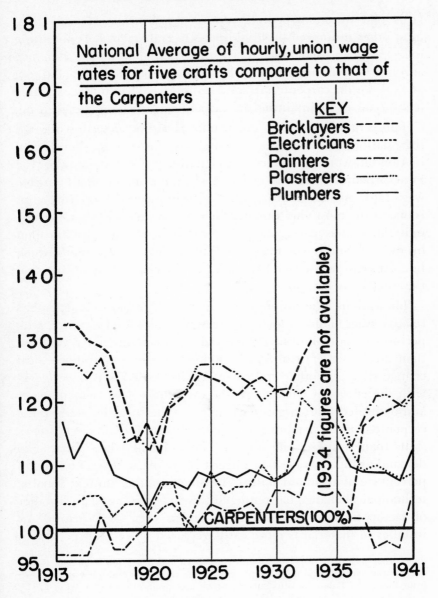

National Average of hourly, union wage rates for five crafts compared to that of the Carpenters

KEY
Bricklayers ------
Electricians ....
Painters -.-.-.-
Plasterers -..-..-
Plumbers ———

(1934 figures are not available)

CARPENTERS (100%)

veals that union carpenters receive a lower hourly wage than most other unionized building industry craftsmen. It is one thing to keep a sick patient alive; it is distinctly another to make him hale and hearty. While the United Brotherhood has maintained a pool of work for the carpenter, its local unions have had understandably less success in maintaining the carpenters' relative wage position.

This is understandable. The primary historical function allotted their national union by the carpenters has not been wage determin-ination but work preservation. The national preserves work for the local carpenters, and local unions bargain for the best of all possible wage rates. As was said earlier, "Preserving work for the carpenter is one of the most vital things which the Brotherhood does for the individual dues payer and [William] Hutcheson...[knew] that his own job and power depend[ed] upon the militancy with which he...[fought] any union that claim[ed] jurisdiction over work that the carpenters have always done."[9]

The various local unions have failed to maintain the carpenter's relative wage position for three reasons. First, the carpenter, who performed more building work before the industrial revolution than any other craftsman, had more to lose from technological change than any other craftsman. While other crafts have coped with the effects of technology, the carpenters have fought longer and dedicated more organized energy to the struggle. Second, the carpenter's trade is more subdivided into separate and subsidiary skills than is any of the others. The union has been unable to demand as high a wage rate since it is unable to deliver as high a percentage of all-round skilled craftsmen as other unions. Finally, technological change has rendered the carpenter more an installer of factory-finished material than he has ever been before. An installer of material is more easily replaced on certain specialized

---

some other means of dispersion might have been based are not available. Conse-quently the averages shown here represent a wide range of rates. They were drawn from Bureau of Labor statistics surveys which are specifically cited in Appendix I, a chart of the figures upon which this graph is based. Complete details on the Bureau's sources of information and methods of compiling can be found in each of the individual surveys.

[9]See above, p. 12. It will be recalled that this quotation was drawn from a personal interview with the late president, William L. Hutcheson, and probably represents his informed views on this subject.

jobs than is the craftsman. As a result, a huge and semiskilled labor force (often nonunion) competes with the carpenter for large portions of his work and makes his leaders' bargaining position less tenable than that of other building trades union leaders.[10]

Unionism which sacrifices the wage to preserve the work is what Professor Perlman has called "job conscious" unionism, with a vengeance. Job consciousness which has taken the basic form of work preservation is the dominant theme in the history of the United Brotherhood.

The carpenters are not ignorant of this theme. In 1946, at the twilight of William Hutcheson's long career as president, a resolution of thanks was presented to him. Wages, hours, and working conditions went unmentioned. The resolution simply thanked Hutcheson for preserving the craft:

New methods of construction have come into being since our inception and many new materials commonly used today were unknown when our local [No. 47 of St. Louis] was chartered [in the 1880's]. Thus, a new peril arose to confront carpenters. Our organization was faced with the peril of having our field of operations narrowed which, in turn, would bring economic ruin to our membership at large. When the members...compare what could have happened to our trade...to what it is today, it gives us more cause to appreciate our Brotherhood.[11]

In 1952 William L. Hutcheson retired from the presidency of the United Brotherhood. When he stepped down, the first vice-president became the new general president, as provided in the constitution. This man had entered the service of the union in 1914 as a clerk. Later he became a carpenter in an Indianapolis local, and still later he became a special representative of the national office. He was employed in this capacity when First Vice-President George H. Lakey died, in April of 1938. William L. Hutcheson appointed the man who was later to succeed him to fill Lakey's unexpired term. Exactly how and why this appointment was made has been placed on public record by Frank Duffy.

[10]For the most recent and detailed analysis of the present-day carpenters, see Department of Labor, Bureau of Labor Statistics, *Employment Outlook in the Building Trades* (Bulletin No. 967), *passim*. Each of these three points is supported by this article.

[11]UBCJA, *1946 Convention Proceedings*, p. 356.

After our good friend George Lakey...passed to his final reward... there was a vacancy. I am looking out for the best interests of this organization all the time. I want to see the best men elected to positions nationally and locally. I went to see General President Hutcheson and I said, 'Bill, I want to talk to you, I have a recommendation to make to you. In accordance with our laws you will have to nominate some person to fill the position of First General Vice-President....I have nothing to do with that, that is your business, but when you do name your man then it must be submitted to the General Executive Board for approval. The one I have in mind is Maurice A. Hutcheson.' And, in the language of the street, Bill Hutcheson hit the ceiling. He wouldn't listen to me. He said, 'Nothing doing, that is out of the question,' and I said, 'Wait a minute, Bill.' He said, 'If I do and it is approved by the General Executive Board, then they will say it is a Hutcheson family affair.' I said 'Well they say that anyhow. They say we have a Hutcheson-Duffy machine. Of course there is nothing to that, but some of them say it just the same.'

Maurice A. Hutcheson is my protege.[12]

When the protégé of the man who had helped to overthrow Peter J. McGuire in 1902 became president of the United Brotherhood exactly a half-century later, the carpenters had thoroughly buried their dead past. Only one souvenir remains to remind the curious that this union was once steeped in the impractical, idealistic radicalism of nineteenth-century America. On the back cover of the 1949 constitution there is inscribed an old demand about which the musty odor of nineteenth-century radicalism still faintly hovers. It calls for "Public Ownership of all public utilities and transportation to be conducted in the interest of the people."

And Peter J. McGuire now has an elaborate stone monument in Camden; he is called "The Father of Labor Day," and every year officials high in the American labor movement come to his grave and tell of what a great and fine man he was.

[12]UBCJA, *1940 Convention Proceedings*, p. 234.

Appendix

Hourly Union Wage Rates for Carpenters and Five Other Skilled Trades, 1913–1941, Expressed in Dollar Terms

Year		Trade				
	B'layers	Carpenters	Elect.	Painters	Plasterers	Plumbers
1913	$ .69	$ .53	$ .55	$ .51	$ .67	$ .62
1914	.70	.54	.56	.52	.68	.63
1915	.71	.55	.58	.53	.68	.63
1916	.71	.56	.59	.57	.71	.64
1917	.73	.61	.62	.59	.73	.66
1918	.80	.67	.70	.65	.76	.72
1919	.88	.77	.80	.76	.88	.82
1920	1.20	1.03	1.05	1.04	1.15	1.06
1921	1.19	1.05	1.10	1.07	1.22	1.12
1922	1.16	.97	1.04	1.01	1.17	1.04
1923	1.32	1.08	1.08	1.11	1.31	1.15
1924	1.40	1.16	1.21	1.17	1.46	1.26
1925	1.48	1.18	1.27	1.23	1.49	1.28
1926	1.57	1.27	1.34	1.31	1.60	1.38
1927	1.60	1.31	1.40	1.35	1.63	1.41
1928	1.62	1.32	1.41	1.37	1.63	1.44
1929	1.66	1.34	1.47	1.37	1.61	1.45
1930	1.70	1.39	1.48	1.47	1.69	1.49
1931	1.70	1.40	1.51	1.48	1.71	1.51
1932	1.47	1.17	1.44	1.23	1.42	1.30
1933	1.44	1.11	1.32	1.24	1.36	1.30
1934			(No figures available)			
1935	1.23	1.16	1.34	1.19	1.39	1.32
1936	1.27	1.23	1.36	1.25	1.39	1.35
1937	1.49	1.29	1.41	1.31	1.51	1.41
1938	1.65	1.40	1.54	1.36	1.69	1.52
1939	1.66	1.40	1.53	1.37	1.69	1.53
1940	1.71	1.43	1.55	1.39	1.70	1.54
1941	1.73	1.42	1.55	1.47	1.72	1.59

Source: U. S. Department of Labor, Bureau of Labor Statistics, *Union Scales of Wages and Hours in the Building Trades, May 15, 1936* (Bulletin No. 626), p. 9; *Union Scales of Wages and Hours in the Building Trades in Seventy Cities, May 15, 1937* (Bulletin No. 657),

p. 28; *Union Wages, Hours, and Working Conditions in the Building Trades, June 1, 1939* (Bulletin No. 674), p. 18; *Union Wages, Hours, and Working Conditions in the Building Trades, June 1, 1941* (Bulletin No. 680), p. 15; "Average Union Scale of Wage Rates Per Hour and Per Week May 1913 to 1920," *Monthly Labor Review*, Vol. 12, No. 4, April 1921, p. 65; "Average Union Rate of Wages Per Hour in the U.S., May 15, 1921 and 1922," *Monthly Labor Review*, Vol. 15, No. 6, December 1922, p. 110; "Union Scale of Wages and Hours of Labor as of May 15, 1923," *Monthly Labor Review*, Vol. 17, No. 6, December 1923, p. 104; "Union Scale of Wages and Hours of Labor as of May 15, 1924," *Monthly Labor Review*, Vol. 19, No. 6, December 1924, p. 44; "Union Scale of Wages and Hours of Labor in May, 1926, by Occupations," *Monthly Labor Review*, Vol. 23, No. 5, November 1926, p. 107; "Union Scale of Wages and Hours of Labor in May, 1928, by Occupations," *Monthly Labor Review*, Vol. 27, No. 5, November 1928, p. 14; "Union Wage Rates in Time-Work Trades in 1930," *Monthly Labor Review*, Vol. 31, No. 5, November 1930, pp. 179–180; "Union Scales of Wages and Hours of Labor in 1931, Part 2, Average Wage Rates, by Trades," *Monthly Labor Review*, Vol. 33, No. 5, November 1931, p. 187; "Union Scales of Wages and Hours of Labor in 1933, Part 2, Average Wage Rates, by Trades," *Monthly Labor Review*, Vol. 37, No. 5, November 1933, p.1190; "Union Scales of Wages and Hours in the Building Trades, June 1, 1938," *Monthly Labor Review*, Vol. 47, November 1938, p. 1100; "Union Wages and Hour, in the Building Trades, June 1, 1940, *Monthly Labor Review*, Vol. 51, November 1940s p. 1239.

Bibliography

BOOKS

Alinsky, Saul D. *John L. Lewis: an Unauthorized Biography.* New York: Putnam, 1949.

Arnold, Thurman. *Bottlenecks of Business.* New York: Reynal and Hitchcock, 1940.

Blum, Sol. *Jurisdictional Disputes Resulting from Structural Differences in American Trade Unions.* (University of California Publications in Economics, Vol. 3.) Berkeley: University of California Press, 1913.

Brooks, R. R. R. *Unions of Their Own Choosing: an Account of the National Labor Relations Board and Its Work.* New Haven: Yale University Press, 1939.

Bureau of National Affairs. *The Taft-Hartley Act...After One Year.* Washington: Bureau of National Affairs, 1948.

Burke, W. M. *History and Functions of Central Labor Unions.* New York: Macmillan, 1899.

Cahill, M. C. *Shorter Hours: A Study of the Movement since the Civil War.* New York: Columbia University Press, 1932.

Cale, E. B. *The Organization of Labor in Philadelphia, 1850–1870.* Philadelphia: University of Pennsylvania Press, 1940.

Chandler, Frances. *History of the Amalgamated Society of Carpenters and Joiners 1860–1910.* Manchester, England: Cooperative Printing Society, 1910.

Commons, John R., and U. B. Phillips. *Documentary History of American Industrial Society.* 10 vols. Cleveland: A. C. Clark, 1910.

————, et al. *History of Labour in the United States.* 4 vols. New York: Macmillan, 1921–1935.

————, ed. *Trade Unionism and the Labour Problem* (2d series). Boston: Ginn, 1921.

Crosser, P. K. *Ideologies and American Labor.* New York: Oxford University Press, 1941.

David, Henry. *The History of the Haymarket Affair.* New York: Farrar & Rinehart, 1936.

333

Deibler, Frederick. *The Amalgamated Woodworkers' International Union of America: A Historical Study of Trade Unions in Relation to the Development of an Industry.* (Economic and Political Series Bulletin of the University of Wisconsin, Bulletin No. 511.) Madison: University of Wisconsin Press, 1912.

Destler, C. M. *American Radicalism, 1865–1901: Essays and Documents.* New London, Conn.: Connecticut College for Women, 1940.

Egbert, D. D., and Stow Persons. *Socialism and American Life.* (Princeton University Studies in American Civilization, No. 4.) 2 vols. Princeton: Princeton University Press, 1952.

Foner, Philip S. *History of the Labor Movement in the United States.* New York: International Press, 1947.

Galenson, Walter. *Rival Unionism in the United States.* New York: American Council on Public Affairs, 1940.

Glocker, Theodore. *The Government of American Trade Unions.* Baltimore: Johns Hopkins University Press, 1913.

Goldman, Eric. *Rendezvous with Destiny: A History of Modern American Radicalism.* New York: A. A. Knopf, 1952.

Gompers, Samuel. *Seventy Years of Life and Labor: An Autobiography.* 2 vols. New York: E. P. Dutton, 1952.

Gregory, Charles. *Labor and the Law.* New York: W. W. Norton, 1949.

Haber, William. *Industrial Relations in the Building Industry.* Cambridge, Mass.: Harvard University Press, 1930.

Harris, Herbert. *American Labor.* New Haven: Yale University Press, 1939.

Harvey, Rowland. *Samuel Gompers: Champion of the Toiling Masses.* Stanford: Stanford University Press, 1935.

Hass F. J. *The American Labor Movement.* New York: Paulist Press, 1937.

Holbing, A. T. *The Departments of the A. F. of L.* (Johns Hopkins University Studies in Historical and Political Science, Series XLIV, No. 1.) Baltimore: Johns Hopkins University Press, 1931.

Horn, Stanley F. *This Fascinating Lumber Business.* New York: Bobbs-Merrill, 1951.

Hurwitz, H. L. *Theodore Roosevelt and Labor in New York, 1880–1900.* (Columbia University Studies, No. 500.) New York: Columbia University Press, 1943.

Jensen, Vernon. *Lumber and Labor.* New York: Farrar & Rinehart, 1945.

Jernegan, W. W. *Laboring and Dependent Classes in Colonial America, 1607–1783.* Chicago: University of Chicago Press, 1931.

Johnson, Hugh. *The Blue Eagle from Egg to Earth.* Garden City, New York: Doubleday, Doran, 1935.

Long, Clarence D. *Building Cycles and the Theory of Investment.* Princeton: Princeton University Press, 1940.

Lorwin, Lewis. *The American Federation of Labor: History, Policies and Prospects.* Washington: The Institute of Economics of the Brookings Institute, Publication No. 50, 1933.

Lyon, L. L., *et al. The National Recovery Administration: An Analysis and Appraisal.* Washington: The Institute of Economics of the Brookings Institute, Publication No. 60, 1933.

McKee, Samuel, Jr. *Labor in Colonial New York* (Columbia University Economic and Political Science Series No. 410.) New York: Columbia University Press, 1935.

McNeill, G. H., ed. *The Labor Movement: The Problem of Today, The History, Purposes and Possibilities of Labor Organizations in Europe and America.* New York: M. W. Hazen, 1887.

Madison, Charles. *American Labor Leaders.* New York: Harper, 1950.

Merritt, W. G. *Destination Unknown: Fifty Years of Labor Relations.* New York: Prentice-Hall, 1951.

—————. *History of the League for Industrial Rights.* New York: League for Industrial Rights, 1925.

Millis, Harry D., and Emelie Clark. *From Wagner Act to Taft-Hartley.* Chicago: University of Chicago Press, 1950.

Mitchell, Broadus. "Depression Decade" in *Economic History of the United States,* Vol. 9. New York: Rinehart, 1947.

Montgomery, Royal. *Industrial Relations in the Chicago Building Trades.* Chicago: University of Chicago Press, 1927.

Moriss, R. B. *Government and Labor in Early America.* New York: Columbia University Press, 1946.

Newman, W. H. *The Building Industry and Business Cycles.* Chicago: University of Chicago Press, 1935.

Perlman, Selig. *A History of Trade Unionism in the United States.* New York: Macmillan, 1922.

—————. *A Theory of the Labor Movement.* New York: Macmillan, 1928.

Powderly, Terence V. *The Path I Trod: The Autobiography of Terence V. Powderly.* Ed. by Harry J. Carman, *et al.* New York: Columbia University Press, 1940.

—————. *Thirty Years of Labor, 1859–1889.* Columbus: Excelsior, 1889.

Reed, Louis. *The Labor Philosophy of Samuel Gompers.* New York: Columbia University Press, 1930.

Reynolds, L. G., and Charles C. Killingsworth. *Trade Union Publications: The Official Journals, Convention Proceedings, and Constitutions of International Unions and Federations 1850–1941.* 3 vols. Baltimore: Johns Hopkins Press, 1944–1945.

Ryan, F. L. *Industrial Relations in the San Francisco Building Trades.* Norman, Oklahoma: University of Oklahoma Press, 1936.

Saposs, David. *Left-Wing Unionism: A Study of Radical Politics and Tactics.* New York: International, 1926.

Schneider, D. M. *The Workers' Communist Party and American Trade Unions.* (Johns Hopkins Studies in Historical and Political Science, Series XLVI, No.. 2) Baltimore: 1928.

Stekloff, Y. M. *History of the First International.* New York: International, 1928.

Symes, Lillian. *Rebel America: The Story of Social Revolt in the United States.* New York: Harper, 1934.

Vigouroux, Louis. *La Concentration des Forces Ouvrières dans L' Amérique du Nord.* Paris: A. Colin, 1899.

Ware, Norman J. *The Industrial Worker, 1840–1860.* New York: Houghton Mifflin, 1924.

————. *The Labor Movement in the United States, 1860–1895: A Study in Democracy.* New York: D. Appleton, 1929.

Whele, Louis B. *Hidden Threads of History: Wilson Through Roosevelt.* New York: Macmillan, 1953.

Wilson, Edmund. *To the Finland Station.* New York: Harcourt, Brace, 1940.

Woehlke, Walter. *Union Labor in Peace and War.* San Francisco: Sunset, 1918.

Young, Edward. *Labor in America.* Philadelphia: S. A. George, 1875.

Zausner, Philip. *Unvarnished: The Autobiography of a Union Leader.* New York: Brotherhood, 1941.

GOVERNMENT PUBLICATIONS

Committee of the President's Conference on Unemployment. *Reports and Recommendations on Seasonal Operation in the Construction Industries, the Facts and Remedies.* New York: McGraw-Hill, 1924.

Edwards, J. Arnold. *Labor Relations in the United States: A Summary of Historical Events in the World War Period, 1912–1920* (U.S. Department of Labor, Bureau of Labor Statistics, Historical Study No. 2.) Washington: Government Printing Office, 1941.

Hotchkiss, W. H., and H. R. Seager. *History of the Shipbuilding Labor Adjustment Board, 1917–1919* (U.S. Department of Labor, Bureau of Labor Statistics, Bulletin No. 283.) Washington: Government Printing Office, 1921.

Illinois Building Investigating Commission. *Report to the 53rd General Assembly.* Springfield, Illinois: Springfield, 1923.

International Labor Organization. *Reports One Through Three of the*

Building, Civil Engineering and Public Works Committee. Geneva, Switzerland: International Labor Organization, 1950–1951.

National Recovery Administration. *Evidence Study No. 7 of the Construction Industry*. Washington: Government Printing Office, 1935.

National War Labor Board. *Report of the Secretary to the Secretary of Labor* (for the year ending May 31, 1919.) Washington: Government Printing Office, 1920.

New York City. Estimate Board Contract Inquiry. *Stenographer's Minutes*. New York: 1921. Mimeographed.

New York Legislature. Joint Committee on Housing. *Preliminary Report*. Albany, New York: J. B. Lyon, 1920.

————. *Intermediate Report*. Albany: J. B. Lyon, 1921.

————. *Final Report*. Albany: J. B. Lyon, 1923.

————. *Minutes of Hearings, May 16, 1919–August 6, 1920; October 20–November 11, 1920*. 15 vols. New York: 1919–1920. Mimeographed.

United States Commissioner of Labor. *Thirteenth Annual Report on Hand and Machine Labor*. 2 vols. Washington: Government Printing Office, 1899.

United States Congress, House, Select Committee on the Depression in Labor and Business. *Hearings of the Investigation Relative to the Causes of the General Depression in Business and Labor*. 45th Congress, 3rd Session. 4 vols. Washington: Government Printing Office, 1879.

United States Congress, Senate, Committee on Education and Labor. *Hearings on S. 1000, S. 4264, S. 1392, S. 1550, S. 1580 and S. 2139, Bills to Amend the National Labor Relations Act*. 76th Congress, 1st Session. 4 vols. Washington: Government Printing Office, 1939–1940.

United States Congress, Senate, Committee on Education and Labor. *Report of the Committee of the Senate upon the Relations between Labor and Capital and Testimony Taken by the Committee*. 48th Congress, 1st Session. 4 vols. Washington: Government Printing Office, 1885.

United States Department of Commerce, Bureau of the Census. *Fifteenth Census of the United States: 1930. Construction Industry*. Vol. I. Washington: Government Printing Office, 1933.

United States Department of Justice. *Annual Report of the Attorney General*. Washington: Government Printing Office, 1941.

United States Department of Labor, Bureau of Labor Statistics. *Statistics of Building Construction, 1920–1937, as Shown by Building Permits Issued* (Bulletin No. 650.) 2 vols. Washington: Government Printing Office, 1938.

United States Department of Labor, Information and Education Service. *Economics of the Building Industry*. Washington: Government Printing Office, 1919.

United States Department of Labor. *The National War Labor Board: A History of Its Formation and Activities and Documents of Importance in the Record of Its Development*. (Bulletin No. 287.) Washington: Government Printing Office, 1921.

United States Industrial Commission. *Final Report and Hearings*. 19 vols. Washington: Government Printing Office, 1900–1902.

United States Industrial Relations Commission. *Final Report and Testimony*. 11 vols. Washington: Government Printing Office, 1916.

United States, Joint Temporary National Economic Committee. *Hearings and Final Report on the Investigation of the Concentration of Economic Power*. 77th Congress, 1st Session. 24 vols. Washington: Government Printing Office, 1941.

Winslow, C. N. *Conciliation and Arbitration in the New York Building Trades* (U.S. Department of Labor, Bureau of Labor Statistics, Bulletin No. 124.) Washington: Government Printing Office, 1913.

NEWSPAPERS

John Swinton's Paper (New York). November 1884–August 1887 (weekly).

Labor Compendium (St. Louis, official organ of the National Building Trades Council). 1904–1906 (weekly); 1906–1911 (monthly).

Labor Standard (New York). 1877–1881. (Formerly *The Socialist*.)

National Labor Tribune (Pittsburgh). 1875–1885.

National Socialist (Chicago, organ of the Socialist Labor party). April 4, 1878–September 14, 1878.

New York Herald. 1873–1874, 1876.

New York Sun. 1873–1874.

New York Times. 1873–1874, 1916, 1925, 1938, 1948–1949.

New York Tribune. 1873–1874.

New York World. 1873–1874.

Socialist (Chicago, official organ of the Socialistic Labor party). 1878–1879. (Formerly the *National Socialist*.)

Socialist (New York, official organ of the Workingman's party). 1876–1877.

Woodhull and Claflin's Weekly (New York). 1870–1876.

Workmen's Advocate (New Haven, official organ of the Socialist Labor party). 1885–1891.

PERIODICALS AND ARTICLES

"Boss Carpenter," *Fortune*, Vol. 33, No. 4, April 1946, pp. 121–123.

Bruere, R. W. "Industrial Control in the Building Trades?" *Survey*, Vol. 52, Sept. 15, 1924, pp. 621–622.

"The Building Cycle," *Fortune*, Vol. 16, No. 2, February 1937, p. 85.

Bureau of National Affairs, *Labor Relations Reference Manual*, 1937–1953.

Cherney, W. L., and J. A. Fitch, "The Untermeyer Revelations," *Survey*, Vol. 49, January 1921, p. 386 and pp. 491–495.

Commons, John R. "New York Building Trades," *Quarterly Journal of Economics*, Vol. 18, May 1904, pp. 409–436.

Cummins, E. "National Board for Jurisdictional Awards and the Carpenters' Union," *American Economic Review*, Vol. 19, No. 3, September 1929, pp. 363–377.

————. "Philosophy of the Carpenters' Union," *Political Science Quarterly*, Vol. 4, No. 3, September 1927, pp. 397–418.

Donnelly, S. B. "The Trade Agreement in the New York Building Trades," *Annals of the American Academy of Political Science*, Vol. 27, 1916, pp. 510–516.

Douglas, Paul N., and F. Wolfe. "Labor Administration in the Shipbuilding Industry During Wartime," *Journal of Political Economy*, Vol. 2, No. 3, March 1919, pp. 145–187; No. 5, May 1919, pp. 362–396.

Edwards, Corwin. "The New Anti-Trust Procedure as Illustrated in the Construction Industry," *Public Policy*, Vol. 2, 1941, pp. 321–340.

Glocker, Theodore. "Amalgamation of Related Trades in American Unions," *American Economic Review*, Vol. 5, No. 3, September 1915, p. 554.

Goodrich, Carter, and Sol Davison. "The Wage Earner in the Westward Movement," *Political Science Quarterly*, Vol. 50, No. 2, June 1935, pp. 161–165.

"Injunctions in the Building Trades," *Monthly Labor Review*, Vol. 14, No. 4, April 1922, p. 812.

Levinson, E. "Bill Hutcheson's Convention," *Nation*, Vol. 147, No. 1, Jan. 2, 1937, pp. 11–12.

Menefee, Selden C. "How the Lumber Strike Was Broken," *Nation*, Vol. 141, No. 3661, Sept. 4, 1935, pp. 275–276.

————. "Tacoma, Timber and Tear Gas," *Nation*, Vol. 141, No. 3654, July 17, 1935, pp. 76–77.

Piez, Charles. "Labor and Ships," *North American Review*, Vol. 209, No. 760, March 1919, pp. 352–361.

"Proposed Amendments of the 1938 AFL Convention to the National Labor Relations Act," *Monthly Labor Review*, Vol. 47, November 1938, pp. 1035–1036.

Rand School of Social Science, *American Labor Yearbook*, 1916–1932.

Shannon, Fred. "The Homestead Act and the Labor Surplus," *American Historical Review*, Vol. 41, No. 4, July 1936, p. 637.

Whele, Louis B. "Adjustment of Labor Disputes Incident to Production for War in the United States," *Quarterly Journal of Economics*, Vol. 32, November 1917, pp. 122–123.

————. "Labor Problems in the United States During the War," *Quarterly Journal of Economics,* Vol. 32, February 1918, pp. 333–384.

EMPLOYER ASSOCIATION AND TRADE UNION PUBLICATIONS

Amalgamated Woodworkers' International Union of America. *Proceedings, 1896–1904.*

————. *International Woodworker,* Vols. 1–14, 1896–1904.

American Federation of Labor. *American Federationist,* Vols. 1–59, 1894–1953.

————. Building Trades Department. *Proceedings, 1908–1953.*

————. *Interesting Discussion at the Tenth Annual Convention of the Federation, 1890, upon the Question: Should a Charter be Issued by the American Federation of Labor to a Central Labor Union Which Has a Political Party Represented Therein.* New York: Frytag, 1891.

————. *Proceedings, 1894–1953.*

Architects, American Institute of. *Proceedings,* 1918–1925.

Barkin, Solomon, in collaboration with the Building Trades Department of the American Federation of Labor. *Negotiating the Construction Code: A History of the Participation of the Building Trades Department Organizations in the Codes.* Washington: Building Trades Department, 1934.

Blanshard, Paul. *Open Shop Movement.* New York: Amalgamated Clothing Workers of America, 1924.

Bricklayers, Masons, and Plasterers, International Union of America. *Annual Report of the President, 1914–1924.*

————. *Bricklayer, Mason, and Plasterer,* Vols. 16–26, 1914–1924.

————. *Proceedings, 1914–1924.*

Bridge and Structural Iron Workers International Association. *Bridgemen's Magazine,* Vols. 14–17, 1914–1917.

Building Trades Employers Association of New York City. *News and Opinion, 1933–1953* (irregular).

Carpenters and Joiners of America, United Brotherhood of. *Abstract of Evidence Submitted in the Controversy over the Erection of Sheet Metal Trim.* Indianapolis: Allied Printing Trades Council, 1923.

————. *The Carpenter,* Vols. 1–72, 1881–1953.

————. *Constitution and Rules for Local Unions Under Its Jurisdiction,* 1881–1951.

————. *Decision of Umpire Adolph Strasser and Plan of Amalgamation Between the United Brotherhood of Carpenters and Joiners of America and the Amalgamated Society of Carpenters and Joiners.* New York: New York District Council of Carpenters, 1908.

————. *Proceedings, 1881–1950.*

————. New York State Carpenters Council. *Carpenters' Trade Journal.* Vol. II, 1915 (monthly).

Congress of Industrial Organizations. *Proceedings, 1938–1953.*

Corotis, Charles, and Charles Phillips. *The Life Story of a Forgotten Giant—Peter J. McGuire.* Camden, New Jersey: Central Labor Union of Camden, New Jersey, 1946. Twenty-four page pamphlet.

Coyne, J. P. "Jurisdictional Disputes in Building in America," *American Federationist,* Vol. 49, No. 12, December 1939, p. 1298.

Haber, William. "Craftsmanship in Building," *American Federationist,* Vol. 36, No. 12, December 1926, pp. 1446–1451.

Hutcheson, William, *et al. A Survey of Seven Years of Experimentation by Acts, Authorities and Administration.* Indianapolis: United Brotherhood of Carpenters and Joiners of America, 1939.

Industrial Association of San Francisco. *American Plan Open Shop Conference, 1927–1928.* San Francisco: Industrial Association of San Francisco, 1928.

————. *American Plan Progress,* Vols. 1–2, 1925–1926 (semi-monthly, irregular).

Knights of Labor. *Journal of United Labor,* Vols. 5–9, 1884–1889.

————. *Proceedings, 1884–1890.*

League for Industrial Rights, *A-B-A Bulletin,* Vols. 11–15, 1915–1918.

————. *Building Trades Strikes Against Open Shop Products Are Unlawful.* New York: League for Industrial Rights, 1927.

————. *Law and Labor.* Vols. 1–13, 1919–1932.

Machinists, International Association of. *Proceedings, 1911–1924.*

McInareney, Joseph. "Labor's Stake in the Building Revival," *American Federationist,* Vol. 42, No. 6, June 1938, pp. 593–597.

McNeill, George E. *The Eight Hour Primer.* New York: American Federation of Labor, 1889.

National Association of Builders. *Official Reports of the Convention, 1888–1899.*

National Association of Manufacturers of the United States. *Open Shop Bulletin, 1920–1929* (irregular).

National Building Trades Council. *Proceedings, 1900–1904.*

National Carpenters' Union, *Proceedings, 1865–1867.*

Painters, Paperhangers and Decorators of America, Brotherhood of. *Painter and Decorator.* Vol. 33, 1920.

Progressive Building Trades Worker. *What's Wrong with the Carpenters' Union.* Chicago: 1925.

Real Estate Record and Builders' Guide. Vols. 13–50, 1881–1918 (New York, weekly).

Trade Union Committee for Unemployment. *A. F. of L. Rank and File Federationist.* Vols. 1–2, January 1934–October 1935 (Irregularly but monthly).

Index

Administration of the United Brotherhood of Carpenters and Joiners of America, see Structure of the United Brotherhood of Carpenters and Joiners, also specific offices as President, general, etc.

Agreement, see Collective bargaining and Treaties

Alien contract labor law, 72

Alliances, of trade unions, see Treaties

Amalgamated Society of Carpenters and Joiners, history, 56; exchange of cards with United Brotherhood of Carpenters and Joiners of America, 57; jurisdictional dispute with United Brotherhood of Carpenters and Joiners of America, 158–159

Amalgamated Wood Workers' Union, founded, 84–85; McGuire's attitude toward, 82, 84; jurisdictional policy, 126; jurisdictional dispute with United Brotherhood,* 77, 84, 86–89, 106, 110, 112–117, 127, 167, 171, 182, 321; and the AFL, 114, 116–117, 127, 129, 135; jurisdictional dispute with New York Carpenters, 86–87, 115–116, 131; reason for decline, 117–118; amalgamation with U. B., 114–117, 118–119, 135, 194

Amalgamation, as AFL policy, 135, 167, 185; Amalgamated Wood Workers' Union and U. B. agree to (1906), 114–115; AFL forces A. W. W. U. into, with the U. B. (1911), 116; of the Machine Wood Workers' Union and International Furniture Workers Union (1895),

85; of the United Order with U. B., 58; U. B. opposes, with other unions in woodworking industry, 84–85

American Construction Council, 269, 271

American Federation of Labor, formed, 53; and eight-hour strike of 1890, 58–59; Socialist attempt to capture, 93–94; types of unions in, 120; and the building trades unions, 122–136, 176, 179–180, 205–207; craft union policy of, 124–125; McGuire's role in, 53, 91–92; and U. B.'s jurisdictional disputes, 110–117, 176–185; policy toward amalgamation, 167; policy affected by technological change, 182; policy during World War I, 217–232; and creation of CIO, 285–286; dispute with the CIO, 286–300; adapts its policy to U. B.'s demands, 321; Carpenters' withdrawal from (1953), xiii–xiv; see also Building Trades Department and Gompers, Samuel

American Federation of Labor-Congress of Industrial Organizations, 136

American Institute of Architects, 240–242, 244

American plan, 235

Americanism, as U. B. policy, 259

Anheuser-Busch Beer Co., 314–315

Anti-Boycott Association, dispute with U. B., 163–167, 231, 324

Anti-Trust laws, applied to the U. B., 307–319; see also Arnold, Thurman

Apprenticeship, lack of national control over, 5; as a trade union service to the building industry, 10; failure to create national system of, 142

Arbitration, in the New York building trades unions, 161; by the National

---

*United Brotherhood of Carpenters and Joiners of America, hereafter indicated as U. B.

shop drive, 243–244; in lumber industry, 296–299; AFL and CIO, 298–299, 300; as affected by Wagner Act, 305; *see also* Jurisdictional disputes

Duffy, Frank, offices held in U. B., 66–67; social philosophy, 250–252; describes McGuire's administration of national office, 73–74, 96; and the Huber machine, 139; and factional disputes, 90, 96–97, 99, 100, 141–151, 258–263; and jurisdictional disputes, 111, 117–118, 179–181, 245, 297; and Structural Building Trades Alliance, 134; and National Building Trades Council, 131; and employers' associations, 159, 160, 161, 166; and World War I labor policy, 219; edits *The Carpenter*, 251, 300; and Maurice Hutcheson, 329–330

Duplex Case, 315

Edmonston, Gabriel, 39, 41, 42, 50, 51, 53, 62, 83

Education, role of in early U. B., 41–43, 69; abandoned as trade union goal, 167

Eight-hour day, granted by National War Labor Board, 229

Eight-hour movement, 1886–1890, importance of, 46–47, 49–50, 60, 319–320; piecework and, 65; and the Haymarket affair, 49; and the Federation of Organized Trades and Labor Unions, 48–49; philosophers of, 47–48; and employers' resistance, 72

Elections, how influenced by general president, 140; contested, 147, 148–151, 257–258; of 1912, 142; disqualification of votes in, 144; lack of, in the U. B., 1920–1929, 250; of general president uncontested, since 1924, 267; *see also* Referendum vote and Tabulating committee

Electrical Workers, treaty with U. B., 270, 270n, 275, 280, 322; dual Building Trades Department, 276

Elevator Constructors, 270

Elevators, effect of invention of on U. B., 80

Emergency Fleet Corp., 220–221

Employers, form first association in building industry, 70–71, 155–156; served by business agents, 7–10, 65–66; McGuire's view toward, 92; resistance to trade unionism, 74, 77, 159, 164–167, 230–231, 290; role in building industry

racketeering, 157–161; cooperate with building trades unions, 231, 233, 235–236; associations, resist open shop, 236; associations in New York City, 203, 212, 214; protest U. B.'s boycott, 3, 4; *see also* Contractors, Middleman, and Management

Executive board, created, 40; weakness of, 70, 72; is part time, 69, 76; mode of election of, 70, 73, 75; McGuire's power over, 73–74; hostile to McGuire, 76; role of, in P. J. McGuire's ouster, 96–97, 99; reports to convention for first time, 143; powers and duties, 148; general president and general secretary placed on, 151; made full time and salaried, 151; dispute with general president, 72, 138–154; importance in union structure analyzed, 4–5, 142, 151–154, 168; constitutional power of, determined, 138–154; composition, 1920–1930, 250; *see also* Board of Vice Presidents

Featherstone, Dan, 195–196, 212

Federated Woodworkers Union, 297–298

Federation of Organized Trades and Labor Unions, *see* American Federation of Labor

Finances, in the building industry, 9–10; U. B. salary expenditures, 1924–1932, 267; cost of Old Age Home, U. B., 255, 255n; in early U. B., 39–40; *see also* Per capita tax

Furniture Workers' Union, International, 83, 84–85

Furuseth, Andrew, 183–184, 192

Gaynor, N. J., 172, 174

General representatives, 169; *see also* Organizers

Gompers, Samuel, and P. J. McGuire, 30, 83, 92; Tompkins Square Riot, 32; first AFL president, 53; and U. B. jurisdictional disputes, 113, 123–137, 175, 179–180, 181, 184, 242–243, 321; and building trades unions, 123–127; and Anti-Boycott Association, 164–165; and Brindell affair, 205–207; World War I policy, 217–220, 227

Government regulation, of the building industry, 271–274, 280, 280n, 282–283; of labor relations, 269, 295–296, 303–319, 324; of trade unions in New York, 215; of trade unions during World War I, 217–232

Philosophy, social and trade union, of founders, U. B., 29–45; and eight-hour theories, 47–48; of P. J. McGuire, 29–45, 55–56, 61–62, 67–69, 82–83, 106, 167, 316–320; of leaders of U. B. in 1890's, 65–68; of William Huber, 67–68; of William Hutcheson, 198, 249–253; of leaders of U. B. (1920–1929), 251–253

Piecework, among carpenters, 9; as a cause of collective bargaining in building industry, 61–62; fought by the business agent, 64; effect of eight-hour movement on, 65; first application of, 27–28; as a factor in the rise of the U. B., 29; prohibited by the U. B., 40; threatens the early unions' existence, 44–45; see also Middleman and Contractors

Pittsburgh, Pa., 1891 U. B. strike in, 71; Structural Building Trades Alliance formed in, 134; consolidation of U. B. locals, 144, 258; employers' offensive against U. B. (1905), 159; dual carpenters' union formed in, 243; locals protest 1924 vote counting, 257; jurisdictional claims of Bricklayers, Carpenters, and Electrical Workers in, 270; indictment of U. B. for restraint of trade in, 312–313

Plasterers, International Association of, 177, 270

Political action, of P. J. McGuire, 32–34; U. B. refuses, 251–252; see also Socialism

Powderly, Terence V., 48, 50

Preservation of work; see Work preservation, Jurisdiction, Jurisdictional disputes, Technological change

President, general, function and powers, 1–2, 11–12, 77, 87–88, 138, 168, 200, 201, 253, 267; relations with the executive board, 145–146, 151, 250; salary of, 97; see also specific presidents such as Hutcheson, Huber, etc.

Press, the, and labor relations in World War I, 226–227

Progressive Building Trades Worker, 254

Progressive Carpenters' Union, 54–55, 58; see also National Carpenters' Union

Protectives, faction in early U. B., 39

Provisional Committee of the Carpenters and Joiners National Union, 38

Public opinion, 226–228, 231–235, 237

Public Works Administration, 280

"Pure and simple" trade unionism, 92; see also Business unionism

Racketeering, in New York City, 204–205, 207, 214–215, 260–261; in the building industry, 153–163, 233–235; and the open shop, 236

Railroads, see Transportation

Referendum vote, of 1896 supports P. J. McGuire, 78; on McGuire's suspension (1901), 100–101; alleged illegal counting of, 140–142, 144, 148–149; general president tries to eliminate, 147; on home for aged carpenters, 255–256; see also Elections

Reynolds, William, "Bud," 260

Roosevelt, F. D., and U. B. in woodworking industry, 223n; heads American Construction Council, 269, 271; creates Board for Jurisdictional Awards, 267, 281; and building industry depression of 1930's, 271–274, 307; and Carpenters' relations with Building Trades Department, 280; and unorganized workers, 288; and U. B.-I. W. A. dispute, 304; creates Temporary National Economic Committee, 307; and Thurman Arnold's attack on the building industry, 308, 311; and unfair labor practices, 311, 314; attempt to amend Wagner Act, 314

Rosen, Morris, 256, 259–263

Rowland, President, UBCJA, 71–72

Rudinsky, Meyer, 261

Ryan, Thomas, opposition to Huber, 141–142, 146, 147, 148, 254

St. Louis, first written agreement in thirty years (1915), 6; McGuire's activities in, 35, 37–38; indictment of U. B. for restraint of trade, 313–315; and mill jurisdiction, 188, 190, 192; dual carpenters' unions in, 243

St. Louis Federal District Court, 313

St. Louis Trades and Labor Alliance, 35

Salary, of the national officers of the U. B. (1924–1928), 267; of the executive board, 151; of the general president, 97; general secretary is only paid officer, 39–40

San Francisco, 1891 U. B. strike, 71; power of P. H. McCarthy in, 140, 157, 233–234; building trades councils organized in, 156; employers' opposition